PRACTICAL LEGAL RESEARCH

SKILLS & STRATEGIES FOR THE LEGAL ASSISTANT

PRACTICAL LEGAL RESEARCH

SKILLS & STRATEGIES FOR THE LEGAL ASSISTANT

Beth Walston-Dunham

College of Saint Mary
Omaha, Nebraska

WEST PUBLISHING COMPANY

MINNEAPOLIS/ST. PAUL   NEW YORK   LOS ANGELES   SAN FRANCISCO

WEST'S COMMITMENT TO THE ENVIRONMENT

In 1906, West Publishing Company began recycling materials left over from the production of books. This began a tradition of efficient and responsible use of resources. Today, up to 95 percent of our legal books and 70 percent of our college and school texts are printed on recycled, acid free stock. West also recycles nearly 22 million pounds of scrap paper annually— the equivalent of 181,717 trees. Since the 1960s, West has devised ways to capture and recycle waste inks, solvents, oils, and vapors created in the printing process. We also recycle plastics of all kinds, wood, glass, corrugated cardboard, and batteries, and have eliminated the use of Styrofoam book packaging. We at West are proud of the longevity and the scope of our commitment to the environment.

Production, Prepress, Printing and Binding by West Publishing Company.

 TEXT IS PRINTED ON 10% POST CONSUMER RECYCLED PAPER

British Library Cataloguing-in-Publication Data. A catalogue record for this book is available from the British Library.

Composition - Carlisle Communications
Copyediting - Deborah Cady
Interior Design - John Edeen
Cover Design - John Edeen
Cover Image - David Chalk, Chalkmark Graphics

COPYRIGHT ©1995   By WEST PUBLISHING COMPANY
                     610 Opperman Drive
                     P.O. Box 64526
                     St. Paul, MN 55164–0526

02 01 00 99 98 97 96 95   8 7 6 5 4 3 2 1 0

Library of Congress Cataloging-in-Publication Data

Walston-Dunham, Beth.
    Practical legal research: skills & strategies for the legal assistant / Beth Walston-Dunham.
        p. cm.
    Includes index.
    ISBN 0–314–04388–8 (soft)
    1. Legal research—United States. 2. Legal assistants—United States—Handbooks, manuals, etc. I. Title.
340 ' .072073—dc20

                                                                94-22668
                                                                CIP

DEDICATION

To my very greatest resources,
George and Sam.

PREFACE

Practical Legal Research: Skills and Strategies for the Legal Assistant is directed toward the novice student of legal research. Its purpose is to thoroughly acquaint the student with all aspects of legal research and to facilitate a basic working knowledge and level of skill through various applications and assignments. At the conclusion of the course, students should be able to perform basic research in all areas of primary and secondary legal authority. In addition, they should be able to validate, cite, and evaluate applicability and strength of the authorities located.

Incorporated into the text are applications and assignments that pertain to legal analysis and writing. To develop the necessary skills for properly presenting the products of research, the student should be encouraged to integrate research assignments with basic legal writing. Most assignments are nonjurisdiction specific. The subjects of assignments either are based on federal law or emanate from areas of law that have been addressed in a majority of jurisdictions. This allows the student to perform research in a limited library setting, for example, a collection of law from only one jurisdiction. Because most resources have a similar basis or organization, such as the West key number system (explained more fully in Chapter 7), limited access to materials should not limit one's ability to develop adequate research skills.

At the conclusion of the course, students should have skills necessary to perform basic-level research and analysis. This in turn prepares the student for either a more advanced course of study or practical application in the workplace. As with many skills, the amount of hands-on experience is a fundamental component of learning, and this text encourages this through a progressively difficult series of assignments. Completion and critique of student performance will enable the student to better refine a basic knowledge of the elements of legal research.

FEATURES OF THE TEXT

Content

The text begins with a brief introduction to the concept of law and the various resources available in the law library. The preliminary chapters

address the methods of proper citation and validation of authority. Before beginning actual research of specific authorities, the text presents a chapter that explains legal analysis and the basic steps of legal research. In Chapter 5, which begins the more in-depth examination of research into specific resources, students are introduced to the legal dictionary/thesaurus and encyclopedia. While discussion of other secondary authorities is reserved for later chapters, this discussion precedes that of primary authorities, such as reporters and statutes, because of the need to emphasize the importance of a command of relevant terminology and concepts in legal research. Because the novice researcher typically does not have an extensive vocabulary of legal terms, learning proper use and benefits of the legal dictionary and thesaurus provides the necessary tools for successfully completing future research assignments in virtually any resource.

Subsequent chapters address the characteristics and methods of research for each of the basic elements of the law library, including both primary and secondary resources. The final chapter of the text introduces the student to computer research. By first establishing a basic level of skill in legal research (i.e., the basic steps of research and familiarity with the likely sources of authority), the student is now ready to expand those skills to incorporate the search methods for computer-assisted research.

Chapter Objectives

Each chapter begins with a series of objectives—fundamental skills and/or concepts that the student should be able to master by the conclusion of the chapter. By reading these objectives before beginning the chapter, students are provided with a basic outline of chapter content and points of focus to use as they study the chapter.

Exhibits

The text includes numerous exhibits that are actual reproductions from other resources. These exhibits allow the student to visualize the content of a variety of legal research resources that may or may not be readily available in the student's own library setting. Through these illustrations, students are able to see realistic examples of the material that is the topic of discussion and thereby better understand the text that is presented.

Applications

The text also includes several applications that are actual demonstrations of concepts presented in the text. By providing these in addition to the textual format, it is hoped that the ideas within the text will take on a more relevant purpose that can be readily applied in realistic research settings.

Assignments

Throughout the text are assignments designed to reinforce the material of each chapter while building basic research skills. Many of the assignments are based upon actual cases or research issues. All assignments incorporate steps necessary in legal research. The chapter assignments assist the student in

developing skills with regard to particular resources. The student may then combine these skills when called upon to perform more comprehensive research.

Strategies

Many chapters of the text conclude the substantive content with a list of strategies that summarize the essential skills that are the focus of the particular chapter. When followed, these strategies should guide students through the basic steps taken during the phase of research the chapter addresses. While the strategies are general in nature and subject to exception, once the chapter content is fully understood, the student should be able to follow these basic steps as a general checklist in research.

Self-Test

Every chapter concludes with a self-test, which examines the depth with which the student has examined the material in the text. The questions also serve as a general review of concepts. The answers to the chapter self-tests are included in the text to enable the student to identify any areas that he or she may not have thoroughly addressed.

Appendix

The text includes two appendixes. The first is a brief introduction to forms of legal writing. This, in conjunction with legal writing examples in Chapter 4, provides the student with a foundation upon which to build personal legal-writing skills. The second appendix consists of twenty separate legal research assignments, given in graduated levels of difficulty, with later assignments also requiring legal writing.

Support Material

This edition is accompanied by a support package that will assist students in learning and aid instructors in teaching. The following supplements accompany this text:

   A study guide by Beth Walston-Dunham that can be used by student
      as they proceed through the text to strengthen research skills and their
      command of the content addressed by the text. Because much of legal
      research must be accomplished independently, the study guide allows
      the student to track the research trail and, with the assistance of proper
      instruction, develop efficient and comprehensive research skills.
   An instructor's manual and test bank by Beth Walston-Dunham that
      includes all the necessary tools for presenting the material in an orga-
      nized and comprehensive manner. The instructor's manual includes
      sample syllabi, a detailed lesson plan, chapter objectives, key terms, a
      lecture key for each chapter, teaching suggestions, and answers to

most of the assignments. A comprehensive test bank contains over 200 objective test questions and answers.

"The Making of a Case" videotape, narrated by Richard Dysart, star of *L.A. Law,* which introduces the student to the meaning and importance of caselaw. The video explains how cases are published and, in the process, provides an introduction to significant aspects of our legal system.

West's legal research videos, which teach the basis and rationale for legal research. The videos cover the three types of legal research tools—primary tools, secondary tools, and finding tools. They include such topics as caselaw reporters, digests, computer assistance, statutes, special searches, and CD-ROM libraries.

"I Never Said I Was a Lawyer" videotape, produced by the Colorado Bar Association Committee on legal Assistants. The video uses a variety of scenarios to inspire discussion and give students experience dealing with ethical dilemmas.

"Drama of the Law II: Paralegal Issues" videotape, which includes a series of five separate dramatizations intended to simulate classroom discussion about various issues and problems paralegals face on the job today.

West's Law Finder and *West's Sample Pages,* which cover the major research materials of West Publishing Company.

How to Shepardize: Your Guide to Complete Legal Research Through Shepard's Citations, 1993 WESTLAW Edition. This 64-page pamphlet helps students understand the difficult legal research technique of Shepardizing case citations.

Citation-at-a-Glance, an 8-1/2 × 11 reference card that illustrates the basics of citation, using the bluebook method.

West's *Legal CLERK* software, which simulates computerized legal research programs commonly used in the law office.

WESTLAW. Qualified adopters can receive ten free hours of WESTLAW, which runs on most computers with a modem.

ACKNOWLEDGMENTS

While the original ideas for this text are predominately my own, the professional presentation of the material would be wholly impossible without the continued support, guidance, and assistance of the editorial and production staff at West Publishing Company. In particular, I would like to pesonally thank Elizabeth Hannan, Patty Bryant, and Stephanie Syata. Their hours of hard work, imagination, and attention to detail deserve much more recognition than these three people ever seem to receive. I would also like to acknowledge the many supportive comments and suggestions from the reviewers on this project (named below). Thanks are due also to my parents, Keith and Betty Walston, authors in their own right, and to Terry Breden and Eric Walston, who continually support and encourage my work. Finally, and as always, I would like to thank Cindy Burns, of Fremont, Nebraska, whose constant support and flexibility allow me to pursue these projects.

Melody K. Brown
College of Great Falls

Janet Taylor Cox
Northeast Mississippi Community College

Robert R. Cummins, J.D.
Southern College

Wendy Geertz
Kirkwood Community College

Wayne J. Horner
Interstate Business College

Jane Kaplan
New York City Technical College

John J. Keller
Paralegal Institute

Cheryl Kirschner
Bentley College

Pamela Kleinkauf
San Diego State University
Palomar College

Lisa M. Logan
American Institute

Ronald G. Marquardt
University of Southern Mississippi

Constance Ford Mungle
Oklahoma City University

Anthony M. Piazza
Dyke College

Kathleen Mercer Reed
University of Toledo

Laurie Sarnella
Denver Business College

Laurel A. Vietzen
Elgin Community College

Leo Villalobos
El Paso Community College

Jean Volk, Esq.
Middlesex County College

J. Lynne Wood
Anne Arundel Community College

Norma K. Wooten,. J.D.
Johnson County Community College

CONTENTS

CHAPTER **1**

SOURCES OF LEGAL AUTHORITY   1

CHAPTER **2**

CITATION OF AUTHORITY   19

CHAPTER **3**

VALIDATION OF AUTHORITY   42

CHAPTER **4**

LEGAL ANALYSIS AND BEGINNING THE RESEARCH PROCESS   60

CHAPTER **5**

LEGAL DICTIONARIES/THESAURUSES/ ENCYCLOPEDIAS   93

CHAPTER **6**

THE SEARCH FOR STATUTORY AUTHORITY   113

CHAPTER **7**

THE SEARCH FOR JUDICIAL AUTHORITY   152

CHAPTER **8**

THE SEARCH FOR ADMINISTRATIVE AUTHORITY   172

CHAPTER **9**

RESTATEMENTS AND TREATISES   191

CHAPTER **10**

ANNOTATED LAW REPORTS   206

CHAPTER **11**

LEGAL PERIODICALS   226

CHAPTER **12**

LOOSELEAF SERVICES   247

CHAPTER 1

SOURCES OF LEGAL AUTHORITY

CHAPTER OBJECTIVES

Upon completion of this chapter, you should be able to accomplish the following:

- Describe the characteristics unique to legal research.

- Discuss the hierarchy of the different types of legal authorities.

- Describe statutory, administrative, and judicial law.

- Distinguish between mandatory and persuasive authority.

- Distinguish between primary and secondary authority.

- Explain the different effects of mandatory, persuasive, primary, and secondary authorities.

- Describe the types of authorities found in the typical law library.

- Describe the different uses of the authorities found in a typical law library.

- Distinguish a code from an annotated code.

- Distinguish a report from a reporter.

The obvious goal of any research project is to locate the answer to a question. Before starting the actual process of legal research, you should understand its unique characteristics. In legal research, this is only the beginning. As the legal researcher, you must take into account many factors, such as how to find the most influential legal authority. Because legal research answers questions with respect to disputes over legal rights, another factor to consider is any adverse authority that might also influence the outcome of the issues. Finally, because the law will determine the result of a particular case, and because law can change without notice, you must be certain that the results of legal research include the most current pronouncements.

Legal research is more complicated than the ordinary task of locating information on a given topic. The research must be relevant and current and must take into account conflicting views. Consequently, it is important to understand the hierarchy and organization of legal authorities that you may encounter in legal research. Simply put, some authorities are stronger than others. Some are binding law, and others are used only as persuasive logic. This chapter addresses not only the hierarchy but also the many resources that are utilized in the location of information. In subsequent chapters, each type of resource will be examined more closely. A detailed description and discussion of methods of research will be given for each resource. At this point, the purpose is to gain perspective of the law library as a whole.

TYPES OF LAW

It is important for the student new to legal research and the study of legal principles to understand the sources of law. Quite often there is the misconception that the only authorities that can be categorized as law are statutes from legislatures such as the U.S. Congress. While it is true that these statutes have the effect of law, they are not the only legal standards that influence a court when a case between two litigants is decided.

statutory law
A primary authority created by a legislative body. Has the effect of law that is generally superior to other types of primary authority.

Law comes from three sources: the legislative branch, the executive branch, and the judicial branch. Not surprisingly, each branch of government at the state and federal levels have some type of discretion to create rules with the effect of law. In accordance with the U.S. Constitution, at the federal level, only the Congress has the authority to create **statutory law.** Also under the Constitution, the executive branch has the duty to enforce the law. The Congress passes what are known as enabling acts that authorize the president to create administrative agencies, which then have the task of enforcement. The law implemented through administrative rules, regulations, and decisions that explain in detail how a statute applies in a specific situation. The judicial branch serves the function of determining the applicability of law to individual parties to a suit. Because parties to a suit are legally bound to obey the order of a court, judicial opinions have the effect of law when determining the legal rights of litigants. When conducting legal research, you should always examine each of the types of law that may contain authority applicable to the situation at hand.

Constitutional Law

The ultimate law of any jurisdiction is the constitution. At the national level is the U.S. Constitution, which provides the basic structure for all forms of government in the United States. The U.S. Constitution also guarantees consistency in the way law is administered and protects what are considered to be the fundamental rights of all citizens. The U.S. Constitution establishes the three branches of government and outlines their functions. The amendments to the Constitution protect individuals from unnecessary or unjust governmental interference with personal freedom.

Each state also has a constitution. Like a charter, a state constitution outlines the structure and function of the branches of state government and enumerates limitations on government influence over individuals. Neither state constitutions nor state laws (as well as federal laws) may conflict with the U.S. Constitution. In cases where courts find this to be true, the courts have the authority to strike down the law in favor of the Constitution. This principle is discussed further in the section on hierarchy of law.

Statutory Law

As stated previously, statutory law emanates from a legislative body. These legal standards are created by elected representatives of the general population. Ideally, statutory law is created by legislators in direct response to the needs and demands of the majority of citizens. As a result, legal standards from the legislatures are given the greatest weight when applying different types of law to a situation. Generally, statutes are written in a fairly broad manner to encompass a wide variety of citizens and occurrences. However, statutes must be specific enough to allow citizens to determine whether they are in compliance with the law. If a statute is found to be applicable to a specific situation, the statute will dictate the outcome. In other words, the result of the lawsuit can be controlled by the language of the statute. Although greater discussion to legal analysis of statutes is given in a separate chapter, the basic process consists of breaking the language down into conditions or elements of the statute that must be identified in the facts of the case. If the elements are not present, the statute would probably not apply.

 APPLICATION 1.1

STATUTE:

203 U.S.C. Section 1. "It shall be unlawful for any person to dispense Class C Narcotics unless such person has been licensed as a registered pharmacist by the State Board of Pharmacy in the State where the drug is dispensed."

FACT SITUATION:

Francis O'Hara is a registered pharmacist who works in a small pharmacy. She is expecting a regular customer to pick up a weekly supply of prescription medicine. The customer is elderly and has no means of transportation other than during a weekly visit from a home health nurse who takes the customer out to get groceries and medicine. While waiting, Francis receives a phone call from the local hospital stating that her son

has been in an accident. Francis instructs the clerk (who is not a pharmacist) to give the prescription to the customer and collect payment. Francis then leaves the pharmacy. Later the customer comes in and gets the prescription from the clerk. Subsequently, the visiting nurse who accompanied the customer turned the clerk in to the authorities and the clerk was arrested.

Based on the exact language of the statute, the clerk violated the law. Without other legal authority that applies to the situation, the clerk would probably be convicted.

Ordinarily, statutes must be given preference over any other type of law that might address the dispute between the parties. The exception is when the statute is deemed unconstitutional. An example would be if the statute were written so vaguely that citizens could not reasonably ascertain whether their conduct was prohibited by the statute. In addition, other types of law such as regulations and judicial opinions serve the purpose of clarifying how the language of a statute should apply to a more specific situation.

In the situation described above, a possible argument could be made about the constitutionality of the statute. Even though the clerk knew she was not a registered pharmacist, the statute does not address whether acting under the direction of a registered pharmacist would still be a violation. Because the clerk did not prepare the prescription and only handed it to the proper person in exchange for payment, is that conduct still considered "dispensing"? What if the clerk did not even know that the bag contained a Class C narcotic? Because the statute does not discuss any requirement of knowledge or intent, nor does it mention anything other than a blanket prohibition to dispense, the clerk may have a viable claim that the law, as written, is too broad to be considered constitutional because the clerk was incapable under the circumstances of determining whether her conduct was illegal.

The U.S. Congress makes statutes that apply to all persons within the jurisdiction of the United States. Additionally, each state has a legislature that creates statutes for the persons within the boundaries of the state or for those who are engaged in certain types of activity within the state. An example of the latter might be a company that sells products within a state even though the manufacturer is located elsewhere. Subsequent chapters will give a more detailed discussion of statutory law and methods of locating it.

Administrative Law

administrative law

Legal standards including regulations, rules, and administrative decisions that issue from administrative agencies as a function of the executive branch duty to enforce the law.

Administrative law is created by administrative agencies, which are under the supervision of the executive branch following creation as the result of a congressional enabling act. At the federal level, this is the president. At the state level, the head of the executive branch is the governor. The chief executive is obligated to see that the laws of the jurisdiction are enforced. Agencies assist in this process by issuing regulations that attempt to clarify and enforce the meaning of statutes that are broadly written. Administrative rules are promulgated as the procedures to be followed by an agency when it creates and issues regulations. Although technically distinct, some jurisdictions use the terms *regulation* and *rule* interchangeably. Administrative decisions are written by hearing officers known as administrative law judges, who determine how a regulation applies to a specific party or situation.

Because administrative law is a direct attempt to clarify and enforce statutory law, it is subordinate to statutory law when the statute and regulation appear to be in conflict. If a court must apply either a statute or a regulation, it will apply the statute. Also, administrative law can be enacted only when it supports or clarifies an existing statute. Without a statute, the agency has no power to create law of any kind, because the function of the executive branch and ultimately the agency is to enforce existing statutory law through clarification, definition, and application. Recall that the U.S. Constitution allows only the legislature to create statutory law.

⚖ APPLICATION 1.2

Refer to the fictional statutory language in Application 1.1. Assume the Federal Food and Drug Administration issues the following regulation: "It shall not be considered a violation of 203 U.S.C. Section 1 if such narcotics are dispensed by one under the supervision of a duly registered pharmacist."

The regulation is a clear attempt to clarify the types of situations that the statutory law attempts to prohibit, namely, the dispensing of controlled substances by persons other than registered pharmacists. The fact situation described above is not one that is intended for criminal prosecution according to the regulation that is derivative of the statute.

Judicial Law

Judicial law is issued in the form of judicial opinions commonly known as cases, opinions, or case law. In many instances, when the outcome of a trial is appealed, a panel of judges from an appellate court will review any irregularities or errors that allegedly occurred in the trial court where lawsuits are initially filed and tried. The appellate court will then issue a decision that affirms, modifies, or reverses the previous outcome at the trial court level. The decision will cite applicable legal authorities and explain the reason for the outcome in the appellate court. These appellate decisions have the force of law and are frequently published for reference by parties and courts in similar cases. Published opinions are of great value. You can conduct a search for a previous case to compare to a current situation. Based on a detailed analysis of the similarities and differences, a determination can be made as to whether the client's case is likely to have the same or a different result. Using this type of legal analysis, you can assess with a certain degree of accuracy how a statute or principle of common law is likely to be interpreted under similar circumstances.

judicial law
Legal standards established by the judicial branch in the form of court orders and judicial opinions.

⚖ APPLICATION 1.3

Refer to the ongoing situation discussed in Applications 1.1 and 1.2. Assume that the lawyer for the pharmacy clerk located a case in which the issue of what constituted "supervision" of an employee was discussed. The opinion made clear that "supervision" did not require constant physical presence of the employer. That would defeat the need for the employee. Rather, as long as the employer gave clear direction of the tasks to the employee, reviewed the actions of the employee, and was ultimately responsible for those acts, the employee would be considered supervised.

With this judicial opinion and the above regulation, the likelihood that the clerk would be convicted is greatly diminished. Note how the three sources of law complement one another and are used jointly to resolve the application of law to the issue of whether, under these specific circumstances, the clerk violated a federal criminal statute.

Some judicial opinions are considered commonlaw. In the traditional sense, commonlaw is created by the judiciary in the absence of any applicable legal authorities. Today, however, commonlaw is often used to describe the application of any type of law in a judicial opinion. Because it is not possible or practical for the legislature to enact legal standards for every conceivable situation, the judiciary serves the role of establishing legal principles or applying existing legal authorities to very specific circumstances. The term *commonlaw* comes from the belief that courts deal directly with individuals and thereby create law for the common man in accordance with what the common man would expect to be acceptable conduct.

Judicial law, although the final word in a case, is the lowest in the hierarchy of legal authorities with regard to influence on a court. It is focused on very specific situations. However, in the event a judge interprets a statute or administrative law to be unconstitutional in some respect, the court has the authority to overrule the statute or administrative law and to give the greatest weight to any applicable case law.

☐ ASSIGNMENT 1.1

Elise is the pilot of an airplane operated by a tour company for sightseeing. Prior to flying, Elise consumes four alcoholic beverages. The plane crashes, and all aboard are killed. Write a sample statute, administrative regulation, and paragraph from a judicial opinion that would apply to this situation and demonstrate the basic differences between these types of legal standards. Refer to the previous illustrations for examples.

WEIGHT OF AUTHORITY: WHAT STANDARDS HAVE THE GREATEST STRENGTH?

legal standard
A principle of law.

The preceding discussion explained that law comes in various forms. The principles of law, also known as **legal standards,** come from a variety of sources. As discussed, statutes are created by the state and federal legislatures. Administrative regulations, rules, and decisions come from many different state and federal agencies. Judicial opinions come from the different levels of courts within the state and federal judicial systems. Other legal authorities exist that do not have the impact of law on a case but are helpful in reaching a logical and fair result. Thus, when attempting to complete legal research on an issue, the question arises, How do you locate the most influential authority?

The discussion of the types of law—statutory, administrative, and judicial—stated that there is a distinct hierarchy of these three. When a statute and judicial opinion would indicate different results on an issue, the statutory result prevails (unless the statute is ruled unconstitutional). Accordingly, nonlaw resources would have less influence than law. A problem arises,

however, when there appear to be two authorities that are similar in origin but dictate different results (e.g., two seemingly contradictory statutes). Many times, this can be resolved by examining the exact source of the authorities. All legal authorities can be classified as primary or secondary and as mandatory or persuasive. To be considered primary, the legal authority must be some form of law, either statutory, administrative, or judicial. Secondary authority is generated by a private source, such as a legal dictionary. Such authority is not law, but it is sometimes helpful when clarifying the meaning of a legal term relevant to the issue between the parties.

Mandatory and persuasive authority indicate the degree of influence of a legal standard on a deciding court. As the name implies, **mandatory authority** is a legal standard that the court is required to follow. An example of mandatory authority for all courts in the American legal system is the U.S. Constitution. Another example is a statute from the same state in which the state court in a case is located. Because the court must follow mandatory authority, it is logical to assume that all mandatory authority must be some form of law (primary authority). Additionally, mandatory authority must be law that comes from a source superior to the deciding court. Hence, mandatory authority is law that is created by a superior primary authority. Examples of mandatory primary authority for all courts would include the U.S. Congress, state legislatures and administrative agencies of the same state whose law is being applied by the deciding court, federal administrative agencies, and the U.S. Supreme Court. Depending upon the status of the particular deciding court, there may also be other courts that issue law that a lower court must follow. An example would be that a state trial court would have to follow the law set down by the highest appellate court of the same state. For example, the courts of Kansas must follow the statutory law of the Kansas legislature. This statutory law would be mandatory on the courts of Kansas. The statutory law of Arizona would not, however, be mandatory, because the law of Arizona does not have to be applied in Kansas.

Persuasive authority is that which the court has no obligation to follow but which may have a logical reasoning that the court is persuaded to follow. An example would include all secondary authority. Also included is primary authority from other jurisdictions or subordinate courts. These other jurisdictions or lower courts cannot dictate to the deciding court how to rule in a given case. However, in the absence of mandatory primary authority, if the deciding court is convinced that a secondary authority, the law of another **jurisdiction,** or a lower court ruling is logical, the deciding court may be persuaded to issue a similar ruling. In Application 1.5, the statutory law of Arizona would be considered a persuasive authority in a Kansas court.

The four methods of classifying authority can be summarized in the following way:

> **Primary Authority** - always law.
> **Secondary Authority** - always private opinion.
> **Mandatory Authority** - always law (primary authority); the court must apply this authority to the issue.
> **Persuasive Authority** - may be law or private opinion; the court may choose to apply it to the issue.

mandatory authority
Primary authority or law that comes from a superior source and that must be adhered to.

persuasive authority
Primary or secondary authority from a collateral or subordinate source that may be given deference.

jurisdiction
Limits of authority of a particular court or branch of government.

primary authority
A legal standard having the effect of law.

secondary authority
Published reference from a private (nongovernmental) source. Does not have the effect of law but can be used as persuasive authority.

⚖️ **APPLICATION 1.4**

Max Rogers is conducting legal research on the question of whether the state of Orion has adopted the felony-murder rule. Totally unfamiliar with the subject, Max consults a legal dictionary and a legal encyclopedia. After gaining a working knowledge of the topic, he moves on in search of law. Max locates a statute from Orion that indicates the felony murder rule is applied in very specific circumstances. He also locates a judicial opinion from the highest court of a neighboring state, which clearly defines the type of situations in which the felony murder rule should be applied.

_____ ▪

📋 **ASSIGNMENT 1.2**

Evaluate the legal authorities underlined in Application 1.4. For each, list the term(s) that could be used to describe the authority:

  a. mandatory
  b. persuasive
  c. primary
  d. secondary

When conducting legal research, you must understand the various ways of classifying authority and the methods needed to locate that which will have the greatest impact on the case at hand. Ideally, you would always find primary mandatory authority in the form of statutes from the jurisdiction of the pending case. Unfortunately, this is seldom the case. Therefore, you must always evaluate the authority found in terms of weight or strength when placed against the legal authorities offered by the opposing party. This will enable you to arrive at an educated opinion as to the probable outcome of the issues in the case.

OVERVIEW OF THE LAW LIBRARY

Although each of the following will be addressed at length in subsequent chapters, it is helpful at this point to briefly tour the resources found in the typical law library. What follows is a listing and brief discussion of the types of materials that you can expect to encounter.

Primary Authority—Law

Codes and Annotated Statutes.   Codes (also referred to by other names such as "Revised Statutes") are collections of all the currently effective statutes of a jurisdiction. One example of a Code would be the United States Code (U.S.C.), which houses all the statutes passed by the U.S. Congress and which are currently in effect. Annotated statutes are similar to codes but have an added feature. An annotated code contains for each statute one- or two-sentence summaries of judicial opinions in which the courts have examined the constitutionality of the statute or the applicability of the statute to a given

situation. Additionally, the annotated code (and sometimes general codes) may have background information about the statute that helps you to understand the intent of the legislature when the statute was originally enacted as well as cross-references to other relevant information. Understanding the purpose of the statute assists you and, ultimately, a court to determine whether and how the statute should apply in a case.

Generally, updated statutory information is published in the interim between new issues of hardbound volumes. The updates appear in the form of a separate book, usually softcover supplements, or pocket parts. (Pocket parts are pamphlets that fit into a pocket located on the inside cover of the hardbound volume. When the pamphlet becomes too cumbersome to fit within the pocket of the book, a softcover supplement or newly updated hardbound volume may be issued.)

It is extremely important to consult both the hardbound statutes and the supplements, since the latter contains changes in the law since the last issuance of a hardbound volume. This might be illustrated in the following way: A law has been on the books in the state of Geriard for several years that states you must be 21 to obtain a license as a practical nurse. However, because many high school vocational programs offer practical nursing training, the high schools want the legal age changed to 18. The legislature considers this, finds it a valid request, and amends the law. Shortly thereafter, a supplement to the statutory code is published that includes all amendments to the law. Donna is a 19-year-old woman licensed as a practical nurse in another state. She moves to Geriard and wants to know whether she can obtain a nursing license. By consulting the statutory code, the answer to her question would be no. But by also consulting the supplement for amendments to the laws within the code, Donna would find that there is no longer an age barrier to her obtaining the license.

Administrative Regulations, Rules, and Decisions.   These authorities are issued by administrative agencies. Each type of administrative authority has a distinct purpose. Regulations are issued by the agency to clarify the meaning of the statute as it applies to individual situations. For example, the National Environmental Protection Act of 1969 is a group of statutes passed by Congress that essentially state the various goals of cleaning up the environment. The Environmental Protection Agency (E.P.A) has issued and continues to issue regulations that explain in detail just what Congress meant by the language of these statutes. In this way, individuals and businesses can determine whether their particular conduct is in compliance with or in violation of federal law.

Rules, on the other hand, explain the process of a particular agency when creating or amending regulations. By having established procedures for the creation of administrative law and the operation of an administrative agency, everyone can have a voice in the process of an administrative agency because the agency is required to follow its rules of procedure.

Administrative decisions are issued when an individual party takes exception to the way a particular regulation or rule is applied. The party has a right to challenge the agency's creation or application of a rule or regulation and to have the challenge considered by an administrative law judge and ultimately a court from the judicial system.

Federal administrative law is generally published in two sources. First, it appears in the Federal Register, a daily publication for all federal agencies. The

Federal Register includes proposed and permanent regulations, rules, and some decisions. Secondly, federal regulations and rules are routinely published in the Code of Federal Regulations (C.F.R.). Like statutory codes, the C.F.R. contains all currently effective law. The distinction is that the C.F.R. is confined to administrative rules and regulations. The C.F.R. is updated annually to remove the text of repealed regulations or rules and to incorporate new or amended ones. While these are the most commonly used administrative resources, other similar publications exist at the state and federal levels.

⚖ APPLICATION 1.5

The Economic Recovery Agency issues a rule that no regulations shall be imposed on private businesses without at least 90 days' notice to the business and 120 days' notice from the date the regulation takes effect to achieve compliance. On April 1, the agency issues a regulation that requires businesses to provide the opportunity for a one-month salary advance to all full-time employees if the advance is used to purchase or build a home. The regulation takes effect on July 1, and businesses have the obligation to offer the advance option to employees as of November 1. The first publication of the rule and regulation appear in Federal Register. Subsequently, the regulation would be included in the Code of Federal Regulations with other effective rules and regulations.

Judicial Authority.   Judicial authority appears in the form of case law, also known as judicial opinion. Primarily, appellate cases are published. These are cases that have been introduced at the trial court level and are appealed on the basis that something occurred at the lower court level that allegedly prevented a proper legal result. Typically, a panel of judges (usually three) reviews the case and issues a joint opinion as to whether the lower court reached an appropriate result.

Case law is published in reports and reporters (discussed in greater detail in subsequent chapters). Cases are published in chronological order by court; that is, as opinions are handed down, they are published with other recent opinions from the same court or jurisdiction. When presented in this way, the publication is known as a report. Also, in many instances, all recent decisions of several courts or jurisdictions will be combined into a single volume known as a reporter. In the case of a report or reporter, volumes of cases accumulate as time passes. These volumes are numbered in the order they are issued, and an entire collection is known as a series. An example would be the Federal Reporter Second Series. This includes several hundred volumes of cases from the U.S. Circuit Courts of Appeals in the federal system over many years.

⚖ APPLICATION 1.6

Refer to the preceding application. Assume a small business challenges the agency regulation in court on the basis that the government is illegally forcing businesses to make employee loans. The case is tried, lost, and appealed to a U.S. Circuit Court of Appeals. The opinion of the court that resolves the issue will be published along with other recent U.S. Courts of Appeals opinions in the next hardbound volume of the Federal Reporter Second Series.

☐ ASSIGNMENT 1.3

Matthew is conducting a legal research project. He has the option of consulting several primary authorities. One consists of pronouncements by the legislature. Another is a combination of legislative pronouncements and summaries of judicial opinions dealing with the legislative pronouncements. He also has access to legal authority issued by the executive branch, which is often more specific than the legislative pronouncements, and to publications with the complete language of judicial opinions as they apply to extremely specific situations.

Identify each of the primary authorities described above.

Secondary Authority/Research Aides

Restatements.   A Restatement is a publication that summarizes all the significant rules of law that are followed by the majority of jurisdictions on a particular subject (e.g., Restatement of the Law of Contracts). Restatements are a rather peculiar secondary source. Technically, they are not considered law. They are authored and published by the American Law Institute. Because Restatements are not issued by a lawmaking authority, they do not have the required effect of law. It is important to note, however, that the members of the American Law Institute are highly regarded as some of the finest legal scholars in the nation. Consequently, in the absence of primary authority, a court may be strongly persuaded by an applicable section of a Restatement for a case. Restatements are published for each of a number of specific subjects in law. They are discussed further in Chapter 9 of the text.

⚖ APPLICATION 1.7

A lawsuit is pending as the result of an auto accident involving a driver of a delivery-company car and an individual. The individual sues the driver and the delivery company for the injuries. There is some question as to whether the driver was under the supervision of the delivery company at the time of the accident. By consulting the Restatement of the Law of Agency, you can determine whether the generally accepted rules of law would deem the company liable for injuries caused by the acts of its drivers under similar circumstances.

Treatises.   The inexperienced legal researcher may confuse the terms *treatise* and *treaty*, the latter being an agreement between two nations. The term *treatise* has an entirely different meaning. A treatise is a detailed and thorough discussion of a subject by a scholar or scholars on the topic. It generally examines the historical background and development of the subject. Legal treatises often speak in terms of generally accepted theories rather than follow the law of a particular jurisdiction.

⚖ APPLICATION 1.8

You have been hired by a law firm that specializes in automobile products liability. Having had limited training in such a specific area, you want to learn as much as

possible. By reading a treatise on products liability, you can develop a much better understanding of how these cases differ from standard personal injury litigation.

Legal Encylopedias.   A legal encyclopedia is similar in many ways to an ordinary encyclopedia. It gives a brief report on various topics. The primary difference is that a legal encyclopedia addresses only subjects of a legal nature. Secondly, the legal encyclopedia includes numerous footnotes that reference other legal authorities on a subject such as cases and statutes. Legal encyclopedias are periodically updated through the use of supplements or pocket parts in the same way statutes are updated. In this way, the text can be modified to reflect changes in the law as they occur.

⚖ APPLICATION 1.9

In Application 1.4, a researcher looked in a legal encyclopedia to gain a basic understanding of the felony murder rule. By doing so, the researcher was able to locate a brief description of the legal standard that enabled further specific research in a specific jurisdiction. The encyclopedia also included footnotes to other authorities on the subject.

Annotated Law Reports (A.L.R.).   These reports are especially useful in legal research on topics of law that are new or changing. In an A.L.R. annotation, a judicial opinion that typifies the current issues on the particular topic of law and a detailed analysis of the treatment of these issues in various jurisdictions are included. This allows the researcher to follow trends and possibly to anticipate a change of law in a jurisdiction. Like legal encyclopedias, Annotated Law Reports are periodically updated through the use of pocket part supplements.

⚖ APPLICATION 1.10

You want to know whether a court has authority to impose child support obligations on a party for the college education of children after they reach the age of majority. Because the law of domestic relations is constantly undergoing change, the A.L.R. is an excellent resource for this issue. By looking for annotations on this subject, you can examine an actual judicial opinion that details the reasoning of a court on the issue, and you can identify all the jurisdictions that have already addressed the issue and the position taken by these courts.

Legal Periodicals.   There are numerous periodic publications such as local, regional, and national legal newspapers and legal journals or magazines. These may be published by commercial companies, special interest groups, bar associations, or law schools. They generally include the same categories of information found in ordinary newspapers and magazines. They contain articles, sometimes news of recent events, and classified advertisements. They differ from a general publication in that they contain information on legal

topics. Such topics include analysis of changes occurring in subjects of law or recent legislative, administrative, and court pronouncements.

 APPLICATION 1.11

You have recently become aware of a new federal law that is likely to affect a number of cases at the law firm where you are employed. The senior partner wants an analysis of the issues that the law will create for pending cases of the firm and the likely results. Rather than start from scratch, you may find that a legal periodical will outline all major issues and give you insight and specific resources to determine the effects of the law on the pending cases in your firm.

Looseleaf Services. A looseleaf service is a combination of many other legal resources. The looseleaf service typically contains primary authority and commentary by private authors (secondary authority) on a particular subject of law. Because the information is contained in a looseleaf binder, specific pages can be individually removed and replaced as the law changes. Looseleafs are frequently published for complex or rapidly changing areas of law (e.g., the federal tax code). Periodic supplements are published on a subscription basis. They generally come out weekly, monthly, semiannually, or annually.

 APPLICATION 1.12

You work for a firm that handles tax issues for several large corporations. The Treasury Department has just issued a new regulation that makes mileage to and from work a deductible business expense as long as the employer confirms the expense with an annual report for each employee. The regulation further states that any business with more than 50 employees must provide this service if the employees request it. The corporations your firm represents want to know whether they can claim a deduction for the cost of preparing the reports. A looseleaf service will provide not only the exact language of the regulation but also an analysis and opinion by tax experts on any resulting issues such as the one just described.

Legal Dictionaries and Thesauruses. These resources are helpful not only in legal research but also in legal writing. The legal dictionary provides definitions of terms as their meanings are interpreted by the legislatures, administrative agencies, and courts. Often these are quite different from the everyday meaning of a word or phrase. The legal thesaurus provides synonyms and related terms for a word or phrase. Because most resources in the law library are indexed by subject, this is helpful when trying to locate information on a particular topic. Often the topic will be indexed by a term other than what you might expect. To illustrate this, assume a client has no funds to pay for a lawyer in a case where the client wants to appeal a decision of a lower court. Procedural laws that have been written to explain how the federal courts are accessible to the poor and indigent are found by looking in the index to the federal statutes under the term *in forma pauperis*. This term is

unfamiliar to most beginning researchers. However, it would appear under the term *indigent* in many legal thesauruses. The thesaurus also helps to make legal writing more interesting by allowing the writer to avoid redundant terms.

Digests. The digest is the companion to and primary finding tool of judicial report(er)s. In a sense, the digest is a large and detailed subject index of cases. A digest takes a judicial opinion and breaks it down into the subjects discussed. For each subject, a short summary is prepared. Usually, it is a one-sentence summary and thus should never be relied on out of context. The summary is commonly called a **headnote,** or annotation. All of the headnotes for all of the opinions in a particular report or reporter are grouped by topic. Consequently, to find a number of judicial opinions on a particular topic for a specific jurisdiction (mandatory primary authority), one needs only to consult that topic in the digest that parallels the appropriate report(er). Because hundreds of thousands of judicial opinions are published, it is a necessary skill to determine the appropriate report(er), digest, topic, and subtopic. Methods to develop the skill of making efficient use of digests are addressed later in the text.

headnote
Also known as an annotation. A brief summary of a judicial opinion.

In Application 1.4, a researcher was examining the felony murder rule. To locate judicial opinions on the topic, the researcher would have to go to the digest and look up the topic and subtopics that deal with homicide and, specifically, felony murder. By reading headnotes, the researcher can narrow the search to include only cases that mention felony murder circumstances as opposed to other categories of homicide.

Reference and Form Books. Essential to any law library are reference and form books. Reference books are like those found in any library. They are books of general information written about the development and status of particular topics of law. An example is a book on the development of civil law from its inception in feudal England to its status in the American legal system today. Form books contain models for the myriad of legal documents and proceedings that one encounters or is required to produce when working within the law or in law-related professions. They include everything from contracts to court pleadings.

⚖ APPLICATION 1.13

As a first-year law student, I was assigned to prepare a motion in limine for class the following day. My first concern was that I had not so much as a clue as to what a motion in limine was, much less how to prepare one. After some preliminary research, I was able to establish the purpose and function of such a motion. However, it was still unclear just exactly what the proper form for such a document should be. By consulting a form book subject index (with the use of synonyms found in a legal thesaurus), I found a sample document. By conforming this to the particular case from my assignment, I was able to prepare the motion adequately (and I received an A on the assignment!!!).

Citators. Citators are used to confirm the current validity of a legal authority. Because law can change quickly and without notice, citators and frequent supplements are published for legal authorities. The appropriate citator can be consulted to determine whether the legal standard of a

particular case or statute or regulation has been changed in any way. It also indicates any other authority that has made reference to the particular source examined. Using a citator is often a useful method to expand your research.

⚖ APPLICATION 1.14

You are conducting research and find a 20-year-old statute that directly supports your position. You look at the supplements and find that the statute has not been amended or repealed by the legislature. You give the statute to the supervising attorney, who presents it to the court. However, the opposition also located the statute and consulted not only the statutory supplement but also a citator. The citator revealed that 14 years ago the state supreme court found that statute to be unconstitutional and deemed it invalid since that time. The legislature never officially repealed the ineffective statute, and the code supplements did not reflect the court ruling.

▢ ASSIGNMENT 1.4

Evaluate the following research assignment. Determine which secondary authorities would be helpful. Explain your answers. ** For the purposes of this assignment, you do not need to complete the research. Rather, identify the secondary sources that would be of assistance in the research and explain why.

The client owns a business with two other partners. While the partners' verbal agreement is that each partner will be responsible for one third of the duties associated with the business, one of the partners has failed almost completely to honor the arrangement. However, this partner does not hesitate to draw one third of the profits each month from the partnership account. You are required to determine whether a partnership in fact exists and, if so, whether the two working partners have any recourse against the third partner.

CHAPTER SUMMARY

The process of legal research can be both frustrating and exciting. There is nothing quite like the discovery of the perfect case to answer a legal question on behalf of a client. Similarly, there is nothing quite so exasperating as a seemingly endless search for authority that should exist but cannot be found. By having a thorough knowledge of the resources available and how to use them, the rewards can immensely outweigh the frustrations.

When conducting research, you must always keep in mind that when a conflict exists, statutes take precedence over administrative law that takes similar precedence over case law. Also, mandatory primary authority is the first priority in locating information. Next would be persuasive primary authority, followed by persuasive secondary authority. Failure to follow these rules can result in authority that is applicable but inferior to that produced by the opposition in the case. Third, the authority located must be validated as current and effective. It does no good to rely on a statute that has been repealed.

It is important to recognize all of the resources available in a law library. Even though the goal may be to locate only mandatory primary authority, sometimes this can be done more efficiently and quickly when secondary resources are consulted first. The competent researcher knows what assistance is available in the law library and uses it fully and to the best advantage of the client.

KEY TERMS

administrative law
headnote
judicial law
jurisdiction

legal standard
mandatory authority
persuasive authority

primary authority
secondary authority
statutory law

SELF-TEST

MULTIPLE CHOICE

1. _____ is the only basis upon which judicial law takes precedence over statutory law.
   a) Constitutionality
   b) Legality
   c) Administrative law
   c) none of the above

2. A _____ is a publication of all current effective legislative law.
   a) reporter
   b) supplement
   c) code
   d) digest

3. _____ and _____ describe the degree of influence an authority has on a court.
   a) Mandatory, persuasive
   b) Mandatory, secondary
   c) Primary, mandatory
   d) Primary, secondary

4. _____ and _____ describe the source of an authority.
   a) Mandatory, primary
   b) Mandatory, secondary
   c) Primary, mandatory
   d) Primary, secondary

5. Any principle of law can be properly referred to as a _____ .

   a) legal standard
   b) regulation
   c) statute
   d) judicial standard

TRUE/FALSE

_____ 6. A short summary of a judicial opinion is referred to as an annotation or a headnote.

_____ 7. Legal standards emanating from the executive branch constitute statutory law.

_____ 8. No secondary authority has the effect of mandatory law.

_____ 9. Knowledge of terms relevant to the topic is essential to begin research.

_____10. Legal research ends when you locate a decisive authority.

FILL-IN THE BLANKS

11–13. Factors to consider when conducting legal research as opposed to other research include

_____

_____

_____

14. _____ authority is that which the court has no obligation to follow.

15. Judicial law is officially published in a
_____ .

16. _____ law can be created only
by the legislature.

17. Primary authority includes
_____, _____ ,
and _____ law.

18. Judicial law is published
_____ .

19. Statutory law is updated by the issuance
of _____.

20. Secondary authority does not have the
effect of _____ .

CHAPTER 2

CITATION OF AUTHORITY

At the conclusion of this chapter, you should be able to accomplish the following competencies:

- Identify the purpose of citation of legal authority.

- Explain the need and benefits of uniformity of rules of citation.

- Demonstrate the process for preparing citations of legal standards.

- Properly capitalize, punctuate, and abbreviate citations of authority.

- Explain the rules of citation and presentation for quotations of legal authorities.

- Prepare citations of authority for secondary authorities.

- Prepare several consecutive citations of authority.

- Incorporate citations of authority into grammatical sentences.

- Prepare citations of procedural law.

- Explain the proper use and positioning of parallel authorities.

Purpose and Benefits of Rules of Citation

A necessary element in any type of professional writing is reference to the sources providing information and authority for the content of the document. When you identify your sources of authority or information in your writing, you should use a specific format for notation within the text, in footnotes, and in bibliographies. Legal writing has rules designed exclusively for reference to legal authorities. These rules are commonly known as rules of **citation**. The phrase "to cite an authority" means to make a proper reference to the source. Basic rules of citation have been designed to allow easy identification and location of the source.

citation
Reference note containing information necessary to locate an authority.

When everyone uses an essentially uniform system of referring to sources of information, locating those sources becomes quite easy. This is similar to basic language or directional information, such as the street system in a city. If we all assigned different words to meanings, we would be unable to communicate. If everyone used his or her own set of street names or other methods of identifying location, travel to a designated point based on information from another person would be virtually impossible. However, by using a commonly accepted language or method of organization, communication of ideas or travel to any point is conducted with relative ease. Similarly, in citation, accepted methods of referring to information allow individuals and governments to communicate and locate information with little chance of confusion or mistake.

An example of how rules of citation work is found in the rules of statutory law citation. The federal government and all state statutory codes are arranged by general topic. (Certain broad areas such as the many subtypes of procedural law may be placed together and then subcategorized by exact topic.) Each topic is given a number. Next, each individual statute within a topic is assigned another number. The proper method to cite a statute includes the name of the code, the topic number, the number representing the specific law on the topic, and the year of the publication. The topic number generally appears somewhere prior to the statute number in the citation. With this information, you can determine the exact location of the statute by identifying the topic number, name and year of the publication, and the specific statute number in the citation. You would take that information to the statutes in the library and find the correct publication and topic number (this information appears on the book binding). You would then open the volume of the correct topic number to the specific statutory number. By doing this, you can locate the exact statutory language that was referred to in the legal writing.

The year of publication of a statute is very important, as statutes may be amended from time to time and their meaning may change. While the arrangement of statutory information may vary somewhat from state to state or in federal publications, citations generally give information in descending order of specificity. For example, the first number given would be the general topic, and the second number would be the specific statute within a topic. The year is generally last and in parentheses. NOTE: Throughout this chapter (and the text), examples and assignments are used to illustrate and to reinforce the concepts associated with proper citation form. Many are fictitious but represent proper elements of citation.

⚖️ APPLICATION 2.1

SAMPLE STATUTORY CITATION
Ill.Rev.Stat. ch. 28, para. 201 (1985)

This citation provides the following information:

Code: (statutory publication) Illinois Revised Statutes.
Subject number: chapter 28.
Individual law: paragraph 201.
Year of publication: 1985.

☐ ASSIGNMENT 2.1

Using the information in Application 2.1, break down the following citations using the same format as used in Application 2.1:

1. 21 Mo.Rev.Stat. 849 (1986).
2. Ala.Code 34-562 (1980).
3. Minn.Stat. 101-1132 (1990).

Rules of citation are essential to a uniform method of communicating information. For example, by having established rules of citation, a court in New Jersey can easily read an opinion from a court in California and determine what legal authorities were relied on by the California court. The New Jersey court can then consult the same authorities relied upon by the California court and make a decision regarding whether these authorities and the California opinion are applicable in the New Jersey case as well. This uniformity allows legal professionals of all types to exchange and obtain information in any jurisdiction. This is increasingly important as society becomes more mobile and as the volume of legal precedents increases.

The benefits of citation are obvious. The legal professional can easily determine the sources of authority when conducting research or when evaluating the research put forth by the opposition. Uniform rules ease the task of legal writing by using established forms for reference to authorities within text or in footnotes. Well-organized methods of reference create a widely accepted method of abbreviation which shortens the task of reference to authority in an acceptable and professional manner.

The following sections contain explanations and examples of the rules of citation for the most commonly cited authorities. *This chapter is not exhaustive, and you should always consult the appropriate rule of citation when making reference to a particular authority.* In this text, the rules discussed are based on a respected authority known as "Harvard Law Review Association, The Bluebook, A Uniform System of Citation," 15th ed. (1991). As exemplified by the 14 prior editions, the bluebook, as it is commonly called, has a long-standing reputation for its pursuit of consistency in the process of creating accepted methods of citation. Other authorities exist that also establish such rules. However, for the sake of consistency throughout this text, the rules according to the bluebook will be followed. Because changes in rules of citation do occur

from time to time, you should always consult the most current version of citation authority, such as the bluebook, when you make reference to a legal authority.

In addition to containing explanatory rules for virtually every primary and secondary legal authority, the bluebook includes tables that contain the abbreviations and citation forms for statutory, judicial, and administrative law, international law, federal law, and the law of each state. The bluebook also has an extensive index that you can use to locate specific information on the preparation of virtually any kind of citation. The index is used for both the explanatory rules and the tables. Once you are familiar with the format, the bluebook's numerous explanations, examples, and tables make the bluebook a very quick and easy-to-use reference tool for citation questions.

BASIC RULES OF CITATION

General Information

Before beginning the process of examining methods of citation for specific authorities, some general rules might be helpful. What follows is a brief description of citation practices employed for most authorities.

Capitalization and Sentence Structure.   In legal writing, citations are treated as phrases that constitute complete sentences. Consequently, they should start with a capital letter and end with a period. However, if the cite is incorporated into a longer sentence, appropriate use of other punctuation should be made, just as when adding a phrase to an existing sentence. Similarly, because citations can stand alone grammatically as independent sentences, when two or more citations are joined, they should be connected with a semicolon.

Another general rule regards capitalization. As in ordinary writing, proper nouns or titles should have the first letter of each word capitalized. The exception to this rule would be if one of the words within a name or title is used as a connecting term such as *or, and,* or *the.* If you are familiar with the proper capitalization of titles, the preparation of citations is much simpler because the rules for capitalization are much the same. Application 2.2 and the text that follows Assignment 2.2 include a number of sample citations that should help you understand the sentence structure and capitalization format. Keep in mind, however, that these are very basic rules and should not supersede the formal rules of citation regarding sentence structure, capitalization, abbreviations, or other organization of information. Also, while the bluebook rules are basically consistent, there is some variation for the different types of authorities. For this reason, the bluebook or other citation reference source should be consulted to confirm the proper format.

In the bluebook, General Rule 8 addresses capitalization. The rule reads as follows:

> In headings and titles, capitalize the initial word, the word immediately following a colon (if any), and all other words except articles, conjunctions, and prepositions of four or fewer letters. . . . Capitalize nouns referring to people or

groups only when they identify specific persons, officials, groups, government offices, or government bodies. . . .

In summary, you should follow the premise that the names of cases refer to the specific parties, and consequently, the first letter of each word should be capitalized. The exception, as previously mentioned, are such terms as *and, the,* and *or* as well as short prepositions, unless the title or name begins with one of these words. A similar rule applies to the names of statutes and statutory publications.

⚖ APPLICATION 2.2

SAMPLES OF CAPITALIZATION IN CITATIONS

1. Zeller v. First National Bank and Trust Co. of Evanston, 323 Ill. 2d 1021, 398 N.E. 2d 148 (Ill. 1979).
2. Aster v. Gross, 371 S.E.2d 833 (Va. 1988); *Pommerenke v. Pommerenke,* 372 S.E.2d 630 (Va. 1988).
3. Martin, et.al. v. The Port of Seattle, 64 Wash. 2d 309, 91 P. 2d. 540 (1964).
4. Oklahoma Statutes Annotated
5. Ohio Revised Code

☐ ASSIGNMENT 2.2

Properly capitalize each of the following case and code names:

1. opheim v. united mobile homes inc.
2. united states v. causby
3. lachman v. sperry-sun well and surveying co.
4. bigvee v. pacific telephone and telegraph co.
5. browning ferris indus. of vermont v. kelso disposal, inc.
6. ernst and ernst v. hochfelder
7. the standard oil co. of new jersey v. united states
8. united states code
9. vernon's annotated missouri statutes
10. arizona revised statutes annotated

The following are samples of proper sentence structure in various types of citations:

1. Single citation as an independent sentence: Federal Trade Commission v. Procter & Gamble Co., 386 U.S. 568 (1986).
2. Single citation as part of another sentence: In the case of Raitt v. Johns Hopkins Hospital, 274 Md. 489, 336 A. 2d 90 (1985), the court stated that the fact that one has never practiced medicine in the jurisdiction of the alleged incident of malpractice does not prevent one from being qualified as an expert witness.
3. Two consecutive citations of authority: Kortus v. Jensen, 195 Neb. 261, 237 N.W. 2d 845 (1976); McCay v. Mitchell, 62 Tenn. App. 424, 463 S. 2d. 710 (1st Dist. App. 1990).

☐ ASSIGNMENT 2.3

Assemble the following information into the designated citation forms. Use the preceding discussion of rules and examples to form your citations.

1. Citation as a single independent sentence:

Parties: state v. state board of equalization and assessment

Source of publication: 123 ark.app. 259, 242 sw2d 609

Court/year: (1982)

2. Citation as part of a textual sentence:

Parties: simon v. st. elizabeth medical center

Court/year: 1974 2nd dist.app. (second district court of appeals)

This principle was overruled in the opinion of *Source of publication:* 347 Ohio Misc. 63, 355 N.E. 2d 903

3. Two consecutive citations:

a) Parties: comiskey v. arlen

a) Court/year: 1976

a) Source of publication: 390 N.Y.S. 2d 122, 55 A. 2d 304

b) Source of publication: 445 f. 2d 1333

b) Court/year: 1958 5th Cir.

b) Parties: oklahoma v. broadrick

Abbreviations.   You may have noticed some abbreviation in the names of cases or statutory publications in the preceding examples. Proper abbreviation of an authority is probably one of the easiest decisions to make when forming a citation. This is because the bluebook clearly defines what terms are properly abbreviated and exactly how the abbreviation should appear. Generally, abbreviations are addressed in Rule 6.1 of the bluebook. However, throughout the bluebook are tables and references for proper abbreviation in specific types of citation such as statutory, cases, and periodicals. The bluebook contains more than 15 tables of abbreviations for use in the various types of citation. An index to the location of these tables is included in General Rule 6. For our purposes, we will confine the discussion to abbreviation of cases and statutory publications, as these are the most commonly cited.

The table of United States jurisdictions contains the proper abbreviations for all primary authority publications (judicial, statutory, and administrative), arranged by jurisdiction. For example, if you would like to know how to cite the official publication of the New Mexico statutes, you would look in the United States jurisdiction table and then follow the alphabetized table to primary authorities of New Mexico. Each jurisdiction represented in the table includes the following information in the order listed:

1. Judicial
   a. The proper abbreviation for the appellate courts in descending order of authority, e.g. Supreme Court, Appellate Court.

     b. The proper abbreviation for the current official report and unofficial reporter (if any).

     c. A table showing the report(er)s published in the history of the jurisdiction and the years of publication.

  2. Statutory

     a. The proper abbreviation for statutory compilations (publications), including the current code, any unofficial publication, and session laws (publications of statute arranged by the session of the legislature in which they were passed).

  3. Administrative

     a. The proper abbreviation for administrative law publications.

An example using the table just described would be citation of a New Mexico statute. You would find in the table that the proper abbreviation for the New Mexico Statutes Annotated is N.M.Stat.Ann. Sometimes, more than one statutory compilation is listed. Generally, the compilations appear in the order of current official publication (government sanctioned), followed by any unofficial (commercially published) or former publications. If a period of years is given after the name of the publication, this is to indicate in what years the authority has been published. Based on the year of the statute you are citing, you can easily determine the proper abbreviation of the authority to identify in your citation. Unlike case citations, you do not cite both an official and an unofficial (parallel) reference for the statutory citation. Rather, cite the first authority listed that was in publication in the year of the statute you are citing, because official authorities are listed before unofficial commercial publications.

With respect to case citation abbreviations, the table of jurisdictions also provides you with information for proper abbreviation of the report(er)s. Listed are all of the report(er)s that have ever regularly published the case law of the jurisdiction and the years of publication. Like statutory compilations, you can compare the year of the decision you are citing to the table and determine the proper publication(s) and abbreviation of the publication(s) for your citation.

You should generally cite the official (listed first) and the first listed unofficial publication. While there is no direct distinction between the two, recall that official publications are typically called **reports** and unofficial publications are called reporters. The exception is if the jurisdiction has no publication of a report and has adopted a reporter as the official source for judicial law. This can be determined by examining what publications existed during the year of the case you are citing. An example of an adoption of a reporter as the official publication is in Minnesota. Until 1977, the official judicial publication was Minnesota Reports. The unofficial source where cases could also be found (known as a parallel citation) was North Western Reporter and, subsequently, North Western Reporter Second Series. In 1977, the publication of Minnesota Reports ceased, and North Western Reporter was adopted as the official publication. Therefore, any citations to Minnesota case law after 1977 would include only reference to North Western Reporter Second Series.

Regarding abbreviations in case names (parties involved in litigation), the information is found in a table prepared specifically for case names. In the table is an alphabetical listing of common names or terms found in case names, followed by the proper abbreviation. Abbreviation of terms not

report
Official publication of judicial law for a jurisdiction.

included in this table should be avoided because future readers may not be able to decipher the abbreviation. An example of a case name abbreviation from the table is the word *National*, a common term in the names of businesses, banks, and organizations. The proper abbreviation for this term is *Nat'l*. In addition to the rule that abbreviations not included in the table should not be used is the rule that if a term has a proper abbreviation, that abbreviation should be used. Thus, when you are preparing a citation, you should always consult the proper table of abbreviations to determine the proper form of the case name.

 APPLICATION 2.3

IMPROPERLY STATED CASE NAME

United Publishers of America v. National Public Investment Authority.

PROPERLY STATED CASE NAME

United Publishers of Am. v. Nat'l Pub. Inv. Auth.

ASSIGNMENT 2.4

Consult Table 6, Case Names, in the bluebook and properly state each of the following case names.
(NOTE: Take this opportunity to familiarize yourself with the organization of the Bluebook. Remember that the abbreviations table can be found by consulting the index of tables in General Rule 6.)

1. Peterson Engineering Association v. Steamboat Industries Limited
2. Stephens v. Department of Public Health
3. Owen National Market Analysts v. Common Baking Corporation
4. Threshermen & Farmers Mutual Casualty Insurance Company v. Giliam Pacific Steamship Transport Incorporated.
5. Butter Cup Company v. Nickle Plate Distributing
6. Committee for Better Municipal Roadways v. Metropolitan Transportation District
7. Atlantic News and Review v. Simington Brothers Securities
8. Brown v. Southall Railway and Telegraph Company
9. Della City Housing Commission v. MacPherson Construction and Equipment Manufacturing
10. Mastriano Savings and Loan Association v. International Tubular Environmental Systems

Quotations.   Details about the proper form used to quote another authority is included in General Rule 5 of the bluebook. The rule also discusses variations, but certain fundamentals should generally be followed. Usually, the quote is incorporated into the general text and is signaled by the use of quotation marks ("/"). However, anytime the text of the quotation is fifty or more words (or numbers), the quote should appear as a separate block of information, with each line indented five spaces on the left and right.

Quotation marks are not necessary at the beginning and end of a block of quoted text. However, if the quoted material contains a quote of yet another authority, quotation marks should be used within the block to set the secondary quotation apart from the primary quotation.

APPLICATION 2.4

Short quotation within ordinary text

When a party seeks an injunction, it should be prepared to offer significant support for its claim that a court order is necessary to prevent a potential danger by the defendant. This was made clear in the decision of Nicholson, et. al. v. The Connecticut Half-way House, Inc. 153 Conn. 507, 510, 218 A. 2d 383 (1966), which stated, "It is clear that the power of equity to grant injunctive relief may be exercised only under demanding circumstances."

Long quotation

It is clear that the power of equity to grant injunctive relief may be exercised only under demanding circumstances. Leo Foundation v. Cabelus, 151 Conn. 655, 657, 201 A.2d 654 (1964). The fears and apprehensions of the plaintiffs in the present case, based as they are on speculation, cannot justify the granting of injunctive relief.

Long quotation with an internal quote

It is clear that the power of equity to grant injunctive relief may be exercised only under demanding circumstances. . . . "No court or equity should ever grant an injunction merely because of the fears or apprehensions of the party applying for it. Those fears or apprehensions may exist without any substantial reason. Indeed they may be absolutely groundless." Goodwin v. New York, N.H. & H.R. Co., 43 Conn. 494, 500 (1966). . . . The fears and apprehensions of the plaintiffs in the present case, based as they are on speculation, cannot justify the granting of injunctive relief.

In addition to the preceding general rules, there are rules specific to the proper forms of citation for all legal authorities. The following is a discussion of form for the proper citation of the various types of authorities addressed in the text.

CITATION FORMS FOR SPECIFIC AUTHORITIES

Codes and Annotated Statutes

Some discussion has already been given to the citation of statutory authorities. A review of that discussion discloses that the typical statutory citation contains the numbers representing the topic and particular statute, the name that identifies the code, and the year of publication of the code in which the statute is located. You should consult the table of U.S. jurisdictions for proper abbreviation of the code name. However, several variations in the possible citations of statutory authority require further examination.

Citation of statutes is addressed in Rule 12 of the bluebook. The rule discusses such things as basic citation and citation of recent enactments,

session laws, and constitutions. The discussion here is confined to the most commonly cited statutory authorities, such as codes and annotated statutes.

Two items that affect citation of statutory materials are supplements and procedural laws. As discussed earlier, because new editions of statutory publications are typically issued several years apart (sometimes even decades), laws enacted, amended, or repealed (cancelled) in the interim are published in periodic **supplements** or **pocket parts.** Consequently, when citing a statute located in a supplement or pocket part, the proper form is to note that the statute is located there by including the proper abbreviation within the parentheses containing the year of publication. The year should reflect the year of the supplement rather than the year of the hardbound publication. Recall that the year designates the version of the statute you are citing. Consequently, it is important to cite the supplement, since the text of the statute you located there is probably different from that in the hardbound, if the statute exists in the hardbound at all. You might arrange such a citation in the following manner:

Utah Code Ann. 34-1506(a) (Supp. 1993).

The second item regards procedural laws. Often these laws are identified as rules, even though they have the same effect as any other statutory law. Also, there are different types of procedural law. These typically include rules of civil procedure, criminal procedure, evidence, appellate procedure, and sometimes other rules, such as supreme court or bankruptcy rules. In some jurisdictions, rules are numbered differently than other statutes in a code. They may be set apart and numbered with consecutive single and double digits, e.g., 1, 2, 3, 10, 20, 30, rather than the more common form of numbering statutes in 3- or 4-digit numbers, such as 101, 102, 1001, 1002.

According to the bluebook, rules of evidence or procedure should be identified as such in the citation rather than citing the statutory publication. For example, the Federal Rules of Civil Procedure are located in title 28 of the U.S. Code. But rather than citing 28 U.S.C. and the rule number, the proper form is to cite the type of rule cited, such as Fed. R. Civ. P. This abbreviation is followed by the specific rule number. The reason is that most rules are contained in title 28. However, different types of rules may have the same rule number. For example, Rule 12 of the Supreme Court Rules is not the same as Rule 12 of the Criminal Rules of Procedure. Citing the topic of procedure and procedural rule number alone may create confusion as to which rule is being cited.

Some commonly employed abbreviations of procedural rules follow. Please note, however, that the statutory publication may contain a preferred method of abbreviation, and in such a case, the suggested form in the publication should be followed.

Appellate - App.
Civil - Civ.
Criminal - Crim.
Evidence - Evid.
Federal - Fed.
Procedure - P.
Rule(s) - R.
Supreme Court - Sup. Ct.

Because the standard method is to cite the most current procedural rule (unless there is a specific reason to cite a prior publication), there is no need to cite the year of publication in a procedural citation.

supplement
Method used to update materials without total revision of a publication. A pocket part is a type of supplement.

pocket part
Method of updating an authority by preparing a pamphlet of updated information for the authority. A pocket part fits into a pocket inside the cover of the book in which the original authority is contained.

⚖️ **APPLICATION 2.5**

SAMPLE RULE CITATION:1
Fed. R. Civ. P. 36.

Administrative Regulations, Rules, and Decisions

A difference exists between the type of authority you must include in a citation of an administrative decision and administrative rules and regulations. The administrative decision contains the complete name of the first party listed (usually the contestant to the agency). The name of the agency generally is not included. The citation should also include the volume number, page number, abbreviated name of the publication where the decision appears, and year of the decision. For example, a decision by the Department of Immigration and Naturalization would appear in the publication *Administrative Decisions under Immigration and Nationality Laws,* abbreviated as "I. & N. Dec." A decision cited from this publication might appear as follows:

> Charles M. Smith, 86 I. & N. Dec. 461 (1983).

An administrative rule or regulation bears a closer resemblance to a statutory citation. Administrative rules and regulations are typically cited by the title (topic or agency), number, the Code of Federal Regulations, and the number of the specific regulation. If the regulation is commonly known by a particular name, the name can be included preceding the other information. The year cited should be the most recently issued publication unless reference is made to a specific version of the rule or regulation in a specific year.

⚖️ **APPLICATION 2.6**

ADMINISTRATIVE RULES AND REGULATIONS
58 C.F.R. 14.506 (1991)

or

FTC Credit Practice Rule, 16 C.F.R. 444 (1993)

Judicial Law

Probably the most often cited legal authority is judicial law. The citation form is fairly standard and easy to learn. The following general rules should be followed when citing judicial authority in legal writing (examples are not complete citations, but rather illustrate the immediately preceding rule):

1. Case names appear in the order given at the top of the published decision, **e.g.,** Mowry v. Jackson.
2. Case names should be properly abbreviated and capitalized. EXCEPTION: Do not abbreviate United States, **e.g.,** United States v. Eagle Tool & Die, Inc.

3. Case names of opposing parties should be separated by the symbol "v." and should be underlined, with a comma after the last letter of the last name, **e.g.,** Breden v. Breden,.

4. The official publication should be given and be followed by the unofficial publication (known as parallel citation), if any. Both should be properly abbreviated, **e.g.,** Oppenhiemer v. Transfer Moving Co., 444 Neb. 321, 568 N.W. 2d 652.
   EXCEPTIONS:
   a. Citations to the U.S. Supreme Court are properly cited only to the publication United States Reports (U.S.), **e.g.,** McGhee v. Arkansas, 392 U.S. 1031.
   b. If a commercial (typically unofficial) reporter is the only publication of judicial law from a jurisdiction in the year of the decision, you can presume that the commercial publication has been adopted as the official location for judicial law of the jurisdiction, **e.g.,** 271 P. 2d 972.

5. Each abbreviated publication should be preceded by the volume number and followed by the page number of the publication in which the decision appears, **e.g.,** 455 So. 900.

6. Direct quotations from the decision should be identified by including the actual page of the quotation immediately following the first page of the decision in the citation, **e.g.,** 561 Ala. 789, 794, 333 S.E. 2d 220, 226.

7. The last element of information in the citation is parentheses that contain the year of the decision, **e.g., (1981).** If the official publication publishes decisions from more than one court, the proper abbreviation for the court should also be included in the parentheses before the year, **e.g.,** Alabama:(Ala. 1991).

8. Case citations should end with a period unless included within a sentence, in which case a comma should be used, or if listed in consecutive order with other citations, in which case the citations should be connected with a semicolon. For example,
   a. Technica Inc. v. Smitty, 804 P. 2d 110, 111 (1987).
   b. In the case of Technica Inc. v. Smitty, 804 P. 2d 110, 111 (1987), the court expressed. . . .
   c. Technica Inc. v. Smitty, 804 P. 2d 110, 111 (1987); Lowenstein v. Maxwell, 392 Neb. 222, 225, 501 N.E. 2d 992, 994 (1988).

9. When citing a decision that was subsequently considered on appeal to a higher court, this information should be duly noted following the parenthetical information of year and court of origin, **e.g.,** Technica Inc. v. Smitty, 804 P. 2d 110, 111 (1987), aff'd. 818 P. 2d 233 (Alaska 1989).

△△ APPLICATION 2.7

SAMPLE CASE CITATIONS

Markowitz v. Shelby Motor Co., 456 P. 2d 1023 (Alaska 1993).

Perma-Siding Mfg. v. Kentucky, 341 U.S. 508 (1972); Union Specialty Stores Inc. v. New Mexico, 258 N.M. 692, 444 P. 2d 328 (1991).

Three Steps Bar & Grill v. City of Lagusa, 375 So. 2d 991 (Ala. 1977).
Porter v. Harrison, 468 F.Supp. 888 (E.D.Pa. 1981), aff'd. 393 F.2d. 937 (3rd Cir. 1983). (This citation indicates that the case was considered in the U.S. District Court of Pennsylvania and the decision was subsequently affirmed by the Third Circuit U.S. Court of Appeals.

☐ ASSIGNMENT 2.5

Use the following information to prepare proper citations:

1. 1983
    Carpenter v.
    Volume 281
    Northwestern Reporter Second Series (publishes opinions of several states)
    19
    Iowa Supreme Court
    Moser
2. v. National Paper and Plastics Incorporated
    633
    Federal Supplement (publishes opinions of all U.S. district courts)
    1981
    United States District Court, District of Nebraska
    Page 1017
    Marvin Johnson
3. v. National Paper and Plastics Incorporated
    Volume 633
    United States District Court, District of Wyoming
    James Johnson and Associates Company
    1981
    Federal Supplement (publishes opinions of all U.S. district courts)
    1796
4. Canary v.
    Eighth Circuit Court of Appeals
    823
    Kaiser
    Federal Reporter Second Series (publishes opinions of all U.S. circuit courts of appeals)
    1979
    Page 722
5. 1986
    Federal Reporter Second Series (publishes opinions of all U.S. circuit courts of appeals)
    Vol. 802
    Page 1025
    8th Circuit Court of Appeals
    Yancy v. McDevitt
6. Donovan v. Dewey
    United States Reports (publishes opinions of U.S. Supreme Court)

Volume 352
Page 594
1981

7. Harrison v. Arrow Metal Products Corporation
Volume 174
Page 875
Northwestern Reporter Second Series (publishes opinions from
several states)
1978
20 Mich.App. 570 (publishes opinions of Michigan court of appeals)

8. Vol. 632
N.D. Ga. (U.S. District Court Northern District of Georgia)
Page 1481
Everett v. Naper
Federal Supplement (publishes decisions of all U.S. district courts)
1961

9. Jones v. Smith
Volume 722 Michigan Appeals 911 (publishes decisions of Michigan
court of appeals)
324 North Eastern Reporter 2d 819
1975

10. Calhoun v. Cook
522 F.2d. 717 (publishes opinions of all U.S. circuit courts of
appeals)
5th Circuit Court of Appeals 1975
362 F. Supp. 1249 (publishes opinions of all U.S. district courts)
Northern District of Georgia 1973
Affirmed

Restatements

As discussed in Chapter 1, a Restatement is a highly regarded form of
secondary authority. Because it is frequently looked to by courts for guidance,
the citation is a fairly common one in judicial opinions. Consequently, it is
important that you be able to easily recognize and prepare the citation to a
Restatement.

Because each Restatement is prepared and published by subject, the full
name of the publication should be included in the citation to distinguish it
from the other Restatement publications. Also included should be the volume
number (each publication includes multiple volumes) and specific section
number (the fundamentals of law discussed in the Restatements are
numbered by section). It is also important to note the year that the particular
section was proposed or adopted, as the ALI (American Law Institute) from
time to time will change its position on a particular point of law. Periodically,
an entirely new publication of a Restatement will be issued to incorporate all
modified sections that occurred since the last edition. As a result, the citation
should include not only the volume number, Restatement title, and section
number but also the edition of the publication as a whole and the actual year
the particular section was proposed or adopted.

APPLICATION 2.8

Restatement (Second) of Torts Sec.847A (Tent. Draft. No. 17, 1974)

This citation includes the following information:

Restatement title and edition

Subject: Torts
Edition: Second

Section number

847A (which refers you to a particular fundamental of law within the Restatement)

Date and number of proposed draft for approval by the ALI

Date: 1974
Draft number: 17

ASSIGNMENT 2.6

From the following information, prepare proper citations:

1. Restatement of Agency
   Second Edition
   Section 142
   Adopted 1964
2. Restatement of Conflict of Laws
   Section 305
   Adopted 1953
3. Restatement of Contracts
   Second Edition
   Tentative Draft Number 11
   Proposed 1977
   Section 141B

Treatises

Chapter 1 defined a treatise as an in-depth body of work in a particular area of law. The treatise is generally a quite lengthy document that thoroughly addresses all aspects of a subject of law. The citation of a treatise is relatively simple and uses the same format as for citation of other books. This type of legal citation is probably the most similar to ordinary reference to authority in other types of nonlegal writing.

There are basic rules to follow when citing a treatise or other book. The following information is to be included:

Volume (if more than one)
Author and editor (if given)
Title of the work
Edition or series number

Year of publication
Publisher (if a subsequent publication is other than the original publisher)

As with other forms of legal citation, the information is presented in a descending order from broad to specific. Also, common to other legal citations, the year of publication is given at the end of the citation.

⚖️ APPLICATION 2.9

5 Samuel Williston, A Treatise on the Law of Contracts (3d ed. 1961)

This citation includes the following information:

Volume number: 5
Author: Samuel Williston
Title: A Treatise on the Law of Contracts
Edition: Third
Year of publication: 1961

(In this particular publication, no editor was listed, and the publisher was the same as in the first edition and thus was omitted from the citation.)

Legal Encylopedias

Legal encyclopedias are cited with some frequency in legal writing. They are a recognized source of definition and discussion of legal terms and concepts. Because they are commonly accepted and well-known sources of secondary authority, the citation of legal encyclopedias is somewhat less formal than other lesser cited references. For example, while the book in a legal citation may include such detailed information as the full name of the author and even the editor or translator, a legal encyclopedia omits such specifics.

The citation of a legal encyclopedia is focused on the exact point of law being cited. Thus, the citation is relatively short. Periodically, legal encyclopedias are revised and a new edition is issued. The revision may include new subjects, omit obsolete subjects, and update changing areas of law. Consequently, to direct the reader to the edition containing the information you have referenced, you should always include the edition in your citation. Also, because legal encyclopedias are almost always multivolume publications, it is very important to direct the reader to the proper volume to locate the information in the citation. Similarly, you should include the name of the topic of discussion and the section number, which will lead the reader to the exact point of citation. You should note that unlike statutory citations, legal encyclopedias do not generally assign a number to the topic. Rather, the number preceding the topic represents the volume that may contain several topics or only part of one topic.

A common practice in the citation of legal encyclopedias is to abbreviate the name of the more commonly used encyclopedias. The most commonly used general encyclopedias that cover nearly all legal topics are Corpus Juris and American Jurisprudence, both of which have also had second editions published. There are many more specific encyclopedias that address the

various aspects of particular areas of law, such as practice and procedure in the federal courts and property law. Application 2.10 shows sample citations of commonly referenced legal encyclopedias.

 APPLICATION 2.10

24 Am.Jur.2d, Divorce and Separation, § 328 (1964)

This citation includes the following information:

Volume: 24
Title and edition: American Jurisprudence Second Edition
Topic: Divorce and Separation
Section number within topic: 328
Year of publication: 1964

25 C.J.S., Dower, § 1 (1955)

This citation includes the following information:

Volume: 25
Title and edition: Corpus Juris Secundum (Secundum = second edition)
Topic: Dower
Section number: 1
Year of publication: 1955

As with any publication that issues periodic supplements, a citation to a legal encyclopedia supplement or pocket part should be so indicated in parentheses. Also, the year in this type of citation should reflect the year of the supplement rather than the year of publication of the hardbound text.

 APPLICATION 2.11

17 Am. Jur. 2d, Contracts, § 10 (Supp. 1987)

Annotated Law Reports

A somewhat less prevalent citation in formal legal writing is the annotated law report. However, this resource is frequently found in legal periodicals and other reference publications. Also, because annotated law reports are often included in legal research, it is very important to understand the citation format in order to locate particular annotations that can assist you in research.

Annotated law reports include the name of the author, the title of the annotation, and the annotation's location within a published **series** of annotations. Remember that a series (unlike an edition) is a completely new publication of new materials in a continuation of the previous publication rather than a revision of the previous publication. It might be helpful to think of a series in terms of a newspaper: each new publication is merely a continuation of the prior, with new information. This is unlike an edition, such

series
Continuation of a chronological publication. A subsequent series does not change the content, but rather revises the format of presentation.

as a third edition of a dictionary, which contains the same information as the previous publication but is updated to modify or delete previously used terms and may include some new terms and definitions.

 APPLICATION 2.12

J. A. Bryant, Jr., Annotation, _Liability of Insane Person for His Own Negligence_, 49 A.L.R. 3d 189 (1978)

This citation includes the following information:

Author: J. A. Bryant, Jr.
Identification and title:
Annotation
Liability of Insane Person for His Own Negligence
Volume number: 49
Publication A.L.R.3d (American Law Reports, Third Edition)
Page: 189
Year of publication: 1989

While American Law Reports is very commonly referenced, there are many other published annotations, and the citation form is essentially the same.

Legal Periodicals

Because of the great variety in types and number of legal periodical publications, the bluebook gives extensive direction in the preparation of these citations. Citation of periodicals is generally discussed in Rule 16 of the bluebook. Commonly, periodical citations contain much the same information as citations to books. The citation includes the author, title of the article, volume and page of the periodical, abbreviated name of the periodical, and year of publication. The title of the article (rather than the publication) is underscored. Also, the name of the publication should be properly abbreviated. Accepted abbreviations for legal periodicals appear in Table 13 of the bluebook. Legal periodicals not listed should be completely spelled out.

One rule of thumb that applies to citation of legal periodicals has to do with the volume and year of publication. Usually in citations the year is included in parentheses at the end of the cite. This is also true for legal periodicals, with one exception. If there is no volume number in a legal periodical, the year in parentheses should be dropped from the citation, and the year should then be inserted where the volume number would ordinarily appear. The first example in Application 2.13 illustrates a citation in which the legal periodical is published by volume. The second example shows the citation as if the publisher did not issue a volume number for each issue of the periodical.

If the periodical is one that is _not_ consecutively paginated from issue to issue throughout the year (each issue begins with page 1), the actual date of publication (rather than the year alone) should be included.

APPLICATION 2.13

G. Hornblower, <u>Insanity and the Law of Negligence,</u> 5 Modern Legal Issues 278 (1992).

G. Hornblower, <u>Insanity and the Law of Negligence,</u> 1992 Modern Legal Issues 278.

G. Hornblower, <u>Insanity and the Law of Negligence,</u> Modern Legal Issues, Apr. 4, 1992, at 278.

Another distinctive feature of legal periodical citations has to do with the name of the author. Typically, if an article is authored by a student, the term "Comment" or "Note" is used in addition to the author's name in the citation. Otherwise, the author's name is used, as with legal texts.

 APPLICATION 2.14

G. Hornblower, Comment, <u>Insanity and the Law of Negligence,</u> 1905 Columbia Law Review 278.

Looseleaf Services

Rule 18 of the bluebook details the citation for a looseleaf service, a cross between a book and a periodical. While the ordinary legal publication is generally contained in a hardbound book, the looseleaf service is constructed as a looseleaf binder to permit constant updating rather than periodic revision. Each section, and often each page, of a looseleaf service bears a date of publication. This date is used in the citation of a looseleaf service. Also included is the volume number, abbreviated title of the service, publisher, page number, and any section heading or more specific heading (if available) to identify the source.

 APPLICATION 2.15

***Maxim Transit Corp. v. Dept. of Treasury,* 5 U.S. Tax Reports 10,702 (Finley Pub. Oct. 17, 1993)**

This citation includes the following information:

Heading of article: Maxim Transit Corp. v. Dept. of Treasury
Volume: 5
Title of publication: U.S. Tax Reports
Page: 10,702
Publisher: Finley Publishing
Date of publication of Specific Article: October 17, 1993

Periodically, all the pages of a looseleaf will be contained in a permanent binder known as a "transfer binder." The process of accumulating information then begins all over again. If you are citing information contained within a

transfer binder, the citation should note this by including the years included and the words *Transfer Binder* in parentheses.

Legal Dictionaries and Thesauruses

Finally, citation of a legal dictionary/thesaurus is fairly common in legal writing. This appears when a particular word or phrase is discussed in terms of its legal rather than its common definition. To properly cite a legal dictionary/thesaurus, you should include the title of the publication, the page, and the year. Multiple editions or volumes should also be included. Because the purpose of citing such a work is to clarify the meaning of a particular term, it is not necessary to include the term in the citation.

⚖ APPLICATION 2.16

West's Legal Thesaurus/Dictionary 473 (1985)

This citation includes the following information:

Title: West's Legal Thesaurus/Dictionary
Page: 473
Year of publication: 1985

▢ ASSIGNMENT 2.7

Assemble the following information into proper citation form. Not all information provided may be necessary for the citation.

1. Missouri Revised Statutes
   Chapter 58
   Law passed 1986
   Section 1014(1)(a)(i)
   1991 Cumulative supplement
   Law amended in 1990
   Volume IV of the Revised Statutes
2. "attorney licensure: is it a license to steal?"
   Published by the American Trial Lawyers Association
   ATLA Magazine
   1969
   Authored by Morgan M. Morgan
   Page 104
   Volume 56
3. "attorney licensure: is it a license to steal?"
   Published by the University of Iowa School of Law
   1969
   Authored by Senior Class Editor Morgan M. Morgan
   Page 104
4. 211 Nebraska Reports 44
   State v. Brehmer

317 Northwest Reporter Second Series 893
1985
5. James Handleman, student
University of Pittsburgh Law Review
1973
"The Coercive Social Worker"
Page 102
6. 1967
Black's Law Dictionary
"Agent"
Page 12
7. Second Edition
Volume 28
Section 1123
"Husband and Wife"
American Jurisprudence
1964
8. A.L.R. Third Series
Page 62
Employment Discrimination in Bakeries
Volume 34
1987
Jane Obrine
9. Volume 6
Diega v. New Mexico
Unemployment Insurance Reports
Publisher: CCH
739
January 3, 1994
10. Arthur Schlesinger, Jr.
Boston Press
1958
"The Coming of the New Deal"

CHAPTER SUMMARY

This chapter has discussed various rules that demonstrate the organization lent to legal research by the use of a standard citation system. Because of accepted rules for reference to legal authorities, any legal professional anywhere in the United States can locate authority from his or her own or other jurisdictions. In addition, armed with a basic knowledge of citation fundamentals, even the layperson can read a legal document and make sense of the otherwise seemingly incoherent system of numbers and letters used to provide quick reference to authorities. Typically, rules of citation are prepared for the different categories of authority, but a common thread is that the information in a citation is generally presented in descending order of specificity.

KEY TERMS

citation	report	supplement
pocket part	series	

SELF-TEST

MULTIPLE CHOICE

1. In legal writing, there are rules designed exclusively for reference to legal authorities, commonly known as rules of _____ .
   a) research
   b) query
   c) validation
   d) citation

2. Citations generally give information in descending order of _____ .
   a) delegation
   b) specificity
   c) authority
   d) validity

3. Rules of citation are essential to a _____ method of communicating information.
   a) uniform
   b) statutory
   c) constitutional
   d) none of the above

4. In legal writing, citations are treated as phrases that constitute _____ .
   a) paragraphs
   b) concepts
   c) complete sentences
   d) all of the above

5. _____ usually have the first letter of each word capitalized.
   a) Verbs
   b) Language
   c) Proper nouns
   d) Adjectives

TRUE/FALSE

_____ 6. Terms that should not be abbreviated in a title are connecting terms.

_____ 7. Parallel authorities are listed before official publications in citations.

_____ 8. A secondary citation (additional publication of a reference) is known as an official citation.

_____ 9. The court of a judicial opinion should always be designated in the citation.

_____ 10. If the text of a quotation is fifty or more words (or numbers), the quote should appear as a separate block of information, with each line indented.

FILL-IN THE BLANKS

11. Two items that affect citation of statutory materials are _____ and _____ laws.

12. The standard method is to cite the _____ _____ procedural rule (unless there is a specific reason to cite a prior publication).

13. The administrative decision does not usually contain the name of the _____ .

14. Administrative rules and regulations are typically cited by the _____ (topic or agency) number, the Code of Federal Regulations, and the number of the specific regulation.

15. Case names should be _____ , with a comma after the last letter of the last name.

16. No unofficial reporter should be included in a citation to the _____ _____ _____ .

17. In a _____ citation, it is important to note the year that the particular section was proposed or adopted.

18. The citation of a _____ is the same format used for citation of other books.

19. In the citation of a legal encyclopedia, the focus is on the exact _____ _____ _____ being cited.

20. If there is no _____ _____ in a legal periodical, the year in parentheses should be dropped from the citation and the year should then be inserted where the volume number would ordinarily appear.

CHAPTER 3

VALIDATION OF AUTHORITY

CHAPTER OBJECTIVES

Upon completion of this chapter, you should be able to accomplish the following competencies:

- Discuss the necessity for research validation.

- Demonstrate the process of validation through use of a citator.

- Explain the common features and purpose of a citator.

- Update validation through use of citator supplements.

- Explain the unique benefits of citators.

- Discuss the reasoning and reason for regular issues of supplemental citators.

- Explain the purpose of citators for secondary authority.

- Describe the issuance of citators by jurisdiction and publication.

- Explain the benefits and limitations of using citators for research in addition to validation.

- Describe the contents of a citator.

Chapter 1 made reference to the necessity of **validation.** While you may locate a point of law that appears to clearly resolve an issue, of equal importance is the need to determine that the precedent is still valid and accepted. You must establish that the legal principle has not been altered or even rescinded since it was first enunciated. This was clearly demonstrated one day when, in oral argument of a motion, the opposition presented a case that unequivocally directed that my client's case be dismissed. My response was simple. While at one time, the defense's authority was the ruling of the supreme court of the state, that case had been overruled some fourteen years earlier. The opposition was chastised by the judge, and my client's case was permitted to proceed, with the other lawyer justifiably embarrassed. Further, the other lawyer's client was caused unnecessary expense, and everyone was unnecessarily delayed in the case. All of this could have been easily avoided had the opposing counsel completed the very simple task of validating his authority.

Because there are so many legal precedents in the form of statute, case law, and administrative law, a system to track the development and treatment of these precedents is essential. As noted in the example in the preceding paragraph, when conducting legal research, an integral element is the determination of whether the law is still effective. This process has been facilitated by the development of what are known as **citators.** The most commonly used hardbound citators are the *Shepard's Citators* publications, which consist of different sources for each jurisdiction and are broken into categories of judicial, statutory/constitutional, and administrative law. Citators are also published for a variety of secondary authorities, such as legal periodicals. For example, there are "Shepard's Citations of Federal Cases," "Shepard's Citations of Florida Statutes," "Shepard's Citations of Legal Periodicals," and so on.

Contrary to what the name might imply, a citator has little in common with the actual citation of, or reference to, an authority. Rather, the term *citator* describes the content included within the citator text or citator computer software, which are essentially nothing more than legal citations. Typically, to

validation
Process of establishing whether an authority is current and effective or whether it has been subsequently reversed, overruled, repealed, or amended. This process is completed through the use of a citator.

citator
Publication used to provide reference to all authorities that have referred to a prior authority.

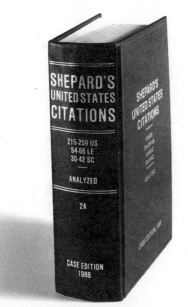

Shepard's United States Citations: Case Edition

validate an authority, you will look up a legal citation in the appropriate citator (e.g., a citator for the jurisdiction of a state court's judicial opinions). There, symbols or notations will indicate how that authority has been dealt with since it was originally issued. The citator will list every subsequent published authority that has mentioned the authority you are validating.

⚖️ **APPLICATION 3.1**

The state legislature of state A passed a law making the wearing of helmets mandatory when bicycling (regardless of whether the cyclist is on public roads or private property). This law took effect on January 1, 1994. The law is challenged as invading the right to privacy. On March 13, 1995, the state supreme court reviews the case and holds that the law violates the constitutional right to privacy, and consequently the law is determined to be invalid. In conducting research on this law in May 1995, if you were to look in a citator by locating the statutory citation in the citator for the legislation of state A, you would find a notation next to a citation of the state supreme court opinion that states the statute was invalidated as unconstitutional. If you did not check the citator, you may assume (wrongly) that the law is still in effect.

While many authorities such as statutory publications indicate whether an authority has been upheld or invalidated, citators are generally published more frequently and thus are more current. Also, when checking validity of a long list of citations, it is usually easier to use a citator than to look up the source of every citation, which may or may not contain validating information. Judicial opinions are published only at the time they are issued and thus do not contain any language about subsequent treatment by higher authorities.

Another significant benefit for the beginning researcher is that the citator furnishes the researcher with a list of additional authorities to check that he or she may not have encountered during initial research. Be cautioned, however, that the citator is by no means the only source that one should examine simply because it is confined to authorities that have mentioned prior authorities. Indeed, there may be a definitive answer to a particular legal question that has not been cited by other authorities. Citators do, however, have the advantage of listing authorities that have been deliberately linked.

USING A CITATOR

While the use of computers for all aspects of legal research, including validation of authority, is the trend, many still use the bound citators that are found in virtually all law libraries. When you first open a citator, it may appear that you are looking at some sort of foreign language. On each page are columns of numbers and letters with virtually no actual words other than an occasional heading such as "Volume 252" (see Exhibit 3.1). In reality, these columns are a very orderly presentation of a large number of citations, which are surprisingly simple to decipher.

EXHIBIT 3.1 Sample page from Shepard's United States Citations: Case Edition.
Reproduced by permission of Shepard's McGraw-Hill, Inc. Further reproduction is strictly prohibited.

LAWYERS' EDITION, UNITED STATES SUPREME COURT REPORTS

Vol. 90

—2006—	**—2079—**	**—2092—**	572A2d332	**—95—**	718FS1218	703FS²1253	860F2d²1513
Case 13	Cir. DC	92LE⁴762		94LE²100	720FS²28	705FS²314	861F2d²1161
Cir. 6	849F2d644	94LE¹151	**—34—**	94LE²107	731FS¹¹591	706FS²319	863F2d²1440
701FS624	857F2d²825	j94LE67	Cir. 10	98LE²427	732FS²1273	706FS²515	871F2d²1528
Conn	890F2d²460	Cir. DC	108BRW767	122FRD64	125FRD²575	f714FS²223	f872F2d286
205Ct241	Cir. 1	863F2d⁵81	N Y	Cir. DC	97BRW¹⁴160	723FS²379	f872F2d²287
	892F2d¹1125	Cir. 1	554NYS2d	807F2d222	107BRW¹¹	728FS²443	873F2d²1259
—2007—	707FS²33	853F2d¹13	[389	860F2d²462	[469	Cir. 6	f885F2d²519
Case 2	710FS²868	Cir. 9	Okla	894F2d²456	Cir. 3	875F2d1216	d885F2d²1413
N J	719FS²71	880F2d⁶1053	756P2d595	686FS²922	869F2d²766	882F2d²1089	885F2d⁵1414
238NJS63	722FS¹879	898F2d1386		686FS⁵922	897F2d²690	e882F2d⁷1091	892F2d1411
	724FS¹4	Ill	**—47—**	686FS⁸922	f897F2d²699	f885F2d¹¹	897F2d²380
—2007—	725FS114	181Il**a**747	Cir. 2	691FS²381	683FS²117	[1298	901F2d²737
Case 4	Cir. 2	181Il**a**748	e687FS⁵138	691FS²1559	685FS293	f885F2d²1299	685FS²60
N J	f889F2d¹426	537NE332	Cir. 7	700FS¹¹61	e685FS²448	f888F2d²464	699FS²804
568A2d1224	692FS¹287	537NE333	895F2d⁷317	700FS²61	690FS²319	898F2d²1151	f699FS²805
	700FS¹92	Tex	Cir. Fed.	700FS⁵61	693FS⁵187	685FS²1017	716FS²440
—2013—	708FS²480	766SW332	848F2d²1222	701FS⁸854	f699FS²68	685FS⁵1017	716FS²476
92LE¹⁶576	711FS¹1197		Calif	f704FS²304	700FS¹247	687FS²353	723FS²534
92LE³576	f724FS236	**—2103—**	213CA3d220	706FS²2	702FS⁸1168	689FS²791	727FS²1339
Cir. DC	727FS¹123	Cir. DC	215CA3d273	Cir. 1	702FS²1169	f695FS²920	728FS²1432
j876F2d943	125FRD359	854F2d²486	261CaR492	857F2d²29	703FS²355	711FS381	122FRD²260
Cir. 2	103BRW473	Cir. 3		e857F2d30	708FS²643	f711FS²382	f127FRD²176
857F2d⁶71	Cir. 3	900F2d¹³671	**—56—**	886F2d²3	708FS²666	716FS²6	104BRW²293
873F2d597	862F2d34	Cir. 5	Cir. 5	888F2d²219	709FS²524	717FS²530	Cir. 10
Cir. 3	876F2d330	866F2d746	896F2d¹161	f889F2d1179	712FS⁶49	719FS²632	858F2d²623
898F2d928	698FS¹1235	898F2d1055	692FS¹709	f889F2d²1180	f712FS²51	d725FS915	887F2d1375
698FS¹73	723FS¹361	Cir. 5	Cir. 6	f889F2d⁵1180	f712FS²459	85BRW434	896F2d²1237
715FS¹⁴634	Cir. 5	856F2d1221	861F2d¹963	893F2d²462	719FS²1252	Cir. 7	f685FS²774
92BRW²990	887F2d¹617	j856F2d1235	870F2d¹340	894F2d²11	721FS⁵707	686FS²225	f685FS⁵775
Cir. 4	f894F2d²704	896F2d¹³1183	898F2d¹496	684FS²1131	722FS²1164	692FS²957	685FS²822
720FS1191	Cir. 6	714FS⁴1074	702FS630	687FS²697	f723FS⁹338	694FS²536	694FS²812
Cir. 5	887F2d705	f714FS1082	Cir. 7	f692FS¹1446	723FS²1101	694FS⁸1369	698FS²216
d846F2d291	688FS¹1256	727FS562	f96BRW¹847	693FS²1335	726FS²110	f698FS727	710FS²1318
695FS¹²269	e716FS²1029		Cir. 9	699FS12	729FS⁵466	698FS²728	f716FS²509
Cir. 8	Cir. 7	**—2128—**	896F2d379	699FS²14	f731FS²182	698FS²1456	f716FS⁵509
867F2d⁷1561	860F2d1425	Cir. 2	81BRW¹56	f701FS²274	733FS²953	699FS²674	f716FS⁵530
Cir. 9	717FS1385	867F2d772	Cir. 10	704FS⁹317	96BRW²596	707FS²377	f716FS⁵530
714FS1078	124FRD192		866F2d¹1244	f708FS²234	Cir. 4	713FS1210	f716FS²542
Cir. 10	Cir. 9	**Vol. 90**	Cir. 11	f709FS²41	862F2d²1046	f714FS²373	716FS⁵543
698FS¹³1538	863F2d²646	**—6—**	691FS1341	709FS²275	885F2d²1200	f714FS²954	716FS²1377
708FS¹⁰1182	864F2d1464	N D	S D	709FS⁸277	886F2d²656	717FS²1338	728FS²1526
Cir. 11	892F2d¹59	440NW520	424NW660	715FS²1156	886F2d⁵661	f717FS²1367	729FS²758
717FS¹⁰1536	d684FS633	Va	424NW663	715FS⁶1156	901F2d²39	f720FS¹711	729FS⁵758
717FS¹¹1536	691FS1272	238Va154	**—61—**	f717FS971	683FS535	d720FS⁵713	729FS²1319
Calif	699FS229	380SE913	Cir. 11	719FS²47	683FS²537	723FS²386	Cir. 11
248CaR203	731FS¹956	Wash	686FS⁵1551	719FS²63	685FS²116	723FS²1271	f847F2d²743
	122FRD585	57WAp446		721FS²397	686FS²106	f729FS²593	f854F2d²391
—2051—	Cir. 10	788P2d1109	**—67—**	f727FS²682	686FS²121	f730FS²133	f877F2d²919
La	729FS¹742	79LE930n	Cir. DC	728FS²823	f689FS²566	730FS1447	d877F2d921
549So2d853	Cir. 11		733FS²399	732FS⁸1207	689FS⁸567	733FS²1183	880F2d²388
	877F2d917	**—25—**	Cir. 2	f123FRD²426	692FS²604	94BRW²497	f901F2d²1055
—2065—	695FS548	ClCt	893F2d²532	Cir. 2	693FS²422	Cir. 8	685FS⁹1226
Cir. 7	695FS¹1188	14ClC120	Cir. 6	854F2d²20	694FS²195	849F2d²1108	691FS338
897F2d871	721FS1260		887F2d²1304	685FS²334	694FS²1250	851F2d²1030	693FS²1076
	723FS¹689	**—26—**	Cir. 9	687FS²880	696FS²177	884F2d²1118	699FS266
—2072—	Ala	Ill	861F2d565	689FS⁷162	699FS²1213	884F2d⁸1118	699FS⁹880
Cir. 1	539So2d205	132Il2d315	Cir. 11	689FS²307	712FS²1226	891F2d²673	699FS²911
701FS11	Colo	184Il**a**10	850F2d²1513	f692FS²326	717FS⁵375	895F2d²1228	699FS²1549
708FS13	761P2d219	540NE542		d693FS²1553	f717FS²1117	900F2d²1198	699FS⁹1550
Cir. 3	Ill	547NE442	**—78—**	695FS²733	717FS²1123	f683FS⁵1291	699FS²1580
697FS¹1369	122Il2d526		Cir. 7	695FS³1461	f720FS²536	f688FS²1381	f705FS²572
709FS¹1334	524NE559	N H	871F2d⁴66	697FS²1343	726FS629	690FS²833	712FS²1576
Cir. 5	N H	131NH24	Conn	d698FS²493	732FS²42	f700FS¹1038	715FS⁴1565
685FS1352	131NH24	549A2d1198	207Ct540	698FS²1090	128FRD²642	f702FS²1426	717FS²817
732FS¹708	549A2d1198	N C	542A2d1121	700FS²123	Cir. 5	702FS²1438	717FS²830
Cir. 6	N C	870F2d111		712FS²30	861F2d²1361	708FS²1069	722FS²728
864F2d1275	96NCA662	893F2d609	**—85—**	f712FS²390	864F2d²385	712FS²156	f724FS²1368
Cir. 7	387SE60	Cir. 4	Mass	712FS²1117	884F2d²202	715FS²1450	f730FS²1574
700FS427	P R	f690FS488	405Mas20	712FS1141	890F2d²773	f723FS²410	731FS²1538
Cir. 8	2TPR509	Cir. 5	537NE1220	712FS²1145	895F2d²216	726FS²755	119FRD²456
857F2d426	W Va	895F2d1512		714FS²97	897F2d²1361	726FS²768	104BRW²550
713FS¹1286	387SE285	Cir. 8		714FS²674	683FS⁸1096	731FS²926	Ala
Cir. 10		686FS¹768		716FS²786	693FS513	f731FS²1434	533So2d610
713FS²1384		731FS367		717FS¹³186	693FS²514	Cir. 9	
713FS⁴1384		Conn		718FS²228	d693FS¹¹515	854F2d²1194	*Continued*

315

Rather than being a complete and formal citation of authority, a citator uses only the numbers and abbreviated name of the publication (e.g., 465 N.W.2d 899). It does not include case names, years, courts, or other descriptive information. For example, a statutory citator will contain in boldface the topic number, abbreviated statutory publication name, and section number of the specific statute (e.g., 111 Il.Rev.Stat.405). Below this is a list of citations. Each of these is in some way related to the statute cited in boldface type. For example, a volume number, abbreviated report name, and page number may appear immediately below the boldface statutory citation. If this is the case, the volume, report, and page refer to the exact page of a judicial opinion in which the statute was mentioned, discussed, or interpreted. Letters immediately to the left of any one of the subsequent lists of citations are often used to indicate exactly what the position was of the subsequent authority, such as a court toward the statutory citation. The same process is used for judicial law.

Perhaps a bit of background on the example given at the beginning of the chapter will make this more clear. A complaint was filed on behalf of the plaintiff. The defense responded with a motion to dismiss on the basis that the plaintiff's cause of action (basis for the lawsuit) was not legally recognized in that jurisdiction. In preparing to fight the motion, the first step was to look at the defendant's authority. Indeed, the case listed by the defendant in the motion clearly stated that the plaintiff's cause of action was not allowed in the jurisdiction. The next step was to verify the validity of the defendant's authority. By looking to the citator for judicial opinions of the jurisdiction and locating the page that contained the volume and page number for that particular opinion, a series of citations was listed in which the opinion was referred to and relied upon in later cases. Looking down the list of citations was a citation with the letter *o* next to it. The table of abbreviations at the front of the citator (see Exhibit 3.2) indicated that the "o" meant overruled. By then locating and reading the judicial opinion cited after the "o" in the citator, it was clear that the state supreme court had reversed its position and no longer prohibited but, rather, endorsed the type of suit such as the plaintiff's. Had the opposing counsel undertaken the simple task of looking up his own researched authority in a citator (a process of about two minutes, including getting the book from the library), he would have known that the motion to dismiss on this basis was futile.

To make validation of authority even more efficient, certain features have been developed in citators. The process of using letters to denote certain actions taken by subsequent authorities was mentioned previously. An additional feature allows the validation search to be narrowed to very specific points of law. For example, a judicial opinion may contain many different points of law and be very lengthy. In West publications, such as regional reporters in the West National Reporter System, judicial opinions are broken into segments and numbered. Similarly, a statute is often a long and detailed statement of law broken into numerous parts and subparts. When validating an authority, these numbered or lettered segments or parts can be very helpful in minimizing the time necessary to check a citator.

As you know, when you locate a particular citation in a citator, the citation is followed by a series of citations. Frequently, there will be a lower-case letter (in the case of statutes or administrative law) or a number that appears superscript (above and immediately to the right) to some of the subsequent citations. These superscript letters or numbers indicate the exact portion of the

EXHIBIT   3.2   Sample Page from the Table of Abbreviations from Shepard's United States Citations: Case Edition.

Reproduced by permission of Shepard's McGraw-Hill, Inc. Further reproduction is strictly prohibited.

ABBREVIATIONS

Unless an abbreviation appeared in the case name itself (as where the party's official name might be "Jones Bros."), the case names were reprinted in full with the following exceptions:

> Assoc.–Association
> Co.–Company
> Cos.–Companies
> Corp.–Corporation
> Inc.–Incorporated
> Ltd.–Limited
> No.–Number

In the citations themselves, the following abbreviations were used:

> U.S.–United States Reports
> L.Ed.–Lawyers' Edition, United States Supreme Court Reports
> L.Ed.2d–Lawyers' Edition, United States Supreme Court Reports, Second Series
> S̶ ̶ ̶me ̶ ̶ourt Rep̶ ̶ter

---

precedent that is referenced in the subsequent citation. However, these superscripts are only finding aids and can be incorrect or incomplete. To be certain, you should consult the actual authorities listed. For example, assume a statute lists all the conditions for proper service of a summons on a defendant. You are interested only in whether a landlord can accept a summons for a tenant in a small apartment building. The various parts of the statute, however, deal with service by mail, service in person, service on the state attorney general, service on a registered agent for business, etc. By locating the statute in the citator and looking to the citations below part (c) of the statute (the section dealing with substitute service), you can avoid looking up every case in which the statute was ever dealt with, including those with circumstances totally different from that of your client.

☐ ASSIGNMENT 3.1

Exhibit 3.1 is an excerpt from a citator. Using Chapter Exhibits, complete the following exercises:

1. Give a judicial citation subsequent to an authority in the citator (as provided in the citator, the citation will be incomplete) and identify where it is located on the page.
2. Give a dissenting opinion citation (as provided in the citator, it will be incomplete) and identify where it is located on the page.

EXHIBIT 3.3 Sample page from the table of abbreviations from Shepard's United States Citations: Statute Edition.
Reproduced by permission of Shepard's McGraw-Hill, Inc. Further reproduction is strictly prohibited.

ABBREVIATIONS—ANALYSIS

Form of Statute

Amend.	Amendment	Proc.	Proclamation
App.	Appendix	Pt.	Part
Art.	Article	Res.	Resolution
Ch.	Chapter	§	Section
Cl.	Clause	St.	Statutes at Large
Ex. Ord.	Executive Order	Subch.	Subchapter
H.C.R.	House Concurrent	Subcl.	Subclause
	Resolution	Subd.	Subdivision
No.	Number	Sub ¶	Subparagraph
¶	Paragraph	Subsec.	Subsection
P.L.	Public Law	Vet. Reg.	Veterans' Regulations
Pr.L.	Private Law		

Operation of Statute
    Legislative

A	(amended)	Statute amended.
Ad	(added)	New section added.
E	(extended)	Provisions of an existing statute extended in their application to a later statute, or allowance of additional time for performance of duties required by a statute within a limited time.
L	(limited)	Provisions of an existing statute declared not to be extended in their application to a later statute.
R	(repealed)	Abrogation of an existing statute.
Re-en	(re-enacted)	Statute re-enacted.
Rn	(renumbered)	Renumbering of existing sections.
Rp	(repealed in	Abrogation of part of an existing statute.

---

3. List all of the notations that appear on the page to the left of the citations.
4. Give a judicial citation that is listed in the citator as an authority to be validated (appears in boldface type).
5. Identify the publication for which the citator was prepared.

SUPPLEMENTS

As mentioned earlier, citators are published with more frequency than most statutory, judicial, or administrative publications of legal standards. To enable a very current validation of authority, supplements are published between

EXHIBIT 3.4   Sample Page of Shepard's United States Citations: Case Edition.
Reproduced by permission of Shepard's McGraw-Hill, Inc. Further reproduction is strictly prohibited.

volume

opinion followed

page

LAWYERS' EDITION, UNITED STATES SUPREME COURT REPORTS								
								Vol. 95
—619—	**—632—**	**—651—**	**—685—**	f731FS⁵1326	18ClC¹416	259CaR204	D C
Case 3	Case 3	Case 3	Case 10	732FS⁵69	91LE596n	D C	549A2d345
Pa	Conn	Cir. 2	Cir. 2	122FRD³23		558A2d309	Ill
568A2d605	15CtA406	98BRW673	687FS53	85BRW¹¹420	**—740—**	Fla	194Ilä164
	546A2d291			Cir. 7	N Y	528So2d53	550NE1158
—620—		**—654—**	**—686—**	854F2d924	136NYAD	Haw	Miss
Case 1	**—632—**	Case 3	Case 6	f685FS⁵1078	[176	70Haw603	531So2d809
Cir. 7	Case 7	Cir. 3	N H	f685FS³1080		778P2d720	N Y
688FS349	Kan	93BRW376	130NH275	f685FS¹1081	**—774—**	784P2d870	150NYAD
	244Kan625	94BRW364		f701FS⁵648	Cir. 2	Ill	[459
—621—	772P2d750	110BRW181	**—687—**	Cir. 8	683FS¹941	135Il2d398	541NYS2d69
Case 4			Case 1	684FS⁵1025	719FS¹267	170Ilä326	Pa
Nebr	**—632—**	**—656—**	Cir. 7	698FS⁵794	Cir. 7	524NE669	120PaC532
232Neb681	Case 8	Case 8	113FRD81	702FS⁵1420	872F2d195	La	549A2d253
	Fla	Cir. 10		702FS⁶1420	Cir. 9	525So2d120	Vt
—623—	555So2d375	884F2d535	**—687—**	703FS²825	d878F2d¹1149	Md	568A2d361
Case 1			Case 5	Cir. 9	Minn	313Md493	W Va
Calif	**—637—**	**—657—**	Cir. 5	f846F2d⁵1197	449NW475	317Md596	369SE467
236CaR819	Case 5	Case 3	696FS1113	846F2d¹⁰1215	449NW476	545A2d1337	
	Cir. 2	Cir. 5		847F2d¹⁰602	N J	565A2d1026	**—912—**
—623—	98BRW673	725FS292	**—688—**	863F2d⁶664	225NJS447	Mich	90LE⁵951
Case 6	102BRW930		Case 7	d863F2d⁵664	542A2d956	430Mch618	Cir. DC
Cir. 4		**—663—**	Cir. 8	d863F2d⁷664	W Va	424NW285	864F2d829
711FS290	**—638—**	Case 4	853F2d596	j863F2d666	369SE705	Mont	874F2d836
	Case 1	Ill		864F2d⁷87		211Mt108	Cir. 1
—624—	174Ilä462		**—702—**	694FS⁹1483	**—788—**	N Y	856F2d368
Case 1	110NJ390	528NE1053	97LE⁴397	700FS7497	Cir. 9	73NY364	Cir. 3
Cir. 2	233NJS318		98LE⁵732	Cir. 10	693FS¹881	538NE84	862F2d73
865F2d520	238NJS62	**—665—**	Cir. DC	851F2d⁹1252	693FS³883	540NYS2d	Cir. 4
	239NJS650	Case 5	716FS30	854F2d⁵1259	Calif	[765	881F2d197
—624—	518A2d1130	Cir. 5	Cir. 1	716FS⁵1385	48C3d830	N D	Cir. 7
Case 4	541A2d695	315Md86	850F2d813	716FS⁶1387	258CaR176	429NW743	874F2d1181
Calif	558A2d1344	553A2d679	706FS⁵961	Cir. 11	771P2d1262	P R	Cir. 8
46C3d286	568A2d1224		f726FS⁵13	700FS¹⁰535	87LE794n	1990JTS29	850F2d¹1265
250CaR266	571A2d1375	**—670—**	Cir. 2	700FS⁸535		Tex	Cir. 11
758P2d594		Case 6	900F2d⁹503	700FS⁹535	**—809—**	761SW845	731FS²1072
D C	**—639—**	Cir. DC	d707FS⁵655	d700FS⁷536	N Y	Va	731FS⁴1072
546A2d372	Case 6	849F2d666	Cir. 3	f700FS⁵536	73NY644	235Va114	Iowa
Haw	Calif	Cir. 9	872F2d⁷1138	f704FS⁵224	541NE25	Wyo	432NW152
69Haw197	208CA3d	868F2d1051	872F2d¹⁰1139	712FS180	543NYS2d25	771P2d809	Pa
Md	256CaR675		690FS404	713FS389	89LE1006n	62Aä408n	561A2d50
[1228		**—673—**	708FS694	f717FS⁵821		62Aä500n	
316Md19	**—640—**	Case 8	708FS³695	f730FS⁵408	**—817—**		**—927—**
557A2d211	Case 2	N Y	729FS⁵1522	MFP§ 2.5	91LE243	**—879—**	Cir. 1
Utah	Wash	137NYAD	Cir. 4		j95LE260	Cir. DC	f838F2d621
765P2d870	756P2d131	[122	j865F2d1441	**—713—**	j96LE542	708FS404	f847F2d⁸936
		137NYAD	703FS483	96LE114	Cir. DC	727FS1508	847F2d⁸940
—625—	**—640—**	[962	704FS¹639	N J	d861F2d¹285	Cir. 2	Cir. 2
Case 4	Case 3	138NYAD	f704FS⁶640	111NJ407	j863F2d982	j856F2d486	87BRW⁷235
Cir. 6	Va	[597	704FS³641	545A2d136	692FS1414	Cir. 3	107BRW817
881F2d256	237Va97		713FS⁹900	W Va	Cir. 2	701FS²485	e112BRW576
	376SE530	**—680—**	f713FS⁹901	370SE144	690FS273	701FS³485	112BRW¹580
—625—		Case 3	713FS²902		716FS²⁶78	f729FS⁵1481	Cir. 3
Case 6	**—641—**	Cir. 7	724FS396	**—729—**	717FS¹⁶1045	Cir. 4	94BRW¹861
Cir. 6	Case 4	684FS603	728FS403	Cir. DC	Cir. 3	856F2d²622	96BRW523
881F2d251	Cir. DC		Cir. 5	860F2d1111	717FS³⁷309	884F2d⁷774	Cir. 4
	j880F2d505	**—682—**	882F2d⁵192	Cir. 1	Cir. 4	884F2d²777	c95BRW¹394
—628—		Case 9	882F2d⁶192	725FS104	883F2d1260	884F2d³777	Cir. 5
Case 2	**—646—**	Cir. 2	886F2d⁵96	Cir. 5	885F2d1218	Cir. 9	86BRW776
Cir. 9	Case 1	92BRW93	688FS³1168	870F2d⁵62	Cir. 5	707FS⁶1218	86BRW⁸77
j859F2d626	Cir. 9		694FS⁵229	j870F2d65	685FS1001	Cir. 10	86BRW⁹77
	861F2d546	**—683—**	700FS⁵325	Cir. 6	Cir. 6	857F2d709	86BRW¹81
—631—		Case 6	701FS³567	873F2d²913	856F2d746	D C	97BRW860
Case 5	**—646—**	Cir. 11	703FS⁵502	95ARF272n	Cir. 7	567A2d427	112BRW181
Cir. 11	Case 5	849F2d560	706FS²116	95ARF286n	731FS¹850		Cir. 6
696FS1466	Cir. 9		d718FS⁸486		Cir. 10	**—886—**	99BRW⁷845
	870F2d549	**—684—**	f733FS⁷238	**—738—**	890F2d³⁴270	Cir. 6	Cir. 7
—631—		Case 3	Cir. 6	92LE¹259	690FS945	718FS³1561	121FRD71
Case 7	**—647—**	La	865F2d⁹784	Cir. 2	703FS1487	Cir. 8	87BRW⁵45
Cir. 11	Case 4	555So2d1333	692FS⁸798	719FS¹148	Cir. 11	894F2d³987	101BRW13
702FS891	Haw		696FS⁵1143	Cir. 6	j862F2d1470	Cir. 9	Cir. 8
	6HA326		699FS⁵125	97BRW¹884	j864F2d748	880F2d³1052	104BRW240
			e716FS⁵306	Cir. 11	871F2d²⁶1043	Cir. 11	Cir. 9
			e716FS⁶306	707FS¹1297	686FS1559	863F2d³1527	795F2d⁷730
			e716FS7306	ClCt	Calif	Ala	
			728FS¹⁰1310	16ClC¹675	211CA3d141	558So2d914	*Continued*

EXHIBIT 3.5 Sample Page of Shepard's United States Citations: Case Edition.
Reproduced by permission of Shepard's McGraw-Hill, Inc. Further reproduction is strictly prohibited.

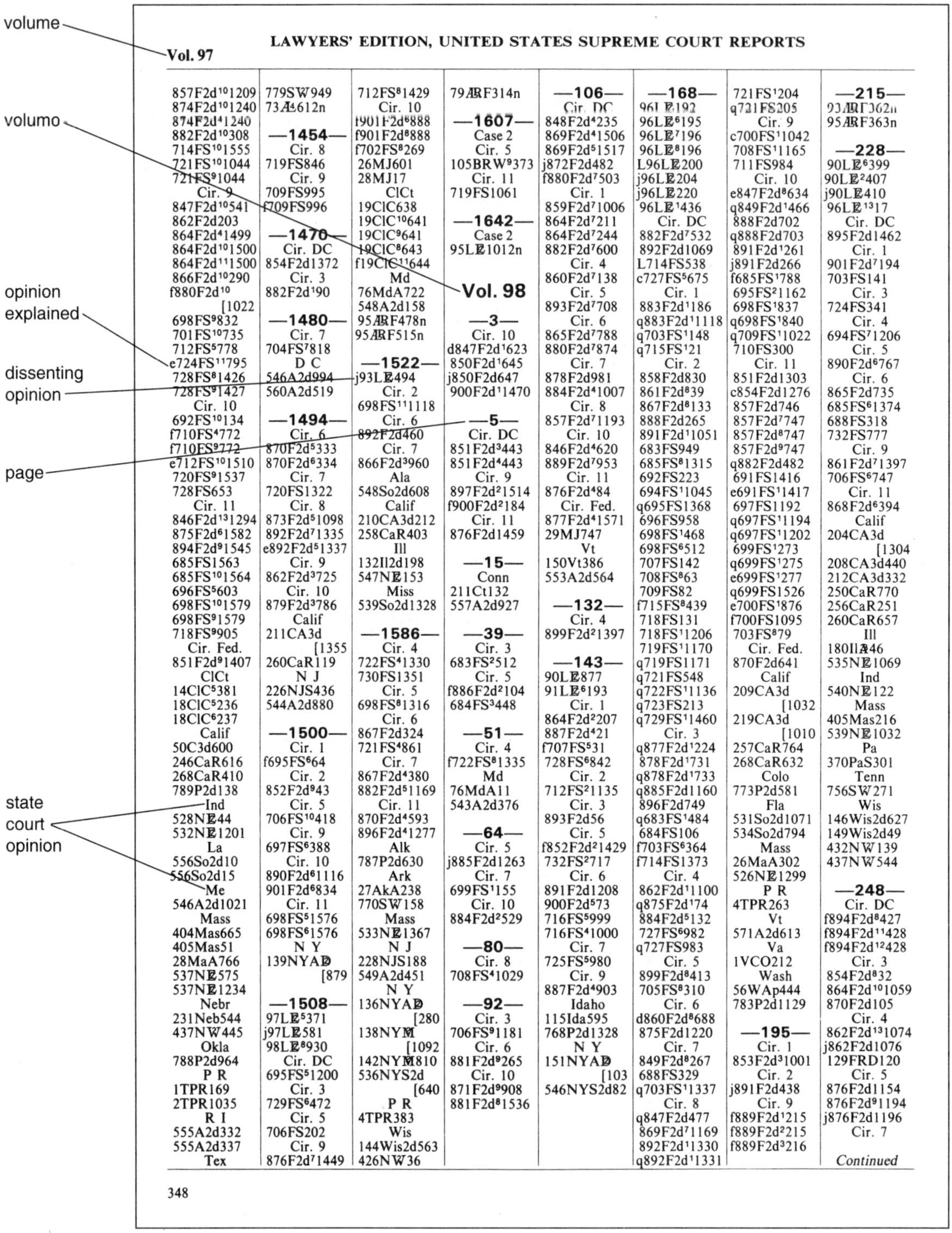
volume
volumo
opinion explained
dissenting opinion
page
state court opinion

Vol. 97

LAWYERS' EDITION, UNITED STATES SUPREME COURT REPORTS

857F2d[10]1209
874F2d[10]1240
874F2d[4]1240
882F2d[10]308
714FS[10]1555
721FS[10]1044
721FS[9]1044
Cir. 9
847F2d[10]541
862F2d203
864F2d[4]1499
864F2d[10]1500
864F2d[11]1500
866F2d[10]290
f880F2d[10]
[1022
698FS[9]832
701FS[10]735
712FS[5]778
e724FS[11]795
728FS[8]1426
728FS[9]1427
Cir. 10
692FS[10]134
f710FS[4]772
f710FS[9]772
e712FS[10]1510
720FS[9]1537
728FS653
Cir. 11
846F2d[13]1294
875F2d[6]1582
894F2d[9]1545
685FS1563
685FS[10]1564
696FS[5]603
698FS[10]1579
698FS[9]1579
718FS[9]905
Cir. Fed.
851F2d[9]1407
ClCt
14ClC[5]381
18ClC[5]236
18ClC[6]237
Calif
50C3d600
246CaR616
268CaR410
789P2d138
Ind
528NE44
532NE1201
La
556So2d10
556So2d15
Me
546A2d1021
Mass
404Mas665
405Mas51
28MaA766
537NE575
537NE1234
Nebr
231Neb544
437NW445
Okla
788P2d964
P R
1TPR169
2TPR1035
R I
555A2d332
555A2d337
Tex

779SW949
73A4612n

—1454—
Cir. 8
719FS846
Cir. 9
709FS995
f709FS996

—1470—
Cir. DC
854F2d1372
Cir. 3
882F2d[1]90

—1480—
Cir. 7
704FS[7]818
D C
546A2d994
560A2d519

—1494—
Cir. 6
870F2d[5]333
870F2d[6]334
Cir. 7
720FS1322
Cir. 8
873F2d[5]1098
892F2d[7]1335
e892F2d[5]1337
Cir. 9
862F2d[3]725
Cir. 10
879F2d[3]786
Calif
211CA3d
[1355
260CaR119
N J
226NJS436
544A2d880

—1500—
Cir. 1
f695FS[6]64
Cir. 2
852F2d[9]43
Cir. 5
706FS[10]418
Cir. 9
697FS[6]388
Cir. 10
890F2d[6]1116
901F2d[6]834
Cir. 11
698FS[5]1576
698FS[6]1576
N Y
139NYAD
[879

—1508—
97LE[5]371
j97LE581
98LE[8]930
Cir. DC
695FS[5]1200
Cir. 3
729FS[6]472
Cir. 5
706FS202
Cir. 9
876F2d[7]1449

712FS[8]1429
Cir. 10
f901F2d[6]888
f901F2d[8]888
f702FS[8]269
26MJ601
28MJ17
ClCt
19ClC638
19ClC[10]641
19ClC[9]641
19ClC[8]643
f19ClC[11]644
Md
76MdA722
548A2d158
95ARF478n
95ARF515n

—1522—
j93LE494
Cir. 2
698FS[11]1118
Cir. 6
892F2d460
Cir. 7
866F2d[3]960
Ala
548So2d608
Calif
210CA3d212
258CaR403
Ill
132Il2d198
547NE153
Miss
539So2d1328

—1586—
Cir. 4
722FS[4]1330
730FS1351
Cir. 5
698FS[8]1316
Cir. 6
867F2d324
721FS[4]861
Cir. 7
867F2d[4]380
882F2d[5]1169
Cir. 11
870F2d[4]593
896F2d[4]1277
Alk
787P2d630
Ark
27AkA238
770SW158
Mass
533NE1367
N J
228NJS188
549A2d451
N Y
136NYAD
[280
138NYM
[1092
142NYM810
536NYS2d
[640
P R
4TPR383
Wis
144Wis2d563
426NW36

79ARF314n

—1607—
Case 2
Cir. 5
105BRW[9]373
Cir. 11
719FS1061

—1642—
Case 2
95LE1012n

Vol. 98

—3—
Cir. 10
d847F2d[1]623
850F2d[1]645
j850F2d647
900F2d[1]1470

—5—
Cir. DC
851F2d[3]443
851F2d[4]443
Cir. 9
897F2d[2]1514
f900F2d[2]184
Cir. 11
876F2d1459

—15—
Conn
211Ct132
557A2d927

—39—
Cir. 3
683FS[2]512
Cir. 5
f886F2d[2]104
684FS[3]448

—51—
Cir. 4
f722FS[8]1335
Md
76MdA11
543A2d376

—64—
Cir. 5
j885F2d1263
Cir. 7
699FS[1]155
Cir. 10
884F2d[2]529

—80—
Cir. 8
708FS[4]1029

—92—
Cir. 3
706FS[9]1181
Cir. 6
881F2d[9]265
Cir. 10
871F2d[9]908
881F2d[8]1536

—106—
Cir. DC
848F2d[4]235
869F2d[4]1506
869F2d[5]1517
j872F2d482
f880F2d[7]503
Cir. 1
859F2d[7]1006
864F2d[7]211
864F2d[7]244
882F2d[7]600
Cir. 4
860F2d[7]138
Cir. 5
893F2d[7]708
Cir. 6
865F2d[7]788
880F2d[7]874
Cir. 7
878F2d981
884F2d[4]1007
Cir. 8
857F2d[7]1193
Cir. 10
846F2d[4]620
889F2d[7]953
Cir. 11
876F2d[4]84
Cir. Fed.
877F2d[4]1571
29MJ747
Vt
150Vt386
553A2d564

—132—
Cir. 4
899F2d[2]1397

—143—
90LE877
91LE[6]193
Cir. 1
864F2d[2]207
887F2d[4]21
f707FS[5]31
728FS[6]842
Cir. 2
712FS[2]1135
Cir. 3
893F2d56
Cir. 5
f852F2d[2]1429
732FS[2]717
Cir. 6
891F2d1208
900F2d[5]73
716FS[5]999
716FS[4]1000
Cir. 7
725FS[5]980
Cir. 9
887F2d[4]903
Idaho
115Ida595
768P2d1328
N Y
151NYAD
[103
546NYS2d82

—168—
96LE192
96LE[6]195
96LE[7]196
96LE[8]196
L96LE200
j96LE204
j96LE220
96LE[1]436
Cir. DC
882F2d[7]532
892F2d1069
L714FS538
c727FS[5]675
Cir. 1
883F2d[1]186
q883F2d[1]1118
q703FS[1]148
q715FS[1]21
Cir. 2
858F2d830
861F2d[8]39
867F2d[8]133
888F2d265
891F2d[1]1051
683FS949
685FS[8]1315
692FS223
694FS[1]1045
q695FS1368
696FS958
698FS[1]468
698FS[6]512
707FS142
708FS[8]63
709FS82
f715FS[8]439
718FS131
718FS[1]1206
719FS[1]1170
q719FS1171
q721FS548
q722FS[1]1136
q723FS213
q729FS[1]1460
Cir. 3
q877F2d[1]224
878F2d[1]731
q878F2d[1]733
q885F2d1160
896F2d749
q683FS[1]484
684FS106
f703FS[6]364
f714FS1373
Cir. 4
862F2d[1]1100
q875F2d[1]74
884F2d[5]132
727FS[6]982
q727FS983
Cir. 5
899F2d[8]413
705FS[8]310
Cir. 6
d860F2d[8]688
875F2d1220
Cir. 7
849F2d[8]267
688FS329
q703FS[1]1337
Cir. 8
q847F2d477
869F2d[7]1169
892F2d[1]1330
q892F2d[1]1331

721FS[1]204
q721FS205
Cir. 9
c700FS[1]1042
708FS[1]1165
711FS984
Cir. 10
e847F2d[8]634
q849F2d[1]466
888F2d702
q888F2d703
891F2d[1]261
j891F2d266
f685FS[1]788
695FS[2]1162
698FS[1]837
q698FS[1]840
q709FS[1]1022
710FS300
Cir. 11
851F2d1303
c854F2d1276
857F2d746
857F2d[7]747
857F2d[8]747
857F2d[9]747
q882F2d482
691FS1416
e691FS[1]1417
697FS1192
q697FS[1]1194
q697FS[1]1202
699FS[1]273
q699FS[1]275
e699FS[1]277
q699FS1526
e700FS[1]876
f700FS1095
703FS[8]79
Cir. Fed.
870F2d641
Calif
209CA3d
[1032
219CA3d
[1010
257CaR764
268CaR632
Colo
773P2d581
Fla
531So2d1071
534So2d794
Mass
26MaA302
526NE1299
P R
4TPR263
Vt
571A2d613
Va
1VCO212
Wash
56WAp444
783P2d1129

—195—
Cir. 1
853F2d[3]1001
Cir. 2
j891F2d438
Cir. 9
f889F2d[1]215
f889F2d[2]215
f889F2d[3]216

—215—
93ARF362n
95ARF363n

—228—
90LE[6]399
90LE[2]407
j90LE410
96LE[1]317
Cir. DC
895F2d1462
Cir. 1
901F2d[7]194
703FS141
Cir. 3
724FS341
Cir. 4
694FS[7]1206
Cir. 5
890F2d[6]767
Cir. 6
865F2d735
685FS[6]1374
688FS318
732FS777
Cir. 9
861F2d[7]1397
706FS[6]747
Cir. 11
868F2d[6]394
Calif
204CA3d
[1304
208CA3d440
212CA3d332
250CaR770
256CaR251
260CaR657
Ill
180IlA46
535NE1069
Ind
540NE122
Mass
405Mas216
539NE1032
Pa
370PaS301
Tenn
756SW271
Wis
146Wis2d627
149Wis2d49
432NW139
437NW544

—248—
Cir. DC
f894F2d[8]427
f894F2d[11]428
f894F2d[12]428
Cir. 3
854F2d[8]32
864F2d[10]1059
870F2d105
Cir. 4
862F2d[13]1074
j862F2d1076
129FRD120
Cir. 5
876F2d1154
876F2d[9]1194
j876F2d1196
Cir. 7

Continued

348

Shepard's United States Citations Cumulative Supplement

hardbound issues on a weekly, monthly, quarterly, and annual basis. When validating an authority, you should consult each issue of the citator and supplements that contain the most current information about the citation. In some cases, supplements are cumulative, which shortens your task.

APPLICATION 3.2

Assume you are attempting to validate a judicial opinion issued in 1978. You will locate the first hardbound edition for the reporters of the jurisdiction to include that opinion. This covers all opinions from 1977 to 1981. You should then consult all additional hardbound editions necessary to bring your search to the most current volume. Next consult the paperback supplements to bring your search for validation current. While these supplements may be issued weekly, they may also be compiled into monthly, quarterly and annual cumulative supplements. Assume the last hardbound edition was issued in 1992. You would then consult each annual supplement up to the current year. Then consult each quarterly supplement up to the preceding quarter. Then consult each weekly supplement up to the current week. As you can see, your validation is much more up-to-date than statutes or digests, which are published only annually and which may or may not contain validating information.

The frequency with which supplements are published is based on the level of activity of a jurisdiction. Citator publishers do not issue a supplement every time a statute is passed or a judicial opinion is rendered. Rather, citators are issued at regular intervals (e.g., weekly, quarterly). The duration of such an interval is determined by how many statutes, opinions, administrative pronouncements, etc., are issued on a regular basis in the jurisdiction. In very active jurisdictions (usually with a large population and consequently a need for extensive legal precedents), supplements may be issued weekly. In jurisdictions that do not issue large volumes of law in a given period of time, the

EXHIBIT 3.6 Sample Pages from the Shepard's United States Citations Cumulative Supplement.
Reproduced by permission of Shepard's McGraw-Hill, Inc. Further reproduction is strictly prohibited.

—410—
j490US1029
491US[1]28
j491US92
j494US622
496US[1]28
Cir. 1
804FS[1]422
Cir. 7
jDk7 91-2722
Cir. 9
980F2d593
980F2d599
Cir. 10
f799FS1099
Md
329Md135
617A2d1068
Pa
414PaS355
S D
494NW642

—450—
493US[1]562
494US[1]351
j494US362
Cir. 8
975F2d[1]1361
1992MC2436
Ariz
846P2d847
Calif
9CA4th1340
12CaR2d162
Ill
148Il2d310
153Il2d362
606NE1200
N Y
80NY331
604NE726
590NYS2d
[177
Va
14VaA614
Wash
67WAp170

—472—
490US222
j61USLW
[4321
Cir. 7
798FS509
Cir. 8
Dk8 91-3396
Cir. 9
Dk9 91-
[70116
eDk9 91-
[70116
Dk9 91-
[70116
Cir. 10
975F2d727
ClCt
e26ClC1058
27FedCl 47
27FedCl[1] 196
98TCt109
f98TCt150
98TCt432

—490—
491US[1]466
491US[1]611
j491US643
61USLW
[4065
Dk3 91-6058
Cir. 3
976F2d168
Cir. 9
805FS806
Mass
411Mas206

—519—
493US110
j493US119
Cir. 7
Dk7 91-3717
dDk7 91-3717
Dk7 91-3717

—568—
490US[2]651
j490US668
Cir. DC
980F2d1460
Cir. 6
799FS728
Cir. 9
803FS322

—625—
Cir. DC
j979F2d221
Cir. 1
806FS307
f807FS[1]15
Cir. 3
802FS1244
Cir. 9
Dk9 91-
[16583
Dk9 91-
[35790
Dk9 92-
[36611
979F2d[1]1379
f980F2d[1]580
Haw
73Haw227
N M
113NM287

—648—
489US[2]614
j489US638
489US672
j489US684
494US[2]331
d496US[2]454
j496US457
j496US463
497US186
Cir. 2
807FS[2]26
Cir. 5
Dk5 92-4822
Cir. 6
jDk6 92-5202
Dk6 91-1852
Cir. 7
803FS1354
803FS[2]1355
Cir. 8
Dk8 92-3001
Cir. 9
981F2d1087
804FS[2]1334
Ariz
845P2d1122
Ark
38AkA161
Calif
11CA4th167
13CaR2d920
17CaR2d337
Conn
24CtA441
D C
619A2d519
Ill
225IlA818
227IlA352
235IlA695
602NE96
607NE158
607NE162
Minn
491NW675
Mo
840SW221
Nebr
239Neb500
242Neb430
242Neb497
495NW478
495NW642
N J
259NJS135
N Y
178NYAD
[1019
179NYAD
[235
183NYAD
[210
152NYM858
152NYM964
579NYS2d
[573
579NYS2d
[856
584NYS2d
[783
587NYS2d
[531
590NYS2d
[627
N D
492NW300
Ohio
75OA525
76OA198
77OA463
78OA143
79OA502
79OA610
79OA611
601NE191
601NE695
602NE706
604NE179
607NE866
607NE935
Pa
415PaS400
615A2d312
615A2d317
Tex
838SW654
838SW882
Utah
841P2d729
844P2d362
844P2d982
Va
14VaA90
Wash
119Wsh2d238
67WAp46
Wis
171Wis2d750
492NW374

—668—
Cir. 10
Dk10 92-
[1209
Ill
229IlA510
S D
490NW729

—689—
Cir. 11
806FS1553

—715—
Cir. 1
808FS44
Cir. 2
Dk2 92-7325
f807FS[2]1140
147BRW[2]64
Cir. 4
144FRD309
Cir. 5
804FS895
f808FS1276
Cir. 6
d806FS[2]190
Cir. 7
Dk7 91-3009
Dk7 91-3673
978F2d339
Cir. 8
807FS[1]564
Cir. 10
Dk10 92-
[7068
Dk10 91-
[6149
Mont
845P2d741
Tex
840SW159
Wis
172Wis2d366
493NW391

—741—
Cir. 1
975F2d16
Cir. 2
Dk2 92-4021
Cir. 4
f978F2d[1]853
e803FS[1]1090
Cir. 9
802FS324
Cir. 10
f804FS203
98TCt503
Ariz
171Az524
Colo
843P2d20
Wash
119Wsh2d197
63WAp727
68WAp64
841P2d1254

—907—
Case 5
P R
17TPR712

—908—
Case 2
Cir. 2
Dk2 92-5010
798FS106
1992MC290

—909—
Case 5
Conn
220Ct524

—911—
Case 5
Haw
8HA117

—916—
Case 7
1992MC162

—921—
Case 12
Mass
413Mas76
N Y
179NYAD
[814
579NYS2d
[157

—922—
Case 3
Conn
220Ct636

—922—
Case 4
Conn
220Ct636
28CtA829

—923—
Case 13
Conn
220Ct280
223Ct191

—927—
Case 5
Mass
411Mas654

—927—
Case 11
Ore
113OrA498

—930—
Case 3
Cir. 7
977F2d276

—930—
Case 4
Iowa
494NW689

—931—
Case 1
Cir. 1
799FS225

—935—
Case 5
N Y
579NYS2d
[428

—937—
Case 6
Minn
490NW96

—938—
Case 1
Ill
221IlA153

—938—
Case 9
Ill
221IlA153

—945—
Case 9
Cir. 8
Dk8 91-1250

—947—
Case 11
Dk3 91-5841
Cir. 3
976F2d141

—959—
Case 2
1992MC940
1992MC1282

—959—
Case 4
Dk3 91-5841
Cir. 3
976F2d142

—966—
Case 8
Cir. DC
798FS31

—967—
Case 9
92CIT90
92CIT92
W Va
173WV41

—968—
Case 4
N Y
584NYS2d
[257

—971—
Case 2
Ore
116OrA484

—972—
Case 2
N Y
180NYAD
[188
180NYAD
[189
180NYAD
[191
586NYS2d
[440
586NYS2d
[441
586NYS2d
[442

—972—
Case 11
Dk2 91-1549

—975—
Case 5
P R
17TPR595

—976—
Case 6
494US757
j494US757

—978—
Case 2
Iowa
495NW749

—980—
Case 5
Ohio
72OA57

—981—
Case 8
1992MC1561

—987—
495US154
j495US179

—1301—
495US[1]154

Vol. 441

—1—
j493US452
Cir. 3
805FS299
805FS[1]300
Cir. 6
806FS1313
806FS[1]1314
Cir. 7
981F2d1517
Wash
66WAp325

—68—
Cir. 3
Dk3 92-1359
Nebr
241Neb956
492NW48
N Y
152NYM725
578NYS2d
[976
Vt
615A2d502

—91—
f490US[2]616
493US335
Cir. 2
Dk2 91-9288
801FS[2]1229
Cir. 3
fDk3 92-1195
804FS692
Cir. 5
Dk5 91-1083
975F2d1183
f979F2d1108
980F2d[1]1050
Cir. 6
803FS118
Cir. 7
978F2d293
f982F2d1094
982F2d[2]1095
Cir. 9
Dk9 89-
[55358
979F2d171
Cir. 11
809FS93
P R
1992JTS9933
30COA675§ 6

—130—
489US[1]299
j493US510
j494US468
Cir. 5
805FS[1]1339
805FS1349
e805FS[1]1352
Conn
224Ct453
25CtA174
619A2d457
W Va
173WV629

—153—
j490US425
491US530
491US668
493US201
Cir. 4
982F2d141
805FS1305
144FRD70
ClCt
26ClC214
26ClC686
Pa
414PaS146
Vt
157Vt90

Continued

EXHIBIT 3.6   Continued

UNITED STATES CODE '88 Ed.

T. 42 § 7477

Column 1

Subsec. f
Cir. 9
731FS1452
Subd. 1
A104St2634
Subsec. g
Cir. 6
889F2d1518
941F2d1360
Subd. 1
Cir. 6
889F2d1518
Subsecs. k to n
Ad104St2406
Subsec. k
Cir. 2
769FS486
Subsec. n
Cir. 2
769FS487
Cir. 9
775FS1296
Subd. 1
Cir. 9
775FS1296
Subsec. o
Ad104St2464
Subsec. p
Ad104St2466

§ 7411
A104St2467
A104St2574
Cir. 1
888F2d182
Cir. 2
885F2d1070
Cir. 4
770FS1105
Cir. 7
893F2d904
Cir. 9
748FS734
74A4666n
94ARF752n
Subsec. a
Subd. 1
A104St2631
Cir. 3
732FS539
¶ C
Cir. 7
893F2d904
Subd. 2
Cir. 7
893F2d904
94ARF752n
Subd. 3
EP§ 3.27
94ARF751n
Subd. 4
Cir. 1
889F2d294
Cir. 7
893F2d904
EP§ 3.27
94ARF751n
Subsec. b
Subd. 6
EP§ 3.27

Column 2

Subsec. c
Subd. 2
Cir. 3
757FS513
Subsec. d
94ARF755n
Subsec. e
Cir. 3
732FS539

§ 7412
A104St2531
Cir. DC
886F2d361
902F2d973
Cir. 1
888F2d182
731FS1140
769FS436
777FS1038
Cir. 2
885F2d1069
755FS536
766FS185
Cir. 3
724FS1159
Cir. 5
889F2d669
Cir. 6
727FS1550
Cir. 8
739FS465
Cir. 9
915F2d1360
748FS734
Cir. 10
763FS490
767FS232
Subsec. a
885F2d1070
Subd. 1
731FS1140
Cir. 2
885F2d1070
Subsec. b
Cir. 1
731FS1138
Cir. 3
724FS1160
Cir. 8
739FS468
EP§ 3.27
Subd. 1
Cir. 2
766FS185
Cir. 10
770FS581
¶ A
885F2d1069
Cir. 4
770FS1103
¶ B
Cir. DC
886F2d362
Cir. 1
731FS1140
Cir. 2
885F2d1069

Column 3

Subsec. c
Cir. 1
731FS1137
Cir. 3
724FS1160
732FS539
Cir. 6
934F2d88
Cir. 8
739FS466
EP§ 3.27
Subd. 1
¶ B
Cir. 1
731FS1138
Cir. 6
934F2d86
Cir. 8
739FS468
Subsec. d
Cir. 6
926F2d588
Subd. 2
Cir. 3
757FS513
Subsec. e
Cir. 3
724FS1161
Cir. 6
926F2d588
773FS20
Cir. 8
739FS466
Subd. 1
Cir. 1
731FS1140
Cir. 3
724FS1160
Subd. 5
Cir. 1
731FS1140
Cir. 3
724FS1160
Subsec. l
Subd. 2
Cir. 2
769FS488

§ 7413
A104St2672
Cir. 5
755FS721
Cir. 6
889F2d1517
941F2d1360
Cir. 8
736FS1546
Cir. 9
748FS734
EP§ 3.07
74A4585n
Subsec. a
58USLW
[4804
Cir. 6
889F2d1515
Cir. 9
748FS734
Subd. 1
Cir. 3
732FS537
Cir. 5
755FS722
Cir. 8
736FS1550
EP§ 3.07

Column 4

Subd. 2
Cir. 9
775FS355
Subd. 3
Cir. 1
731FS1136
Subd. 4
Cir. 3
732FS537
Subsec. b
58USLW
[4804
59USLW
[4182
Cir. 1
731FS1136
Cir. 2
730FS483
Cir. 3
732FS535
Cir. 6
889F2d1520
941F2d1352
Cir. 7
733FS1267
Cir. 8
736FS1547
Cir. 10
763FS490
763FS492
767FS232
EP§ 3.07
PLDM§ 1.08
Subd. 1
Cir. 1
731FS1137
Cir. 3
732FS537
Subd. 2
58USLW
[4806
Subd. 3
Cir. 1
731FS1137
Subd. 4
Cir. 1
731FS1137
Subsec. c
58USLW
[4804
Cir. 6
941F2d1361
Cir. 8
736FS1546
PLDM§ 1.08
Subd. 1
¶ C
Cir. 6
934F2d86
Subsec. d
Cir. 6
889F2d1519
Subd. 2
58USLW
[4805
Subd. 10
58USLW
[4806
Subsec. e
EP§ 3.35A

Column 5

§ 7414
Cir. 3
724FS1159
Cir. 9
728FS627
Cir. 10
763FS490
767FS232
EP§ 3.10
Subsec. a
A104St2574
A104St2680
Cir. 1
731FS1137
Cir. 9
728FS627
EP§ 3.10
Subd. 1
¶ A
Cir. 1
731FS1143
¶ B
Cir. 1
731FS1143
¶ E
Cir. 1
731FS1143
Subd. 2
EP§ 3.68
¶ B
Cir. 9
728FS627
Subd. 3
Ad104St2681
Subsec. c
EP§ 3.12

§ 7415
Cir. DC
912F2d1527
Subsec. a
Cir. DC
912F2d1528
Subsec. b
Cir. DC
912F2d1528
Subsec. c
Cir. DC
912F2d1528

§ 7416
Cir. 1
728FS833
Cir. 6
926F2d587
773FS19
Cir. 8
736FS1550
Cir. 9
748FS734
74A4578n

§ 7418
Cir. 2
772FS95
Cir. 9
748FS736
779FS487
Cir. 10
728FS1517
Subsec. a
A104St2409
480US600
107SC1434
Cir. 2
772FS95

Column 6

Cir. 7
722FS1571
Cir. 9
914F2d1550
748FS736
Cir. 10
903F2d1295
Subsec. b
A104St2574
Cir. 9
748FS736
Subsec. c
Ad104St2530
Cir. 2
772FS95
Subsec. d
Ad104St2530

§ 7420
Cir. DC
937F2d643
Cir. 6
889F2d1518
941F2d1352
941F2d1360
Cir. 8
736FS1546
EP§ 8.09
Subsec. a
Subd. 2
¶ A
A104St2684

§ 7421
A104St2467

§ 7422
Subsec. a
Cir. 2
885F2d1071

§ 7423
96ARF473n
Subsec. a
74A4598n
Subsec. b
74A4598n
Subsec. c
96ARF473n

§ 7426
A104St2469
EP§ 3.18

§ 7429
Ad104St2577
Cir. 6
941F2d1355
Subsec. c
Cir. 6
941F2d1355

§ 7430
Ad104St2689

§ 7431
Ad104St2689

§ 7450
Rs104St2648

Column 7

§ 7451
Rs104St2648
§ 7452
Rs104St2648
§ 7453
Rs104St2648
§ 7454
Rs104St2648
§ 7455
Rs104St2648
§ 7456
Rs104St2648
§ 7457
Rs104St2648
§ 7458
Rs104St2648
§ 7459
Rs104St2648
Cir. 5
718FS484

§ 7470
et seq.
Cir. DC
937F2d643

§§ 7470 to
7491
74A4684n

§§ 7470 to
7479
Cir. DC
898F2d184
902F2d966
902F2d976
Cir. 1
889F2d294
Cir. 6
916F2d320

§ 7470
Cir. DC
898F2d184
937F2d645
Subsec. 3
Cir. DC
937F2d645
Subsec. 5
Cir. DC
937F2d645

§§ 7471 to
7473
Cir. 10
908F2d632

§ 7471
A104St2470

§ 7472
Cir. DC
898F2d185

Column 8

Subsec. a
A104St2469
Subsec. b
A104St2470

§ 7473
Cir. DC
898F2d184
902F2d976
Cir. 8
736FS1543
Subsec. b
Cir. DC
898F2d186
902F2d966

§ 7474
Cir. DC
898F2d185
Subsec. a
A104St2469
Subsec. d
EP§ 3.37

§ 7475
Cir. DC
902F2d976
937F2d643
Cir. 1
888F2d182
889F2d293
Subsec. a
Cir. DC
898F2d184
Subd. 1
Cir. 7
893F2d905
Subd. 3
Cir. 6
916F2d320
Subd. 4
Cir. 3
732FS538
Cir. 6
916F2d320
Subsec. c
EP§ 3.14

§ 7476
Cir. DC
898F2d184
902F2d977
Subsec. c
Cir. DC
898F2d184
Subsec. d
Cir. DC
898F2d184
Subsec. e
Cir. DC
898F2d188
Subsec. f
Ad104St2462

§ 7477
A104St2470
A104St2684
Cir. 1
889F2d295
Cir. 3
732FS535

supplements may be issued only quarterly. There are also citators and supplements issued for secondary authorities, such as certain legal periodicals, Restatements, and other resources commonly consulted in legal research.

VALIDATION BY COMPUTER

An increasing amount of legal research is done by computer, and validation of authority has understandably been included in the services available to the computer researcher. The process is essentially the same, however. Access to citator information is obtained through the use of a computer rather than an actual book. (The actual procedure for using computer-based citators such as West's Insta-Cite is discussed in Chapter 14.)

☐ ASSIGNMENT 3.2

Using Exhibits 3.7 and 3.8, complete the following questions for each of the citations given (you may need to refer to Exhibit 3.2 showing citator abbreviations):

1. List any citation that has been overruled ("o") or dissented ("j") by a subsequent court. Also give the "o" or "j" citation.
2. Identify any citation that has been followed ("f") and the citator that issued the citation.
3. For the judicial citator page, indicate the very first and last reporter volume covered (in whole or in part) by the page.
4. Determine whether any statute has been amended. If so, give the statute and the citation for the amendment.
5. Explain each abbreviation representing a note about a citation (e.g., "o").

⫸ S T R A T E G Y

Locating Information in a Citator

1. Narrow the citation you are examining as much as possible (e.g., the exact lettered paragraph of a statute or numbered paragraph of a case).
2. Obtain the proper citator for the publication of your cited authority (e.g., Shepard's Citations of Northwestern 2d).
3. Locate each volume and supplement that contain information about the volume or chapter you are examining. The chapters or volumes included in a particular Shepard's Citations volume are given on the front cover.
4. Locate the portion of Shepard's Citations that contains information about the publication. (Remember, some Shepard's contain information about more than one reporter or statutory publication.)
5. Find the volume or chapter number (this information appears at the top of the page). This volume or chapter number will be in large, boldface type.
6. Find the page or section number following the volume or chapter number. This information will be in slightly smaller boldface type.

EXHIBIT 3.7 Sample page from Shepard's United States Citations: Case Edition (1971-1976).
Reproduced by permission of Shepard's McGraw-Hill, Inc. Further reproduction is strictly prohibited.

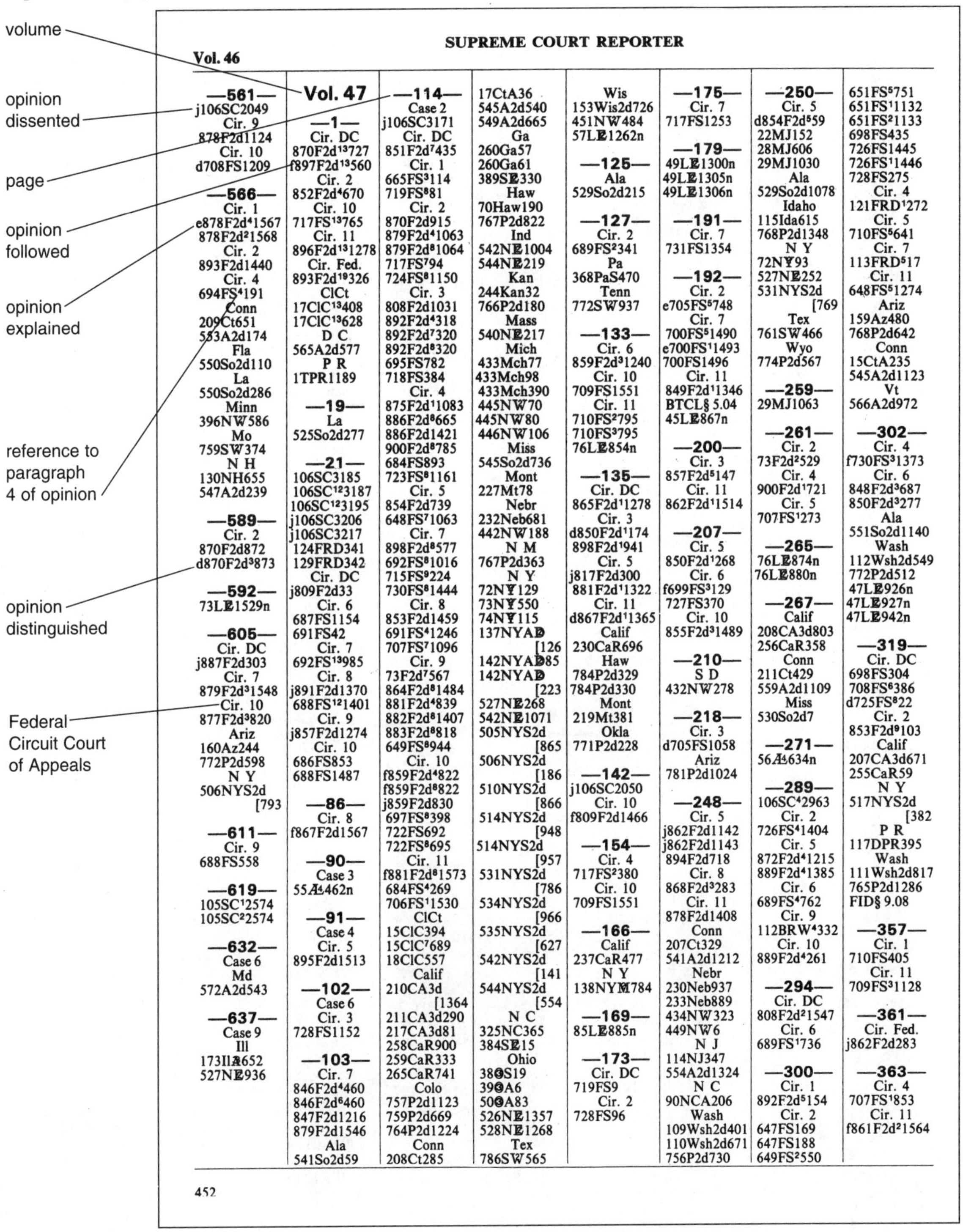
volume
opinion dissented
page
opinion followed
opinion explained
reference to paragraph 4 of opinion
opinion distinguished
Federal Circuit Court of Appeals

SUPREME COURT REPORTER

Vol. 46

—561—
j106SC2049
Cir. 9
878F2d1124
Cir. 10
d708FS1209
—566—
Cir. 1
e878F2d[4]1567
878F2d[2]1568
Cir. 2
893F2d1440
Cir. 4
694FS[4]191
Conn
209Ct651
553A2d174
Fla
550So2d110
La
550So2d286
Minn
396NW586
Mo
759SW374
N H
130NH655
547A2d239
—589—
Cir. 2
870F2d872
d870F2d[3]873
—592—
73LE1529n
—605—
Cir. DC
j887F2d303
Cir. 7
879F2d[3]1548
Cir. 10
877F2d[3]820
Ariz
160Az244
772P2d598
N Y
506NYS2d
[793
—611—
Cir. 9
688FS558
—619—
105SC[1]2574
105SC[2]2574
—632—
Case 6
Md
572A2d543
—637—
Case 9
Ill
173IlA652
527NE936

Vol. 47

—1—
Cir. DC
870F2d[13]727
f897F2d[13]560
Cir. 2
852F2d[4]670
Cir. 10
717FS[13]765
Cir. 11
896F2d[13]1278
Cir. Fed.
893F2d[19]326
ClCt
17ClC[13]408
17ClC[13]628
D C
565A2d577
P R
1TPR1189
—19—
La
525So2d277
—21—
106SC3185
106SC[12]3187
106SC[12]3195
j106SC3206
j106SC3217
124FRD341
129FRD342
Cir. DC
j809F2d33
Cir. 6
687FS1154
691FS42
Cir. 7
692FS[13]985
Cir. 8
j891F2d1370
688FS[12]1401
Cir. 9
j857F2d1274
Cir. 10
686FS853
688FS1487
—86—
Cir. 8
f867F2d1567
—90—
Case 3
55A4462n
—91—
Case 4
Cir. 5
895F2d1513
—102—
Case 6
Cir. 3
728FS1152
—103—
Cir. 7
846F2d[4]460
846F2d[6]460
847F2d1216
879F2d1546
Ala
541So2d59

—114—
Case 2
j106SC3171
Cir. DC
851F2d[7]435
Cir. 1
665FS[3]114
719FS[8]81
Cir. 2
870F2d915
879F2d[4]1063
879F2d[8]1064
717FS794
724FS[8]1150
Cir. 3
808F2d1031
892F2d[4]318
892F2d[7]320
892F2d[8]320
695FS782
718FS384
Cir. 4
875F2d[1]1083
886F2d[8]665
886F2d1421
900F2d[8]785
684FS893
723FS[8]1161
Cir. 5
854F2d739
648FS[7]1063
Cir. 7
898F2d[8]577
692FS[8]1016
715FS[8]224
730FS[8]1444
Cir. 8
853F2d1459
691FS[4]1246
707FS[7]1096
Cir. 9
73F2d[7]567
864F2d[8]1484
881F2d[4]839
882F2d[8]1407
883F2d[8]818
649FS[8]944
Cir. 10
f859F2d[4]822
f859F2d[8]822
j859F2d830
697FS[8]398
722FS692
722FS[8]695
Cir. 11
f881F2d[8]1573
684FS[4]269
706FS[1]1530
ClCt
15ClC394
15ClC[7]689
18ClC557
Calif
210CA3d
[1364
211CA3d290
217CA3d81
258CaR900
259CaR333
265CaR741
Colo
757P2d1123
759P2d669
764P2d1224
Conn
208Ct285

17CtA36
545A2d540
549A2d665
Ga
260Ga57
260Ga61
389SE330
Haw
70Haw190
767P2d822
Ind
542NE1004
544NE219
Kan
244Kan32
766P2d180
Mass
540NE217
Mich
433Mch77
433Mch98
433Mch390
445NW70
445NW80
446NW106
Miss
545So2d736
Mont
227Mt78
Nebr
232Neb681
442NW188
N M
767P2d363
N Y
72NY129
73NY550
74NY115
137NYAD
[126
142NYAD85
142NYAD
[223
527NE268
542NE1071
505NYS2d
[865
506NYS2d
[186
510NYS2d
[866
514NYS2d
[948
514NYS2d
[957
531NYS2d
[786
534NYS2d
[966
535NYS2d
[627
542NYS2d
[141
544NYS2d
[554
N C
325NC365
384SE15
Ohio
38OS19
39OA6
50OA83
526NE1357
528NE1268
Tex
786SW565

Wis
153Wis2d726
451NW484
57LE1262n
—125—
Ala
529So2d215
—127—
Cir. 2
689FS[2]341
Pa
368PaS470
Tenn
772SW937
—133—
Cir. 6
859F2d[3]1240
Cir. 10
709FS1551
Cir. 11
710FS[2]795
710FS[3]795
76LE854n
—135—
Cir. DC
865F2d[1]1278
Cir. 3
d850F2d[1]174
898F2d[1]941
Cir. 5
j817F2d300
881F2d[1]1322
Cir. 11
d867F2d[1]1365
Calif
230CaR696
Haw
784P2d329
784P2d330
Mont
219Mt381
Okla
771P2d228
—142—
j106SC2050
Cir. 10
f809F2d1466
—154—
Cir. 4
717FS[2]380
Cir. 10
709FS1551
—166—
Calif
237CaR477
N Y
138NYM784
—169—
85LE885n
—173—
Cir. DC
719FS9
Cir. 2
728FS96

—175—
Cir. 7
717FS1253
—179—
49LE1300n
49LE1305n
49LE1306n
—191—
Cir. 7
731FS1354
—192—
Cir. 2
e705FS[5]748
Cir. 7
700FS[5]1490
e700FS[1]1493
700FS1496
Cir. 11
849F2d[1]1346
BTCL§ 5.04
45LE867n
—200—
Cir. 3
857F2d[5]147
Cir. 11
862F2d[1]1514
—207—
Cir. 5
850F2d[1]268
Cir. 6
f699FS[3]129
727FS370
Cir. 10
855F2d[3]1489
—210—
S D
432NW278
—218—
Cir. 3
d705FS1058
Ariz
781P2d1024
—248—
Cir. 5
j862F2d1142
j862F2d1143
894F2d718
Cir. 8
868F2d[3]283
Cir. 11
878F2d1408
Conn
207Ct329
541A2d1212
Nebr
230Neb937
233Neb889
434NW323
449NW6
N J
114NJ347
554A2d1324
N C
90NCA206
Wash
109Wsh2d401
110Wsh2d671
756P2d730

—250—
Cir. 5
d854F2d[5]59
22MJ152
28MJ606
29MJ1030
Ala
529So2d1078
Idaho
115Ida615
768P2d1348
N Y
72NY93
527NE252
531NYS2d
[769
Tex
761SW466
Wyo
774P2d567
—259—
29MJ1063
—261—
Cir. 2
73F2d[2]529
Cir. 4
900F2d[1]721
Cir. 5
707FS[1]273
—265—
76LE874n
76LE880n
—267—
Calif
208CA3d803
256CaR358
Conn
211Ct429
559A2d1109
Miss
530So2d7
—271—
56A4634n
—289—
106SC[4]2963
Cir. 2
726FS[4]1404
Cir. 5
872F2d[4]1215
889F2d[4]1385
Cir. 6
689FS[4]762
Cir. 9
112BRW[4]332
Cir. 10
889F2d[4]261
—294—
Cir. DC
808F2d[2]1547
Cir. 6
689FS[1]736
—300—
Cir. 1
892F2d[5]154
Cir. 2
647FS169
647FS188
649FS[2]550

651FS[5]751
651FS[1]1132
651FS[2]1133
698FS435
726FS1445
726FS[1]1446
728FS275
Cir. 4
121FRD[1]272
Cir. 5
710FS[5]641
Cir. 7
113FRD[5]17
Cir. 11
648FS[5]1274
Ariz
159Az480
768P2d642
Conn
15CtA235
545A2d1123
Vt
566A2d972
—302—
Cir. 4
f730FS[3]1373
Cir. 6
848F2d[3]687
850F2d[3]277
Ala
551So2d1140
Wash
112Wsh2d549
772P2d512
47LE926n
47LE927n
47LE942n
—319—
Cir. DC
698FS304
708FS[6]386
d725FS[8]22
Cir. 2
853F2d[9]103
Calif
207CA3d671
255CaR59
N Y
517NYS2d
[382
P R
117DPR395
Wash
111Wsh2d817
765P2d1286
FID§ 9.08
—357—
Cir. 1
710FS405
Cir. 11
709FS[3]1128
—361—
Cir. Fed.
j862F2d283
—363—
Cir. 4
707FS[1]853
Cir. 11
f861F2d[2]1564

452

Cir. 8
750FS1003
Subsec. a
Cir. 1
907F2d1245
721FS1509
Cir. 7
780FS513
Subd. 1
Cir. 1
721FS1510
Subd. 2
¶ B
Cl. 1
A104St4194
Subsec. b
Cir. 1
907F2d1245
721FS1508
Cir. 7
780FS513
Subd. 1
A104St4159
Cir. 1
907F2d1244
721FS1510
Subd. 2
Cir. 1
907F2d1244
721FS1510
Subd. 3
Cir. 1
907F2d1244
721FS1510
Cir. 5
912F2d830
¶ A
L104St4195
Cir. 5
C734FS1276
Cl. v
Cir. 5
912F2d824
¶ B
L104St4145
Cir. 5
912F2d824
C734FS1281
¶ D
Cir. 1
907F2d1244
721FS1514
Subsec. c
Subd. 2
A104St4195
Subd. 3
Rs104St4196
Subsec. d
Cir. 1
907F2d1245
721FS1508
Cir. 7
780FS513
Subsec. e
Ad104St4160

§ 1437r
Subsec. f
Subd. 3
A104St4196
Subd. 4
Ad104St4160

§ 1437s
Subsec. a
A104St4161

§ 1437t
Ad104St4196

§ 1437u
Ad104St4225

§ 1437bb
Subsec. b
A104St4199

**§§ 1437aaa to
1437aaa-8**
Ad104St4148

§ 1439
Subsec. a
A104St4303
Subd. 1
A103St1990
Subd. 5
A104St4238
Subsec. d
A103St1988
Subd. 1
¶ A
A104St1186
A104St4233
A104St4323
Subd. 4
A103St1998

§ 1441
et seq.
Cir. 2
733FS777
Cir. 7
780FS512

§ 1441
Cir. DC
928F2d417
731FS1105
Cir. 1
767FS1160
Cir. 2
733FS785
Cir. 3
110BRW700

§ 1441a
Cir. 9
741FS830
103ARF770n

§ 1442
Subsec. a
Cir. 3
719FS340

§ 1450
et seq.
Cir. 2
779FS685

§ 1452b
Cir. 1
764FS695

Subsec. e
Cir. 1
764FS698

§ 1453
et seq.
909F2d90

§ 1456
Subsec. c
Cir. Fed.
939F2d1551

§ 1471
et seq.
Cir. 5
721FS116

§ 1471
Subsec. a
Cir. 8
767FS1477
Subd. 3
Cir. 2
733FS778
Subsec. b
Subd. 4
A104St4282
Subsec. e
A104St4283

§ 1472
et seq.
945F2d455

§ 1472
Cir. 1
945F2d455
Cir. 11
950F2d1551
Subsec. c
Cir. 8
767FS1478
Subd. 1
A103St2041
¶ B
A104St4297
Subd. 3
Cir. 8
767FS1478
Subd. 4
¶ A
Cir. 8
767FS1478
¶ B
Cir. 8
767FS1478
Subd. 5
¶ A
Cir. 8
767FS1478
Cl. 1
Cir. 8
767FS1487
Cl. 2
Cir. 8
767FS1478
¶ G
Cir. 8
767FS1479

Cl. 1
Subcl. 1
Cir. 8
767FS1479
Subcl. 2
Cir. 8
767FS1479
Cl. 2
Subcl. 1
Cir. 8
767FS1477
Cir. 11
950F2d1548
741FS1564
Subsec. f
Ad104St4283
Subsec. g
Ad104St4283
Subsec. h
Ad104St4284
Subd. 3
¶ C
A105St915

§ 1473f
Subsec. t
Subd. 1
Cir. 4
955F2d253

§ 1475
A104St4287
Cir. 2
733FS778
Cir. 1

§ 1479
Subsec. d
RnSubsec e
[104St4287
Subsec. d
(104St4287)
Ad104St4287
Subsec. f
Ad104St4288

§ 1480
Subsec. e
A104St4291
Subsec. g
A104St4291
Subd. 1
945F2d451
Cir. 2
733FS785
Cir. 8
767FS1490
Cir. 11
950F2d1549
741FS1564
Subd. 5
¶ A
Cir. 8
767FS1478

§ 1483
Subsec. a
Subd. 1
A104St4281
Subsec. b
A104St4281
Subsec. c
Subd. 1
A104St4282
Subsec. d
A104St4282

§ 1485
A104St4291
Cir. 1
945F2d451
Cir. 2
742FS805
Cir. 5
725FS897
Cir. 8
767FS1477
Cir. 11
950F2d1548
741FS1564
Subsec. b
Subd. 4
A103St825
A104St4282
A105St915
Subsec. t
Ad103St2042
Subsec. u
Ad103St2048
Subsec. w
Ad104St4292

§ 1486
Subsec. k
Ad104St4292

§ 1490
A103St826
A104St4296

§ 1490a
Subsec. a
Subd. 2
¶ C
A104St4296

§ 1490c
Subsec. f
A103St826
A104St4282
A105St915

§ 1490g
Ad104St4404

§ 1490m
Subsec. c
Subd. 1
A104St4296
Subsec. g
A104St4296

§ 1490o
A105St280
Subsec. b
A103St2044
A104St4297

§ 1490p
Ad103St2045
Subsec. h
A104St4297

§ 1491
et seq.
ClCt
20ClC134

§ 1501
et seq.
Cir. 7
750FS914
Cir. 11
764FS175

§ 1502
Cir. 6
776FS321

§ 1571
Cir. 9
911F2d1318

§ 1581
Subsec. d
Subd. 1
A105St280

§ 1587
Subsec. b
A105St281

§ 1592a
Subsec. a
A105St281
Subsec. c
A105St281

§ 1592n
Subsec. h
A105St281

§ 1594
Cir. 6
769FS222
Subsec. a
Cir. 6
769FS222

**§§ 1651 to
1654**
930F2d1112
Cir. 5
780FS1214

§ 1651
Cir. 5
930F2d1112
Subsec. a
Cir. 5
930F2d1112
Cir. 7
780FS1214

§ 1653
Cir. 5
930F2d1116
Subsec. a
Cir. 5
930F2d1113
Subsec. b
Cir. 5
930F2d1112
Cir. 7
780FS1215

§ 1705
Subsec. a
58USLW
[4368

§ 1715
Cir. 8
927F2d1032

§ 1716
Cir. 8
927F2d1032

§ 1717
Cir. 5
943F2d1445
Cir. 6
114BRW546
Cir. 7
111BRW733
Cir. 9
105BRW39
Cir. 10
107BRW315
Cir. 11
119BRW835

§ 1751
et seq.
Cir. 9
952F2d1175

**§§ 1751 to
1779**
Cir. 4
768FS1157

**§§ 1751 to
1769c**
A103St916

§ 1755
Subsec. a
A103St913
Subsec. e
Subd. 1
A103St906
Subd. 2
A103St907

§ 1756
Subsec. a
A103St913

§ 1757
A103St908
A103St914

§ 1758
A103St908
A103St914
Subsec. a
Cir. 5
A103St878
Subsec. b
A103St908
Subd. 1
¶ A
A103St908

§ 1759a
Subsec. e
Subd. 1
A103St909

§ 1760
A103St914

§ 1761
A103St879
A103St915

§ 1762
R103St915

§ 1762a
A103St882
Subsec. g
A103St882
Subd. 3
A103St882

§ 1763
R103St883

§ 1766
A103St883
Subsec. d
A103St909
Subsec. h
Subd. 1
A103St907

§ 1766a
Ad103St885

§ 1769
A103St916
Subsec. e
Subd. 1
A103St886
Subsec. f
Ad103St886
Subsec. g
Ad103St910

§ 1769a
A103St887

§ 1769b-1
Ad103St887

§ 1769c
(103St889)
Ad103St889

§ 1771
et seq.
Cir. 9
952F2d1175

§ 1772
Subsec. a
A103St911
Subd. 10
Ad103St911

§ 1773
A103St891
A103St916
Subsec. b
A103St912

EXHIBIT 3.8 Sample page from Shepard's United States Citations: Statute Edition.
Reproduced by permission of Shepard's McGraw-Hill, Inc. Further reproduction is strictly prohibited.

7. If you are looking at a particular paragraph or section number, look at the numbers superscript to the citations below the boldface page or section number.
8. Examine the letters to the left of the citations for any indication of subsequent treatment that affects the authority (e.g., "a" in a statutory citator would indicate the statute was amended).
9. Follow these steps for each citator and supplement that contain information about the citation of authority you are examining.

||||▶ S T R A T E G Y

Validation of a Statutory Authority

1. Obtain the complete citation (topic number, name and year of publication or supplement, statute number).
2. Locate the proper citator for the statutory publication; the year of the citation will indicate in which hardbound volume the statute first appears. The cover of the citator should provide you with the years of publication addressed. Begin with the first hardbound citator that includes the year of the statute you are validating. Complete the following steps in each subsequent citator publication.
3. Open the citator to the proper pages for your statutory publication. Statutory citators may include more than one statutory publication for a jurisdiction. Follow the pages in numerical sequence until you locate the page that contains the topic number of your citation. Topic numbers are in large, boldface type.
4. Once you have located the proper topic number, look for the statute number. It should appear in proper numerical sequence with regard to the other statutes within a particular topic and should appear in a boldface type slightly smaller than that used for topic numbers.
5. After you locate the proper statute page number, any citations below it are references to authorities that mention the statute. Letters to the left indicate how the statute was addressed (e.g., amended, followed, repealed). Numbers or letters superscript to a citation indicate reference to a particular subpart of the statute that was mentioned. (Administrative law is validated in a similar manner using the code chapter and regulation/rule section.)

||||▶ S T R A T E G Y

Validation of a Judicial Authority

1. Obtain the publication information for the judicial opinion (volume number, name of publication, page number of the first page of the opinion).
2. Locate the proper citator for the judicial publication. The volume numbers of a judicial report(er) included in a citator are indicated on the cover of the citator. Start with the first hardbound citator that includes the volume number you are validating. Complete the following steps for each subsequent citator publication.
3. Open the citator to the proper pages for your reporter (judicial citators may include more than one reporter). Follow the pages in numerical sequence until you locate the page that contains the volume number of your citation. Volume numbers are in large, boldface type and are preceded by the abbreviation "Vol."
4. Once you have located the proper volume number, look for the page number. It should appear in proper numerical sequence with regard to the other pages within a particular volume and should appear in a boldface type slightly smaller than that used for volume numbers.

5. After you locate the proper page number, any citations below it are references to authorities that mention the opinion. Letters to the left indicate how the opinion was addressed (e.g., affirmed, followed, overruled). Numbers or letters superscript to a citation indicate reference to a particular paragraph of the opinion that was mentioned.

Note: If an authority is not included in a citator (e.g., a particular judicial opinion first page number does not appear), it means that there was no reference made to the authority during the time period covered by that citator. For this reason, all citators issued since the publication of the original authority must be consulted to determine whether any subsequent reference has been made to the authority from its inception.)

Chapter Summary

This chapter has demonstrated the importance of validation of authority. It is necessary to accurately assess the current force and effect of a legal authority. Citators make this task a manageable one and are organized in such a way as to minimize the time spent on the process. Citators are also published with much greater frequency and are often the only source that provides information about the subsequent treatment of a legal standard following its issuance. Citators are published by jurisdiction and further by type of authority (e.g., report, statute, administrative law). There are also citators for certain secondary authorities, such as legal periodicals. The citator can be used as a research aid to locate materials on related topics. In short, the citator is an absolutely integral element of all legal research.

Key Terms

citator   validation

Self-Test

MULTIPLE CHOICE

1. When conducting legal research, an integral element is the determination of whether the law is still _____ .
   a) primary
   b) mandatory

   c) citated
   d) valid
2. Typically, to validate an authority, you will look up a legal citation in the appropriate _____ .
   a) report
   b) code

c) register
d) citator
3. Citators are generally published
_____ and thus are more
current.
   a) more often than primary authorities
   b) daily
   c) at the time statutes are updated
   d) none of the above
4. The citator should not be the only source
that you should use in research, because
_____.
   a) it is based only on authorities that have
   mentioned prior authorities
   b) it may be an incomplete source
   c) it may be limited in scope
   d) all of the above
5. A citator uses only the
_____ numbers of the citation.
   a) volume and publication
   b) page and publication
   c) volume, page, and publication
   c) court and publication

TRUE/FALSE

_____ 6. A citator contains complete citations.
_____ 7. Letters to the left of the list of
citations are used to indicate exactly
where the citation appeared in
subsequent authority.
_____ 8. Superscript numbers or letters
indicate the exact portion of the
precedent that is referenced in the
subsequent citation.
_____ 9. Citators are published on a weekly,
monthly, quarterly, and annual basis
to enable a very current validation
of authority.
_____ 10. When validating an authority, you
need consult only the most recent
issue of the citator or its
supplements.

FILL-IN THE BLANKS

11. Usually supplements are
_____ .
12. The frequency with which supplements
are published is based on the level of
activity of a _____.
13. In jurisdictions that do not issue large
volumes of law in a given period of time,
the supplements may be issued less
_____ .
14. There are also citators for
_____ _____ ,
such as certain legal periodicals.
15. Citators are available electronically to
the _____ researcher.
16. A specific point of authority within a
citation is designated by a small number
or letter _____
_____ _____
_____ the citation.
17. _____ to the left of a
subsequent citation denote action taken
with respect to the authority you are
validating.
18. Supplements may be published
_____, _____, and
_____ .
19. Supplements published within the same
year and between issuance of hardbound
volumes are generally _____ .
20. Citators do not include
_____ information about the
authority you are attempting to validate.

CHAPTER 4

LEGAL ANALYSIS AND BEGINNING THE RESEARCH PROCESS

Upon completion of this chapter, you should be able to accomplish the following competencies:

- Define the term *legal analysis.*

- Discuss the purposes of legal analysis.

- Explain the benefits of legal analysis.

- Analyze statutory and administrative law.

- Analyze case law.

- Prepare a case brief.

- Compare and contrast precedent with a current situation.

- Explain the purpose of the basic steps of research.

- Discuss the need for each of the basic steps of research.

- Complete each of the basic steps of research.

LEGAL ANALYSIS

When you watch a courtroom scene on television or in the movies, the movement is swift and smooth. The players speak with authority and accomplish their goals. In this respect (allowing, of course, for great dramatization and some distinctions between fiction and fact), the scene is not much different in an actual courtroom. The reason for this is that trials are basically consistent. Through established rules of procedure and principles of law, the lawyers, judge, court reporters, legal assistants, and other legal professionals know what to expect and when to expect it. This is all the product of legal research. Even the most novice beginners, if they can adequately research, can prepare themselves to move a case through the legal system.

The ability to research is not confined to simply looking up information. As mentioned in Chapter 1, you must look up the right information that has the greatest impact, and the information must be valid. Even having accomplished this, legal research is still unlike any other. It uses an entire language, sometimes called "legalese," to which you must become accustomed. The law is not deliberately vague. Rather, the language of the law has been carried over for centuries. And, while everyday language has changed and developed and intermingled with different languages of different countries, lawyers and judges have been reluctant to adopt such changes because they might be interpreted as changing the legal effect of documents. Consequently, much of the language and definition of legal terms can be traced back to sixteenth-century England and earlier.

Fortunately, the trend in the latter part of the twentieth century has been to adopt a more straightforward and current approach to drafting legal documents. Many terms and definitions from the past are still commonly used. Whenever possible, however, legal writing more and more frequently is written in ordinary language that the layperson can understand. Because these two standards are so intermingled, it is necessary for you to develop an understanding of the legal terminology that is still prevalent in law. A legal dictionary, such as West's Legal Thesaurus/Dictionary, can be an invaluable companion in legal research.

Breaking Down the Authority

The actual process of **legal analysis** includes appreciating the meaning of a legal standard and its potential impact on a situation. To do this, you must first disassemble the legal standard into its basic components. Following this, it becomes much easier to distinguish the significant information and to apply that information to another situation.

legal analysis
Method of extracting significant information from a legal authority for comparison purposes.

⚖ **A P P L I C A T I O N   4 . 1**

A client of the firm where you are employed has been arrested for driving under the influence. The client claims that she came out of a bar on a cold night and, knowing that

she was too drunk to drive just then, got into the car, started the ignition for heat, cracked the window, and fell asleep. She was abruptly awakened by a police officer, who administered a field sobriety test and arrested her for driving under the influence.

Your first reaction might be that the client committed no offense. However, by researching the drunken driving statute, you find that a person can be charged who is legally drunk and "in control" of the vehicle. Further research produces cases that describe the various acts that can legally constitute "in control." By comparing each issue and circumstance of these cases to the client's case, you can determine whether the client is likely to be convicted of driving under the influence.

Statutory Law and Administrative Regulations. Because the organization of a judicial opinion is so different from that of a statute or administrative regulation, each is discussed separately. As mentioned earlier in the text, a statute is generally written in terms broad enough to encompass a variety of situations. Statutory law (and administrative regulations) does not, as a rule, describe very specific factual circumstances. Rather, it usually gives conditions or elements that must be present for the statute to apply. Whether the facts of a person's case match the elements of the statute determines whether the outcome of the case will be governed by the statute. Consequently, it is an essential part of legal analysis and legal research to locate all relevant statutory or administrative law and to effectively break it down into components that can be accurately assessed in terms of whether they are present in the facts of a particular situation.

Because statutory and administrative law by their nature must be written in such a way as to encompass a variety of circumstances, the language is sometimes lengthy and appears quite vague. However, breaking each part into manageable portions allows you to reduce a complicated document into an easily understood list of conditions. You should, however, remember that every word in a statute is there for a reason. For example the difference between the words *shall* and *may* is significant. If a statute states that something *shall* occur, it is mandatory. However, if the word *may* is used, the condition is left to the discretion of the authority, such as a court, as to whether it should be applied. The two terms *and* and *or* are used to determine whether conditions are both required or are alternatives. As a result, when you are breaking down statutes or administrative regulations, pay special attention to every word and do not discard words, assuming they are only present for purposes of grammar. You must look to determine whether the word impacts the meaning of the legal standard. Also, be certain to examine any definitions given within the statute to particular terms. In the case of an act, which is a collection of statutes on a particular topic, there is frequently a statute within the act that gives definition to terms used in the language of other statutes contained within the act.

APPLICATION 4.2

STATUTORY LANGUAGE
Federal Rule of Evidence 403

"Although relevant, evidence may be excluded if its probative value is substantially outweighed by the danger of unfair prejudice, confusion of the issues, or misleading the

jury, or by considerations of undue delay, waste of time, or needless presentation of cumulative evidence."

F.R.E. Rule 403 Analyzed

Even relevant evidence can be withheld from a jury if the opposition can demonstrate any *one* of the following:

a. The benefit of the evidence is not stronger than the damage it could do by confusing, misleading, or causing an emotional reaction by the jury rather than an objective verdict based on the facts and evidence.

b. The benefit of the evidence is not justified by the amount of time it will take to present, such as taking the jury to view an accident scene a great distance away.

c. The evidence merely duplicates other evidence that can be offered.

☐ ASSIGNMENT 4.1

Break the following statutory language into its components:

Federal Rule of Evidence 608

F.R.E. Rule 608 "(a) Opinion and reputation evidence of character. The credibility of a witness may be attacked or supported by evidence in the form of opinion or reputation, but subject to these limitations: (1) the evidence may refer only to character for truthfulness or untruthfulness, and (2) evidence of truthful character is admissible only after the character of the witness for truthfulness has been attacked by opinion or reputation evidence or other-wise."

Once you have become accustomed to breaking a legal standard down into individual elements or conditions, you must then develop an ability to apply the legal standard to a particular circumstance. With statutes and administrative regulations, this may take some practice, because the terminology does not usually speak in terms of individual facts. Usually, however, when you summarize the language in plain terms (without changing its meaning), the task of comparison becomes easier. Refer to the analysis of Rule 403 in Application 4.2 and see how it is compared in the following application.

⚖ APPLICATION 4.3

The defendant objects to certain graphic photographs of an accident scene involving a train in which officials are seen collecting the dismembered body of the victim. The defendant claims that F.R.E. Rule 403 applies.

Summarized F.R.E. Rule 403

Even relevant evidence can be withheld from a jury if the opposition can demonstrate any *one* of the following:

a. The benefit of the evidence is not stronger than the damage it could do by confusing, misleading, or causing an emotional reaction by the jury rather than an objective verdict based on the facts and evidence.

b. The benefit of the evidence is not justified by the amount of time it will take to present, such as taking the jury to view an accident scene a great distance away.

c. The evidence merely duplicates other evidence that can be offered.

F.R.E. Rule 403 Compared

The evidence is relevant to prove the victim was fatally injured when run over by the train.

a. Could the jury remain objective about the liability of the railroad for the accident after seeing such gruesome photographs? Probably, unless it is claimed that the railroad somehow intentionally or knowingly caused this type of injury.

b. Is time an issue in viewing the evidence? No. The evidence can be presented in the courtroom with all of the other evidence.

c. Does the evidence duplicate other evidence? Probably. The autopsy report and coroner's inquest reports undoubtedly describe the condition of the victim's body.

---

objective
Unbiased presentation of facts.

Based on the foregoing, it is very possible that a judge would exclude the photographs. There is at least the possibility of an emotional reaction of viewing photos. This possibility is not as great when reading an objectively written medical description of the injuries. Secondly, because more **objective** evidence is available to prove the same facts (the extent of injuries), a court may opt to apply F.R.E. Rule 403 and exclude the evidence.

If you were actually researching the case in Application 4.3, you would also want to look at judicial opinions in which similar issues were decided. Based on your position in the case, you could then argue whether the court should follow the precedent of other cases involving photographic evidence or, for some reason, should view this case as distinct.

⬜ ASSIGNMENT 4.2

Use the synopsis of the statutory law you prepared in Assignment 4.1 and (1) apply it to the following situation and (2) explain why the testimony of the employer should or should not be admitted as evidence under Rule 608.

Mark is on trial for selling drugs. In fact, he was present in a car when one of the other passengers in the car got out and made a drug deal with an undercover agent. Because Mark was present, he was also arrested and charged. Mark claims that he did not know the passenger (it was a friend of the driver whom Mark did know). Mark also testifies that he did not know that the passenger asked to stop at the parking lot to sell drugs. During trial, the prosecution offers evidence that three years ago, Mark received one year probation for using his older brother's driver's license to buy alcohol. Mark's lawyer wants to have Mark's employer testify that for two years, Mark's job has included handling large sums of cash for the business and that Mark has an impeccable record with the company. (Mark's job is to collect daily receipts from several laundromats' coin-operated machines and to total the money and deposit it at the bank.)

Judicial Law.   While judicial opinions contain much more precise applications of law than statutes or regulations, additional factors need to be considered in determining whether a situation will be dealt with in the same

way as a similar situation in a published opinion. Consequently, the process of case analysis (legal analysis of a judicial opinion) is quite different from that of statutory analysis. When you break down a judicial opinion and put your analysis into written form, it is known as a **case brief.** There are many types of briefs in legal writing, and the case brief is just one.

case brief
Legal analysis of a judicial opinion. Case analysis.

The components of a judicial opinion are quite distinct from those of a statute. While statutes describe situations that might arise, cases are written descriptions by courts of the manner in which law was applied to a situation that has already occurred. Opinions are essentially detailed descriptions of a lawsuit and how the law was interpreted to resolve the issues of the case. While there are many methods of breaking a judicial opinion into components, the distinction between methods is largely a matter of semantics and labeling. The method used in this text is designed to be straightforward and relatively simple to use. As stated, these components can be reorganized or given different headings, but the elements present in virtually all judicial opinions remain the same.

Framework for Case Analysis or a Case Brief

The Facts.   The first step in a case brief is to identify the key facts. In many situations, this will control whether the legal principles of a previous case would be applicable to another situation.

There are two types of facts in a case brief. First are the "occurrence" facts—the things that happened between the parties to create a dispute and ultimately produced a lawsuit. An example would be of a contract made between two parties for the sale of a house, and subsequently the buyer claimed that the seller misrepresented certain facts that, if known, would have prevented the buyer from accepting the contract. Second are the legal facts (procedural history)—the things that occurred during the lawsuit that led the case to an appellate court. An example would be a decision by the judge stating that the buyer did not ask specific enough questions prior to the sale and therefore had no claim against the seller. The buyer might take the decision to an appellate court to determine whether the court properly applied the law in reaching its verdict.

Often, cases will include a great deal of background information, which is helpful but not a pivotal part of the decision. Those facts that did not play a part in the outcome of the case should generally be disregarded for the purposes of case analysis. For example, most cases will indicate the date and often the time of an occurrence. While this helps to set the scene, usually this information is not of the utmost importance. An exception to this might be the date in a contract case or the time of day in an accident case (to determine whether light or darkness was an important factor). But in most situations, this type of information is not relevant to the legal effect of the decision. The value of such information is to explain more thoroughly the nature of the dispute and the issues involved. Consequently, in case analysis, only information that is absolutely necessary to understand the dispute, verdict, and reasons for appeal should be included.

The Issue.   Once the important facts have been determined, you should proceed to determine the issue of the case. It is important to understand that the issue in most judicial opinions is not the guilt or innocence of a party in

the suit. Rather, the issue in the vast majority of lawsuits is whether or not the correct legal standards were applied and/or whether they were applied properly at the trial level. Consequently, the determination of guilt or innocence is relevant only with respect to why or how that result was achieved. The goal of case analysis is to identify what precedent was used and how these legal standards were applied so that the case can be compared to other situations. Therefore, you should not be unduly concerned with who won or lost in the previous case, other than as a legal fact and an indicator of who would win under an application of the same legal standards under similar facts.

When identifying the issue, your focus should be on what the appellate court actually considered when it examined the trial court's selection and application of legal standards. The issue is identified by determining what question or questions the appellate court answered in the opinion. The exception, of course, would be if you are reading a trial court opinion. Relatively few of these are published, however, and those that are, generally center around a particular issue between the parties and how the law should be applied to resolve it.

One method to assist the inexperienced person to identify the issue in a judicial opinion is completing the issue in the form of a question: *The appellant (party who appeals the verdict) alleges the trial court abused (exceeded or improperly used) its discretion (authority) when it_____ .*

This completed sentence should be the issue that was addressed by the appellate court in the opinion.

The Law. The third step in case analysis is to determine what legal standards the ultimate result in the opinion was based upon. Judges always search for some guidance from existing legal standards. If there are none, the judge looks to the beliefs of society and the fundamentals of right and wrong as seen by society (common law). Often the latter is determined by looking to the opinions of legal scholars and other noted authorities on a subject. In any event, the decision in a case will be based upon some existing statement of law or wisdom. The court uses this as authority and applies it to the occurrence and legal facts of the case. This determines the answer to the issue before the court.

Most often the court will use an established legal standard as authority. But if the judge applies an opinion of a scholar, this is private opinion and not law. However, by incorporating this second authority into the judicial authority, that opinion becomes the new legal standard in that court, and the point takes on the effect of law. Consequently, the use of the term *law* describes the authority adopted and applied by a judge as the guiding legal standard in deciding a case.

In a case brief, you should indicate the source of the "law" (legal principle) used to determine a case. Just as importantly, the actual principle should be stated. You would serve no purpose by giving one without the other. When analyzing the effects of a case, you need to know not only the source of the legal standard but also the content. When identifying the law during case analysis, you should look for those legal standards that directly address the issue. An example of legal authority is the following excerpt from a judicial opinion that responds to the issue in that opinion:

Issue: Can a person be convicted of assisting in a robbery when there is evidence that the person's life was threatened in order to coerce assistance?

Law: "When a party is forced, under threat of serious harm, to perform an illegal act, then that party cannot be held accountable for committing a criminal act." *People of the State of Maine v. Jezbera*, 402 A.2d 777 (Me 1980).

The quotation is the legal standard. The information that follows is the source. Specifically given is the name of the case, the volume number, the name of the reporter series where the opinion is published, and the page number where the case begins. The information in the parentheses indicates the court that decided the case and the year of the opinion.

If you were to go to a library containing Atlantic Reports, 2d Series, located volume 402, and opened it to page 777, you would see the case of *Maine v. Jezbera*. You would also find information indicating that this opinion was handed down by the supreme court of Maine in 1980. As you can see, the legal standard applied by a court is of little use to someone who later analyzes the case for comparison to another situation unless the source of the legal standard is also given. This is because the standard in the opinion may be either persuasive or mandatory, and only the knowledge of the origin of the standard can determine this. Similarly, if only a citation and the result of the case were given, you would have no way of knowing whether the legal standard represented by the citation would apply in your case.

The Rule or Holding or Reasoning of the Decision. Finally, judicial opinions do not merely state the law (both principle and its source) and then follow with a blanket statement of the winner. Rather, the court will give some explanation of why and/or how the legal standard applies to the facts and issue of that particular case. In case analysis, this information is essential. You cannot predict the likelihood of similar results between an opinion and another situation without understanding what the reasoning of the court was in the judicial opinion. Unless this information is included in the case analysis, it could not be determined whether the same legal standards would apply in the present situation to the present facts and issue.

Once the facts, issue, law, and rule have been determined, your analysis can be completed through comparison with other situations of similar facts and issue. Similarities and differences should be identified. You should then determine whether the similarities are strong enough to create a likelihood that the same legal standards would be applied in the same way in the other situation. You can do this in large part by examining the rule of the case. Ask yourself just how and why the previous court applied the particular legal standard to the case. If the case is analyzed for purposes of comparison to another situation, the next question to explore is the likelihood that the law would be applied in the same way under the facts and issue of the other situation.

In the following example, an edited (for purposes of clarity) judicial opinion is given and is followed by a case analysis (brief).

CASE

JOEY AVERSA, etc., et al., Appellants,
v. HARVEY TAUBES, et al., Defendants,
RUBY MALVA, et al., Respondents.

Supreme Court, Appellate Division,
Second Department.
June 7, 1993.
598 N.Y. 2d 804

**Before Mango, P.J., and ROSENBLATT,
LAWRENCE, COPERTINO AND JOY, JJ.**

MEMORANDUM BY THE COURT

In consolidated actions to recover damages for
medical malpractice, the plaintiffs appeal from an
order of the Supreme Court, Queens County (Rut-
ledge, J.), dated September 30, 1991, which denied
their motion to disqualify Lawrence Burnett and the
firm of Belair & Evans as the ATTORNEYS for the
defendants Ruby Malva and Alan Haber.

ORDERED that the order is reversed, on the law,
with costs, the plaintiffs' motion is granted,
Lawrence Burnett and the law firm of Belair &
Evans are disqualified from representing the defendants Ruby Malva and Alan Haber in these actions,
and no further proceedings shall be taken against
the defendants Ruby Malva and Alan Haber in
these actions without leave of the court, until the
expiration of 30 days after the service upon them
personally of a copy of this decision and order, with
notice of entry, which shall constitute notice to
appoint another ATTORNEY under CPLR 321(c).

The underlying action herein was commenced to
recover damages sustained by the infant plaintiff, as
a result, inter alia, of the alleged malpractice of the
defendants Ruby Malva and Alan Haber. The record
indicates that (1) Lawrence Burnett, an ATTORNEY
representing the defendants Malva and Haber, was
formerly associated with the law firm representing
the plaintiffs, and (2) during that period, Burnett
appeared in court on behalf of the plaintiffs in order
to submit a motion for a further deposition of
another defendant. Under these circumstances, Burnett cannot continue to represent the defendants
Malva and Haber. The Court of Appeals has stated
(Cardinale v. Golinello, 43 N.Y.2d 288, 296, 401
N.Y.S.2d 191, 372 N.E.2d 26):

"Irrespective of any actual detriment, the first
CLIENT is entitled to freedom from apprehension
and to certainty that his interests will not be
prejudiced in consequence of representation of the
opposing litigant by the CLIENT's former ATTOR-
NEY. (Drinker, Legal ETHICS, pp. 109, 115.) The

standards of the profession exist for the protection
and assurance of the CLIENTS and are demanding;
an ATTORNEY must avoid not only the fact, but
even the appearance, of representing conflicting
interests (Rotante v. Lawrence Hosp., 46 AD2d 199
[361 N.Y.S.2d 372]; Edelman v. Levy, 42 AD2d 758
[346 N.Y.S.2d 347]). '[W]ith rare and conditional
exceptions, the lawyer may not inadvertently, affect,
or give the appearance of affecting, the obligations
of the professional relationship' (Matter of Kelly, 23
NY2d 368, 376 [296 N.Y.S.2d 937, 244 N.E.2d 456])".

Moreover, the law firm of Belair & Evans, with
whom Burnett is presently associated, must also be
disqualified from representing the defendants Ruby
Malva and Alan Haber, under "the principle of
attribution" (see, Cardinale v. Golinello, supra;
Greene v. Greene, 47 N.Y.2d 447, 452, n. 3, 418
N.Y.S.2d 379, 391 N.E.2d 1355). Accordingly, the
plaintiffs' motion to disqualify Lawrence Burnett
and the firm of Belair & Evans from representing
Malva and Haber is granted.

SAMPLE CASE BRIEF

Averse v. Taubes, et. al., 598 NYS 2d 804 (1993)

FACTS Plaintiffs filed an action against defendants for medical malpractice. One of the attorneys
associated with the firm representing the plaintiff's
and who had some involvement with the representation, subsequently became involved with the
representation of defendants. Plaintiffs took exception to this and filed a motion to disqualify the
attorney from representing defendants. The trial
court denied the motion and the plaintiffs appealed.

ISSUE The appellant alleges the trial court
abused its discretion when it found that membership by an attorney in a firm representing a client
and appearing on behalf of the client in procedural
matters is not sufficient to create a conflict of
interest when the same attorney becomes associated
with the opposing party in the same action as
involving the former representation of a client.

LAW Clients are entitled to certainty of fairness
in litigation and attorneys must avoid not only the
fact but even the appearance of a conflict of interest.
Rotante v. Lawrence Hosp., 46 A2d 199, 361 N.Y.S.
2d 372.

RULE In this case, the fact that the attorney
had access to plaintiff's file and actually was
involved (even in a minor capacity) in representation and subsequently became involved in representation of the opposing party gives rise to the
question of whether the attorney had access to

privileged information of plaintiffs that might be used against them in litigation. Attorneys not only have an ethical duty to avoid actual conflict of interest wherein they use information of the opposing party that would otherwise be privileged, attorneys must avoid even the appearance or possiblity of such a conflict. In the present case there was clear evidence of such a possibility and therefore the attorney should not have been permitted by the trial court to represent the defense. The trial court abused its discretion when the plaintiff's motion to disqualify was denied.

Reversed.

Applications 4.4 (a), (b), (c), and (d) are examples of several different types of legal writing. Each incorporates legal research and analysis in a different way. Some of the documents are written objectively, while others have a more **argumentative** approach. The tone of the document is based on the document's purpose. The reason for including these examples here is to demonstrate how the initial steps of research are used to produce the final result.

argumentative
Method used to persuade. Language is presented in a fashion that leads the reader and indicates the desired result.

⚖️ APPLICATION 4.4 (a)

EXTERNAL MEMORANDUM OF LAW

A memorandum written in support of a party's position on a particular issue in a case. The memorandum presents arguments to the court of what law is applicable and the result it suggests.

MEMORANDUM OF LAW IN SUPPORT OF PLAINTIFF'S RESPONSE TO DEFENDANT'S MOTION FOR SUMMARY JUDGMENT

Present before the Court is a Motion for Summary Judgment by movant Defendant. The operative facts which gave rise to this lawsuit and ultimately the current motion are as follows:

FACTS

On or about March 11, 1985, at approximately 9:00 p.m. the Plaintiff was playing volleyball at the Activity Center owned and operated by the City of Nowahsville. At the aforementioned place and time the Plaintiff was caused to fall and suffer serious and permanent injuries. Thereafter, the Plaintiff went to the Activity Center office where Defendant Santiago was located. Defendant Santiago was then and there, and at all times pertinent hereto, employed by the City of Nowahsville. The Defendant Santiago refused to permit the Plaintiff to call for medical assistance and/or leave the office unless she first signed a release of liability for the City. She refused, but was unable, due to her injuries, to go elsewhere in search of assistance. Finally, she was permitted to call for help and was taken from the facility to a nearby hospital.

Thereafter, the Plaintiff brought this suit against Defendants City of Nowahsville and Mike Ford for conduct related to her injuries, and also against Defendant Santiago for false imprisonment. Following Answer and Discovery, Defendant Santiago filed a Motion for Summary Judgment. A discussion of the propriety of such a motion follows.

ARGUMENT

Illinois Revised Statutes, Chapter 110, Section 1005(c) states in pertinent part that a Motion for Summary Judgment should only be granted when "[there] is no genuine issue as to any material fact and that the moving party is entitled to a judgment as a matter of law." Consequently, in a case such as that presently before the Court

involving allegations of liability against numerous parties, there simply is no basis to support a finding of no genuine issue of material fact.

The defendant Santiago sets forth numerous facts in its Motion for Summary Judgment which it contends are uncontroverted. Two points should be made regarding Defendant's assertion. First, the fact which Defendant asserts is the basis of plaintiff's complaint as to cause of injury is only one of numerous facts pled which alone or with other conduct caused plaintiff's initial physical injury. Secondly, whether these facts are or are not "uncontroverted" is immaterial to the consideration of the Motion before this Court. The Motion of the Defendant places before the Court the issue of whether or not any genuine issue of fact exists to support the Plaintiff's claim of false imprisonment against Defendant Santiago, which allegedly occurred after the initial physical injury. It will be demonstrated in the discussion that follows, that such a conclusion cannot be reasonably reached under applicable standards.

Long ago, the Illinois Supreme Court enunciated its interpretation of the legislative intention of the Summary Judgment statute when it held, "the section manifests an intention to limit summary proceedings to cases simple in their nature." *Ward v. Sampson, et. al.,* 391 Ill. 585, 63 N.E.2d 751 (1945). By no interpretation can the issues in the present case be characterized as simple ones. The present case involves multiple questions of fact, many of which involve several defendants concurrently.

In furtherance of the prior holding expressing the necessity for selecting only appropriate circumstances for summary judgment it has been recognized in Illinois Law that "Summary Judgment is a drastic remedy and is to be awarded with caution; only if the right of the movant is free from doubt, may it be granted. *Burks Drywall, Inc. v. Washington Bank Etc.,* 110 Ill.App.3d 569, 442 N.E.2d 648, 66 Ill.Dec. 222 (1982).

The basis for the caution exercised by the courts are the extensive ramifications of any order for Summary Judgment. Such an order in effect releases a party from liability in a particular action. Therefore, the courts are rightfully cautious in granting these orders.

Having examined the standards previously prescribed for Summary Judgment, it becomes necessary to examine the applicability of such a motion to the present case. In addition to the multiple complexities involving the present case which would render Summary Judgment inappropriate, there are also numerous issues of material fact present which in the past have been recognized by the courts as questions to be determined by a jury and which consequently, would preclude Summary Judgment with respect to Defendant Santiago.

The Defendant Santiago claims that there is no genuine issue of fact as to the Plaintiff's claim for false imprisonment. In support of that, he states that the Plaintiff did not testify that Defendant "confined" her to the office at the Activity Center. As authority, the Defendant quotes the Restatement of Torts which gives a broad definition of false imprisonment. Defendant neglects however, to interpret that definition under applicable law. A matter which, when done here, will show that a question of fact does exist to support the Plaintiff's claim that she was in fact confined until such time as she succumbed to the Defendant's demands.

In *Marcus v. Liebman,* 59 Ill.App.3d 337, 375 N.E.2d 486 (1978), the following was stated with respect to a claim for false imprisonment:

> False imprisonment consists of an unlawful restraint of individual personal liberty or freedom of locomotion against a person's will. This unlawful restraint may be effected by words alone, by acts alone, or both. Actual force is unnecessary to an action in false imprisonment. However, the submission must be to a threatened and reasonably apprehended force.

As can be seen above, the case is not as clearcut as the Defendant Santiago would lead this Court to believe. It has not and cannot be established as a matter of law in this case that Defendant Santiago did not restrain the Plaintiff's liberty by acts and or words that caused her, at the time of the occurrence, to reasonably apprehend the use of force.

The Defendant himself testified that the Plaintiff did not appear to be completely coherent in his estimation, prior to and during the alleged false imprisonment. (Deposition of Defendant, p. 14–16).

The Plaintiff testified that the Defendant Santiago insisted that she sign a "release" form of some sort before she would be allowed to make a phone call for someone to take her to the hospital. (Deposition of Plaintiff p. 32; 75; 76). It is obvious from this testimony that she perceived some use of force to prevent her from obtaining help to leave the facility. Plaintiff also testified that the phone in Defendant Santiago's office was the only one in the facility. (Deposition of Plaintiff p. 74). The Plaintiff testified that she was somewhat incoherent following her injury, but understood what was going on around her although she felt unable to respond, and at one point she fainted. (Deposition of Plaintiff, p. 32; 68; 70). Finally, Plaintiff testified that she was in Defendant Santiago's office approximately 20 minutes. (Deposition of Plaintiff, p. 80). This is relatively consistent with Defendant Santiago's testimony that Plaintiff was in his office for approximately fifteen minutes. (Deposition of Defendant, p. 15).

An eyewitness to the accident, and also a Defendant in this action, Mike Ford also testified that the Plaintiff remained in the office for approximately twenty minutes. (Deposition of Mike Ford, p. 19). And, Mike Ford testified that another individual who had been in the office with the Plaintiff, had told him Defendant Santiago would not let the Plaintiff leave the office until she signed a paper (the alleged release). (Deposition of Mike Ford, p. 20).

The foregoing would demonstrate that a genuine issue of fact exists as to whether, by the Defendant's words or acts, the Plaintiff, in a somewhat reduced condition of which Defendant was admittedly aware, reasonably apprehended that she would not be allowed to physically leave or seek assistance to leave until such time as she signed the "release".

It is a further question of fact as to whether Defendant's refusal to let the incoherent and injured Plaintiff, call for help from the only phone in the facility unless she signed a release, was a use of force which could reasonably have led her to believe she was confined.

Clearly, the Defendant Santiago has not even addressed these pertinent facts, nor has he alleged and proven them to be uncontroverted. As a result, several questions of fact exist and the Motion for Summary Judgment cannot succeed.

WHEREFORE, the plaintiff prays that defendant's Motion for Summary Judgment be properly denied and this cause be permitted to proceed without further delay.

Respectfully submitted,

_____

Attorneys for Plaintiffs

 APPLICATION 4.4 (b)

Answer to Petition for Leave to Appeal is an argumentative document presented to an appellate level court in support or in opposition to acceptance for review of a trial court case by an appellate level court.

ANSWER TO PETITION FOR LEAVE TO APPEAL

Come now the Plaintiffs-Respondents by their attorneys, and submit the following for their answer to Defendant-Petitioner's Petition brought pursuant to Illinois Revised Statutes, Chapter 110, Paragraph 306.

ARGUMENT

Defendant brings this Petition pursuant to a denial in the trial court of its Motion to Decline Jurisdiction Based on Forum Non Conveniens. In its petition defendant makes numerous statements which are inaccurate and in some cases blatant misstatements of

both the applicable law as well as the facts involved in this present case. These will be outlined in detail in the discussion which follows.

Purpose of the Doctrine

The first and perhaps most important error of defendant is its statement that the purpose of the Doctrine of Forum Non Conveniens is "convenience," (See Defendant's Petition for Leave to Appeal, page 3). The Doctrine of Forum Non Conveniens was addressed at length by our United States Supreme Court in the case of *Gulf Oil v. Gilbert,* 330 U.S. 501, 67 S.Ct. 839, 91 L.Ed. 1055 (1947). This landmark case has been the framework upon which subsequent decisions across the country including Illinois, have been based in applying the doctrine to various factual situations and developments of the law. As this Court is well aware, while convenience is a consideration, the purpose of the doctrine clearly stated in *Gulf Oil, supra,* is fundamental fairness and efficient judicial administration. This holding was adopted by Illinois's highest court in the case of *Adkins v. Chicago Rock Island & Pacific R.R. Company,* 54 Ill.2d 511, 514, 301 N.E2d 729 (1973).

In furtherance of serving the goal of fairness in the Doctrine of Forum Non Conveniens, the United States Supreme Court clearly and unequivocally stated, "unless the balance is strongly in favor of the defendant, the plaintiff's choice of forum should rarely be disturbed." *Gulf Oil Company, supra.* The fact that the Supreme Court was compelled to comment upon the degree of the balancing test serves to only further emphasize that even a balance appearing to be somewhat in the defendant's favor will not suffice.

Application of the Unequal Balancing Test

Secondly, and of vital importance to this Court's consideration is the test to be applied in a determination based on the Doctrine of Forum Non Conveniens. In its Petition Defendant boldly states that the determination is based upon what jurisdiction has the significant factual connections. (See Defendant's Petition, page 4). This statement merely glosses over the actual test which has been developed by the courts and attempts to greatly simplify a much more complex question. The test is not as defendant would imply as "who has the most factual connections," but rather and again as this Court is well aware, is an unequal balancing test expressed by the Supreme Court in *Gulf Oil, supra.* In speaking of the "balance" above, the Court was not addressing factual connections but rather a number of balancing factors which have been developed for application in a case involving the issue of forum non conveniens.

The most commonly enunciated factors by the Illinois courts in applying this unequal balancing test are as follows:

1. private interest of the litigant;
2. relative ease of access to sources of proof;
3. availability of compulsory process for attendance of unwilling witnesses;
4. cost of obtaining willing witnesses;
5. possibility of view of premises when appropriate;
6. factors of public interest such as congested dockets and jury duty; and,
7. availability of another more appropriate forum.

Espinosa v. Norfolk and Western Railway Company,
86 Ill.2d 111, 427 N.E.2d 111, 56 Ill.Dec. 31 (1981).
Evaluation of these factors in the present case will reveal that the balance is clearly not in the defendant's favor sufficient to meet the requirements of the unequal balancing test.

Evaluation of Factors of Private Interest

It was held in *Piper Aircraft Company v. Reyno,* 454 U.S. 235, 70 L.E.2d 419, 102 S.Ct. 252 (1981), by the Supreme Court that there is a strong presumption in favor of the

Plaintiff's choice of forum. Further, the Court held that the consideration is within the discretion of the trial court and can only be reversed upon a "clear abuse of discretion". *Piper, supra.* Consequently, the plaintiff's choice of forum, especially in a case such as this where the alternative forum is located less than one hundred miles from the Defendant's preferred alternative and all witnesses are located across three counties all of which are also proximally located, the plaintiffs are entitled to deference in their choice of forum.

Relative Ease of Access to Sources of Proof

There are, in addition to witnesses, only three actual sources of proof to be considered. And, it is notable that defendant did not so much as address these in its Petition. None of these sources of proof can be said to favor the Defendant's preferred forum over and above the pending jurisdiction in this court.

Initially to be addressed is the situs of the conduct complained of. The incident which precipitated plaintiff's injuries took place in a rural area. However, a view of the premises by jurors is not permitted in a case such as this. Rather, this has been held only appropriate in condemnation cases in Illinois. *Looft v. Missouri Pacific Railroad,* 104 Ill.App.3d, 432 N.E.2d 1152, 60 Ill.Dec. 253 (1982). Therefore, this is not a factor to be considered under the current facts.

The two remaining sources of proof (other than witnesses), consist of medical and employment records of Plaintiff Donald Nance. Plaintiff's medical records are located predominately in the county where this court is situated. This has been the site of ongoing treatment for a significant period of time since the date of his injuries. The medical records in the Defendant's preferred forum, consist of emergency room and associated records which reflect a less than two hour stay at an area hospital prior to his transfer to a metropolitan hospital, in another County. It should be noted that minimal treatment was given until the transfer but even this is less significant and more remote than that rendered in this county.

With respect to his employment records, the plaintiff was employed in the county where defendant proposes jurisdiction, at the time of the injuries. However, plaintiff had only been employed there for a few months and had over the previous several years been employed at several locations, many of which were outside that county in other adjacent counties in Central and Southern Illinois. Consequently, the value of such employment records in the defendant's proposed forum is minimal at best.

Availability of Compulsory Process and Cost of Presenting Testimony

As pertains to the witnesses in this action the following should be noted. To plaintiff's knowledge there are no existing occurrence witnesses. And to date, none have been disclosed by the defendant even though discovery by plaintiff regarding this was initiated as much as 2 years ago and continues. Thus, remaining witnesses would consist of post-occurrence testimonial evidence which is comprised of predominately medical testimony from physicians located in this county.

Defendant in its petition lists numerous individuals all of whom conveniently for defendant are residents in and around defendant's proposed forum. However, defendant has not disclosed these individuals before as persons having relevant knowledge of the occurrence or post-occurrence facts, nor has the defendant even intimated as to what this knowledge might be or how it might be relevant. Given that the plaintiff was alone at the time of the incident and no individuals have been discovered who were eyewitnesses, the credibility of defendant's claim of knowledge of these various persons is clearly in issue.

Further, Defendant lists individuals who reside in the proposed forum whom defendant contends can testify as to plaintiff's present condition. This is of little significance since plaintiff has been and continues to be under the care of qualified health care professionals who can more competently testify to his condition and all of whom are located in the county where the case now pends.

Defendant also indicates the accident was investigated by members (plural) of the Sheriff's Department of the proposed forum and that these persons are residents of that county. Defendant does not indicate who these persons are, whether they are still employed by the Sheriff's Department, or any other evidence that might support its contention that they still reside in that County or what relevant knowledge they might have regarding the incident. They obviously arrived on the scene after the accident, there were no witnesses and plaintiff was suffering from a fractured skull and head injuries so severe as to require brain surgery, which injuries would have precluded him from offering any information at that time.

Next, Defendant contends that ambulance and local hospital personnel are significant contacts to be considered for their contribution of testimony in this matter. However, Defendant conveniently omits to point out that the plaintiff was unconscious for the vast majority of time while under their care and that no significant treatment was rendered until his transfer to a large metropolitan hospital in another county. Defendant also neglects to point out that the entire contact of these persons with the plaintiff lasted no more than four hours of his more than two years of subsequent medical treatment.

In its Petition, Defendant also states that the only medical witnesses in this county are the possible medical experts there. This, as Defendant is well aware is not an accurate statement of the facts. Defendant has been receiving treatment from a physician in this county as his primary treating physician since a short time after his injuries. Further, he has been hospitalized at a hospital in this county and has received medical treatment/services from two other physicians both of whom practice in this county. Thus, these physicians, as well as the hospital personnel are all individuals with relevant knowledge as to the plaintiff's condition and progress.

In addition, as stated previously, the Plaintiff received treatment in a county other than the jurisdiction proposed by defendant. This treatment began on the day of the incident complained of and continued for several months. Such treatment included that by the physicians listed by defendant as well as hospital personnel at the hospital, where plaintiff was originally transferred to, and on two occasions following the incident.

Consequently, it is readily apparent that the witness factor of the unequal balancing test would not support the defendant's proposed court of jurisdiction as a more appropriate forum. It has at the very least witnesses who have actual relevant knowledge of the facts pertaining to this action. And, Defendant's attempt to bolster its position by listing numerous individuals who might have some statement to offer on defendant's behalf, without even intimating what relevant knowledge they might have that other witnesses would not, is not proper for the trial court's nor this Court's determination.

Finally, Defendant's bold statement that seven of eight potential witnesses are located in the proposed forum and one is located in another county than where the case currently pends is wholly without basis. (See Defendant's Petition page 5.) Defendant itself does not even continue this argument to indicate who these "seven of eight" witnesses are and later lists more than fifteen witnesses located in three different counties.

All witnesses are located close enough to, or within this county, so that the cost of obtaining the presence of those not within the county would not be prohibitive and compulsory process would be available for all.

View of Premises When Appropriate

As pointed out previously, this consideration does not favor the defendant in this case. As stated, a view of the premises is only considered in condemnation cases in Illinois. *Looft, supra.*

Factors of Public Interest

Finally, this court is presented with the impact of a case such as this on matters of public interest. While the actual incident took place in Macoupin County, it was unwitnessed. Further, the Defendant has not denied plaintiff's allegation that it does

business in the county where the case currently pends. Therefore, the citizens of this county, would have an interest in determining what is and is not acceptable conduct by a person such as Defendant within their boundaries. But, it should also be noted, that as all alternative forums are in Illinois, the decision of the court would be binding across the state.

With respect to Defendant's allegations regarding the time necessary to reach trial several things should be noted. First, the defendant does not indicate where its figures are derived from or any other basis which might lend them some validity. Additionally, assuming arguendo that they are accurate reflections of the court dockets, the Defendant provides figures which are some three years old. By Defendant's very own statement these figures are subject to change from year to year and consequently, it cannot be said that figures from such a remote point in time are in any way applicable for consideration today.

Finally, Defendant places great weight on the time necessary to reach trial. It should be noted that Defendant did not respond to the Complaint until more than four months after service of the Complaint and then only after it requested that an order of default entered against it be vacated. These are factors which Defendant omitted to include in its Petition but which are relevant when it requests that the Court give deference to the time it will be required to defend this action in various counties.

Inapplicability of Case Law Cited by Defendant

Defendant cites numerous cases as authority for its position. While these cases are certainly relevant to the extent that they address the doctrine of forum non conveniens, they are in no way analogous to the present situation. With one exception, the cases cited involve alternative jurisdictions in different states and in some cases different countries rather than the present situation where the defendant seeks to have the case transferred approximately 50 miles to a court in an adjacent county.

Defendant does cite *Torres v. Walsh,* 98 Ill.2d 338, 74 Ill.Dec. 880, 456 601 (1983). While this case applies forum non conveniens intrastate, it is so factually distinct, it is in no way analogous to the present case. In *Torres, supra,* the plaintiffs were not residents of Illinois and all defendants, all witnesses, the situs of each of the complained of incidents, and all sources of proof were located in Sangamon County. Cook County, where the lawsuit originated was more than 200 miles north of Sangamon County, and its sole connection with the case was that it was the location of one registered agent for one of several defendants. Obviously, this is not pertinent to the current situation where all three alternative forums are proximally located and where the subjects of consideration by this Court are dispersed across them.

CONCLUSION

It is apparent that defendant's conclusion that the "heart of this lawsuit is in or about Macoupin County, Illinois . . ." (See Defendant's Petition p. 7), is obviously a contrived notion of the facts under the unequal balancing test. Witnesses are located in all three alternative forums. Since there are no occurrence witnesses, the most important testimony would be those post-occurrence which includes medical testimony. The least of this is in Macoupin County, Defendant's preferred forum. Much is located in Sangamon County, but the most recent and most relevant information regarding plaintiff's current condition and progress for most of the time since his accident is located in Madison County. And, as stated, compulsory process is available for all, and since the pertinent jurisdictions are all within 100 miles of one another cost would not be a significant factor.

Sources of proof are located in all three alternate forums as well as other jurisdictions in Illinois. Consequently, ease of access is a neutral factor since regardless of where the action proceeds some testimony and proof will have to be be gathered from other jurisdictions.

As stated, the public interest factors do not favor the Defendant. First, the citizens of Madison County have just as much interest in the matter as citizens of the other

counties and would benefit from trial in their jurisdiction. And, the length of time necessary to reach trial in this matter is not an issue to be properly raised by the Defendant for this Court's consideration as the Defendant has unclean hands by creating delay of this matter from its outset.

Thus, it is unequivocally clear that following a proper application of the unequal balancing test that the trial court was properly exercising its discretion when it found that the factors did not so strongly favor the defendant that it required defeating the plaintiff's choice of forum, which is the standard imposed by the United States Supreme Court in *Gulf Oil, supra.* Therefore, there was no clear abuse of discretion by the trial court and on that basis the Defendant's Petition should be denied.

Respectfully Submitted,

_____

Attorneys for Plaintiffs-Respondents

 A P P L I C A T I O N   4 . 4 (c)

Opinion Letter (These are letters prepared to answer the legal questions of clients).
Dear Mr. Moriarty:

Upon consideration and research of your question regarding liability for the injuries suffered by someone who recently fell at your home, we have reached the following conclusions:

Under current applicable law, a business owner who invites persons onto the premises has a duty to exercise reasonable care for safety of the invitees. *Cawley v. Quick-Save Grocery Inc.,* 146 Conn. 543, 546, 152 A.2d. 923; (1986). By holding a garage sale on your property, you invited individuals onto the property for the express purpose of transacting business. Consequently, you were under a legal obligation to act reasonably for the safety of your customers.

As you explained it, the injury to your invitee occurred when she was standing on an underground sprinkler head which was activated by a timing device. The weight of the invitee's body against the sprinkler head caused a build-up in pressure which ultimately propelled the invitee into the air some 5-7 feet. Upon landing on the nearby concrete driveway she suffered several broken bones and a concussion. While we were unable to locate any law that was factually similar, we have made the following analysis. Property which contains a potentially dangerous condition which is not readily discoverable by others, constitutes a patent defect. According to the legal standards of this jurisdiction, a property owner is responsible to disclose patent defects and/or to take other reasonable precautions to prevent such defects from injuring the invitee. *Leo v. Brainard,* 177 Conn. 548, 122 A.2d 245 (1990).

In the present case, the underground sprinkler heads lay beneath the grass and were not readily visible. Secondly, the invitee had no reasonable means of knowing that a timing device was about to activate the sprinkler system. However, in your defense, the invitee probably felt the pressure of the sprinkler head and possibly saw other sprinkler heads emerging. These facts should have put her on notice that the system was in operation.

It is our conclusion that if presented to a jury, it is quite possible that you would be found liable. Consequently, we must advise you to take action to defend yourself and negotiate a reasonable settlement. If you would like our representation in this matter, please contact us immediately. Regardless of your decision with respect to representation, please be advised that the response to the plaintiff's (injured party) complaint must be filed no later than July 20, 1994.

Sincerely,

⚖ **A P P L I C A T I O N   4 . 4 (d)**

Internal Memorandum—an objective document prepared by one party for consideration by another on the same side of an issue, e.g. by a paralegal for a supervising attorney. The internal memorandum examines the law and clearly states the strengths and weaknesses of a position on a legal issue.

MEMO

TO: Legal professional staff

FROM: J. Ellias, paralegal

RE: Diligent Service of Process

Per request of the senior staff attorneys, I have researched the question of diligent service. Essentially, the issue is this: if a case is filed within the statute of limitations, must the plaintiff then take all reasonable steps to immediately serve notice of the action upon the defendant? My research has produced the answer that a plaintiff is indeed obligated to attempt notice of a pending action through appropriate service of process, as soon as reasonably possible on the defendant.

In the case of *Hackeny v. Grabenstein,* 365 Mo.App. 231, 385 N.W.2d 297 (1983), the defendant was not served until nearly 18 months after the statute of limitations had run and the suit had been filed. In that instance, the court reasoned that the purpose of the statute of limitations is to impose a duty upon the plaintiff to reasonably discover causes of action and to limit the extent to which a defendant must preserve evidence and other records relevant to any situations which might ultimately produce litigation. By the plaintiff's action, it was clear that plaintiff's intent was to delay notice of the claim until such time as defendant's ability to produce evidence in his behalf was impeded. This attempt to circumvent the purpose of the statute of limitations was considered inappropriate by the court and the action was dismissed in the defendant's favor.

The extent to which a plaintiff must pursue service of process was addressed in the case of *Gudgel v. Bryant,* 386 Mo.App. 297, 399 N.W2d 1012 (1985). In that case the court held that what is "reasonably diligent service" is influenced by the circumstances such as whether the statute of limitations is near conclusion at the time the suit is filed. But, the court made it clear that in all instances, the plaintiff is not reasonable when suit is filed and attempts at notice to defendant through proper service of process are delayed for no other reason than to gain an upper hand in the action.

Based on the foregoing, it is my recommendation that all actions originating in this office on behalf of plaintiffs be presented to the clerk of the court for proper service of process on defendants no later than 30 days from the date the action is filed.

Respectfully Submitted,

J. Ellias, paralegal

BASIC STEPS IN RESEARCH

Conducting legal research is quite unlike other types of research. If, for example, you want to locate information on the Civil War, you would simply go to the subject index at the library and look for publications under that topic. However, as discussed in Chapter 1, in legal research, the task is generally much more involved than locating information on a particular topic. You must take into account the jurisdiction and whether authority is mandatory or persuasive, primary or secondary, current, and valid. Often,

you will need to do preliminary research to prepare yourself to locate the research you are ultimately seeking.

Something that few of us like to admit is just how limited our ordinary vocabulary can be. Many times research can be fruitless because of either the lack of familiarity with relevant terms or the habit of using the same terminology repeatedly and ignoring terminology that will assist in the research process. Something that you should always be willing to consider throughout your research, no matter how experienced you may become, is the need to search for additional terms that will assist you in finding the desired information. Of course, assembling the necessary information is contingent on properly constructing your research question.

Identification of the Issue

research issue
General question to be addressed by research.

The first step in any research seems obvious. Before you can find the answer, you must know the question. In legal research, proper completion of this step is crucial. By incorrectly stating the **research issue** in question, hours and hours can be wasted on useless research. For example, in a criminal case, the question is seldom whether or not X committed the crime. Rather, the question is whether, under the specific circumstances of this case, X can be convicted of the crime. The two may be very different.

 A P P L I C A T I O N   4 . 5

Juan Amos was walking down the street when he saw Marco Arello coming out of a store. Juan yelled at Marco, "Stop or I'll shoot!" Marco began to run. Juan repeated his command and then fired a fatal shot into Marco's back. Did Juan shoot and kill Marco? Yes. Can Juan be convicted of the murder of Marco? No. Juan was an off-duty police officer who was familiar with Marco as a serial killer. Marco had taken hostages and killed them the day before when attempting to escape police.

As you can see, the circumstances of each case influence the case's legal effect and result. Thus, when you are framing an issue for research, you must include all necessary circumstances. In the preceding situation, the question should not have been simply a question of guilt or innocence. It should have been stated something like this: Can an off-duty police officer be convicted of murder when, after giving warning, the officer takes the life of a known and dangerous criminal?

As you can see, the special circumstances of this situation have tremendous impact on the findings of your research. When identifying the issue that you are attempting to answer, you should be as specific as possible. It is always easier and less time consuming to slowly broaden the research if it is too narrow than to scale down the research if it is too broad. If your question is too narrow, you will find little or nothing to answer your questions. However, if it is too broad, you may find literally hundreds of sources, cases, statutes, regulations, and secondary authorities. Much time can be wasted as you attempt to wade through these and select those that are truly applicable.

☐ **ASSIGNMENT 4.3**

Assume you are employed by the attorney for the plaintiff (party alleging injury). Evaluate the following situations and write what you think the issues for research should be.

Situation A

Keith Timmons invited his best friend Joseph Bryant on a ski trip. While on the trip, Keith offered to give Joe some pointers to save Joe the cost of skiing lessons. Everything went well, and Joe progressed quickly. On the third day of the trip, Joe decided to attempt some of the more difficult ski runs. Keith advised Joe that he was ready. Joe made one trip safely. The second trip down the mountain, Joe fell and slid into the path of a rope lift. Several skiers were knocked from the lift and seriously injured. Joe also was injured. Joe and the other skiers want to sue Keith Timmons for being the ultimate cause of their injuries.

Situation B

Catherine Braden and her husband Bill went to their favorite bar late on a Monday afternoon. They went there regularly on Mondays, as did several other patrons, to watch Monday night football. On this particular night in January, the temperature was dropping quickly. Snow had fallen Sunday. During the day on Monday the temperatures rose enough to turn the snow into a heavy slush. As the temperatures dropped that night, the slush turned to ice.

The owners of the bar had pushed the snow to the edges of the parking lot during the day. However, as it began to melt, it ran all over the parking lot. When Catherine and Bill arrived, the lot had numerous areas of standing water. When Catherine and Bill left the lot, they had a very difficult time getting to their car because the water had turned to ice. As they drove from the lot, Bill lost control of the car and struck two pedestrians on the sidewalk in front of the lot and the bar. No alcohol was involved in the accident. The pedestrians want to sue Bill.

Situation C

20-year-old Boyd Polson attended the wedding reception of Dennis and Carla Gold at the home of Carla's parents. During the reception, Boyd drank several alcoholic beverages. He danced frequently with many of the guests. Late in the evening, Boyd became enamoured of a young woman who had been a bridesmaid in the wedding. He wanted to tell her of her beauty. He asked the leader of the band to give her the message. The bandleader invited Boyd to give the message personally. He stumbled up to the stage and took the microphone. Just as he started to speak, he lost his balance and fell from the stage. In addition to sustaining his own injuries, he fell on the ring bearer (a professional who was paid much money for his services at many society weddings) and broke the ring bearer's hand. The ring bearer thinks the bride's parents should be held responsible, as they provided Boyd with the alcohol that caused his drunkenness.

As stated before, having an adequate command of relevant terminology can greatly shorten and ease the research process. An invaluable tool is a legal dictionary and/or legal thesaurus, which can provide you with alternate legal terms that you may not think of when formulating your **research query** based on your issue. If you are having difficulty in framing your issue, or even in knowing where to begin, a preliminary brainstorming session may help. Without preparing complete questions, simply list all of the words that come into your head when you think of the situation you want to research. If you have trouble getting started, consult a dictionary or thesaurus. The more terms you come up with, the more extensive your research will probably be. Next, prioritize your list. Arrange the terms in the order that you think is most likely to produce results.

research query
Words, phrases, and questions used in sources of authority to obtain the answer to a research issue.

If you are totally unfamiliar with your research subject (which happens even to experienced researchers), it may be helpful to first consult a legal encyclopedia, legal periodical (most of which are indexed by subject), or annotated law report. All of these publications typically provide brief discussions of various topics of law. This may be enough to acquaint you with the subject matter and provide you with enough terminology to construct your issues for research.

APPLICATION 4.6

Amanda is a law clerk who is just starting out. Her employer tells her that their client is charged under the felony murder rule. The employer wants Amanda to find out just exactly what the courts in the jurisdiction consider to be felony murder.

Amanda thinks to herself, "Well, a felony is a serious crime, and I would think any murder would be serious. This should be a breeze to research." As Amanda looks to the statutes, she sees nothing called the "felony murder rule." After several hours, she backs up and goes to a legal encyclopedia. Looking in the subject index, she finds murder. She locates felony murder as a subheading. Upon reading this section, she discovers that felony murder does not involve murder as most people would interpret it. Rather, the felony murder rule applies in some jurisdictions when a person commits a felony and as a direct result the victim dies within a certain period of time (e.g., one year). The felony does not even have to be a direct physical attack, such as shooting. It only has to proximately cause death within the given time period.

By approaching legal research without sufficient command of relevant terminology, a great deal of time can be wasted, as in the previous example. A good legal researcher never overestimates his or her own knowledge of legal terms. Too often, a crucial factor in research is time. The amount used between receiving the assignment and locating the *correct* answer must be kept to only that which is necessary to be thorough and accurate.

ASSIGNMENT 4.4

Read the following scenario, identify the issue, and prepare a list of terms you think will lead you to the answer.

Carlos comes to your office in a wheelchair. Five years ago he was seriously injured in an accident and was left paralyzed. While in the hospital,

the person responsible for the accident, the Reverend Mr. White, came to Carlos with an attorney, who happened to be Mr. White's brother. The attorney told Carlos that he would represent Carlos free of charge. The attorney then negotiated a settlement between Carlos and Mr. White for the cost of Carlos's medical bills and $10,000 for pain and suffering. Carlos accepted the settlement and signed a contract to that effect. He has since married, and his wife feels the attorney representation in this circumstance was improper. Your employer feels the same. He wants you to research whether a lawsuit can be brought on a contract that was signed and completed five years ago.

Determination of Likely Sources of Authority

Once you have identified your issue and have armed yourself with enough terminology to begin your search, your next step is to locate authority that will have the greatest impact on your case. In doing so, you must answer a number of questions:

   a.   Is the case in state or federal court?
   b.   In which state or federal court is the case located?
   c.   Which appellate (intermediate and supreme) courts have authority if the case is appealed?
   d.   Is the issue likely to be governed by statute (commonly encountered situations), judicial law (very specific and unique circumstances), or administrative law (the issue or at least one party is a person, activity, or organization subject to government regulation). Or is the issue likely to be addressed by all three (quite often this is the case)?
   e.   Are you familiar enough with the subject and issue that you don't need any background information?

Your answer to these questions in advance of your research can save you a great deal of time otherwise spent uselessly moving among authorities in an attempt to locate elusive information. Refer to Application 4.6, which demonstrates how a basic familiarity with the concepts and terms of your research is essential to success.

 APPLICATION 4.7

Research Assignment

Four good friends opened a restaurant together. Each had a specific role in the business and certain responsibilities. Since the restaurant opened six months ago, two of the friends have worked diligently, one friend has put forth some effort, and the remaining friend has done almost nothing except show up every Friday to collect his 1/4 share of the profits. One of the hard-working owners of this restaurant comes to your office and wants to know just how he can legally withdraw his investment and get out of the business altogether.

Preliminary Research Questions

a. Is the case in state or federal court?

ANSWER: Probably state. Operation and investment in small businesses (that are not corporations) are usually matters not covered by federal law.

b. In which state or federal court is the case located?

ANSWER: Probably the county in which the business is located or the county in which the owners reside.

c. Which appellate (intermediate and supreme) courts have authority if the case is appealed?

ANSWER: The state supreme court and any Intermediate level court that has authority over the local trial court.

d. Is the issue likely to be governed by statute (commonly encountered situations), judicial law (very specific and unique circumstances), or administrative law (the issue or at least one party is a person, activity, or organization subject to government regulation). Or is the issue likely to be addressed by all three (quite often this is the case).

ANSWER: The issue is likely to be governed by laws of business. Most often these are statutory. So this should be your starting point. However, there may also be regulations and/or judicial law that help you clarify and understand how the statutory law applies to this type of circumstance.

e. Are you familiar enough with the subject and issue that you don't need any background information?

ANSWER: If you can list at least six terms or subjects that you could consult in the statutes to begin your research, you are probably ready to at least begin looking for applicable law.

☐ ASSIGNMENT 4.5

Complete the questions as presented in Application 4.7. With respect to question (e), however, actually list those terms that you think would lead you in your research.

Research Assignment

Elmo Hart has come to your office with the following problem: Elmo's grandmother recently died. In the last ten years of her life, Elmo cared for his grandmother in his home, paid many of her medical bills, and even paid for her funeral. In addition, Elmo provided a home for his grandmother's two Great Dane dogs, Elmer and Elvira. During the last year of his grandmother's life, someone from a local animal shelter visited regularly and often brought information about the shelter and other documents. Upon his grandmother's death, Elmo discovered that she had willed her entire estate of $500,000 and had left Elmo only Elmer and Elvira (animals whose food consumption alone exceeds $15 per day). Can Elmo, the sole surviving heir, have the will invalidated?

a. Is the case in state or federal court?
b. In which state or federal court is the case located?
c. Which appellate (intermediate and supreme) courts have authority if the case is appealed?
d. Is the issue likely to be governed by statute (commonly encountered situations), judicial law (very specific and unique circumstances), or administrative law (the issue or at least one party is a person,

activity, or organization subject to government regulation). Or is the issue likely to be addressed by all three (quite often this is the case).

e. Are you familiar enough with the subject and issue that you don't need any background information?

Preparing the Query

Now that you are ready to begin your research, it is necessary to take a few minutes to formulate your questions. Query preparation for computer research is addressed in a subsequent chapter. However, as with computer research, traditional law library research requires that you properly state your question and use relevant terminology.

This step in research will become easier as your skills grow. You will become more familiar with the arrangement of law and common phrases. This in turn will eliminate much of the time that a novice researcher might spend looking up terms that simply are not used much in legal writing. For example, if you are conducting research on the right of a client who is poor, you may have little success locating any applicable law using the term *poor,* or even *poverty.* However, if you look under such headings as *destitute, indigent,* and *in forma pauperis,* you are likely to find a substantial amount of law with respect to the rights and options within the legal system for the financially disadvantaged.

 APPLICATION 4.8

Your client wants to file an action against his landlord for discrimination. Because discrimination is covered by federal civil rights laws, you may file the suit in federal court. However, your client cannot even afford the initial filing fees. Is there a remedy? How would you research this?

Research Query

Can a person without funds file a lawsuit even though he/she cannot pay the filing fees at the time the complaint is presented to the court?

Terms for Use in Research

poor	indigent	bankrupt
poverty	in forma pauperis	impoverished
destitute	filing fees	needy

ASSIGNMENT 4.6

Complete the following as presented in Application 4.8.

Research Assignment

Your client's daughter is in a persistent vegetative state as the result of an accident. Your client has brought in his daughter's diary, which in one entry states, "I hope I never have to live without knowing what is going on around me." Is this sufficient to constitute a document that will permit life support to be discontinued?

Research Query

Terms for Use in Research

As in determining the general issue of your case, the key to an effective research query is to be specific. The more specific your query, the more likely you are to avoid wasting time reading statutes, cases, or regulations that are only marginally related to the actual issue you are trying to answer. If you find that your query is too narrow and you are unable to locate anything, broaden it very gradually. One step at a time, expand your research until you begin to locate relevant information.

⚖ APPLICATION 4.9

A neighbor borrows a riding lawn mower in exchange for mowing the owner neighbor's lawn. The owner spends her summers in Minnesota with her elderly mother. After three summers, the mother dies and the owner of the lawn mower requests that it be returned, as she plans to mow her own lawn. The neighbor refuses to return the mower.

Research Query

Can the borrower of a lawn mower obtain ownership of the mower after possessing it for three years and giving a service to the owner in exchange for the possession?

Terms for Use in Research

lawn mower	bailment	possession
personal property	ownership	contract
borrowed	payment	agreement

Broadened Research Query

Can one keep personal property after possessing and delivering a service in exchange for possession?

☐ ASSIGNMENT 4.7

Evaluate the following and prepare a specific and a broadened research query and list research terms:

A local city council passes an ordinance making it illegal to display any flag other than the American flag on the Fourth of July. This includes state flags, foreign flags, and even decorative windsocks. Your client (a former immigrant and naturalized citizen) has always displayed the flag of his home country alongside the American flag in front of his home. Is the ordinance legal?

Research Query

Terms for Use in Research

Broadened Research Query

Analysis and Prioritization of Products of Research

Once you have employed your research query and have located sufficient authority to respond to the issue, you must then determine which of the authorities found are going to be used to answer the issue. This requires close legal analysis and prioritization. Many beginning research students find this step the most difficult. Even moreso than actually locating the information, until you have developed a sense of what is significant, you will often be faced with the nagging doubt of whether an authority you had but discarded will reappear in the form of opposing authority put forth by the other side. Fortunately, prioritization skills are based upon certain principles that, if followed, should relieve most doubt.

As indicated, the first step is legal analysis. Earlier in this chapter, the process of statutory, regulatory, and case analysis was discussed. This is an element of research that should never be overlooked or hurried through. For example, even if a case with very similar facts turns out favorably, it may not be at all applicable. You must examine and understand the reasoning of the court before you can propose that the court in your client's case follow a similar reasoning.

APPLICATION 4.10

A state statute indicates that a natural father of an illegitimate child must file an allegation of paternity within thirty days of the birth to preserve any rights with respect to the child. A leading case in the state was based on circumstances in which the father knew of the pregnancy and birth, yet he did not file any documents alleging paternity until, at age six months, the child was placed for adoption. The court held that under the statute, the father had notice of his obligations and failed to file the proper documents. Consequently, the father lost all rights of paternity, and the child was placed for adoption with another family.

Assume your client is the hopeful adoptive mother of an illegitimate child. The child is four months old, and the natural father has appeared and wants custody, claiming he has just learned of the birth. The father knew of the

pregnancy but had no contact with the mother since the third month of her pregnancy, when he dropped her off at a clinic where she scheduled herself for an abortion against the father's will.

Does the father have any rights regarding the child? At first glance it would appear that he does not. However, a closer look at the applicable law, specifically the case that interpreted the statute, will show that the court clearly identifies a number of facts in that case, such as ongoing communications with the mother, visits with the child at the hospital, discussions with the mother about placing the child for adoption, etc. According to the court, all of these support the finding that the father waived his rights with respect to the child. In the present case, the facts are very dissimilar. The father did not even know about the birth and was in fact led to believe that the child had not been born at full term.

As you can see, the facts of the opinion might actually be used to distinguish the present case and propose a different ruling. Only legal analysis (a comparison of facts and law) will provide you with the information necessary to determine whether an authority applies to your case and the result such authority would implicate. Consequently, you should always analyze the authorities you find. While at first this is time consuming, it is necessary and should be done in writing. After time and practice, you will develop the ability to analyze as you read. However, in cases of complicated issues, the best method is still to prepare written analysis of your authorities.

The next step is prioritization. As stated, a few rules of thumb will help you determine what authorities will have the most impact and should be concentrated on in the presentation of your research, whether it is in the form of a memo to your employer, a legal opinion letter to a client, or a trial brief. The following general priority list is to be used when assessing value to your authorities. This list assumes all authorities have been analyzed and those that remain are relevant to the issue(s).

Cases in State Court
1. U.S. Supreme Court opinions.
2. State statutes (followed by derivative regulations).
3. State supreme court opinions.
4. State intermediate appellate court opinions from the appellate court with jurisdiction over the trial court where the case is pending.
5. Other intermediate appellate court opinions from the same state.
6. Trial court opinions or orders or law from other jurisdictions.

Cases in Federal Court
1. U.S. Supreme Court opinions.
2. Federal statutes (followed by derivative regulations).
3. Federal court of appeals decisions from the appellate court with jurisdiction over the U.S. District Court where the case is pending.
4. Other federal court of appeals decisions.
5. U.S. District Court opinions from the court where the case is pending.
6. Other U.S. District Court opinions.

DO NOT FORGET THE RULE THAT A JUDICIAL OPINION CAN TAKE PRECEDENCE OVER OTHER LAW IF THE LAW IS FOUND TO BE UNCONSTITUTIONAL.

⚖ APPLICATION 4.11

Your research has produced the following authorities, all of which state approximately the same legal principle. The authorities are in the order that they should be prioritized.

a. Statute of State X, which states, "One who unlawfully enters the property of another, with the intent to commit a felony therein, is guilty of burglary."

b. Case from the Supreme Court of State X, which states, "It is the opinion of this court that the crime of burglary requires not only intentional unlawful entry but also the intent to commit additional felonious criminal acts."

c. Case from another jurisdiction that espouses the same legal principle but is virtually factually identical to your case.

In Application 4.11, the case that is most similar was ranked last in priority. Why is this? The rationale is quite simple. Law from another jurisdiction or jurisdiction of equal or subordinate authority (such as a lower court) is primary persuasive. These legal standards are primary authority in that they have the effect of law. However, the authority to whom they are presented is not bound by them. Therefore, they are only persuasive. Assume Application 4.11 was based on Michigan law. The case described in (c) was from Wisconsin. The courts of Michigan are in no way bound by the law of the courts of Wisconsin. Indeed, the courts of Michigan have every right to apply Michigan law even if it is in direct conflict with a legal standard of Wisconsin that seems to apply exactly to the case at hand.

The prioritization of authority does not mean that you must choose only one authority to present. Quite the contrary. It is often helpful to use a variety of applicable legal standards to fully explain your position. However, many times you will locate so many authorities that you need to select only those that are most relevant. This may include persuasive authority. However, do not omit all discussion of applicable mandatory authority because (as in Application 4.11) a persuasive authority appears to be more factually on point.

The next step in prioritization is to distinguish the importance of several authorities from the same source, such as the state supreme court. How can you prioritize ten opinions from the same court? Don't they all have essentially the same weight? Quite the contrary. Prioritization of authorities from the same authority is not as clear-cut as prioritization of different types of authority. A number of factors must be weighed to reach your result, including the following:

   a. How old is each of the authorities? It is just as misleading to say that recent rulings are the strongest as to state that old rulings are the most stable. In fact, the age of a ruling is not the major factor. A very real possibility is that the particular issues have not come before the court recently or that they only just came before the court for the very first time. However, when examining an opinion issued before 10 or 15 years prior, consider the ruling very carefully. Has anything changed in related issues or society that might prompt the court to change its position? A good way to check this in terms of national trends is to consult an Annotated Law Report or a Legal Periodical that contains a segment on the point of law. Often these

publications will discuss how the law is evolving and in what
direction the courts are heading.

b. If you are ranking judicial opinions, are any of them en banc? The
term *en banc* is used to describe cases that were considered by the
entire appellate court. While quite often an appellate court consists
of nine to eleven judges, the judges usually sit in panels of three or
more to hear cases. This still provides a degree of collective wisdom
while allowing the court to hear more cases on appeal. However,
periodically, the entire court will consider and vote on an issue.
These occurrences are somewhat rare and typically have greater
effect because of the unified position of the court with regard to the
importance of the legal issues involved. Consequently, if you encounter an en banc opinion in your research and it is relevant, it
should be accorded due weight.

c. Would any of the opinions be considered landmark? This is a very
gray area, and you will need practice to identify these decisions
readily. A landmark decision is one that clearly establishes a legal
standard for a jurisdiction. Perhaps the issue has not been appealed
previously, or possibly various intermediate appellate courts have
ruled differently on the issue. When the high court of a jurisdiction
hands down an opinion to resolve any doubt about the application
of a legal standard, that opinion is considered to be landmark.
Often, the name of the case will become quite familiar. As you read
other authorities, you will see that they repeatedly rely on this
opinion as a guidepost. Occasionally, even the media will discuss
the case.

⚖ APPLICATION 4.12

In 1964, the U.S. Supreme Court issued an opinion that essentially clarified the rights of
all citizens interrogated or placed under arrest by law enforcement. The standard set up
by the court was designed to inform citizens who might otherwise be unaware of or
have forgotten their constitutional rights. These rights included the right to remain silent,
a warning that anything said could be used against the person in court, and the right to
an attorney even if the person is indigent and cannot afford an attorney. Today, if you
ask any child over the age of ten who has watched an average amount of television
what this is all about, that child will likely say, "Miranda." *Miranda v. Arizona* was the
name of that landmark case.

d. Do any of the opinions change the legal standard from its previous
application in the jurisdiction? An important part of your research is
to look back into the law. Has the law changed, and why? This
information can be found in judicial opinions and legislative
histories (discussions of the reasoning behind statutory law). If, for
example, an opinion changes the legal standard of a jurisdiction to
expand the rights of a natural father toward an illegitimate child,
you must determine whether that variance is a total reversal or a
very limited and conditional exception to the rule. For example,
does the opinion overrule the statute with regard to rights of the

natural father, or does it state that in this case, the natural father was misled to the point he was prevented from exercising his rights and for that reason those rights should be restored to him. The statute, as written, however, is still constitutional.

e. How factually similar is each authority to your client's case?

All of these questions should be answered in addition to legal analysis of each authority and comparison to your own circumstances. After you have done this, you should select those authorities that have the greatest impact (e.g., mandatory, which are landmark, which are similar in facts and issues, and which have a reasoning that is applicable to your case).

Validation of Research

The final step in research is validation. As discussed in the previous chapter on the use of citators, validation is absolutely imperative to good and thorough research. You must select those authorities that are relevant and then verify that these authorities will be accepted as sound statements of the applicable law. When validating through the use of a citator, be conscious of the notations provided about subsequent citations. Often such notations provide a great deal of insight.

⚖ APPLICATION 4.13

In the state of M, a particular legal standard came before the supreme court on appeal on several occasions over a period of years. In each case, one justice in particular dissented (disagreed) with the ruling on the point. Often, he was accompanied by other justices, but not to the point that the law could be changed. Over time, the members of the court changed, and eventually the judge who had consistently dissented on that particular issue became the chief justice. Within a fairly short time, the issue came before the court again. The judges could not reach a majority opinion, and so the chief justice was required to cast the deciding vote. He did so, and the law of the jurisdiction changed.

If you are validating an authority that indicates it has been consistently disagreed with or distinguished as inapplicable for some reason, you should consider that a trial court, or even an appellate court, might not continue to uphold the position. If that result would harm your case, you may choose to look for another authority upon which to rest your position and seek to again distinguish the potentially negative case from your own.

Finally, Chapter 3 mentioned that validation can actually be a source for research. This is true. If you are able to locate one authority on your issue, you might want to validate to obtain a quick listing of citations that might also address the issue. However, as stated in Chapter 3, this is only a by-product of validation and not its purpose. Remember, the only citations that appear are those that mention the authority. There may be many others that do not appear simply because they do not include a reference to the authority that you are validating.

IIII➡ STRATEGY

Legal Analysis

Statutory/Administrative

1. Break the statute into each element/condition that must be satisfied to render the statute applicable to a particular fact situation.
2. Compare your fact scenario to the elements and identify which elements are satisfied and which are not.
3. Determine whether any unsatisfied elements of the statute or additional facts in the case are so significant as to render the statute inapplicable.

Judicial

1. Identify the pivotal facts (those that played an influential role in the outcome of the case). Include occurrence facts (those circumstances that resulted in a lawsuit) and legal facts (those circumstances that occurred during litigation and contributed to the current issue decided by the court).
2. Identify the issue. As the majority of published opinions are appellate, the issue would be whether a particular error occurred in the lower court that caused an allegedly improper result under applicable law.
3. Identify those sources of authority used by the court to resolve the issue. Include the citation and a brief statement of the principle of law.
4. Examine and explain briefly how the principles of law apply to the facts of the current case to resolve the issue. State the outcome of the case.
5. Compare the elements of the case brief (Steps 1–4) to the factual circumstances of your own case. Identify differences and similarities in facts and whether the same legal standards are controlling in your jurisdiction. Determine whether the differences and similarities are likely to produce a distinct or similar result.

IIII➡ STRATEGY

Steps in Legal Research

1. Issue: Determine the basis of the actual legal dispute between the parties (e.g., custody of a child).
2. Determine the likely sources of authority: Identify the jurisdiction, the venue, and whether the case is likely to be controlled by statutory, administrative, or judicial law or a combination of all three.
3. Prepare the query: What is the actual question for your research (e.g., what does a court consider when determining proper custody of a child)?
4. Establish relevant terms: What legal terminology is relevant to the issue and likely to lead you to the applicable legal standards (e.g., custody, best interest doctrine, husband & wife, infant, divorce)?
5. Modify query: Broaden, narrow, or amend your query and list of relevant terms as necessary to focus research more closely on your issue.
6. Analyze & prioritize: Examine the products of your research, selecting those most pertinent to your issue. Of those selected, arrange them in order of influence on a deciding court. First apply the general hierarchy of law and then arrange in order of importance (e.g., landmark and recent cases generally have greater influence than older cases or cases from another jurisdiction).
7. VALIDATE! For each authority you intend to rely upon to support your position or any authority you intend to oppose or distinguish, validate to determine the current status of the authority.

NOTE: At each stage of research, you should evaluate your own level of competence. For example, if you are uncertain as to the issue, consult an authority with a general discussion of the topic. This will help to familiarize or expand your knowledge of the common questions and terminology in this particular area of law.

CHAPTER SUMMARY

This chapter has examined the need for and process of legal analysis. Without it, erroneous conclusions may be drawn about a legal authority and its effect. Examples were presented to illustrate not only the different types of legal writing but also how legal authority and legal analysis are incorporated into them. While one type of document may be objective and another persuasive in nature, both require an examination of authority and its applicability to a given set of circumstances.

The second part of the chapter addressed the steps of research regardless of the source. While subsequent chapters will provide actual strategies for research in the various types of authority, this chapter focused on the overall preparation and implementation of the research plan to ensure comprehensive and accurate results. To enable you to adequately research a legal question, you must first understand the legal issue that is in dispute. To do so, it is absolutely necessary that you distinguish the legal (rather than the ordinary) meaning of the question as well as any relevant terminology. The second element is to plan the research by identifying the most likely sources of relevant primary authority. Third, you must prepare the actual query for research. This involves framing specific questions, using information about the issue and relevant terminology. Finally, upon completing the research, you should always conclude by validating your authority. Without this final step, your authority cannot be relied upon as current and effective.

KEY TERMS

argumentative	legal analysis	research issue
case brief	objective	research query

SELF-TEST

MULTIPLE CHOICE

1. Judges and lawyers have been reluctant to adopt changes in _____ because such changes might be interpreted as changing the legal effect of documents.
   a) statutes
   b) terminology

c) judicial opinions
d) regulations
2. The actual process of legal analysis includes appreciating the meaning of a legal standard and its _____ .
a) author's commentary
b) legislative history
c) potential impact
d) none of the above
3. A _____ is generally written in terms broad enough to encompass a variety of situations.
a) judicial opinion
b) headnote
c) statute
d) none of the above
4. The words in a statute _____ .
a) usually all have significance
b) may be present only for proper grammar
c) have the same meaning as in any other type of writing
c) all of the above
5. The elements considered in legal authority include _____ .
a) mandatory, persuasive
b) primary, secondary
c) validity
d) all of the above

TRUE/FALSE

_____ 6. Consideration of whether authority is (1) mandatory or persuasive and (2) primary or secondary is essentially the same thing.
_____ 7. The facts of a case do not influence its legal effect on future cases.
_____ 8. When you are framing an issue for research, you must include all necessary circumstances.
_____ 9. Having an adequate command of relevant terminology can greatly affect efficiency and accuracy in the research process.

_____ 10. If you are totally unfamiliar with your research subject, it may be helpful to first consult statutes.

FILL-IN THE BLANKS

11. Once you have identified your issue and have armed yourself with enough terminology to begin your search, your next step is to locate _____ that will have the greatest impact on your case.
12. Once you have employed your research _____ and have located sufficient authority to respond to the issue, you must then determine the priority of the authorities.
13. The facts of the opinion might actually be used to _____ the present case and propose a different ruling.
14. Only _____ _____ will provide you with the information necessary to determine whether an authority applies to your case and the result implicated.
15. Law from another jurisdiction or an equal or subordinate authority (such as a lower court) is _____ _____ .
16. The _____ of authority does not mean that you must choose only one authority to present.
17. The term _____ _____ is used to describe cases that were considered by the entire appellate court.
18. A _____ decision is one that clearly establishes a legal standard for a jurisdiction.
19. If an opinion changes a _____ _____ of a jurisdiction, you must determine whether that variance is a total reversal or a very limited and conditional exception to the rule.
20. The final step in research is _____ .

CHAPTER 5

LEGAL DICTIONARIES/ THESAURUSES/ENCYCLOPEDIAS

CHAPTER OBJECTIVES

Upon completion of this chapter, you should have developed the following competencies:

- Explain the purpose and benefits of a legal dictionary.

- Explain the purpose and benefits of a legal thesaurus.

- Describe the process for using a legal dictionary and legal thesaurus in legal research.

- Discuss how a legal dictionary can be used as authority.

- Prepare a citation for a legal dictionary.

- Describe the purpose and benefits of a legal encyclopedia.

- Explain the system of organization of a legal encyclopedia.

- Discuss the supplementation of a legal encyclopedia.

- Explain the steps of research within a legal encyclopedia.

- Explain the role of research in a legal encyclopedia with respect to other sources of authority.

NATURE AND FUNCTION IN LEGAL RESEARCH AND WRITING

As a beginning researcher, you are probably excited about developing the skill to locate specific law to answer legal questions. On the other hand, you may have some anxiety about the size of the task when you first walk into a law library or call up a law library by computer. The choices can be mind boggling. However, by approaching your research in a systematic way and using the resources that are available to you, research quickly becomes an interesting pursuit that rewards you with the results.

One helpful hint to lower your anxiety level is to remember that no matter how many thousands of books or how many hundreds of different resources exist in the law library, nearly all of them are indexed by subject in some way. Consequently, if you can familiarize yourself with the proper terminology and acclimate yourself to the various types of subject indexes, your research skills should develop very quickly.

This chapter focuses on the use of legal dictionaries and thesauruses as secondary authority to expand your base of terminology in research and of legal encyclopedias as a beginning step in research. By the end of the chapter, you should have developed the skills necessary to begin a basic research assignment.

Legal Dictionaries/Thesauruses/Encyclopedias

Legal dictionaries and legal thesauruses are two totally distinct resources with different purposes. But because they are so compatible, it is not unusual to find a text that is a combination legal dictionary/thesaurus. An example is *West's Legal Dictionary/Thesaurus* (1985) by William Statsky. You may also find these resources published separately. Both are helpful in the research process and should always be kept at hand for quick consultation. After many years as a lawyer, teacher, researcher, and writer, this author still keeps a copy within reach.

The Legal Dictionary As a Resource.   The legal dictionary is distinct from an ordinary English-language dictionary. As discussed in prior chapters, the language of legal documents contains a variety of terms, including some that are not even English but are Latin in origin. Additionally, the legal dictionary provides you with the meaning attached to a word by the American legal system rather than the ordinary everyday interpretation. Perhaps the most well known legal dictionary and one that can be found in virtually any law library is *Black's Legal Dictionary*. This publication is probably the most cited legal dictionary in judicial opinions and is widely accepted as a standard authority for definition of legal terms.

⚖ APPLICATION 5.1

SANCTION *NEW WEBSTER'S DICTIONARY & THESAURUS OF THE ENGLISH LANGUAGE, 1992*

1. Explicit permission given by someone in authority.

Sanction *(West's Legal Dictionary/Thesaurus)* 3. A penalty for an infraction or violation. See punishment.

Clearly, the legal definition may involve a totally different meaning from the conversational interpretation of the same term. In ordinary language, when you state that someone has sanctioned another's act, this would probably be understood to mean that the action was approved. If one is sanctioned by a court, however, most lawyers would interpret this to mean that the individual was penalized in some way. Within the context of legal research and writing, you should always consult a legal dictionary for proper use of terminology.

Another tremendous benefit of a legal dictionary is that it often contains definitions for words and terms that are not usually a part of everyday English language and that sometimes do not even appear in ordinary dictionaries. Often these are **terms of art.** This language has carried over for hundreds of years in the legal profession because use of more common or trendy synonyms might result in a different interpretation of the meaning of the word or term. Consequently, it is easier and more prudent for legal professionals to use a term as it has always been used. However, for the person who is not familiar with such a word or term, without the help of a legal dictionary, it may appear to be nonsensical.

terms of art
Language, words, or phrases that have a particular meaning when used within the context of a certain subject, such as law.

⚖ APPLICATION 5.2

A woman whose date was chronically late to pick her up told her boyfriend, "It's over! You're guilty of **laches,** and there's no denying it."
    Translation to present-day language: "It's over! Your lateness is inexcusable."

As you can see, to encounter such terms as *laches, pro bono, putative,* and *sua sponte* not only can confound but also interrupts the research process. Becoming familiar with terminology is not something that you can do all at once. Rather, it takes time, and with regard to legal terminology, quite often the meaning of a term is largely affected by the context in which it appears. For example, a "material" witness is usually someone who has important personal knowledge of the facts of a case, whereas, "material" evidence is related to the case, will not cause an overreaction by the jury, and does not duplicate other evidence.

Using an ordinary legal dictionary will probably be your easiest task in learning to perform legal research. As stated, a legal dictionary is arranged in the same manner as other dictionaries. The difference is that it incorporates legal rather than common definitions. The terms are arranged in alphabetical order, and quite often the legal dictionary will contain phrases, such as "nolo contendre," in addition to single words.

Another type of resource similar to the legal dictionary is a publication known as *Words and Phrases*. Although this publication is arranged much like a legal dictionary, it has two additional features that make it a very useful authority. First, *Words and Phrases* provides a citation for each term in which the term was explained in some form of primary authority. This may be a case, a statute, or an administrative law. The point is that if you were to look up the citation given, you not only would find a discussion of the term but also would see the term used in context. Often this is extremely helpful to gain a thorough understanding of a term.

Secondly, *Words and Phrases* is updated periodically through the use of pocket parts. Over time, the meaning of a term may change somewhat, and when this occurs, the term, current interpretation, and recent citation are printed in the supplement. Periodically, new pocket parts are issued that integrate all previous pocket parts until a revised hardbound edition is published.

The Legal Dictionary As an Authority.   At first, you may not think of something as basic as a legal dictionary as something that you would depend upon as an authority in a legal document. This is something that occurs quite frequently, however. Whenever a party wants to drive a point home, what better way than to start with the basics: define the term. Therefore, you will find as you research that definitions and dictionary citations are common in legal writing, especially in pleadings and other trial-court-level documents. While ordinary terms or terms that are used quite frequently are not usually given formal definition, other terms whose meaning may have only vague application in a case may very well be defined for clarity.

⚖ **APPLICATION 5.3**

The plaintiff maintains that the defendant was not a bona fide purchaser of the automobile and, consequently, knew that he did not have clear title that he could transfer to plaintiff. To constitute a "bona fide purchaser," one must purchase the "property for value without any notice of defects in the title of the seller." *West's Legal Dictionary* 99 (1985). In the present case, the defendant was well aware that the title to the automobile was forged, and as a result, defendant had full knowledge of a defect in the title.

The method of citation for legal dictionaries is found in Rule 15.7 of the bluebook, which essentially requires that the citation include the name of the publication and the page on which the term is found, followed by the year of publication or supplement in parentheses. If the definition is taken from a

supplement or the publication is a second edition (or later), such information should be noted before the year in the parentheses.

☐ ASSIGNMENT 5.1

Using a legal dictionary, match the following terms to the definitions:

_____ placate

_____ bond

_____ color of law

_____ effect

_____ gross

a. That which is produced.
b. Total, before or without diminution or deduction.
c. An obligation to pay a designated amount of money if a certain act is not done.
d. Accommodate, quiet, assuage, mitigate.
e. The appearance of a legal right but without substance.

☐ ASSIGNMENT 5.2

Read the following pairs of sentences and state your opinion (with explanation) as to whether the compared sentences have a different legal meaning. Do not use a dictionary of any kind for this assignment.

A.1 The property of the parties was divided equitably.

A.2 The property of the parties was divided equally.

B.1 Antonia was the victim of robbery at gunpoint.

B.2 Antonia was the victim of theft at gunpoint.

C.1 George was indicted for a crime.

C.2 George was charged with a crime.

☐ ASSIGNMENT 5.3

Using a legal dictionary, locate five terms that are heard in ordinary language but have different meanings when used in a legal context. Do not use terms that appear with definition or discussion in this text.

The Legal Encyclopedia As a Resource.   Some discussion has already been given to the usefulness of a legal encyclopedia. Such a publication is an excellent resource for preliminary research. The disadvantage is that the content is often national in scope (some states have their own legal encyclopedia publications) and thus presents only generally accepted principles. This

is offset, however, by the fact that few jurisdictions have such easily accessible information about legal standards. It not unreasonable to begin research in a legal encyclopedia, even though your ultimate goal is to locate a specific point of law within a particular jurisdiction. After all, the knowledge you gain from the legal encyclopedia may very well enable you to locate very specific law in that single jurisdiction.

Examples in previous chapters demonstrated how a legal encyclopedia can be used to gain a basic understanding of a topic of law. Part of what makes the legal profession so interesting is that even after years of experience, many lawyers encounter unfamiliar questions of law. While there may be similarities of fact patterns, a case is virtually never repeated exactly. There is always some twist, some major or, more often, minor difference that can turn the entire direction of the lawsuit. Partly for this reason, some of the most well worn books in any law library are the legal encyclopedias.

Until you have at least a minimal understanding of your topic, it is impossible to adequately undertake research. After all, if the topic is unfamiliar, how can you know the most relevant terms? The legal encyclopedia can not only acquaint you with the basic principles on a topic of law but also provide any number of words or phrases that you can use when constructing your research queries.

The Legal Encyclopedia As an Authority.   As stated in the previous section, the legal encyclopedia is a helpful tool when beginning the research process. However, it is also frequently cited as a sound authority in legal documents. The same reasons that cause the legal encyclopedia to be a good source for general information make it suitable as an authority. Legal encyclopedias generally focus on well-established and widely accepted principles of law. Therefore, if you are researching an unfamiliar issue or an issue that has not been the subject of much litigation, the legal encyclopedia may be the perfect authority upon which to base your position. For example, assume you are researching the law of a jurisdiction with a total population of less than 2,000,000 people. Consequently, this state does not generate the litigation (and subsequent appeals producing published case law) that a more heavily populated state might have. Also, because the state is largely agricultural, the statutes are not heavily focused on business or other urban concerns. You spend a great deal of time performing your research but simply cannot find any primary authority in the jurisdiction that applies. This is true even though in your preliminary research you found a section in a legal encyclopedia that precisely described the applicable legal standard. If there is no relevant or persuasive primary authority from another jurisdiction that would tend to influence the case, you are perfectly correct in citing a persuasive secondary authority, such as a legal encyclopedia.

case of first impression
A case whose legal issues are considered by the court for the first time. There is no other primary interpretative authority on the issue within the jurisdiction.

Citation of legal encyclopedias is quite common in **cases of first impression,** which deal with issues that have not been previously addressed in the jurisdiction (at least not in published form by a higher court, legislature, or agency). In such a situation, the legal encyclopedia offers a clear statement of the accepted view of a majority of jurisdictions that have addressed the issue.

When referring to a legal encyclopedia, proper citation form should be used, and a clear statement, if not a quotation, of the information in the encyclopedia is necessary. As you will recall in case analysis, you do little good

by repeating a legal principle without its source, and vice versa. Both are necessary elements in citing any legal authority, including a legal encyclopedia.

Methods of Research

Conducting your early research assignments in legal dictionaries and encyclopedias is an excellent way to begin understanding the legal research process. These publications are some of the most "user friendly" in the law library. Undoubtedly, you have used a regular dictionary in the past. Thus, you should have little difficulty in using a legal dictionary, which is arranged in essentially the same way. A legal thesaurus (which is not combined with the definitions of a legal dictionary) is an alphabetical arrangement of terms (words as well as phrases). Each term is followed by synonyms (words of same or similar meaning) and usually antonyms (words of opposite meaning).

Research in the legal encyclopedia is quite simple regardless of the doubt you may have about this when you first see one. It is not unheard of for the volumes of a legal encyclopedia to number in the hundreds. The subject index alone may be 20 or 30 volumes. However, the process is the same. Assume you wanted to locate information in this textbook about how to abbreviate case names in a citation. You would look in the subject index under such terms as *citation, cases, case law, case names,* and *judicial authority*. These terms would lead you to sections of the book where the information you need is located. The legal encyclopedia functions the same way, only on a much larger scale.

When you realize that there are multiple index volumes containing thousands of terms arranged alphabetically to lead you into the encyclopedia, the need for a specific research query becomes a reality. Hopefully, by specifying the issue,—the exact question you wanted to answer will be complete. By formulating your query, you have identified all the key terms and phrases that are likely to lead you to that answer. Even if you have a fairly short list of places to look, these resources, along with help from a legal dictionary or thesaurus, can make this task manageable.

☐ ASSIGNMENT 5.4

Prepare a research query from the following issue. Use the excerpted pages from the legal encyclopedia in Exhibit 5.1 to select those entries that you think are most likely to address the issue.
Issue: If X uses a knife to threaten Y during a rape, but never cuts or stabs Y, and Y dies of a heart attack during the rape, can X be charged with homicide? If so, and X is convicted, is there a presumption of X's guilt on the charge of rape?

Another method of research, in addition to the subject index of the legal encyclopedia, is the use of topical arrangements (see Exhibit 5.2). The actual volumes of the legal encyclopedia are arranged into broad subject categories. These subjects are then arranged alphabetically. At the beginning of each subject is a table of the topics addressed within that topic area. These topics are not arranged alphabetically. Rather, each broad subject is broken up into

EXHIBIT 5.1   Sample pages from Corpus Juris Secundum, index.
Copyright 1994 WEST PUBLISHING COMPANY (1–800–328–9352).

HOMICIDE

HOMICIDE—Continued

Evidence—Continued

Participation, post

Passion,

Admissibility, **Homic § 251**

Sufficiency, **Homic § 313**

Pathologist, **Homic §§ 293, 294**

Personal relations of parties, admissibility, **Homic § 220**

Photographs, admissibility, **Homic § 239**

Physical conditions, admissibility, **Homic §§ 219, 239**

Subsequent conditions, **Homic § 242**

Preparation for crime, admissibility, **Homic § 233**

Preponderance of evidence, generally, post

Presence of accused, admissibility, **Homic § 213**

Presence of and use of persons or articles not introduced into, **Homic § 324**

Presumptions, **Evid § 135**

Layman's knowledge of legal technicalities, **Evid § 132(2)**

Previous attempts, admissibility, **Homic § 233**

Previous difficulties, antecedent circumstances, admissibility, **Homic § 235**

Provocation,

Admissibility, **Homic § 251**

Sufficiency, **Homic § 313**

Reception, rules governing, **Homic § 325**

Relation of parties, **Homic § 217**

Relative positions of parties, admissibility, **Homic § 239**

Relative size and strength of parties, admissibility, **Homic § 219**

Remoteness, generally, post

Searches and seizures, killing of person making, **Homic § 197**

Self-defense, post

State of mind, generally, post

Subsequent circumstances, admissibility, **Homic § 241 et seq.**

Sufficiency, **Homic § 316**

Suicide, admissibility, **Homic § 215**

Surrounding circumstances, admissibility, **Homic § 234 et seq.**

Third persons,

Commission of act, admissibility, **Homic § 216**

Defense against, **Homic § 257**

Threats,

Accused, admissibility, **Homic § 230**

Victim, admissibility, **Homic § 231**

Tracks, admissibility, **Homic § 213**

Unlawful character of act of deceased, admissibility, **Homic § 253**

Variance, generally, post

Vicious humor before homicide, admissibility, **Homic § 234**

View of place of homicide, **Homic § 322**

Weapons, possession of after crime, **Homic § 244**

Weight and sufficiency, **Homic § 295 et seq.**

Excusable homicide. Justifiable or excusable homicide, generally, post

Executors and administrators, beneficiary charged with murder, advancement to hire counsel **Ex&Ad § 491**

Exercise of authority or duty,

Defense, questions of law and fact, **Homic § 330**

Excuse of justification in general, admissibility, **Homic § 254**

Killing in, instruction as to, **Homic § 348**

HOMICIDE—Continued

Expert testimony,

Cause of death, **Homic § 200**

Establishment by, **Homic § 298**

Physical condition of parties, admissibility, **Homic §§ 219, 242**

Position of deceased, admissibility, **Homic § 239**

Explanatory matters, evidence,

Admissibility, **Homic § 234**

Declarations,

Accused, admissibility, **Homic § 247**

Deceased, admissibility, **Homic § 237**

Flight or concealment, evidence as to, **Homic § 246**

Explosives, cause of death, means or instruments used, admissibility, **Homic § 201**

Express malice,

Evidence, admissibility, general provisions, **Homic § 203**

Previous declarations, showing by, **Homic § 204**

Extradition,

Death in United States from blow struck in Mexico, extradition to Mexico, **Extrad § 26**

International extradition, **Extrad § 26**

Extreme emotional disturbance, attempts, **Homic § 95**

Extremist, dying declarations declarant as required to be in, **Homic § 276**

Eyewitnesses,

Circumstantial evidence, participation of accused in crime, **Homic § 307**

Grade or degree of crime, details by, **Homic § 190**

Identity and presence of accused, admissibility, **Homic § 213**

Other crimes, commission of or attempt to commit, **Homic § 309**

False imprisonment, murder, underlying unlawful acts, **Homic § 55**

Family difficulty, prior connection with, admissibility of evidence as to, **Homic § 235**

Family relationship, prior difficulties between persons in, admissibility of evidence as to, **Homic § 206**

Fear,

Incriminating others, evidence, admissibility, **Homic § 216**

Justifiable or excusable homicide, matters not constituting, **Homic § 103**

Federal courts,

Certiorari to supreme court, printing petition, **Fed Cts § 276**

Default judgment, setting aside, **Fed Civ Proc § 1130**

Removal of cause to federal court, **Fed Cts § 164**

Federal prosecutions, punishment for homicide set by federal statute, **Homic § 366**

Felonies,

Attempts, **Homic § 95**

Homicide in commission of other crime, **Homic § 45 et seq.**

Felony murder, **Homic § 45 et seq.**

Killing in perpetration of,

Burden of proof, **Homic § 190**

Evidence, admissibility, **Homic § 196**

Other offenses, commission of or attempt to commit, **Homic § 309**

Premeditation as presumed, **Homic § 182**

Murder,

General provisions, **Homic § 45**

Homicide in commission of other crime, felony murder, **Homic § 45 et seq.**

301

EXHIBIT 5.1 Continued

INNOCENCE

EXHIBIT 5.1   Continued

WEAPONS

EXHIBIT 5.2 Sample pages from the Corpus Juris Secundum topical index. Copyright 1957 WEST PUBLISHING COMPANY (1–800–328–9352).

97 C. J. S.

WITNESSES

This Title includes production of oral testimony at the trial of causes in general, civil or criminal; competency to testify; procuring attendance for that purpose, and production of documents by witnesses; examination of witnesses; their credibility; and corroborating, impeaching, or contradicting their testimony.

Matters not in this Title, treated elsewhere in this work, see Descriptive-Word Index

Analysis

See also descriptive word index for Title "Witnesses" in Volume 98

EXHIBIT 5.2   Continued

WITNESSES   97   C. J. S.

III. COMPETENCY—Continued

See also descriptive word index for Title "Witnesses" in Volume 98

EXHIBIT 5.2   Continued

97 C. J. S.   WITNESSES

III. COMPETENCY—Continued

    D. CONFIDENTIAL RELATIONS AND PRIVILEGED COMMUNICATIONS—Continued

See also descriptive word index for Title "Witnesses" in Volume 98

341

EXHIBIT 5.2   Continued

---

§ 266 WITNESSES   97 C. J. S.

3. Communications Between Husband and Wife

§ 266. Rule of Exclusion

    a. In general
    b. Statutory construction
    c. Privilege of disclosure

a. In General

    The general rule is that communications by one spouse to the other in the confidence, or course, of the marital relation, and not in the presence or hearing of a third person, are privileged communications which neither spouse can disclose, or be required to disclose, in evidence, unless the other spouse waives the privilege.

    The general rule, which existed at common law[47] and is preserved, or re-established by statute,[48] is that communications made by one spouse to the other in the confidence, or course, of the marital relation are protected from disclosure as privileged communications which neither spouse can disclose, or can be required to disclose, in evidence,[49] unless

---

47. U.S.—Rogers v. U. S., C.A.Colo., 179 F.2d 559, affirmed Rogers v. U. S., 71 S.Ct. 438, 340 U.S. 367, 95 L.Ed. 344, 19 A.L.R.2d 378, rehearing denied 71 S.Ct. 619, 341 U.S. 912, 95 L.Ed. 1348—Dickinson v. Abernathy Furniture Co., 89 F.2d 932, certiorari denied Preferred Acc. Ins. Co. v. Marsh, 58 S. Ct. 36, 302 U.S. 715, 82 L.Ed. 552—Marsh v. New York Life Ins. Co., C.C.A.Ohio, 89 F.2d 932, certiorari denied New York Life Ins. Co. v. Marsh, 58 S.Ct. 36, 302 U.S. 716, 82 L.Ed. 553.

Ill.—People v. Palumbo, 125 N.E.2d 518, 5 Ill.2d 409.

Mo.—Sellars v. Sellars, App., 274 S. W.2d 509—Dickinson v. Abernathy Furniture Co., 96 S.W.2d 1086, 231 Mo.App. 303.

N.Y.—People v. McCormack, 104 N.Y. S.2d 139, 278 App.Div. 191, affirmed 103 N.E.2d 895, 303 N.Y. 782.

Pa.—Hunter v. Hunter, 83 A.2d 401, 169 Pa.Super. 498.

Competency of husband and wife as witness see supra §§ 75–104.

Objections to admissibility see infra §§ 302–305.

Waiver of privilege see infra §§ 306–314.

All private and confidential communications

Ariz.—Arizona Title Guarantee & Trust Co. v. Wagner, 251 P.2d 897, 75 Ariz. 82.

Knowledge gained by means of marriage relation

At common law, neither the husband nor the wife could testify as to any fact or transaction the knowledge of which was obtained by means of the marriage relation.

Ill.—Heineman v. Hermann, 52 N.E. 2d 263, 385 Ill. 191.

48. Cal.—Leemhuis v. Leemhuis, 289 P.2d 852, 137 C.A.2d 117.

Ill.—People v. Palumbo, 125 N.E.2d 518, 5 Ill.2d 409—Heineman v. Hermann, 52 N.E.2d 263, 385 Ill. 191 —Dunn v. Heasley, 30 N.E.2d 628, 375 Ill. 43.

Mo.—Sellars v. Sellars, App., 274 S. W.2d 509—Dickinson v. Abernathy Furniture Co., 96 S.W.2d 1086, 231 Mo.App. 303.

N.Y.—People v. McCormack, 104 N.Y. S.2d 139, 278 App.Div. 191, affirmed 103 N.E.2d 895, 303 N.Y. 782.

Pa.—Hunter v. Hunter, 83 A.2d 401, 169 Pa.Super. 498.

March v. Kinchem, Com.Pl., 32 West.L.J. 124.

Utah.—State v. Musser, 175 P.2d 724, 110 Utah 534, vacated on other grounds 68 S.Ct. 397, 333 U.S. 95, 92 L.Ed. 562.

Statute not intended to change common-law rule

U.S.—Marsh v. Preferred Acc. Ins. Co., C.C.A.Ohio, 89 F.2d 932, certiorari denied Preferred Acc. Ins. Co. v. Marsh, 58 S.Ct. 36, 302 U.S. 715, 82 L.Ed. 552—Marsh v. New York Life Ins. Co., C.C.A.Ohio, 89 F.2d 932, certiorari denied New York Life Ins. Co. v. Marsh, 58 S.Ct. 36, 302 U.S. 716, 82 L.Ed. 553.

Removing ground of incompetency; exception

(1) Purpose of statute prohibiting husband and wife from testifying concerning any communication during marriage, but providing that either shall be allowed to testify for the other with respect to any business transacted as agent, is to remove grounds of incompetency and not to increase them.

U.S.—Ramsouer v. Midland Val. R. Co., C.C.A.Ark., 135 F.2d 101.

(2) In interpleader by insurer to determine right to proceeds of life policies, wife of insured, who had been a beneficiary before assignment of policies, held qualified to testify as to assignment, under exception in statute where wife, if unmarried, could have maintained an action on, or for reformation of, the assignment.

U.S.—Penn Mut. Life Ins. Co. v. Meguire, D.C.Ky., 13 F.Supp. 967.

The Uniform Reciprocal Enforcement of Support Act does away with marital disqualifications and the privilege as to confidential communications between husband and wife.

N.J.—Pfueller v. Pfueller, 117 A.2d 30, 37 N.J.Super. 106.

49. U.S.—Blau v. U. S., Colo., 71 S. Ct. 301, 340 U.S. 332, 95 L.Ed. 170.

Rogers v. U. S., C.A.Colo., 179 F.2d 559, affirmed 71 S.Ct. 438, 340

U.S. 367, 95 L.Ed. 344, 19 A.L.R. 2d 378, rehearing denied 71 S.Ct. 619, 341 U.S. 912, 95 L.Ed. 1348— Fraser v. U. S., C.A.Tenn., 145 F. 2d 139, certiorari denied Fraser v. Barton, 65 S.Ct. 684, 324 U.S. 849, 89 L.Ed. 1409—U. S. v. Mitchell, C. C.A.N.Y., 137 F.2d 1006, adhered to 138 F.2d 831, certiorari denied Mitchell v. U. S., 64 S.Ct. 785, 321 U.S. 794, 88 L.Ed. 1083, rehearing denied 64 S.Ct. 1052, 322 U.S. 768, 88 L.Ed. 1594.

Salamon v. Indemnity Ins. Co. of North America, D.C.N.Y., 10 F.R. D. 232.

Cal.—Leemhuis v. Leemhuis, 289 P. 2d 852, 137 C.A.2d 117.

Fla.—Brown v. May, 76 So.2d 652— Mercer v. State, 24 So. 154, 40 Fla. 216, 74 Am.S.R. 135.

Ill.—Hefer v. Thomson, 16 N.E.2d 255, 296 Ill.App. 651.

Ky.—Sewell v. Sewell, 260 S.W.2d 643—Beddow's Adm'r v. Barbourville Water, Ice & Light Co., 66 S.W.2d 821, 252 Ky. 267.

Mass.—Case of Chernick, 189 N.E. 800, 286 Mass. 168.

Miss.—McFadden v. Welch, 170 So. 903, 177 Miss. 451.

Mo.—Forbis v. Forbis, App., 274 S. W.2d 800—Reeve v. Reeve, App., 160 S.W.2d 804.

N.J.—State v. Tune, 110 A.2d 99, 17 N.J. 100, certiorari denied 75 S.Ct. 584, 349 U.S. 907, 99 L.Ed. 1243.

N.Y.—People v. McCormack, 104 N.Y. S.2d 139, 278 App.Div. 191, affirmed 103 N.E.2d 895, 303 N.Y. 782.

People v. Afarian, 108 N.Y.S.2d 533, 202 Misc. 199.

Ohio.—Manning v. Prudential Ins. Co. of America, 118 N.E.2d 421, 95 Ohio App. 172—In re Ruhl's Estate, App., 43 N.E.2d 760.

Okl.—**Corpus Juris cited in** De Wolf v. State, 245 P.2d 107, 121, 95 Okl. Cr. 287.

Or.—McKinnon v. Chenoweth, 155 P. 2d 944, 176 Or. 74.

Pa.—Hunter v. Hunter, 83 A.2d 401, 169 Pa.Super. 498.

March v. Kinchem, Com.Pl., 32 West.L.J. 124.

Tenn.—Hazlett v. Bryant, 241 S.W.2d 121, 192 Tenn. 251.

Petway v. Hoover, 12 Tenn.App. 618.

EXHIBIT 5.2 Continued

the other spouse consents thereto and waives the privilege, as discussed infra §§ 306–314, the incompetence not being absolute,[50] or unless such communication was made in the presence or hearing of a third person competent to be a witness, as discussed infra § 271; but it is not every communication between husband and wife that is privileged[51] or confidential.[52]

This rule on privilege is based on considerations of public policy, which seeks to preserve the peace, confidence, and tranquility of the marital relation;[53] the rule is not dependent on any injunction of

---

Tex.—Smith v. State, 150 S.W.2d 388, 141 Tex.Cr. 577.
Wash.—State v. Americk, 256 P.2d 278, 42 Wash.2d 504—State v. Snyder, 147 P. 38, 84 Wash. 485.
Wis.—Fischer v. State, 276 N.W. 640, 226 Wis. 390.
70 C.J. p 379 note 91.

The reason for the rule is a sound one and springs from the recognition of the fact that marriage bonds are to be protected and not disrupted by a compulsory making known of matters induced by the relation and confided by one spouse to the other under the marriage relation. Induced by such relationship, the wife confides to the husband her most secret thoughts, and likewise the husband in her, which thoughts under no circumstances would be revealed to others. The mainspring to such action is the confidence the one bestows on the other and the confidential nature of the relationship between the two.
Mo.—Dickinson v. Abernathy Furniture Co., 96 S.W.2d 1086, 231 Mo. App. 303.

Conversation; marital communication

Test of whether conversation between spouses is admissible is whether testimony elicited entails a disclosure of any marital communication.
Cal.—Leemhuis v. Leemhuis, 289 P. 2d 852, 137 C.A.2d 117.

Discrediting spouse's testimony

Where a husband or wife has testified, his or her spouse is not qualified to discredit such testimony by testifying concerning information received as a result of the marital relation.
Ga.—Gorman v. State, 188 S.E. 455, 183 Ga. 307—Keaton v. McGwier, 24 Ga. 217.
Stewart v. Wilson, 88 S.E.2d 752, 92 Ga.App. 514.

Communications held not privileged
(1) A question addressed to wife, asking whether she knew that plaintiff was making some claim against her husband, since deceased, did not itself indicate that it called for confidential communication between husband and wife.
Wis.—Zimdars v. Zimdars, 295 N.W. 675, 236 Wis. 484.

(2) In action for injuries sustained by plaintiff while riding in an automobile driven by his son and owned by son's wife, son's written state-

ment, contrary to his testimony and made to liability insurer which carried insurance on automobile, was not inadmissible as privileged.
Ga.—Sweet v. Awtrey, 28 S.E.2d 154, 70 Ga.App. 334. ;

(3) In husband's action to establish trust in land conveyed to divorced wife, for that part of purchase price paid by husband, cross-examination of husband concerning what wife said when she handed certain paper to him was not objectionable on ground that it constituted confidential communication between the husband and wife.
Ga.—Statham v. Council, 9 S.E.2d 768, 190 Ga. 517.

(4) In action by decedent's sons against his wife involving question whether decedent's assignment of his shares in family corporation, amounting to forty per cent of stock, to himself and his wife in joint tenancy was concomitant with agreement that sons should be owners of such shares after wife had enjoyed life estate in them, wherein sons asserted no claim to note which had been placed in joint tenancy of spouses, it was not error to require wife to testify with respect to such note.
Cal.—Leemhuis v. Leemhuis, 289 P. 2d 852, 137 C.A.2d 117.

(5) Bill by divorced wife against husband and second wife for a discovery in aid of alimony and support arrearage due under divorce decree was not demurrable as calling for confidential communications between respondents who were husband and wife.
Ala.—Shaffield v. Shaffield, 34 So.2d 591, 250 Ala. 381.

(6) In proceeding by decedent's nephew against estate based on specific oral contract for labor performed for decedent, wife of decedent was not incompetent under statute relating to communications between husband and wife, to testify to statements made by decedent, where she took no part in conversation and statements were not made to her.
Iowa.—Gardner v. Marquis, 275 N.W. 493, 224 Iowa 458.

(7) Loud quarrel.
N.Y.—People v. McCormack, 104 N. Y.S.2d 139, 278 App.Div. 191, affirmed 103 N.E.2d 895, 303 N.Y. 782.

50. Ind.—Hunt v. State, 133 N.E.2d 48.
Mo.—Chamberlain v. Chamberlain, App., 230 S.W.2d 184.

51. U.S.—Rogers v. U. S., C.A.Colo., 179 F.2d 559, affirmed 71 S.Ct. 438, 340 U.S. 367, 95 L.Ed. 344, 19 A.L.R. 2d 378, rehearing denied 71 S.Ct. 619, 341 U.S. 912, 95 L.Ed. 1348.

52. N.Y.—People v. McCormack, 104 N.Y.S.2d 139, 278 App.Div. 191, affirmed 103 N.E.2d 895, 303 N.Y. 782.

53. Fla.—Mercer v. State, 24 So. 154, 40 Fla. 216, 74 Am.S.R. 135.
Mo.—Dickinson v. Abernathy Furniture Co., 96 S.W.2d 1086, 231 Mo. App. 303.
Pa.—Hunter v. Hunter, 83 A.2d 401, 169 Pa.Super. 498.
Tex.—Smith v. State, 150 S.W.2d 388, 141 Tex.Cr. 577.
70 C.J. p 380 note 94.

"The principle of privileged communications between husband and wife . . . was adopted to encourage mutual confidence between the parties for the preservation of the marital status."
U.S.—Rogers v. U. S., C.A.Colo., 179 F.2d 559, 564, affirmed 71 S.Ct. 438, 340 U.S. 367, 95 L.Ed. 344, 19 A. L.R.2d 378, rehearing denied 71 S. Ct. 619, 341 U.S. 912, 95 L.Ed. 1348.

"The public policy which lies at the foundation of every rule of privileged communications, is satisfied in the privilege accorded by the law to communications between husband and wife. They originate in confidence which is essential to the relation, and the relation is a proper object of encouragement by law, for the injury that would inure to it by disclosure is greater than the benefit that would result in a judicial investigation of the truth. Wigmore on Evidence, 3rd Edition, § 2332. The confidence that attaches to communications between husband and wife has for its purpose free and unrestrained privacy divested of any apprehension of compulsory disclosure."
U.S.—Fraser v. U. S., C.C.A.Tenn., 145 F.2d 139, 143, certiorari denied Fraser v. Barton, 65 S.Ct. 684, 324 U.S. 849, 89 L.Ed. 1409.

The basis of the immunity given to communications between husband and wife is protection of marital confidences, regarded as so essential to preservation of marriage relationship as to outweigh disadvantages to administration of justice which privilege entails.
U.S.—Wolfle v. U. S., Wash., 54 S.Ct. 279, 291 U.S. 7, 78 L.Ed. 617.

subheadings, sub-subheadings, and so on. To use the topical arrangement to locate information, you need to have a sufficient working knowledge of the topic to know approximately how the information would be categorized. Otherwise, the index is still the most efficient method to determine the exact location of the specific information you need.

☐ ASSIGNMENT 5.5

Using the excerpted topical arrangement in Exhibit 5.2, list the order of headings and subheadings you would consult to determine the following: Can a spouse testify against his wife if she is accused in a criminal action?

Supplements. Supplementation of legal dictionaries such as *Words and Phrases* was previously addressed. As a general rule, standard legal dictionaries are not supplemented. Rather, new editions are periodically published to revise and update the definitions. However, supplementation is a necessary component of legal encyclopedias. A legal encyclopedia is made up of hundreds of volumes of books, each containing as many as a thousand pages. The cost to issue a new edition every year would be staggering. Also, because the legal encyclopedias contain widely accepted legal standards, the changes in the law are generally not sweeping ones. Consequently, supplementation is the most efficient method to publish any changes or updating that should be brought to the attention of the reader.

Legal encyclopedias often use annually cumulative (containing all changes in the current year and prior years since the last hardbound publication) pocket parts or other softbound supplements to apprise the researcher of changes in law. When conducting research in a legal encyclopedia, you should always consult both the encyclopedia and the supplement, as even widely accepted legal standards are modified from time to time. Also, the supplement contains more recent citations that demonstrate how the topic has been addressed in more current cases and publications. Such citations are often helpful to give you a clearer understanding of how the standard is actually applied in specific circumstances.

The only information included in the supplement is newer citations to the footnotes and any substantive changes that have occurred in the law. If you consult the supplement for the section you have researched in the legal encyclopedia and find no text—only footnotes—you can assume that as of the date of the supplement, no broad changes in the law have occurred. This does not, however, mean that no changes have occurred in any one jurisdiction (or even several jurisdictions), possibly including your own. It simply means that most states that follow majority rules of law have not addressed the issue or changed their position.

☐ ASSIGNMENT 5.6

Use the excerpt from a legal encyclopedia (see Exhibit 5.3) to determine whether the answer to Assignment 5.5 has changed since publication of the hardbound edition.

EXHIBIT 5.3   Sample pages from the Corpus Juris Secundum pocket part.
Copyright 1993 WEST PUBLISHING COMPANY (1–800–328–9352).

§ 264 WITNESSES   97 CJS 122
Page 758

Va.—Moore v. Warren, 122 S.E.2d 879, 203 Va. 117.

In Minnesota

(6) Other matters.

Minn.—Haugen v. Dick Thayer Motor Co., 91 N.W.2d 585, 253 Minn. 199—Larson v. Montpetit, 147 N.W.2d 580, 275 Minn. 394—Ackerman v. Theis, 160 N.W.2d 583, 281 Minn. 82.

Blood test not in connection with accident report

Fla.—State v. Mitchell, 245 So.2d 618.

Wis.—Luedtke v. Shedivy, 186 N.W.2d 220, 51 Wis.2d 110.

9. Cal.—Security Ins. Co. v. Snyder-Lynch Motors, Inc., 7 Cal.Rptr. 28, 183 C.A.2d 574.

Del.—Halko v. State, 204 A.2d 628, 8 Storey 47.

Testimony of officer

(1) Alaska—Creary v. State, App., 663 P.2d 226.

Fla.—Lobree v. Caporossi, App., 139 So.2d 510—Rosenfeld v. Johnson, App., 161 So.2d 703.

Iowa—Soreide v. Vilas & Co., 78 N.W.2d 41, 247 Iowa 1139—State v. Flack, 101 N.W.2d 535, 251 Iowa 529—Curry v. Jones, 138 N.W.2d 101, 258 Iowa 129—Grocers Wholesale Co-op., Inc. v. Nussberger Trucking Co., 192 N.W.2d 753.

Reports admissible in criminal cases

Iowa—State v. Flack, 101 N.W.2d 535, 251 Iowa 529.

page 759

10. Mich.—Duncan v. Strating, 99 N.W.2d 559, 357 Mich. 654.

Tex.—Spradling v. State, App. 9 Dist., 628 S.W.2d 123, review ref.

Statement to prosecuting attorney

Mich.—Conlon v. Dean, 165 N.W.2d 623, 14 Mich. App. 415.

11. Iowa—State v. Flack, 101 N.W.2d 535, 251 Iowa 529.

In some cases, the fact information was not related to a police officer at the scene of an accident is privileged.[11.5]

11.5 Failure to complain at accident scene was privileged

Fla.—Thomas v. Gottlieb, App.4 Dist., 520 So.2d 622.

12. Cal.—Carroll v. Beavers, App., 270 P.2d 23, vac. 273 P.2d 56, 126 C.A.2d 828, 59 A.L.R.2d 263.

14. Iowa—State v. Flack, 101 N.W.2d 535, 251 Iowa 529—Pinckney v. Watkinson, 116 N.W.2d 258, 254 Iowa 144.

16. U.S.—McConnell v. U.S., C.A.Fla., 428 F.2d 803.

Cal.—Morales v. Thompson, 340 P.2d 700, 171 C.A.2d 405.

Iowa—Hamilton v. Becker, 86 N.W.2d 142, 249 Iowa 516—Meyer v. Schumacher, 160 N.W.2d 433.

N.Y.—Brown v. Adams, 203 N.Y.S.2d 277.

Tex.—Martin v. Jenkins, Civ.App., 381 S.W.2d 115, err. ref. no rev. err., Sup., 384 S.W.2d 123.

Va.—Lee v. Artis, 136 S.E.2d 868, 205 Va. 343—Oliphant v. Snyder, 147 S.E.2d 122, 206 Va. 932.

Disclosures to patrolman not admissible

Fla.—Dinowitz v. Weinrub, App. 4 Dist., 493 So.2d 29.

Iowa—Chandler v. Harger, 113 N.W.2d 250, 253 Iowa 565—Brown v. Lyon, 142 N.W.2d 536, 258 Iowa 1216.

17. U.S.—Davis v. Brooks Transp. Co., D.C.Del., 186 F.Supp. 366.

Cal.—Hodges v. Severns, 20 Cal.Rptr. 129, 201 C.A.2d 99.

Mich.—Jaxon v. City of Detroit, Dept. of St. Railways, 151 N.W.2d 813, 379 Mich. 405.

Ohio—City of Dayton v. Smith, 166 N.E.2d 256, 109 Ohio App. 383.

The statute may not apply where the report is made in pursuance of a military investigation rather than a civilian police investigation.[17.5]

17.5. Blood test

U.S.—Kuklis v. Hancock, C.A.Fla., 428 F.2d 608.

A statute providing confidentiality to accident reports does not preclude release by the state of information generated from confidential accident reports when that disclosure does not reveal the identity or compromise the privacy interest of the reporting parties.[17.10]

17.10. Cal.—Davies v. Superior Court (State), Cal., 204 Cal.Rptr. 154, 682 P.2d 349, 36 C.3d 291 disapproving People ex rel. Department of Transportation v. Superior Court, 60 Cal.App.3d 352, 131 Cal.Rptr. 476; State of California ex rel. Department of Transportation v. Superior Court (Thomsen), 102 Cal.App.3d 25, 162 Cal.Rptr. 78; Edgar v. Superior Court, 84 Cal.App.3d 430, 148 Cal.Rptr. 687.

Other reports have been held not privileged.[21.5]

21.5. Fla.—Stafford v. Southern Bell Tel. & Tel. Co., App., 179 So.2d 232, cert. discharged, Sup., 190 So.2d 339.

Okl.—Perry v. City of Oklahoma City, 470 P.2d 974.

22. Statute construed

(4) Other matters.

U.S.—Israel v. U.S., C.A.N.Y., 247 F.2d 426—Berguido v. Eastern Air Lines, Inc., C.A.Pa., 317 F.2d 628, cert. den. 84 S.Ct. 170, 375 U.S. 895, 11 L.Ed.2d 124.

Fidelity & Cas. Co. of New York v. Frank, D.C.Conn., 227 F.Supp. 948.

Fla.—Ratner v. Arrington, App., 111 So.2d 82.

Mo.—Aviation Enterprises, Inc. v. Cline, App., 395 S.W.2d 306.

page 760

Whether or not other particular accident reports are confidential has been adjudicated by the courts.[24.5]

24.5. Reports not privileged

N.Y.—Linton v. Lehigh Val. R. Co., 269 N.Y.S.2d 490, 25 A.D.2d 334.

25. Kan.—Bingham v. Hillcrest Bowl, Inc., 427 P.2d 591, 199 Kan. 40.

The contents of workmen's compensation claims files have been held not privileged as that concept is used in the statute declaring specified communications privileged.[26.5]

26.5. Tex.—Evans v. Casualty Reciprocal Exchange, Civ.App., 579 S.W.2d 353, err. ref. no rev. err.

Wash.—Mebust v. Mayco Mfg. Co., 506 P.2d 326, 8 Wash.App. 359.

§ 265. Communications to Prosecuting Attorney

27. Ill.—People v. Jarrett, 206 N.E.2d 835, 57 Ill. App.2d 169.

Ind.—**C.J.S.** cited in Anderson v. State, 156 N.E.2d 384, 386, 239 Ind. 372.

F.D.I.C. referrals to U.S. Attorney

U.S.—Federal Deposit Ins. Corp. v. Cherry, Bekaert & Holland, M.D.Fla., 131 F.R.D. 596.

29. Statute inapplicable where no damage to public interest

Minn.—Sprader v. Mueller, 130 N.W.2d 147, 269 Minn. 25.

State's attorney mediator not privileged

Fla.—State v. Castellano, App. 2 Dist., 460 So.2d 480.

page 761

33. Report of store's security officer

Ill.—People v. Jenkins, 309 N.E.2d 397, 18 Ill.App.3d 52.

§ 266. Rule of Exclusion

Library References

Witnesses ⚮188(1) et seq.

page 762

47. Del.—Pierce v. State, 437 A.2d 851.

Predicate for change

U.S.—U.S. v. Owens, D.C.Tenn., 424 F.Supp. 421.

48. Ariz.—State v. Watkins, 614 P.2d 835, 126 Ariz. 293.

Pretrial interspousal communications

Iowa—State v. Pepples, 250 N.W.2d 390.

49. U.S.—Trammel v. U.S., Colo., 100 S.Ct. 906, 445 U.S. 40, 63 L.Ed.2d 186.

U.S. v. Harper, C.A.Miss., 450 F.2d 1032.

Merlin v. Aetna Life Ins. Co., D.C.N.Y., 180 F.Supp. 90.

Ala.—Cooper v. Mann, 143 So.2d 637, 273 Ala. 620.

Ark.—Sumlin v. State, 617 S.W.2d 372, 273 Ark. 185.

Fla.—Ross v. State, App., 202 So.2d 582.

Ill.—People v. Fritz, 417 N.E.2d 612, 48 Ill.Dec. 880, 84 Ill.2d 72.

Mo.—Oliver v. Oliver, App., 325 S.W.2d 33.

Neb.—Blohme v. Blohme, 89 N.W.2d 127, 166 Neb. 369, reh. den. 91 N.W.2d 30, 167 Neb. 1.

N.J.—Touma v. Touma, 357 A.2d 25, 140 N.J.Super. 544.

N.Y.—Prink v. Rockefeller Center, Inc., 398 N.E.2d 517, 48 N.Y.2d 309, 422 N.Y.S.2d 911.

Lewis v. Hynes, 368 N.Y.S.2d 738, 82 Misc.2d 256, affd., 379 N.Y.S.2d 374, 51 A.D.2d 550.

N.C.—State v. Harvell, 262 S.E.2d 850, 45 N.C.App. 243, review den., app. dism., 269 S.E.2d 626, 300 N.C.App. 200.

Okl.—Terry Motor Co. v. Mixon, 336 P.2d 351.

Or.—State v. Lindley, 502 P.2d 390, 11 Or.App. 417.

Pa.—Com. v. Wilkes, 199 A.2d 411, 414 Pa. 246, cert. den. 85 S.Ct. 344, 379 U.S. 939, 13 L.Ed.2d 349.

S.C.—South Carolina State Highway Dept. v. Booker, 195 S.E.2d 615, 260 S.C. 245.

The reason for the rule, etc.

Fla.—Smith v. State, App., 344 So.2d 915.

(2) Other statements.

Md.—Coleman v. State, 380 A.2d 49, 281 Md. 538, 98 A.L.R.3d 1275.

Does not bar evidence that conversation took place

Mass.—Gallagher v. Goldstein, 524 N.E.2d 53, 402 Mass. 457.

Applicable only to communications successfully made

Wash.—State v. Wilder, 529 P.2d 1109, 12 Wash.App. 296.

Unauthorized out-of-court disclosures

Wis.—Muetze v. State, 243 N.W.2d 393, 73 Wis.2d 117.

page 763

50. Kan.—State v. Johnson, 621 P.2d 992, 229 Kan. 42.

51. Ill.—In Interest of Baby Boy Butt, 395 N.E.2d 1, 32 Ill.Dec. 54, 76 Ill.App.3d 587.

Ind.—Shepherd v. State, 277 N.E.2d 165, 257 Ind. 229.

La.—State v. Bennett, 357 So.2d 1136.

N.Y.—People v. Allman, 298 N.Y.S.2d 363, 59 Misc.2d 209.

Tenn.—Burton v. State, Cr., 501 S.W.2d 814.

Wash.—State v. Diana, 604 P.2d 1312, 24 Wash.App. 908.

Marital privilege not applicable to crime against wife

Kan.—State v. Johnson, 621 P.2d 992, 229 Kan. 42.

☐ ASSIGNMENT 5.7

Using the excerpts in Exhibits 5.2 and 5.3 of legal encyclopedia and supplement pages, complete the following:

1. Provide a thorough description of steps you took to locate the answer.
2. Answer each question, giving the citation of the location in the legal encyclopedia where the answer is located.
3. Determine whether the answer to the question has changed based on the supplement, giving the citation to include the supplement.

⫸ STRATEGY

Use of Legal Encyclopedia

1. After preparation of your research query, consult the legal dictionary/thesauruses to confirm that you are using the term properly and that you have enlisted all relevant terminology.
2. Using the list of relevant terms, consult the subject index of the legal encyclopedia. If you are unsuccessful in locating references to specific topics and sections that are pertinent to your query, consult the table of general topics and compare your list of relevant terms to locate similar terminology that may assist you in further narrowing your search.
3. Once you have identified a specific term in the subject index, you will be referred to a topic and section number. Locate the volume containing the general topic (these are arranged alphabetically), then turn to the exact section. There you should find a brief discussion pertinent to your query. Below the discussion will be the footnoted references.
4. After consulting the bound volume, consult the supplement for any recent changes of law on the topic and section.

CHAPTER SUMMARY

The purpose of this chapter has been to acquaint you with the purpose and benefits of legal dictionaries, thesauruses, and encyclopedias. Although such publications are those that you have probably consulted in the past, those prepared for legal subjects are confined primarily to legal issues. The legal dictionary may contain individual words, terms, and even phrases in other languages. The thesaurus is helpful to expand your research query in terms that you may otherwise be unfamiliar with. Finally, the legal encyclopedia is useful to educate you about basic principles of law within a subject; it can also be used as a basis for authority when you want to demonstrate what generally accepted legal standards on a topic have been established. As a general rule, when including research within legal encyclopedias, you should always consult not only the source but also any supplements to ensure that your information remains accurate and current.

KEY TERMS

case of first impression   terms of art

SELF-TEST

MULTIPLE CHOICE

1. Nearly all legal publications are indexed by _____ in some form.
   a) subject
   b) page number
   c) chapter number
   d) book title

2. The legal dictionary provides you with the meaning attached to a word by the _____ .
   a) ethical interpretation
   b) ordinary interpretation
   c) legal interpretation
   d) none of the above

3. A benefit of a legal dictionary is that it often contains definitions for terms, known as _____ , that sometimes do not even appear in ordinary dictionaries.
   a) terms of art
   b) phrases
   c) multiple phraseology
   d) terms of documentation

4. A legal dictionary is _____ in the same manner as other dictionaries.
   a) indexed
   b) described
   c) subdivided
   d) arranged

5. *Words and Phrases* provides reference to _____ for each term in which the term was explained in some form of primary authority.
   a) legal encyclopedia
   b) citation of authority
   c) dictionary
   d) A.L.R.

TRUE/FALSE

_____ 6. *Words and Phrases* is updated periodically through the use of supplements.

_____ 7. Legal encyclopedias focus on well-established and widely accepted statutes.

_____ 8. Citation of legal encyclopedias is quite common in cases of first impression.

_____ 9. Conducting your early research assignments in legal dictionaries and encyclopedias is an excellent way to begin understanding the terms and issues.

_____10. A legal dictionary is an alphabetical arrangement of synonyms.

FILL-IN-THE BLANKS

11. A legal thesaurus contains _____ and _____.

12. The _____ _____ of the legal encyclopedia is arranged alphabetically.

13. Another method of research in a legal encyclopedia is done through the use of _____ _____.

14. Subject categories are arranged _____.

15. _____ within a category are not arranged alphabetically.

16. As a general rule standard legal dictionaries are not _____.

17. Supplementation is the most _____ method to publish any changes or updating that should be brought to the attention of the reader.

18. Legal encyclopedias often use
_____ _____
supplements (containing all changes in
the years since the last hardbound
publication).

19. You should always consult the
encyclopedia and the _____,

as even widely accepted legal standards
change from time to time.

20. Information included in the supplement is
newer citations to the footnotes and any
_____ changes that have
occurred in the law.

CHAPTER **6**

THE SEARCH FOR STATUTORY AUTHORITY

CHAPTER OBJECTIVES

Upon completion of this chapter, you should have developed the following competencies:

- Describe the process of legislation.
- Distinguish a statutory publication from an annotated statutory publication.
- Explain the organization of a statutory publication.
- Describe the various types of statutory publications.
- Compare federal and statutory law.
- Distinguish between substantive and procedural law.
- Identify subjects that are likely to be the subject of statutory law.
- Explain the process of statutory research.
- Identify the finding tool features of statutory law.
- Discuss the purpose and benefits of cumulative supplements to statutory law.

CODES AND ANNOTATED STATUTES

annotated statutes

Statutory compilation with accompanying headnotes (annotations) of judicial opinions that have applied and/or interpreted the statute.

legislative history

Information about the background and rationale for legislation.

In Chapter 1, a distinction was made between codes and **annotated statutes.** Both contain the effective law of a jurisdiction. Both may have similar names incorporating titles such as "Revised Statutes" or "Code." The distinction is the supplemental feature of annotations. A standard statutory publication contains the language of the statutes, the heading, topic and section number, date of enactment, and sometimes legislative history. The **legislative history** describes the actions and intent of the legislature when the law was passed. The statutes may be arranged by topic alphabetically, or they may be grouped into smaller codes, which then arrange information by topic alphabetically within each smaller code.

A statutory publication that is annotated connects the statutory publication to publications of judicial law as well as to other types of legal publications. After each statute are headnotes and citations of cases in which the judicial branch has examined the statute as it applied to parties of a lawsuit. This list of headnotes and citations may include only a few cases, or it may include literally thousands. When there are numerous headnotes, they are generally broken into consecutively numbered subject groupings. By looking at the table of annotated subjects that precede them, you can identify the subject number that represents cases on a particular aspect of the statute. You would then go to this number and it would be followed by those annotations.

If you are concerned only with the language of a statute, annotated statutes can be a cumbersome source for research. Because of all the additional information included, they are generally much more extensive in terms of number and size of volumes than an ordinary statutory code. However, if you are interested in how the statute has been applied, an annotated statute can be an excellent method to connect your statutory and judicial research. In annotated statutes, you are immediately provided with citations of judicial opinions that contain a discussion about the exact statute you are researching. Do not, however, allow the annotated statute to shortcut your research. There may be other cases that address the legal issue without addressing the statutory language. These are not included in the annotations. In another chapter, comprehensive judicial research will be more closely examined.

To properly understand the distinction between statutory and other types of primary authority, you must understand the method by which they are created. It is generally understood that courts apply legal standards to individual parties and thereby establish new legal standards. Surprisingly few, however, actually understand the legislative process and how incredibly well it addresses the needs of society given the size of the task. For purposes of discussion, the legislative procedure will be addressed generally. Most state governments have a legislative process similar to that of the federal government, described next.

The Creation of Statutory Law

The Process of Legislation.   When a proposed law is introduced to the legislature, it is called a bill. A bill is sponsored by a legislator who introduces

it. When a bill is formally proposed as **legislation,** it is registered with the clerk of the legislature and assigned a number. Usually, the number corresponds to the year or session of the legislature in which the bill was introduced and the order in which it was proposed with respect to the other bills proposed during the same year or session. Often, the bill is also known by the name of the legislator(s) who introduce it, e.g., the Gramm-Rudman Act. Officially, however, the bill is referred to by its assigned number. As the bill progresses through the legislative process, it carries the same number for identification until such time as it is voted into law or defeated.

Once a bill has been introduced, it is assigned to the appropriate committee of legislators for consideration of its contents and its potential ramifications as law. Congress has created a number of such continuing committees to study the need for legislation and proposed laws in specific areas of government, commerce, and other appropriate legislative subjects. At times, the bill will be revised while in committee, with additions or deletions that are necessary to make it a complete and effective statute. After committee hearings, the bill is presented to the body of Congress where it originated (House of Representatives or Senate) for a vote by the legislators. The bill must pass by a majority vote before it can be sent to the other body for consideration. Prior to a vote, the bill is discussed and debated by Congress. At this time, changes also may be made in the language of the bill. Often, such changes are necessary to gain the approval of a sufficient number of legislators to pass the bill. If a bill succeeds by a majority vote in the body of Congress where it began, it moves on to the corresponding body. For example, if a bill is introduced in the House of Representatives and passes by a majority vote, the final version is then submitted to the Senate. If the bill passes by a majority in the corresponding body of Congress, it is forwarded to the president for approval or disapproval.

With the exception of Nebraska, which has a unicameral (one body) legislature, the process is quite similar for state statutory law. If passed by the legislature, the law is then presented to the executive officer, which at the state level is the governor.

This is the point when the **veto** power may be exercised. The veto is a key element in the system of checks and balances in a democratic government. Each branch of government has a method to influence the other branches. Such a mechanism is designed to prevent one branch from obtaining too much power or acting in a way that is inconsistent with the U.S. Constitution. According to Article I of the U.S. Constitution, each bill that has received a majority vote in both houses of Congress shall be presented to the president for approval. After the president receives the bill, under the Constitution, it must be acted upon within ten days (excluding Sundays). If nothing is done in this time, the bill automatically becomes law without presidential approval on the date indicated. If the president signs the bill, it becomes law on the date indicated by Congress. If the president returns the bill with objections to the house where it originated, it is vetoed (rejected). Once a bill has been vetoed, a second vote can be taken. If each body of Congress approves the bill by at least a two-thirds majority (rather than the previous simple majority), the bill becomes law regardless of the presidential veto. In actuality, this method is quite effective. Congress passes those laws that the members believe to be the will of the people. If the president considers this belief to be misguided, the executive branch has the power to force a reconsideration by Congress.

legislation
Statutory law created by an elected legislative body (e.g., Congress).

veto
Authority of the executive branch to cancel or reject recently enacted legislation.

However, if a significant majority of senators and representatives hold the position that the public contends the bill should become law, the veto can be overridden. A similar method of approval or rejection exists with the governor at the state level. (See Exhibit 6.1)

Codification and Legislative Publications. Congress meets several months of each year to consider proposed laws. These meetings are collectively called sessions. Each annual session is numbered consecutively, e.g., 85th Congress, 86th Congress. After a full session of Congress has been concluded, all laws passed during the session take on the inclusive name of **session law.** U.S. session laws are published in the **statutes at large.** Most states have similar publications. Each session law is assigned a public law number that represents the session of Congress in which the law was passed and the chronological order of the law in relation to other laws passed during the same session. For example, Public law 92-397 would be the 397th law proposed (and ultimately passed) during the 92nd session of Congress. Each session law is identified by its public law number until such time as it can be incorporated into a code, which is the publication of virtually all statutes currently in effect in the jurisdiction and organized by general topic.

In many jurisdictions, to avoid confusion, the bill number and the session law number are the same. Consequently, there may be gaps in the consecutively numbered session laws, because not all bills introduced become law. The process of incorporating the public law into the existing code is known as codification. At this time, the new laws are renumbered to reflect their location within the code (rather than the previous number, which represented the time of introduction and passage).

session law
A statute that has been passed during a specific term of a legislative body (e.g., the 95th Congress).

statutes at large
Publication of all session laws passed in a given term of a legislative body.

EXHIBIT 6.1
Typical Steps in the Legislative Process.

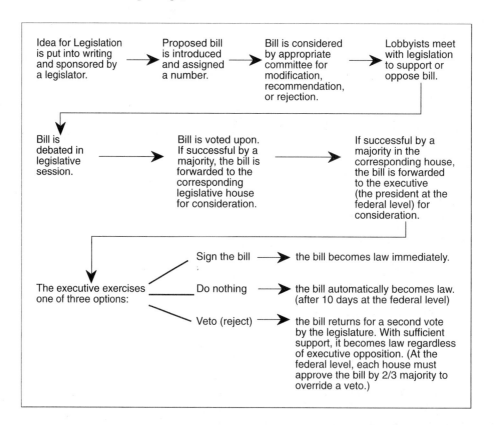

In addition to session laws and codes, copies of recently enacted individual laws may be obtained directly from the clerk of the legislature. These individual copies are referred to as **slip laws.** Slip laws are usually not published for wide distribution, but rather are distributed based upon individual requests.

Sometimes several bills on one subject will be introduced to Congress as a package of related but individual laws for legislation on that subject which addresses various aspects of the subject. When this occurs, the package of bills is known as an act. Other laws may be introduced individually or as additional amendments to laws of an act that has already been passed in a previous session of Congress. Another type of bill is that which has the sole purpose of repealing (cancelling) an existing law.

All federal laws passed by Congress and currently in effect are published in a multivolume set. Federal laws are officially published in the United States Code (commonly referred to as U.S.C.). The annotated version published by West is the United States Code Annotated, or U.S.C.A. Because laws are constantly being added, deleted, or modified, it is a difficult task to keep them organized in a single permanent set of books. Usually, state collections of existing laws are known as Revised Statutes or Codes. State law publications and the U.S.C. are updated through the use of periodic supplements.

The U.S.C. is located in multiple bound volumes, and the method by which it is organized enables the statutes to remain current in light of constant change. Under this method of organization of laws (known as codification), all laws are divided by basic subject. For example, virtually all laws pertaining to banking institutions are located in one section in the statutes, known as a title, e.g, "Banking." (This is similar to chapters in a textbook. Each chapter deals with a different subject and bears a name that indicates what subject is addressed in that part of the text.)

All subjects are arranged in alphabetical order, and each law within a title (subject) is assigned a section number. This way, the organization of the laws can always be revised. If one law exists and is later amended, the amendment is assigned the same number as the previous law. For example, Title 21, Section 1316, can be amended and the new language of Section 1316 printed where the prior language previously appeared. If an additional law is passed on a general subject (title) and that particular law is new to the subject, it is assigned a new section number that is not assigned to any other law on the subject. For example, assume Section 1316 is the last law to appear in Title 21. If a new law is passed, it might be assigned Section 1317. Consequently, the subject of law will lead one to the correct title (grouping of laws on a particular topic). Each title contains a table of contents listing specific sections (laws) of the title and descriptive headings for each section. There is also an extensive subject index to the statutes that makes them even more accessible.

As stated previously, the U.S. Code takes up several volumes. It would be impractical to publish an entirely new set after every session of Congress to incorporate information from laws that are newly passed, amended, or repealed. For this reason, supplements are used between publications of the bound volumes. After each session of Congress, the session laws are codified (given their permanent title and section numbers) and published in supplement volumes to the code. Usually, these are in pocket-part form or pamphlet form located next to the hardbound volume where the codified law will eventually appear. Supplements are published annually to incorporate changes from the most recent session of Congress and all past sessions that

slip law
Singular publication of a statute that generally is not published but must be requested or subscribed to by the clerk of the legislature.

have occurred since the last bound publication. If an existing law cannot be found in the bound code, it is probably located in the corresponding supplement. Periodically, newly bound editions are published that incorporate all prior supplements, and the process of supplementation begins again. Keep in mind that statutory research is never complete until all relevant supplements have been consulted.

Constitutional Law

Earlier in the text, the hierarchy of laws was addressed. In that discussion, the point was made that judicial law is ordinarily subordinate to legislative law. The exception to this rule occurs when the judicial branch, by its interpretation, finds a law to be unconstitutional. In such a case, the judicial branch has the authority to declare the law invalid because it violates the guarantees to all citizens found in the Constitution. When this occurs, there is only one means by which the legislative branch can override the action of the judicial branch, and this is through an amendment to the Constitution.

The process of passing a constitutional amendment is substantially similar to passing statutory law. However, the standards to gain approval are somewhat higher. Because the Constitution is the ultimate law of the land, an amendment must pass both houses by a two-thirds majority, rather than the typical simple majority. Additionally, in the case of a constitutional amendment, two thirds of the states can propose such an amendment to the Congress besides the more traditional method of introduction. Once properly approved by Congress, the amendment must then be approved by three fourths of the state legislatures before it is ratified and becomes part of the U.S. Constitution. This is different from the regular legislative process, which requires law passed by Congress to be reviewed only by the president. By placing such stringent requirements on constitutional amendments, it is extremely difficult to pass a law that is not representative of the will of the people nationwide. In the United States, the original Constitution and Bill of Rights have been amended on only 17 occasions in more than 200 years. However, judicial interpretation of the provisions of the Constitution versus statutory language occurs regularly.

☐ ASSIGNMENT 6.1

Examine each of the following situations and determine how far in the legislative process the bill has proceeded. (Refer to Exhibit 6.1)

1. A statute making the burning of the American flag a violation of the U.S. Constitution is voted on and approved by three fourths of the state legislatures.
2. A bill is under consideration by a congressional committee at the close of a session of Congress.
3. A bill is assigned a permanent number to be included with other effective law.
4. A bill is voted upon by one house of Congress at the end of the congressional session.
5. A bill is rejected by the president.

Substantive and Procedural Law

Constitutional law has certain unique characteristics that distinguish it from other types of law. Similarly, all other statutory law can be categorized by its own characteristics. One such method of distinction is substantive law and procedural law. However, these types of law serve very different functions. Both types impact the legal right of parties, and thus both are frequently the subject of legal research.

Substantive Law.   According to *West's Legal Dictionary/Thesaurus*, 896, 1985, substantive law creates, defines, and regulates rights, as opposed to adjective, procedural, or remedial law, which provides a method of enforcing rights. Substantive law is exactly what its name implies. It is the body, essence, and substance that guides the conduct of citizens. It encompasses principles of right and wrong as well as the principle that wrong will result in penalty. It includes the rights and duties of citizens, and it provides the basis to resolve issues involving those rights and duties. Every citizen has the right to live and enjoy his or her own property free from intrusion by other citizens. All members of a populous society are obligated to respect and to not interfere with the rights of others. Substantive law establishes the extent of this right and obligation to which all persons are subject.

When a person engages in conduct producing an adverse effect or another individual, an injury may occur. The innocent yet injured party wants to be compensated for the damage caused by the injury. The innocent injured party requests assistance from the legal system on the basis that the guilty party acted wrongfully. This wrongful conduct gave rise to the dispute between the two parties. The court will examine the situation to determine whether the conduct of the alleged guilty party was indeed wrongful by society's standards. If it was wrongful, the party will be judged guilty and be penalized. If it was not, the party will be judged not guilty. In either event, the court resolves the issue based on what society has determined to be right and wrong conduct between individuals and entities.

In legal research, quite often the issue you are researching is based on substantive law. The parties to a lawsuit usually have different interpretations of what their conduct should be or should have been based on a legal principle. In research, you will located the legal principle and analyze it as it applies to the current situation. You must also then analyze any other primary authority, such as judicial opinions that have applied the principle in other cases. Then, as discussed in previous chapters, you are in a position to predict how the principle will be applied to produce an outcome in the current situation.

Procedural Law.   According to *Statsky's Legal Dictionary/Thesaurus*, 605, 1985, procedural law prescribes a method of enforcing rights or of obtaining redress for the invasion of rights. The basic function of **procedural law** is to facilitate the movement of a lawsuit through the legal system. Such laws are created to ensure that each party is afforded fair and impartial treatment. Further, procedural law has as its goal that the judge and jury who hear the case will be provided only with evidence that will allow them to make a fair and impartial decision. Procedural rules can be likened to a large piece of machinery that assembles a product. The machinery does not feel or possess

opinions. The function of procedural law is to assemble all of the pieces into a complete product. The parties to the suit provide the pieces to the product at appropriate times and in the appropriate manner. The completed product delivered from the machine is the decision that resolves the dispute. This decision is based upon the pieces of information (substantive law and facts of the case) that have been fed into the machine and assembled.

Procedural law also plays a significant part in litigation that includes the following:

1. The time limit for bringing a lawsuit.
2. The manner in which the lawsuit is begun (e.g., by filing a complaint or petition).
3. The proper way to inform the defendant that a lawsuit has been filed.
4. The types of information that each party must release to the other party.
5. The procedure at trial.
6. The evidence that can be introduced at trial.
7. The method for appealing the decision if the losing party feels it was unfair.

Types of Procedural Law. For the sake of convenience, procedural law has been divided into several categories. A person researching the law has a much easier time finding the particular laws or rules that apply to a given case if the law is organized according to category. Most often, a jurisdiction will divide its procedural law into the following categories:

1. Rules of civil procedure.
2. Rules of criminal procedure.
3. Rules of evidence.
4. Rules of appellate procedure.

Courts generally have the power to create, in addition to the rules that are enacted into law for an entire jurisdiction, local rules. These are rules that apply only to the court that creates them and to no other court. An example would be a county court. The procedural laws of the state apply to all of the state courts, including county courts, but each county court may enact its own local rules as well. Local rules are designed to supplement the state laws of procedure. In the section of this chapter dealing with research methods for statutory law, special attention will be given to the organization of procedural statutory law.

WHAT SUBJECTS OF LAW ARE LIKELY TO BE STATUTORY?

At first you may think, how could someone possibly know what law is statutory and what law is administrative, or case law. Unless you already know the exact legal principle you are researching, this is something you usually can't know for certain. But you will develop a strong sense of what law is likely to be statutory or administrative, or judicial. As you develop this skill, the time necessary to properly research an issue will shorten.

Some rules of thumb exist that will assist you in determining the types of law that are likely to be statutory. First, all primary authorities stating what constitutes a criminal act are statutory. This is guaranteed by the U.S. Constitution. The legislature cannot enact a statute making certain conduct criminal and provide for punishment of persons who performed the conduct before it was declared illegal. The process of punishing someone for conduct that occurred before the conduct was made illegal is known as an ex post facto law and is prohibited by Article I, Section 9, of the Constitution. In our country, a primary element of all criminal laws is the concept of fair warning. Under the U.S. Constitution, this means that one must be capable of determining that a particular conduct would be considered criminal before the fact. Allowing persons to perform some act and then making that act a criminal offense and prosecuting them for it would not be fair. Consequently, all substantive criminal law is statutory as a product of the requirement for fair notice.

A second consideration in determining the likelihood of a principle of law being statutory is activities that are engaged in by a large portion of the population and affect others. The legislative law sets standards for these activities, which in turn guide the general public in their conduct. Examples include traffic laws, licensing laws for various professions, laws for the operation of certain businesses, such as insurance sales. If your research is focused on some aspect of such an activity, you can be reasonably certain that a statutory law exists to cover it.

Finally, a subject closely related to statutory law is administrative law. All administrative regulations are designed to clarify and enforce statutory law. Administrative agencies are constitutionally prohibited from making statutory law. Therefore, any law from an administrative agency ultimately emanates from statutory law. An example would be the Federal Communications Commission (FCC). The FCC regulates all electrical communications across the airwaves. If you are conducting research on the authority of the FCC to regulate a certain subject, persons, or entity, you know that as an administrative agency, the FCC has authority that is ultimately statutory.

In contrast, subjects that are particularly unique or tend to be strongly affected by individual circumstances are likely not be statutory. For example, while there is a statute in virtually every state that prohibits driving at a speed unsafe for existing road and weather conditions (regardless of the statutory speed limit), the issue of whether driving 45 m.p.h. in a 40-m.p.h. zone during snowfall at a rate of one inch per hour constitutes illegal behavior is probably a matter for the courts. While the driver may be guilty of a statutory violation, he or she might not be considered in violation of the "driving too fast for conditions" statute under the totality of the circumstances (e.g., the road was flat and straight, there was no other traffic, the pavement was well lit, and the temperature was such that most of the snow on the road was melting).

☐ ASSIGNMENT 6.2

Evaluate the following topics and state why you think they are (or are not) likely to be addressed by statutory law.

    a. Requirements for a valid will.
    b. Duties of business owners for safety of customers.

   c. Fees charged by attorneys.

   d. Amount of staff per number of visitors required by public facilities (such as arenas) for public functions.

   e. Acceptable methods to serve notice of a divorce action on a spouse.

   f. Rights of an owner who has lent personal property, such as a lawn mower, to a neighbor who damages the property.

   g. Right of lease tenant to adequate notice before a rent increase.

   h. Whether certain evidence is admissible in a trial.

   i. Towing of cars parked on private property without permission.

   j. Circumstances in which a will can be overturned because of improper influence on decedent prior to death.

METHODS OF LOCATING STATUTORY LAW

The preliminary steps of research are essentially the same regardless of the sources you consult. After you have focused on the issue, familiarized yourself with the topic, and framed your query, the preparation is complete. At this point, you must determine to which sources you will apply your query to obtain the answer. This includes both whether the answers are likely to be statutory or judicial and whether the controlling authority is of federal or state law origin. For example, if you have decided that your issue is likely to be addressed at least in part by statutory law, your first stop should be at the appropriate statutory compilation. If the issue is federal (i.e., it involves some branch of federal government, law, or a constitutional right), the issue is likely to be controlled by statutory law. Otherwise, your answer is more than likely found in a state statutory publication. You should go to the appropriate publication to begin your search.

Subject Indexing

Most statutory publications are organized in a similar manner. After all laws are categorized by subject, the general subjects are then arranged alphabetically and numbered consecutively. For example, if agriculture was the first of the alphabetized subjects of law, it would be number one, and so on. Each statute within a subject is given a number. No number is ever used more than once, even if the first law assigned a particular number is repealed.

As mentioned earlier, some jurisdictions categorize the codes into separate smaller subcodes or subcategories, and some simply divide the statutes into topics known as titles or as chapters and even subchapters. The subcode method of organization frequently occurs with procedural law. There are not only a great number of individual procedural laws but also numerous subtypes of procedural law. When a code is broken down this way, the proper citation may be to the smaller code rather than the statutory publication (e.g., Fed. R. Civ. Pro. 4). You should consult the statutory publication and the bluebook for proper citation of a particular subcode, such as that commonly used with procedural law.

Statutory publications usually begin or end with detailed subject indexes. Your research query should contain several terms to be used in research. By

locating these terms in the subject index, you will be referred to a topic and statute number. The first number represents the subject. For example, Title 15 is represented in the citation 15 U.S.C. § 1211. The second number indicates the specific statute within a subject.

Your next step is to locate the statute. By examining the cover of the hardbound volumes, you can identify which volume contains the subject number corresponding to the subject you are searching for. Then, locate that subject within the volume and proceed to the specific statute. While the statutes are arranged in proper numerical order, they may appear to skip forward. This is because as statutes are repealed, they are removed from the next hardbound edition. As a result, the first statute in a topic may be numbered 2,106 rather than 100.

When reading a statute, you should make sure that what you are reading is actually the text of the statute. Quite often the publication will include additional information about the statute, such as annotations. You may also see information about amendments to the statute, legislative history, and other types of related information. Generally, the collateral information will be titled, and frequently, it is in a different style of type. The statutory text will appear directly below a boldface number (statute number) and title of the statute. The text may then be broken into subparts, but these are also usually clearly marked.

☐ ASSIGNMENT 6.3

From the excerpted pages in Exhibit 6.2 of a statutory subject index, identify those statutes that you think would answer the following questions:

1. Is it illegal just to threaten to kidnap the president?
2. What is the government definition of synthetic rubber?
3. How is the Secretary of the Navy appointed?
4. Is there a federal provision for inspection of dead chickens?
5. Is federal money available for grants to improve education for gifted Indian children?
6. Must exported pears be inspected?
7. What is the purpose of the Coast Guard Auxiliary?
8. Is there a mandatory retirement age for firefighters?
9. What is a public aircraft?
10. What law addresses acquisition of atomic energy disposal contracts?
11. Are there laws about anchoring a boat in Pearl Harbor?
12. Is it illegal to sell the eggs of a bald eagle?
13. Are there federal programs to rid cotton fields of the boll weevil?
14. What are the legal holidays of the Internal Revenue Service?
15. Is there a federal law providing monetary grants to remove building barriers to handicapped persons?

Topic Indexing

As you know, statutes are broken down into broad subject categories, which provide an alternative method of researching statutory law. The beginning of most statutory hardbound volumes contains a list of the titles for each subject

EXHIBIT 6.2
U.S.C.A. Statutory
Subject Index
Sample Pages.
Copyright 1994 by
West Publishing
Company
(1–800 328–9352).

ATOMIC ENERGY—Cont'd
Civil penalties—Cont'd
Tailings or wastes produced by extraction of uranium, etc., **42 § 2114**
Violations,
Energy Department regulations, provisions, exceptions, **42 § 2282a**
Licensing requirements, **42 § 2282**
Civil service,
Application to officers and employees, **42 § 2201**
Classification of positions, compensation of officers and employees, **42 § 2201**
Civil Service Commission investigations to permit individual to have access to restricted data, **42 § 2165**
Civilian reactor development, cooperation with other nations as to restricted data, **42 § 2164**
Claim settlements, **42 § 2207**
Claims or judgments for damages resulting from nuclear incident involving reactor of U.S. warship, payments,
Exceptions, terms and conditions, **42 § 2211**
Settlement of, **42 § 2211 nt, EON 11918**
Coastal Zone Management, generally, this index
Combined licenses, construction permits and operating licenses,
Generally, **42 § 2235**
Effect on pending proceedings, **42 § 2235 nt**
Commercial facilities, transfer, etc., of special nuclear material produced in, limitation, **42 § 2077**
Commission,
Atomic Energy Commission, generally, ante, this heading
Defined,
Advanced nuclear reactors, energy policy, **42 § 13491**
EURATOM Cooperation Act, **42 § 2291**
General provisions, **42 § 2014**
Nuclear Regulatory Commission, generally, post, this heading
Commissioner of Patents and Trademarks, application for patents for inventions or discoveries useful in production or utilization of special nuclear material or atomic energy, **42 §§ 2181, 2182**
Common defense and security, defined, **42 § 2014**
Communication, restricted data,
Central Intelligence Agency authorized for intelligence purposes, **42 § 2162 nt, EON 10899**
State Department, authority in accordance with agreement for cooperation, **42 § 2162 nt, EON 11057**
Communist nations, restrictions on assistance of materials to under Foreign Assistance Act, **22 § 2370 nt**
Communities owned,
Generally, **42 § 2301 et seq.**
Administrative review of determinations, **42 § 2309**

ATOMIC ENERGY—Cont'd
Communities owned—Cont'd
Advances to Community Disposal Operations Fund, **42 § 2311**
Amount of indemnity, financing, **42 § 2365**
Apartment houses, priorities, purchase or sale of, **42 § 2348**
Applicability, provisions relating to sales of property for private use, **42 § 2341**
Appraisal of property, **42 § 2322 et seq.**
Appropriations, **42 § 2312**
Assignees of priority interests of occupants, eligibility, priority for purchase of apartment buildings, **42 § 2348**
Assistance in organization, **42 § 2381**
Assumption of lessor's obligations, priority sale of apartment houses, **42 § 2348**
Basis, appraisal of property, **42 § 2323**
Cash sales of property, **42 § 2344**
Classification of property, **42 § 2331**
Community, defined, **42 § 2304**
Community Disposal Operations Fund, establishment, purpose, availability, etc., **42 § 2311**
Compromise of certain claims, **42 § 2310**
Conditions, indemnity payment, etc., **42 § 2366**
Congress,
Findings, **42 § 2302**
Legislation authorizing appropriations, necessity, **42 § 2312**
Considerations, classification of real property within Los Alamos, **42 § 2331**
Constructions of utilities, appropriations, **42 § 2312**
Contents, contracts, mortgages and other instruments, **42 § 2307**
Continuation, assistance payments to governmental agencies, respecting certain localities, after termination period, **42 § 2391**
Contracts,
Acquiring, handling or disposing of property, **42 § 2310**
Assistance payments to governmental entities, **42 § 2394**
Forms, **42 § 2307**
Purchase, payments, **42 § 2361**
Declaration of policy, **42 § 2301**
Deductions from sales price, **42 § 2326**
Applicability of provisions to priority sale of apartment houses, **42 § 2348**
Deeds, leases, etc., as evidence, **42 § 2308**
Delegation of duties and responsibilities to other agencies, etc., **42 § 2313**
Determination,
Administrative review, **42 § 2309**
Amount and recipient of assistance payment to governmental entities, **42 § 2391**
Disposal, property under lease or license agreement, **42 § 2342**
Eligibility to participate in priority purchase of apartment houses, **42 § 2348**
Energy Research and Development Administration, generally, this index

EXHIBIT 6.2
Continued

853   **BALD**

BAILIFFS—Cont'd
District courts,
  Appointment, **28 § 755**
  Crier to perform duties of bailiff, **28 § 755**
United States Court of Federal Claims, appointment and removal, **28 § 795**
United States Court of International Trade, criers to perform duties of, **28 § 872**

BAILMENT
Cargo, safe containers for international cargo. International Cargo Safe Containers, generally, this index
Rules of Civil Procedure, generally, this index
Soldiers' and sailors' civil relief,
  Dependent's right to benefits, **50 Ap § 536**
  Modification, etc., of contract secured, **50 Ap § 517**
  Rescission or termination of contract after receiving deposit or installment of purchase price, **50 Ap § 531**
United States Court of Federal Claims, generally, this index

BAKER BEACH
Golden Gate National Recreation Area, right of occupancy, **16 § 460bb–2**

BAKER ISLAND
District court, jurisdiction, **48 § 644a**
Judicial district of Hawaii, inclusion in, **28 § 91**

BALANCE OF PAYMENTS
Arctic Research and Policy, generally, this index.
Armed Forces, procurement for, goods which are other than American goods, consideration given to, **10 § 2301 nt**
Asian Development Bank, development loans authorized use of U.S. Special Resources, effect on, **22 § 285j**
Customs duties, imposition, supplemental duty for purposes of, **19 nt prec § 1202, PN 4074**
Deep Seabed Hard Mineral Resources, generally, this index
Exports, regulation and control of. Imports and Exports, generally, this index
Inland waterway user taxes and charges, study, **33 § 1803**
International investment and trade in services survey, data collection program to analyze, **22 § 3103**
International Monetary Fund, this index
International Trade, this index
North Atlantic Treaty Organization, sharing of expenses to offset balance-of-payments deficit, **22 § 1928 nt**

BALANCE OF TRADE
Statistics reflecting aggregate values of U.S. imports and exports, reporting, **13 § 301**

U.S.C.A. Gen.In. A–B '94 Pamph.–19

BALANCE SHEET
Securities and Exchange Commission, registered broker and dealer to file with, **15 § 78q**

BALANCED BUDGET AND EMERGENCY DEFICIT CONTROL ACT OF 1985
Text of Act. See Popular Name Table
Budget process of Congress. Concurrent Resolutions, generally, this index
Emergency powers to eliminate deficits, deficits in excess of maximum amount. Budget, generally, this index
Short title, **2 § 900 nt**

BALANCED BUDGET AND EMERGENCY DEFICIT CONTROL REAFFIRMATION ACT OF 1987
Text of Act. See Popular Name Table
Budget, generally, this index
Short title, **2 § 901 nt**

BALANCED GROWTH
See FULL EMPLOYMENT AND BALANCED GROWTH, generally, this index

BALD EAGLE
Agricultural protection, taking for, **16 § 668a**
Appropriations for Migratory Bird Treaty Act available for administration and enforcement of provisions concerning, **16 § 668d**
Arrests, provisions concerning as applicable to, **16 § 668b**
Attorney General, institution, action for sale of, **16 § 668**
Custom duties, applicability of certain custom laws, **16 § 668b**
Damages, cancellation of grazing agreements, **16 § 668**
Definitions, protection, **16 § 668c**
Eggs, sale, penalty, **16 § 668**
Enforcement of provisions for protection of, **16 § 668b**
Evidence, recovery of penalty for violations, **16 § 668**
Execution of law relating to, law applicable, **16 § 668b**
Exhibition, purposes, taking and using for, **16 § 668a**
Exportation, sale, penalties, **16 § 668**
Falconry, permission to take, possess and transport eagles for purposes of, **16 § 668**
Federal Inspector for the Alaska Natural Gas Transportation System, transfer of certain enforcement functions from Secretary of Interior, etc., to, **5, Ap 1, RPN 1 of 1979**
Forfeiture, permit, violations concerning selling, etc., **16 § 668b**
Hearing, penalties for sale, **16 § 668**
Information leading to conviction of person violating protection provisions, payment, **16 § 668**
Interior Department, enforcement of provisions for protection of, **16 § 668b**
Jurisdiction, recovery of penalty for violations, **16 § 668**
Licenses and Permits, this index

EXHIBIT 6.2
Continued

COAST

COAST GUARD AUXILIARY—Cont'd

Assignment to Coast Guard duty, **14 § 831**
Benefits to members, limitation, **14 § 893**
Commandant of the Coast Guard,
    Administration of Auxiliary, **14 § 821**
    Members assigned to specific duties, **14 § 831**
Death of member, **14 § 832**
Disenrollment, **14 § 824**
Eligibility, **14 § 823**
Enrollments, **14 § 823**
Facilities of members, use of, **14 § 826**
Flags, **14 § 891**
    Penalty for unauthorized display, **14 § 892**
Hospital treatment, **14 § 832**
Injury to member, **14 § 832**
Insignia, **14 § 891**
    Penalty for unauthorized display, **14 § 892**
Interest, payment on claims, rate, **14 § 830**
Members,
    Generally, **14 § 823**
    Appointment or enlistment in Reserve, **14 § 825**
    Death, **14 § 832**
    Disenrollment, **14 § 824**
    Eligible to membership in other naval or military organizations, **14 § 825**
    Facilities, use of, **14 § 826**
    Injury, **14 § 832**
Motorboats,
    Flags, pennants, or other insignia, **14 § 891**
        Penalty for unauthorized display, **14 § 892**
    Members' boats assigned to Coast Guard duty, status, **14 § 827**
    Owners as members of Auxiliary, **14 § 823**
    Promoting efficiency in operation, purpose of Auxiliary, **14 § 822**
    Use of members' boats by Coast Guard, **14 § 826**
Nonmilitary organization, **14 § 821**
Obsolete or unneeded material of Coast Guard, disposal to, **14 § 641**
Pennants, **14 § 891**
    Penalty for unauthorized display, **14 § 892**
Per diem, assignment to Coast Guard duty, **14 § 831**
Powers and duties, **14 § 831**
    Limitation on rights and privileges, **14 § 893**
Purposes, **14 § 822**
Radio, this index
Ration allowance, **14 § 830**
Sickness or disease, hospital treatment, **14 § 832**
Temporary members of Reserve, **14 § 706**
Travel between place of assigned duty and residence as including specific duty, **14 § 832**
Traveling expenses, assignment to Coast Guard duty, **14 §§ 830, 831**
Unauthorized use of words "Coast Guard Auxiliary, " etc., penalty, **14 § 639**
Uniforms, **14 § 891**
    Penalty for unauthorized wearing of, **14 § 892**
Yachts, this index

COAST GUARD EXCHANGES

Contracts,
    Express or implied with,
        District courts, concurrent jurisdiction with U.S. Court of Federal Claims, civil action or claim against U.S., **28 § 1346**
        United States Court of Federal Claims, jurisdiction, claims founded on, **28 § 1491**
    Resolution of claims and disputes relating to. Public Contracts, generally, this index
Employment taxes, civilian employees, **26 §§ 3121, 3122**
Federal old-age, survivors and disability insurance benefits, civilian employees,
    As employed within Act, **42 § 410**
    Determinations as to employment, etc., **42 § 405**
    Exemption of, **42 § 410**

COAST GUARD MUTUAL ASSISTANCE

Uniformed services, deductions from pay for amounts owed to, **37 § 1007**

COAST GUARD RESERVE

For other general provisions applicable to. See, also, ARMED FORCES, generally, this index
Active duty or service,
    Agreement to serve on, condition as to designation as student aviation pilot, **14 § 709**
    Annual training requirement, satisfaction of on day to day basis by active duty for emergency augmentation of regular forces, **14 § 712**
Aviation pilots, **14 § 709**
Benefits, entitlement, **14 § 705**
Coast Guard Academy cadet refusing to accept appointment as officer, etc., and transferred to Reserve, **14 § 182**
Emergency augmentation of regular forces, ordering members to, **14 § 712**
Enlistment of members engaged in schooling, **14 § 713**
Grade on entry upon, **14 § 745**
Length of, promotion lists, **14 § 725**
Non-prior service person qualified for induction but not under orders to report under Military Selective Service Act, performance, initial period of, **10 § 511**
Officers, post, this heading
Powers and privileges, **14 § 704**
Promotion lists, precedence when transferred from reserve lists, **14 § 725**
Rank and precedence of officers on promotion lists, **14 § 725**
Recall to duty of member released after wartime appointment or promotion, **14 § 710**
Release of,
    Student aviation pilot from, **14 § 709**

EXHIBIT 6.2
Continued

797 **COTTON**

COTTON—Cont'd

Analyses of fiber properties, spinning tests and other tests, 7 § 473d

Annual revision, cost of production study, 7 § 1441a

Appendix to, Harmonized Tariff Schedules of U.S., 7 § 1444

Apportionment,
 National acreage reserve, 7 § 1344
  Inapplicability to upland cotton, certain crop years, 7 § 1342 nt
 States, counties and farms, national base acreage allotment for upland cotton, certain crop years, 7 § 1350

Appropriations,
 Authorization, cotton research and promotion, 7 § 2101 nt
 Insect eradication programs, 7 § 1444a

Assessments, collection and payment, etc., research and promotion, 7 § 2106

Assignment,
 Option contracts, 7 § 607
 Payments, upland cotton, certain crop years, 7 § 1444-2

Availability for inspection of records pertaining to acreage allotments and marketing quotas, 7 § 1344

Average yield for year, determination, price support, 7 § 1444

Bales,
 National marketing quota, 7 § 1342
 Records and reports of cotton ginners, census, 13 § 43
 Report of number of linter, census, 13 § 42

Barbadenese species or hybrid thereof, "extra long staple cotton" as meaning cotton produced from pure strain varieties of, etc., program beginning with certain crop year, 7 § 1444

Board, consumer advisors appointed to membership, 7 § 2106

Boll weevils, programs to eradicate, 7 § 1444a

Bond, export market acreage, 7 § 1349

Borrowing on cotton, authority of Agriculture Secretary, 7 § 604

Carry-over,
 Defined, 7 § 1301
 Estimation of, 7 § 471

Census,
 Publication of statistics, 13 § 41 et seq.
 Simultaneous publication of cotton reports, 13 § 45

Central filing system, required information, ownership interests of persons in cotton, etc., 7 § 259

Certified mail, request for information forwarded by, 7 § 473

Changes in farming operations determinations by Secretary, limitation on payments for certain crop years, 7 § 1308

Classification,
 Sampling for classification, generally, post, this heading
 Services, availability to producers by Secretary of Agriculture, fees, collection, 7 § 473a

COTTON—Cont'd

Collection and publication of statistics, 13 § 41 et seq.
 Secretary of Agriculture, 7 § 471

Commodity certificates, redemption, limitations, 7 § 1445k nt

Commodity Credit Corporation,
 Authorized program carried out through, upland cotton, certain crop years, 7 § 1444-2
 Cropland set-aside program for certain crop years, duties, 7 § 1444
 Donations to educational institutions, 7 § 1431a
 Export sales program, 7 § 1853
 Insect eradication programs, duties, etc., concerning, 7 § 1444a
 Insurance by, 7 § 1383
 Payment-in-kind certificates, 7 § 1348
  Price supports, 7 § 1444
 Price support program provisions carried out through, 7 § 1444
 Sales, 7 § 1427
  American grown extra long staple cotton, market prices, 7 § 1427
  Export, 7 § 1852
  Extra long staple cotton, unrestricted use, 7 § 1427
  Restrictions, 7 § 1427
  Upland cotton, 7 § 1427
   Unrestricted use, 7 § 1427
 Special grazing and hay program, certain crop years, duties, 7 § 1445d

Commodity Exchanges, generally, this index

Comptroller General, reports, administration, etc., research and promotion, 7 § 2101 nt

Conditions,
 Eligibility for loans and payments on upland cotton, producers to set aside and devote to approved conservation uses, certain acreage, 7 § 1444
 Transfer, acreage allotment, 7 § 1344b

Confidential information, 7 § 472

Conservation,
 Reserve contract, adjustment upon transfer of land covered by, 7 § 1344b
 Uses,
  Condition, eligibility for loans and payments of upland cotton to producers, setting aside and devoting certain acreage to, 7 § 1444
  Production or haying and grazing on acreage devoted to, 7 § 1444-2

Cooperation,
 Federal Government with State governments,
  Investigation of new uses, 7 § 423
  Statistics and estimates, 7 § 474
 With Mexican Government, insect eradication programs, 7 § 1444a

Cooperators,
 Defined, price support, upland cotton, 7 § 1428
 Price supports, 7 § 1444

EXHIBIT 6.2
Continued

HANDICAPPED PERSONS AND CHIL-
DREN—Cont'd
Education—Cont'd
Assistance for education of all children, etc.,
with disabilities—Cont'd
Centers and services to meet special
needs of disabled—Cont'd
Experimental, demonstration, and out-
reach pre-school and intervention
programs, 20 § 1423
Federal Register, notice published in,
intent to accept application for
grants, etc., 20 § 1423
Grants and contracts, experimental programs, development and operation,
20 § 1423
Identification of needs of children with
disabilities, grants or contracts, 20
§ 1423
Indian tribes, experimental programs,
arrangements with, 20 § 1423
Personnel training, grants or contracts,
20 § 1423
Regional resource centers, assistance
from technical assistance center, 20
§ 1421
Technical assistance development program, 20 § 1423
Certification, actual number of children
receiving special education and related services, duties of Secretary, 20
§ 1417
Civil action, complaints by parents, etc.,
20 § 1415
Clearinghouses, dissemination of information to, 20 § 1418
Commingling of Federal funds with State
funds prohibited, contents, State
plan, assurances, 20 § 1413
Complaints, opportunity to present respecting identification, etc., of child,
etc., required procedures, 20 § 1415
Composition, State advisory panel, contents, State plan, 20 § 1413
Comprehensive system of personnel development, requisite feature, State
plan, 20 § 1413
Conclusiveness, Secretary's findings concerning State plans, 20 § 1416
Conditions, qualification for assistance, 20
§ 1412
Congressional committees,
Annual reports by Secretary to,
Deaf-blind infants, toddlers, children
and youth, 20 § 1422
Early education for children with disabilities, 20 § 1423
Progress toward provision of free appropriate public education, 20
§ 1418
Regional resource centers, materials
produced or developed, 20
§ 1421
Research projects, index, 20 § 1441
Training personnel for education of
disabled, 20 § 1434

HANDICAPPED PERSONS AND CHIL-
DREN—Cont'd
Education—Cont'd
Assistance for education of all children, etc.,
with disabilities—Cont'd
Congressional committees—Cont'd
Secretary to provide information concerning programs and projects, 20
§ 1418
Consolidated application for payments to
local educational agency, etc., requirement, submission to State educational agency, grounds for, 20
§ 1414
Consultation with individuals involved,
etc., with education, State to assure,
conditions, eligibility for, 20 § 1412
Contents,
Annual report, Secretary to Congressional committees, progress toward
providing free appropriate public
education, 20 § 1418
Applications for,
Allotment, funds, Indian children, 20
§ 1411
Payments to local educational agencies or intermediate educational
units, 20 § 1414
Biennial report, Indian tribe or tribal
organization to Interior Secretary,
20 § 1411
State plans, 20 § 1413
Contracts. Grants, contracts, or cooperative agreements, generally, post, this
subheading
Control of funds and title to property to
be in public agency for, certain uses,
etc.,
Assurances, contents, application for
payments to local educational
agencies, etc., 20 § 1414
Contents, State plan, assurances, 20
§ 1413
Cooperation, Secretary with states, 20
§ 1417
Cooperative agreements. Grants, contracts or cooperative agreements,
generally, post, this heading
Counselors. Attorneys and counselors,
generally, ante, this subheading
Courts of appeals, jurisdiction, review,
Children in private schools, participation by alternative arrangements, 20 § 1413
Secretary's final action respecting,
Approval of State plan, 20 § 1416
Private schools, participation by alternative arrangements, 20
§ 1413
Crippled Children's Services, early intervention services, evaluation, 20
§ 1418
Data,
Collected, etc.,
By Secretary, etc., protection of
rights and privacy of parents and
students 20 § 1417

EXHIBIT 6.2
Continued

1027   **HOLIDAYS**

HOLDING COMPANIES—Cont'd
Crimes and offenses, embezzlement, theft, or misapplication of funds, penalties, **18 § 656**
Depository Institution Holding Companies, generally, this index
Embezzlement, officers or employees, penalties, **18 § 656**
Federal Reserve banks, member bank, "affiliate" meaning, **12 § 371c**
Foreign Personal Holding Companies, generally, this index
Income tax,
  Accumulated earnings credit, **26 § 535**
  Capital loss deduction, etc., not allowed, **26 § 535**
  Evidence of purpose to avoid, accumulated earnings, **26 § 533**
  Exemptions, certain title holding companies, **26 § 501**
  Foreign Personal Holding Companies, this index
  Personal Holding Companies, this index
  Sale, obedience to SEC orders, gain or loss, basis for determining, **26 § 1082**
Market reform. Securities Exchange Act, generally, this index
Misapplication of funds, officers or employees, penalties, **18 § 656**
Officers or employees, embezzlement, theft, or misapplication of funds, penalties, **18 § 656**
Personal Holding Companies, generally, this index
Public Utility Holding Companies, this index
Registered Holding Company, generally, this index
Savings and Loan Holding Companies, generally, this index
Theft, officers or employees, penalties, **18 § 656**

HOLDING COMPANY REGULATION ACT
Text of Act, **15 § 79 et seq.**
Public Utility Holding Companies, generally, this index

HOLDING PERIOD
Income Tax, this index

HOLIDAYS
See, also, specific index headings
Bankruptcy Rules and Forms, generally, this index
Christmas, generally, this index
Cigar and cigarette tax, time for payment, special rule, **26 § 5703**
Cigarette paper and tubes tax, time for payment, special rule, **26 § 5703**
Columbus Day, **36 § 146**
Compensation, Vice President, Senators, officers, employees of Senate, payday falling on, **2 § 60c–1**
Contested elections, House of Representatives Members, computation of time, **2 § 394**

HOLIDAYS—Cont'd
Courts of appeals,
  Court of Appeals for Fifth Circuit, generally, this index
  Court of Appeals for Eleventh Circuit, generally, this index
  Supplementing FRAP in specific circuit courts of appeals. See specific Circuit Court of Appeals headings in this index
Criminal fine collection, notice required on, procedure, **18 § 3612**
Customs duties, boarding officers, compensation for services rendered on, **19 § 261**
Customs employees, overtime and premium pay for services rendered, **19 § 267**
Daily, hourly and piece-work basis Federal employees, **5 § 6104**
Defined, customs officers, compensation and wages, **19 § 267**
Definitions, this index
Distilled spirits, gallonage tax, time for collection of, special rule, **26 § 5061**
District of Columbia, this index
Emergency employment by Department of Agriculture without regard to holidays, **7 § 2226**
Enumeration of legal public holidays for Federal employees, **5 § 6103**
Extra compensation for overtime of in charge and radio engineers of FCC, **47 § 154**
Field Engineering and Monitoring Bureau of FCC, extra compensation of engineers and radio engineers, **47 § 154**
Government agencies, etc., observance of, **5 § 6103 nt, EON 11582**
Immigration and Naturalization Service officers and employees, extra compensation for services performed on, **8 § 1353a**
Inauguration Day, generally, this index
Independence Day, generally, this index
Internal revenue,
  Legal holiday, defined, **26 § 7503**
  Review, jeopardy levy or assessment procedures, computation of days, **26 § 7429**
  Time for performance of acts, **26 § 7503**
Labor Day, generally, this index
Lading vessels on, **19 § 1452**
Memorial Day, generally, this index
Mondays, uniform annual observance of certain legal public holidays on, **5 § 6103**
Mother's Day,
  Display of flag on buildings, **36 § 141**
  Second Sunday in May, **36 § 142**
National banks, proceedings where election of directors or meetings of shareholders falls on legal holiday, **12 § 75**
National Maritime Day, **36 § 145**
New Year's Day, generally, this index
Office of Personnel Management, delegation, Presidential regulatory authority to prevent or relieve Federal employees from working, **5 § 6104 nt, EON 10552**
Officers and Employees of Government, this index

EXHIBIT 6.2
Continued

INDIANS

INDIANS—Cont'd
Education—Cont'd
Programs for children or students—Cont'd
Financial assistance to local educational
agencies,
Adjustments, appropriations, 25 § 2606
Amendments, grant applications, 25
§ 2604
Amount, grants, 25 § 2602
Applications, grants, 25 § 2604
Appropriations, authorization, 25
§ 2606
Approval, grant applications, 25 § 2604
Auditing, rent applications, 25 § 2604
Congressional declaration of policy, 25
§ 2601
Demonstration projects, grants for, 25
§ 2602
Denial, payments taken into account by
State, 25 § 2605
Eligibility forms, contents, etc., 26
§ 2604
Federal funds, uses, 25 § 2603
Payments, 25 § 2605
Penalties, false information, grant ap-
plications, 25 § 2604
Reallocations, appropriations, 25
§ 2606
Reduction, payments, failure to main-
tain fiscal effort, 25 § 2605
Schools that are not, etc., local edu-
cational agencies, grants to, 25
§ 2603
Use, Federal funds, 25 § 2603
Free public education, defined, 25 § 2651
Funding, National Council on Indian Ed-
ucation, 25 § 2642
Indian, defined, 25 § 2651
Indian preference, Office of Indian Edu-
cation professional staff, 25 § 2641
Information, adult education, 25 § 2631
Local educational agency, defined, 25
§ 2651
National Advisory Council on Indian Ed-
ucation, establishment, composition,
etc., 25 § 2642
Office of Indian Education, establish-
ment, powers, duties, etc., 25 § 2641
Parent, defined, 25 § 2651
Secretary, defined, 25 § 2651
Special programs and projects to improve
educational opportunities,
Additional grants, gifted and talented
students, 25 § 2624
Applications for grants, 25 § 2621
Appropriations,
Authorization, 25 § 2621
Fellowships for Indian students, au-
thorization, 25 § 2623
Gifted and talented students, autho-
rization, 25 § 2624
Teachers, authorization, 25 § 2622
Demonstration projects, gifted and tal-
ented students, 25 § 2624
Evaluation, grants for, 25 § 2621

INDIANS—Cont'd
Education—Cont'd
Programs for children or students—Cont'd
Special programs and projects to improve
educational opportunities—Cont'd
Fellowships,
Indian students, 25 § 2623
Teachers, 25 § 2622
Gifted and talented students, 25 § 2624
Informational network, gifted and tal-
ented students, 25 § 2624
Payment to institutions in lieu of tu-
ition, fellowships for Indian stu-
dents, 25 § 2623
Special rules, fellowships for Indian stu-
dents, 25 § 2623
Stipends, fellowships for Indian stu-
dents, 25 § 2623
Teachers, educational training pro-
grams for, 25 § 2622
Technical assistance, grants for, 25
§ 2621
Traineeships, teachers, 25 § 2622
Training, 25 § 2621
Special programs relating to adult edu-
cation, 25 § 2631
Programs for Indian children. Bureau of
Indian Affairs, generally, this index
Project Headstart. Community Services,
generally, this index
School districts, contracts with for school
construction, 25 § 458
Schools,
Colleges. Tribally controlled community
college assistance, generally, post,
this subheading
Grants. Tribally controlled school grants,
generally, post, this heading
Indian Schools, generally, this index
Secondary and postgraduate forestry pro-
grams, 25 §§ 3113, 3114
State education agency, contracts with for
school construction, 25 § 458
Study and investigation by Secretary of Inte-
rior, 25 § 304a
Tribal Culture and History Programs, provi-
sion for, 25 § 1616f
Tribal development,
Critical needs,
Generally, 25 § 3321 et seq.
Certification of area service agree-
ments, requirement, 25 § 3324
Critical area service agreements, de-
fined, 25 § 3324
Eligible Indian tribe or tribal organiza-
tion, defined, 25 § 3322
Federally funded higher education as-
sistance, defined, 25 § 3322
General provisions, 25 § 3325
Indian, defined, 25 § 3322
Secretary of Interior, generally, post,
this heading
Service agreements, terms, limitations,
waiver, etc., 25 § 3324
Service conditions permitted, area des-
ignation, 25 § 3323

EXHIBIT 6.2
Continued

817   **KIDNEY**

KIDNAPPING—Cont'd
Director and Deputy Director of CIA, kidnapping of or attempts or conspiracy to kidnap, penalties, **18 § 351**
Electronic surveillance, foreign intelligence purposes. Surveillance, generally, this index
Employee retirement income security program, protection of employee benefit rights, fiduciary responsibility, persons convicted of, prohibited from holding certain positions, **29 § 1111**
Federal officials, penalties, **18 § 1201**
Fines and penalties,
    Generally, **18 § 1201**
    Indian country, offense committed by Indians in, **18 § 1153**
    Receiving, possessing and disposing of ransom money, **18 § 1202**
    Transportation of kidnaped persons in interstate commerce, **18 § 1201**
Foreign officials, official guests, or internationally protected persons,
    Congressional statement of findings and declaration of policy concerning U.S. jurisdiction, **18 § 112 nt**
    Penalties, **18 § 1201**
    Protection of, violations, **18 § 878**
Indians, offense committed by, in Indian country,
    Jurisdiction, **18 § 3242**
    Punishment, **18 § 1153**
Interception of wire, etc., communications, authorization, Presidential, Congressional, etc., kidnapping, **18 § 2516**
International Child Abduction Remedies, generally, this index
International parental kidnapping. Parental Kidnapping Prevention, generally, this index
International terrorist activities. Terrorists and Terrorism, generally, this index
Involuntary servitude, intent to sell person kidnaped into, **18 § 1583**
Jurisdiction,
    Indian country, offense committed by Indians in, **18 § 3242**
    Internationally protected persons, victim, **18 § 1201**
Justices of the Supreme Court,
    Interception of wire, etc., communications, authorization, **18 § 2516**
    Kidnapping of or attempts or conspiracy to kidnap, penalties, **18 § 351**
Juvenile justice and delinquency prevention, **42 § 5601 et seq.**
Major Presidential and Vice Presidential candidate, penalty, **18 § 351**
Maritime and territorial jurisdiction of U.S., act against person within, penalties, **18 § 1201**
Missing Children, generally, this index
Parental Kidnapping Prevention, generally, this index

KIDNAPPING—Cont'd
President, Vice-President, etc.,
    Acceptance of contribution from charitable organization by officer or employee injured during offense, **18 § 209**
    Interception of wire, etc., communications, authorization, **18 § 2516**
    Penalties, **18 § 1751**
    Threats against, penalties, **18 § 879**
Proof defendant knew victim was protected official unnecessary, prosecution for kidnapping or attempts or conspiracy to kidnap Congressional member, cabinet department heads, etc., **18 § 351**
Prosecution for offense, **42 § 1987**
Racketeer Influenced and Corrupt Organizations, generally, this index
Ransom or reward for release of kidnapped person,
    Demand or request, in interstate commerce, **18 § 875**
    Demanding or receiving, sentencing guidelines and statutory index, **18 Ap 4**
    Mailing demand or request for, **18 §§ 876, 877**
    Possessing and disposing of, **18 § 1202**
Sentence and punishment,
    Generally, **18 § 1201**
    Children, penalty enhancement, authority of U.S. Sentencing Commission to amend existing guidelines, applicability, **18 § 1201**
    Foreign official, official guests, or internationally protected persons, **18 § 1201**
    Guidelines and statutory index, **18 Ap 4**
    Indian country, offense committed by Indians in, **18 § 1153**
    Receiving, possessing and disposing of ransom money, **18 § 1202**
    Transportation of kidnaped persons in interstate commerce, **18 § 1201**
Slave, kidnaping with intent to hold as, **18 § 1583**
Terrorists and Terrorism, generally, this index
Threat,
    Against President and successors, **18 § 871**
    Communicated in interstate or foreign commerce, penalty, **18 § 875**
    Mailing communication, **18 §§ 876, 877**
Transportation, etc., penalty, **18 § 1201**
Unlawful restraint, sentencing guidelines and statutory index, **18 Ap 4**

KIDNEY DISEASE
End stage renal disease, program, Federal old-age, survivors and disability insurance benefits, **42 § 426–1**
Program, Federal old-age, survivors and disability insurance benefits, **42 § 426–1**
Research, grants for programs for, **29 § 762**
Grants, multigrant projects, administration, PHS, **42 § 235**
Medicare eligibility and reimbursement, Federal old-age, survivors and disability insurance benefits, end stage renal disease program, **42 § 426–1**

EXHIBIT 6.2
Continued

PEANUTS   90

PEANUTS—Cont'd
Private marketings, other, marketing assessment, 7 § 1445c–3
Processing, defined, 7 § 609(d)
Processing tax, 7 § 609(b,d)
Quality improvement, price support, 7 § 1445c–3
Quota peanuts,
  Defined, 7 § 1358–1
  National acreage allotment, 7 § 1358
  National marketing quota, 7 § 1358
    Applicability to certain crop years, 7 § 1358 nt
  Pools, records, 7 § 1445c–3
  Price supports for certain crops years, 7 § 1445–3
Referendum,
  Eligibility of lessor of acreage allotment, 7 § 1358a
  Marketing quotas, 7 § 1358
  Time for, 7 § 1358
Refund of penalty for peanuts kept on farm for seed or home consumption, 7 § 1359
Release and reapportionment, farm acreage allotments, 7 § 1358
Reports and records under Agricultural Adjustment Act of 1938, 7 §§ 1373, 1374
Sale,
  Acreage allotments, 7 § 1358a
  Lease, or transfer of farm poundage quota, certain crop years, 7 § 1358b
Secretary of Agriculture,
  Adjustment of national marketing quota because of emergency or export demand, 7 § 1371
  Administration of special account of marketing penalties collected, 7 § 1359
  Apportionment of acreage allotment among farms, 7 § 1358
  Collection of marketing penalties, 7 § 1359
  Investigation and adjustment to maintain normal supply in case of farm marketing quotas, 7 § 1371
  Marketing agreements with, requirements, inspection and quality control, applicability to persons who have not entered into agreement, 7 § 608b
  Measurement of farms and report of plantings, 7 § 1374
  Proclamation, 7 § 1358
  Referendum on marketing quotas, 7 § 1358
  Regulations,
    Administration of provisions concerning transfer of acreage allotment, 7 § 1358a
    For identification, 7 § 1375
  Transfer of acreage allotment, determination by, 7 § 1358a
Shelling, reports and records of persons engaged in shelling, 7 § 1373
State acreage allotments, apportionment among State farms, 7 § 1358
Statistics. Peanut Statistics, generally, this index
Surrender of acreage allotments, 7 § 1358

PEANUTS—Cont'd
Suspension of marketing quotas and acreage allotments, 7 §§ 1358 nt, 1358a nt, 1359 nt, 1371 nt
Terms and conditions, lease of acreage allotment, 7 § 1358a
Time for referendum, 7 § 1358
Total supply for marketing year, 7 § 1301
Transfer,
  Acreage allotments, 7 § 1358a
    applicability to certain crop years, 7 § 1358a nt
    Natural disaster, 7 § 1358
  Farm poundage quotas, certain crop years, 7 § 1358b
Warehouses and Warehousemen, generally, this index

PEARL HARBOR, HI
Anchorage regulation, 33 § 475
Pearl Harbor Survivors Association, incorporation, etc., 36 § 3601 et seq.
Veterans of attack on, Congressional medal, etc., 31 § 5111 nt

PEARL HARBOR SURVIVORS ASSOCIATION
Incorporation, etc., 36 § 3601 et seq.

PEARLS
Vessels, generally, this index

PEARS
Certification, grade, refusal of certificate on ground of violation of law, 7 § 586
Defined, export standards, 7 § 589
Export standards. See Interstate and Foreign Commerce, generally, this index
Marketing promotion including paid advertising, etc., orders regulating handling of commodity, agricultural adjustment, 7 § 608c(6)
Orders, regulating handling of,
  Applicability, Agricultural Adjustment Act, 7 § 608c(2, 6)
  Terms and conditions of order covering area within two or more States, Agricultural Adjustment Act, 7 § 608c(6)(J)
Penalty for violating export standards law, 7 § 586
Processors and producers,
  Referendum, approval, marketing order applicable to pears for canning or freezing, Agricultural Adjustment Act, 7 § 608c(19)
  Representation on agency selected to administer marketing orders, Agricultural Adjustment Act, 7 § 608c(7)

PEAS
Black-eyed, production for donation, acreage reduction program, upland cotton, conditions permitting, 7 § 1444–2

PEAT
Income tax, percentage depletion, 26 § 613

EXHIBIT 6.2
Continued

283   **POULTRY**

POULTRY AND POULTRY PRODUCTS
—Cont'd
Implementation of policies to encourage full production in periods of short supply at fair and reasonable prices, **7 § 1282a**

Income tax,
Farming syndicates, poultry expenses, limitations on deductions, taxable year taken, **26 § 464**
Taxable year, deductions, limitations, farming expenses, **26 § 464**

Inspection,
Text of Act, **21 § 451 et seq.**
Additives, adulteration, **21 § 453**
Administration, powers available, **21 § 467d**
Administrative detention,
Product believed to violate provisions, **21 § 467a**
Representatives of Secretary of HHS, power, **21 § 467f**
Admiralty proceedings, proceedings to condemn poultry to conform to, **21 § 467b**
Adulterated, defined, **21 § 453**
Advisory committees,
Appointment, **21 § 454**
Consultation with, **21 § 460**
Animal food, necessity for inspection, **21 § 460**
Animal food manufacturer,
Defined, **21 § 453**
Registration, necessity, **21 § 460**
Ante mortem inspection, adulterated poultry, **21 § 454**
Appeal,
Determination of adulteration, **21 § 455**
Inspection service, refusal or withdrawal, **21 § 467**
Labeling determination, **21 § 457**
Application for inspection service, grounds for refusal, **21 § 467**
Appropriations, **21 § 469**
Assault, resistance, etc., person enforcing provisions, **21 § 461**
Boarding houses, exemption, **21 § 464**
Bond, condemned poultry released to owner, **21 § 467b**
Capable of use as human food, defined, **21 § 453**
Carrier, liability, **21 § 461**
Color Additive Amendments of 1960, prohibition against exemption of poultry or poultry products from requirements, **21 § 379e nt**
Color additives,
Adulteration, **21 § 453**
Defined, **21 § 453**
Commerce, defined, **21 § 453**
Concurrent jurisdiction with States, etc., **21 § 467e**
Condemnation,
Adulteration, **21 § 455**
Product violating provisions, **21 § 467b**
Congress,
Declaration of policy, **21 §§ 452, 454**
Statement of findings, **21 § 451**

POULTRY AND POULTRY PRODUCTS
—Cont'd
Inspection—Cont'd
Congressional committees,
Exemption criteria, evaluation and development, etc., results of studies submitted to, **21 § 464 nt**
Reports, **21 §§ 454, 470**
Container,
Defined, **21 § 453**
Standards, **21 § 457**
Costs, **21 § 468**
Custom slaughterers, exemption, **21 § 464**
Definition of poultry products, **21 § 453**
Designation of State as subject to Federal inspection, **21 § 454**
Detention of products believed to violate provisions, **21 § 467a**
Distribution, certain poultry products to charity and public agencies after condemnation, **21 § 467b**
Eggs and Egg Products, generally, this index
Enforcement, powers available, **21 § 467d**
Exemptions, **21 § 464**
Studies, evaluation and development of criteria, etc., results submitted to Congressional committees, **21 § 464 nt**
False and misleading labeling, **21 § 457**
Fine for violations, **21 § 461**
Food, Drug and Cosmetic Act,
Applicability, **21 § 467f**
Defined, **21 § 453**
Imported poultry subject to, **21 § 466**
Labeling standards, consistency with, **21 § 457**
Food additive, defined, **21 § 453**
Governor of State, consultation, inspection requirements, **21 § 454**
Guam, "territory" as including, **21 § 453**
Hotels, exemption, **21 § 464**
Immediate container,
Defined, **21 § 453**
Labeling standards, **21 § 457**
Imports, **21 § 466**
Imprisonment for violations, **21 § 461**
Inspectors,
Ante and post mortem inspection, **21 § 455**
Defined, **21 § 453**
Jurisdiction to enforce provisions, **21 §§ 457, 467b, 467c, 467e**
Killing person enforcing provisions, **21 § 461**
Label, defined, **21 § 453**
Labeling, standards, **21 § 457**
Legislative finding, **21 § 451**
Liability of agents, employees, employers, carriers, **21 § 461**
Major consuming areas, designation, **21 § 451**
Misbranded, defined, **21 § 453**
Miscellaneous activities subject to regulation, **21 § 460**

134   LEGAL RESEARCH

EXHIBIT 6.2
Continued

433   **PUBLIC**

PUBLIC AGENCIES—Cont'd
State governments. State Agencies, generally, this index
Student Literacy Corps, Institutions of Higher Education or Learning, generally, this index
Technology, generally, this index
Technology related assistance for individuals with disabilities. Disability, generally, this index
United States nationals found mentally ill in foreign countries, arrangements for hospitalization, **24 § 322**
Veterans Health Administration, health-care personnel, education, training and research programs, cooperation, **38 §§ 7302, 7303**
Vocational Rehabilitation and Other Rehabilitation Services, generally, this index
Water management for rural areas, activities, cooperation, etc., **7 § 2204c**
Water Pollution Prevention and Control, generally, this index
Youth Conservation Corps, contracts with, **16 § 1703**
Youthbuild programs, HOPE. National Affordable Housing, generally, this index

PUBLIC AIRCRAFT
Defined, Aviation Act of 1958, **49 Ap § 1301**

PUBLIC AIRPORTS
See AIRPORTS AND LANDING AREAS, generally, this index

PUBLIC AND ASSISTED HOUSING DRUG ELIMINATION ACT OF 1990
Text of Act. See Popular Name Table
Housing, generally, this index
Short title, **42 § 11901 nt**

PUBLIC AREAS
See specific index headings

PUBLIC ASSISTANCE
Bankruptcy, local benefit, debtor's right to receive, exemptions, **11 § 522**
Colorado River Floodway, establishment, etc., **43 § 1600 et seq.**
Domestic Volunteer Services, eligibility for other benefits, **42 § 5058**
Food Stamps, generally, this index
Indian child protection and family violence prevention. Child Abuse and Neglect, generally, this index
Industrial facilities, geographical dispersal in interests of national defense, **50 Ap § 2062**
Job Training Partnership, generally, this index
Low-Income Home Energy Assistance, generally, this index
Offices, national voter registration. Registration, generally, this index
Programs, equal credit opportunity. Consumer Credit Protection, generally, this index
Social Security, generally, this index

PUBLIC ASSISTANCE—Cont'd
Supplementary medical insurance benefits for aged and disabled, State agreements, coverage, **42 § 1395v**

PUBLIC AUCTION
See AUCTIONS AND AUCTIONEERS, generally, this index

PUBLIC AUTHORITIES
See specific index headings

PUBLIC BODIES
Certain, Ohio and Utah, transfer of community services programs development loans to nonprofit corporations, provisions, **42 § 9812a nt**
Coal lands, reservation, leasing tracts for lease to, grounds for, **30 § 201**
Coast Guard, navigation aids, contracts for establishment, maintenance, and operation by, authorization, **14 § 81**
Community development, training and fellowship programs for, **20 § 801 et seq.**
Community facilities and advance land acquisition, grants, **42 § 3101 et seq.**
Lower Income Housing, this index
Rural Telephones, generally, this index
Slum Clearance and Urban Renewal, generally, this index
Water Pollution Prevention and Control, generally, this index

PUBLIC BROADCAST SYSTEM
Public telecommunications facilities. See Telecommunications, generally, this index

PUBLIC BROADCASTING ACTS AND AMENDMENTS
Text of Acts. See Popular Name Table
Corporation for Public Broadcasting, generally, this index
Short title of Acts, **47 § 609 nt**
Telecommunications, generally, this index

PUBLIC BROADCASTING ENTITY
Copyrights,
  Educational television and radio program by, limitation on scope of exclusive rights in sound recordings, **17 § 114**
  Infringement,
    Defense of fair use, **17 § 504**
    Remission of statutory damages, defense of fair use, **17 § 504**
Corporation for Public Broadcasting, generally, this index
Defined, noncommercial educational broadcasting facilities, **47 § 397**
Public telecommunications facilities. Telecommunications, generally, this index
Star Schools, generally, this index

PUBLIC BROADCASTING FINANCING ACTS
Text of Acts. See Popular Name Table
Corporation for Public Broadcasting, generally, this index
Short title, Act of 1970 and 1975, **47 § 396 nt**

EXHIBIT 6.2
Continued

RETIREMENT
846

RETIREMENT OF CIVIL SERVICE EM-PLOYEES—Cont'd

Expulsion, Member of Congress, exception, entitlement to annuity upon separation from service at certain age, **5 § 8336**

Extension of coverage, statutes authorizing, unfunded liability created, financing, appropriations to Fund, **5 § 8348**

FBI-DEA Senior Executive Service, removal of member, entitlement to annuity, **5 § 8336**

Federal employees' group health insurance, enrollment,
  Former spouses, eligibility, **5 § 8341 nt**
  Health benefits plan, **5 § 8905**
  Election of coverage, **5 § 8905 nt**

Federal Employees' Retirement System,
  Elections, individual subject to civil service retirement, irrevocability, effect, etc., **5 § 8331 nt**
  Employee or member subject to,
    Exclusion from civil service retirement, **5 § 8331**
    Payment of lump-sum credit, determination, etc., **5 § 8342**
  Exclusion from treatment, deductions, etc., **5 § 8334**
  Thrift Savings Fund,
    Contributions to, election, conditions, etc., **5 § 8351**
    Participation by Foreign Service Retirement and Disability System participants, **22 § 4069**

Federal Prison Industries, employees of. Law enforcement officers, generally, post, this heading

Federal service, defined, offset, certain benefits, etc., **5 § 8349**

Federal wages, defined, deductions, etc., treatment, individuals excluded from Federal Employees' Retirement System, **5 § 8334**

Fees for examinations, **5 § 8347**

Filing,
  Application for disability retirement with OPM, **5 § 8337**
  Survivor annuities, election or waiver respecting, etc., **5 § 8339**
  Waiver of annuity with OPM, **5 § 8345**

Findings by OPM,
  Disability retirement, **5 § 8337**
  Good health of unmarried employee or member at time of retiring, computation of annuities, **5 § 8339**

Firefighters,
  Age, mandatory separation from service, exemptions, **5 § 8335**
  Annuities,
    Computation, **5 § 8339**
      Service in Panama Canal Company or Canal Zone Government, **5 § 8339**
    Entitlement, **5 § 8336**
    Immediate retirement, **5 § 8336**
    Increase, service in Republic of Panama, **5 § 8339**
  Deductions, **5 § 8334**
  Defined, **5 § 8331**

RETIREMENT OF CIVIL SERVICE EM-PLOYEES—Cont'd

Firefighters—Cont'd
  Foreign Service Retirement and Disability System, creditable service, **22 § 4071d**
  Mandatory separation, **5 § 8335**
  Notice, date of separation from service, **5 § 8335**
  Separation from service, annuity,
    Computation of, **5 § 8339**
    Entitlement to, **5 § 8336**
  Tables, deposit, percentage of basic pay, **5 § 8334**
  Time, mandatory separation from service, **5 § 8335**

Foreign Service, this index

Forfeiture of annuities and retired pay, **5 § 8311 et seq.**

Former employees or members, computation of annuity, **5 § 8339**

Former President and former Vice-President, office staff, applicability, **3 § 102 nt**

Former spouse,
  Alternative annuities, eligibility, election, etc., **5 § 8343a**
  Deceased employee, member or annuitant, entitlement to survivor annuity, amount, commencement, etc., **5 § 8341**
  Defined, **5 § 8331**
    Survivor annuities, surviving children, **5 § 8341**
  Entitlement, retirement or death of employee or member before effective date, **5 § 8341 nt**
  Federal employees health benefits plan, enrollment eligibility, **5 § 8341 nt**
  Payment of lump-sum credit subject to terms of court order or decree respecting, etc., **5 § 8342**
  Survivor annuity,
    Election, time, etc., **5 § 8339**
      Additional election, **5 § 8341 nt**
    Increase, cost-of-living adjustment, **5 § 8340**

Fund,
  Officials, prohibition, use for paying employees of, **5 § 5502**
  Payments by U.S. Postal Service, COLAs, **5 § 8348 nt**
  Retirement and Disability Fund, generally, post, this heading

Garnishment, money exempt from, **5 § 8346**

General limitation on cost-of-living adjustment for annuities, formula, **5 § 8340**

Government, defined, **5 § 8331**

Health benefits, Employees Health Benefits Fund, schedule of payments, Postal Service, **5 § 8906 nt**

Health insurance,
  Continuation, **5 § 8706**
  Restored employees and survivor or disability annuitants, coverage of, **5 § 8706**

House of Representatives,
  Beauty Shop, employees, creditable service, **5 § 8332**

EXHIBIT 6.2
Continued

RUBBER   908

RUBBER PRODUCING FACILITIES
—Cont'd
Disposal Commission—Cont'd
Notice and advertisement, purchase propos-
als, **50 Ap § 1941e**
Payment, purchase price, **50 Ap § 1941e**
Period for receipt of purchase proposals, **50
Ap § 1941e**
Prompt disposal, **50 Ap § 1941c**
Report, recommended disposal to Congress,
50 Ap § 1941g
Restriction, activities, members and employ-
ees after leaving Commission, **50 Ap
§ 1941d**
Sales contracts, powers, **50 Ap § 1941a**
Securing, additional information from per-
sons submitting purchase proposals, **50
Ap § 1941e**
Submission, disposal report to Attorney
General, **50 Ap § 1941a**
Termination, **50 Ap § 1941r**
Disposition,
Procedure, **50 Ap § 1941e**
Proceeds from disposal, **50 Ap § 1941j**
Unsold facilities, **50 Ap § 1941f**
Effective date, contracts of sale, **50 Ap
§ 1941e**
Exclusion, Government-owned evaluation lab-
oratory at Akron, OH, from term "rubber
producing facilities", **50 Ap § 1941i**
Failure to complete transfer prior to termi-
nation date, **50 Ap § 1941e**
Federal Facilities Corporation, administration
of matters involving Rubber-Producing
Facilities Disposal Commission, **50 Ap
§ 1941r nt, EON 10678**
Funds, expenses of disposal, **50 Ap § 1941g**
General purpose synthetic rubber, defined, **50
Ap § 1941s**
Institute, WV, disposal, facility at, **50 Ap
§ 1941x**
Limitation on Government rubber sales, **50 Ap
§ 1941e**
Louisville, KY, disposal, facility at, **50 Ap
§ 1941y**
Minimum annual production necessary to sus-
tain disposal report, **50 Ap § 1941v**
National security clause, contracts of sale, **50
Ap § 1941e**
Offer, Government rubber for sale to purchas-
er of facilities after termination of trans-
fer, **50 Ap § 1941e**
Operating agency, defined, **50 Ap § 1941s**
Payment, costs, disposal from operating in-
come, **50 Ap § 1941q**
Person, defined, **50 Ap § 1941s**
President, report, Congress, nation's rubber
requirements and resources, **50 Ap
§ 1941h**
Prior disposal of facilities as unaffected by
Act, **50 Ap § 1941k**
Purchase proposals, **50 Ap § 1941e**
Rejection, recommended sales contract, **50 Ap
§ 1941v**

RUBBER PRODUCING FACILITIES
—Cont'd
Report,
President to Congress, nation's rubber re-
quirements and resources, **50 Ap
§ 1941h**
Recommended disposal to Congress, **50 Ap
§ 1941g**
Restriction, sale or lease of facilities, **50 Ap
§ 1941g**
Small business enterprise, defined, **50 Ap
§ 1941s**
Standby condition, defined, **50 Ap § 1941s**
Standby funds upon transfer of Government
rubber producing facilities to GSA, **50 Ap
§ 1941f**
Synthetic rubber, defined, **50 Ap § 1941s**
Time, transfer, possession of facilities, **50 Ap
§ 1941e**
Transfer, unsold facilities to GSA, **50 Ap
§ 1941f**

RUBELLA
Vaccines, generally, this index

RUBY MOUNTAINS WILDERNESS
Generally, **16 § 1132 nt**

**RUDMAN-GRAMM-HOLLINGS BALANCED
BUDGET ACT**
See BALANCED BUDGET AND EMERGENCY DEFICIT
CONTROL ACT OF 1985, generally, this index

RUGS
Income Tax, generally, this index
Wool Products Labeling Act, exceptions, **15
§ 68j**

RUINS
American Antiquities, generally, this index
Excavation or injury as offense, **16 § 433**
Mesa Verde National Park, **16 §§ 112, 114,
115, 117c**

RULE NISI
Power to issue, **28 § 1651**

**RULES AND ADMINISTRATION COMMIT-
TEE OF SENATE**
See CONGRESSIONAL COMMITTEES, this index

RULES AND REGULATIONS
See specific index headings

**RULES COMMITTEE (HOUSE OF REPRE-
SENTATIVES)**
See CONGRESSIONAL COMMITTEES, this index

RULES OF APPELLATE PROCEDURE
For supplemental rules of circuit courts of
appeals. See specific CIRCUIT COURT
OF APPEALS, headings in this index
Text of Federal Rules of Appellate Proce-
dure, **Title 28 (Rules Volume)**
Acknowledgement, service of papers, **FRAP
R25(d)**

EXHIBIT 6.2
Continued

261   **SECRETARY**

SECRETARY OF LABOR—Cont'd
Women—Cont'd
Task Force on Legal Equity for, nominees
for appointments to, **42 § 2000e nt,
EON 12336**
Worker adjustment and retraining notification,
prescription of regulations, authority, **29
§ 2107**
Working capital fund, comprehensive program
of centralized services, Labor Department, duties, **29 § 563a**

SECRETARY OF NAVY
For other general provisions concerning.
See, also, "Secretaries" development
under Military Departments, this in-
dex
Absence, successors to duties, **10 § 5017**
Accidents, expenditures for prevention, **10
§ 7205**
Accounting,
Accounts, paymasters, lost or captured naval
vessels, **10 § 7862**
Expenditures for obtaining information, **10
§ 7231**
Administration, liberated and occupied areas,
10 § 7207
Administrative Assistant in Office of, appoint-
ment, powers, duties, **10 § 5018**
Admiralty claims by or against U.S., military
claims, settlement or compromise, **10
§§ 7365, 7622**
Advice and aid to Secretary of Transportation
and ship building capability, **46 Ap § 1152**
American Chemical Society, determination in-
ventions involve national defense, vesting
of title in U.S. Government, etc., **36
§ 3204**
American Samoa, transfer of administration to
Secretary of the Interior, **48 § 1662 nt,
EON 10264**
Applications, to disabled persons serving ten
years in Navy or Marine Corps, **10 § 6160**
Appointment,
Generally, **10 § 5013**
Original appointments, service credits upon
limiting amount, **10 § 5600**
Temporary appointments, officers designat-
ed for limited duty, **10 § 5596**
Termination of temporary appointments of
officers and officers designated for lim-
ited duty, **10 § 5596**
Appropriations, passenger carrier use, **31
§ 1344**
Architects or architectural corporations, em-
ployment, purposes, **10 § 7212**
Armed Forces Health Professions Scholarship
and Financial Assistance Program for Active Service, establishment and maintenance, **10 § 2121**
Armed Forces Policy Council, membership, **10
§ 171**
Assistant secretaries,
Appointment, powers, duties, etc., **10
§ 5016**
Assignment of functions, etc., to, **10 § 5013**

SECRETARY OF NAVY—Cont'd
Assistant secretaries—Cont'd
Compensation, **5 § 5315**
Financial Management, appointment, pow-
ers, duties, etc., **10 § 5025**
Manpower and Reserve Affairs,
Membership on Reserve Forces Policy
Board, **10 § 175**
Principal duty, etc., **10 § 5016**
Order of succession of authority to act as, **5
§ 3347 nt, EON 12879**
Part of Office of, **10 § 5014**
Professional assistance to,
By Office of Chief of Naval Operations,
10 § 5032
From Headquarters, Marine Corps, **10
§ 5042**
Secretary of Commerce, assuring training of
future officers, etc., in promoting maxi-
mum integration of total seapower
forces of Nation, **46 Ap § 1126–1**
Secretary of Defense, succession to position
of, **5 § 3347 nt, EON 12787**
Secretary of Transportation, assuring training of future officers, etc., in promoting
maximum integration of total sea power forces of Nation, **46 Ap § 1126–1**
Successors to duties of Secretary, **10 § 5017**
Attorney General to advise, **28 § 513**
Bequests, acceptance for benefit of Office of
Naval Records and History, **10 § 7222**
Bureaus, performance of duties under authori-
ty of, **10 § 5132**
Cemeteries, functions, powers, and duties con-
cerning, unaffected by provisions concern-
ing National Cemetery System, **24 §§ 271
to 276 nt**
Certification, admiralty claims against U.S.
settled or compromised, certification to
Congress, **10 § 7622**
Changes of title, **50 § 401 nt**
Chief of Naval Operations. Navy Depart-
ment, generally, this index
Civilian employees, faculty members, Naval
War College, **10 § 7478**
Civilian life, appointment from, **10 § 5013**
Assistant Secretaries, **10 § 5016**
Under Secretary, **10 § 5015**
Claims, settlement or compromise, **10 § 7621
et seq.**
Admiralty claims,
Against U.S., **10 § 7622**
By U.S., **10 § 7623**
Coast Guard, this index
Collection of captured enemy flags, standards
and colors, **10 § 7216**
Collisions,
At sea, international regulations for pre-
venting. Collision of Vessels, general-
ly, this index
On inland waters of U.S., rules for prevent-
ing. Inland Navigational Rules, gener-
ally, this index
Colonial National Historical Park, transfer of
certain lands to Secretary, **16 § 81j**

of law and the corresponding subject number. If you can determine from this list the topic or topics that are likely to contain relevant statutes, you can go directly to that topic in the publication. At the beginning of a topic in a hardbound volume, you will find a sequential listing of numbers and titles for each of the individual statutes within a topic. If there are very many statutes, they may be grouped into a subtopic, such as a subchapter. In this case, only the subtopics are listed with page numbers. By turning to the proper page number, you can then find a listing of the specific statutes. (See Exhibits 6.3–6.5).

☐ ASSIGNMENT 6.4

Examine each of the excerpts in Exhibit 6.6 and determine where the following statutes are likely to be located:

1. Can a company take a product containing less than one percent wool fibers and label it as woolen?
2. Does federal law determine how fur products must be labeled?
3. Is it legal to import products below their wholesale value?
4. When was the first federal law on magnet schools?
5. Are there any special laws to provide for the education of native Hawaiian children?
6. Is the Panama Canal open to everyone who wants to pass through?
7. Must steamships be inspected?
8. Are members of the board of directors ever liable to the shareholders of a corporation?
9. Is it a federal offense for a store owner to remove the content identification label from pillows before they are sold?
10. Is it illegal to discriminate against neutral Americans engaged in commerce during time of war?

Other Research Methods for Statutory Law

By far, the most common methods of researching statutory law are the subject and topic index methods. However, there are additional methods that are helpful in some situations. First, the popular name table of the U.S.C.A. can help shorten your research time when you are armed with the name that a statute has been commonly identified with. As previously mentioned, this is quite often the name of the legislator who proposed the bill. Other common names include the name of the statute or the subject with which the statute is associated. If you know a common name of a statute, you can find it in the popular name table to obtain the citation.

A second method is the use of law finders, commercial publications that assist you in locating statutory law. Essentially, the law finder is a subject index that incorporates more commonly used terms, whereas statutory indexes often use only the language that actually appears in the statutes. Consequently, if you have not done much statutory research and are not yet familiar with language commonly used in legislation, the law finder can help you find the statute by subject.

EXHIBIT 6.3
**Table of Topics
for U.S.C.A.**
Copyright 1990
West Publishing
Company
(1–800–328–9352).

TITLES OF
UNITED STATES CODE
AND
UNITED STATES CODE ANNOTATED

1. General Provisions.
2. The Congress.
3. The President.
4. Flag and Seal, Seat of Government, and the States.
5. Government Organization and Employees.
6. Surety Bonds (*See Title 31, Money and Finance*).
7. Agriculture.
8. Aliens and Nationality.
9. Arbitration.
10. Armed Forces.
11. Bankruptcy.
12. Banks and Banking.
13. Census.
14. Coast Guard.
15. Commerce and Trade.
16. Conservation.
17. Copyrights.
18. Crimes and Criminal Procedure.
19. Customs Duties.
20. Education.
21. Food and Drugs.
22. Foreign Relations and Intercourse.
23. Highways.
24. Hospitals and Asylums.
25. Indians.
26. Internal Revenue Code.
27. Intoxicating Liquors.
28. Judiciary and Judicial Procedure.
29. Labor.
30. Mineral Lands and Mining.
31. Money and Finance.
32. National Guard.
33. Navigation and Navigable Waters.
34. Navy (*See Title 10, Armed Forces*).
35. Patents.
36. Patriotic Societies and Observances.
37. Pay and Allowances of the Uniformed Services.
38. Veterans' Benefits.
39. Postal Service.
40. Public Buildings, Property, and Works.
41. Public Contracts.
42. The Public Health and Welfare.
43. Public Lands.
44. Public Printing and Documents.
45. Railroads.
46. Shipping.
47. Telegraphs, Telephones, and Radiotelegraphs.
48. Territories and Insular Possessions.
49. Transportation.
50. War and National Defense.

II

EXHIBIT 6.4
Page 1 of the United States Code Annotated volume on Title 11 Bankruptcy (Sections 544-700).
Copyright 1984 West Publishing Company (1-800-328-9352).

UNITED STATES CODE ANNOTATED

TITLE 11

BANKRUPTCY

Sections 544 to 700 appear in this volume

[1] Chapter repealed by Pub.L. 99–554 without corresponding amendment of chapter analysis.

1

EXHIBIT 6.5
Page 2 of the
United States
Code Annotated
volume on Title
11 Bankruptcy
(Sections 544-700).
Copyright 1984 by
West Publishing
Company
(1-800-328-9352).

CHAPTER 5—CREDITORS, THE DEBTOR, AND THE ESTATE

Sections 544 to 700 appear in this Volume

SUBCHAPTER I—CREDITORS AND CLAIMS

[1] So in original. Does not conform to section catchline.

2

**EXHIBIT 6.6
U.S.C.A. Table of
Contents Sample
Pages.**
Reprinted with
permission from
U.S.C.A. Title 15,
Commerce and
Trade copyright
1958 by West
Publishing
Company
(1–800–328–9352).

TABLE OF CONTENTS

TITLE 15

COMMERCE AND TRADE

Complete Chapter Analysis, see page 1.

T. 15 U.S.C.A. §§ 21–77   XV

EXHIBIT 6.6
Continued

TABLE OF CONTENTS

EXHIBIT 6.6
Continued

TABLE OF CONTENTS

T. 15 U.S.C.A. §§ 21–77   **XVII**

EXHIBIT 6.6
Continued

TABLE OF CONTENTS

Index, see volume containing end of Title 15.

EXHIBIT 6.6
Continued
Reprinted from
U.S.C.A. Title 20,
Education
copyright 1990 by
West Publishing
Company
(1–800–328–9352).

TABLE OF CONTENTS

TITLE 20

EDUCATION

Complete Chapter Analysis, see page 1. For Section Analysis, see beginning of each Chapter.

XIX

EXHIBIT 6.6
Continued

TABLE OF CONTENTS

EXHIBIT 6.6
Continued
Reprinted with
permission from
U.S.C.A. Title 46,
Shipping copyright
by West
Publishing
Company
(1–800–328–9352).

TABLE OF CONTENTS

TITLE 46

SHIPPING

Volume containing §§ 1–250

Volume containing §§ 251–681

Finally, **deskbooks** are usually paperback, are published annually, and contain the various types of procedural laws for a jurisdiction. If your work finds you repeatedly looking up questions about procedural law, such as statute of limitations, methods of service of process, voluntary and involuntary dismissals, and discovery, you may want to consult a deskbook. While these publications are arranged in the same manner as a statutory compilation, they contain only procedural law, usually do not contain annotations, and are generally much less cumbersome and complex than a complete statutory publication.

deskbook

Condensed statutory compilation of current procedural laws for a jurisdiction.

▌▌▌▶ STRATEGY

Locating statutory law

1. Identify whether the subject of your query is likely to be one addressed by statutory law.
2. Identify whether the applicable statutory law is likely to be state or federal.
3. Consult the subject index for the proper statutory publication (federal or the particular state, as indicated in step 2).
4. The subject index should refer you to a particular topic (or number representing a topic) and statute number within the topic. If researching procedural law or the law of a jurisdiction that organizes statutes by subcode, you may be referred to a particular topic or law within a subcode.
5. If you are unable to locate any relevant information in the subject index, compare your list of relevant terms to the table of topics to locate any topics that you may not have included in your original list.
6. Once you locate a specific statute, consult supplements for any recent changes.
7. Validate your research with a citator (including current supplements).

CHAPTER SUMMARY

Statutory law is that primary authority that is created solely by the legislative branch. The method of creating statutory law includes voting by the legislature and presentation for approval by the executive authority. This type of law is organized into codes by jurisdiction and is supplemented between publications. Statutory law is indexed by subject. Another method of research is locating law by its topical arrangement. Statutes are grouped by subject, subjects are numbered, and specific laws within a subject are also numbered. The information in a statutory citation appears in descending order of specificity, subject first, then individual statute. Other methods of research exist, including popular name tables, law finders, and deskbooks for procedural law.

Key Terms

annotated statutes	legislative history	slip law
deskbook	procedural law	statutes at large
legislation	session law	veto

Self-Test

MULTIPLE CHOICE

1. A statutory publication that is _____ connects the statutory publication to publications of judicial authority.
   a) indexed
   b) codified
   c) annotated
   d) legislative history

2. When there are numerous headnotes after the statute, they are generally broken into groupings arranged by _____ .
   a) court of origin
   b) subject
   c) digest key number
   d) none of the above

3. By looking at the _____ , you can identify the annotation that represents cases on a particular aspect of the statute.
   a) table of subjects
   b) legislative history
   c) statute index
   d) statutory citation

4. The _____ must pass by a majority vote before it can be sent to the other body of the legislature for consideration.
   a) opinion
   b) regulation
   c) codified statute
   d) bill

5. If passed by the federal legislature, the law is then presented to the _____ .
   a) president
   b) Congress
   c) attorney general
   d) governor

TRUE/FALSE

_____ 6. After a full session of Congress has been concluded, all laws passed during the session take on the collective name of session law.

_____ 7. U.S. session laws are published in the statutes at large.

_____ 8. The process of incorporating a successful bill into the existing code is known as subject indexing.

_____ 9. Supplements are published annually to incorporate changes from the most recent session of Congress and all past sessions that have occurred since the last session.

_____ 10. Because the Constitution is the ultimate law of the land, an amendment must pass both houses by a two-thirds majority rather than the typical simple majority.

FILL–IN THE BLANKS

11. _____ _____ establishes the extent of personal rights and obligations to which all persons are subject.

12. The basic function of _____ is to facilitate the movement of a lawsuit through the legal system.

13. All primary authorities stating what constitutes a _____ act are statutory.

14. All _____ _____ are designed to clarify and enforce statutory law.

15. Subjects that are particularly _____ or tend to be strongly affected by individual circumstances are likely not to be statutory.

16. By examining the cover of the hardbound volumes, you can identify which _____ contains the subject you are searching for.

17. While the statutes are arranged in proper _____ order, they may appear to skip forward.

18. An alternative method to subject index that is also quite frequently used is _____ _____ .

19. _____ _____ and _____ are also methods used in statutory research.

20. Publications of statutory procedural law are known as _____ .

CHAPTER 7

THE SEARCH FOR JUDICIAL AUTHORITY

CHAPTER OBJECTIVES

Upon completion of this chapter, you should be able to accomplish the following competencies:

- Explain how judicial law is created.

- Discuss the functions of judicial law.

- Distinguish common law from statutory law.

- Explain the organization of judicial publications.

- Describe the National Reporter System.

- Distinguish a digest from a reporter.

- Identify those subjects that are likely to be addressed judicially.

- Explain the process of subject index research in judicial law.

- Explain the process of topical research in judicial law.

- Discuss how reference tools could be used to assist in research in judicial law.

THE CREATION OF JUDICIAL LAW

Because every situation is different in some respect, judges are expected to have the knowledge and objectivity to examine individual situations and determine what legal standards should apply and how. The judicial branch is designed to provide fairness and enforcement of rights for all persons.

The only way people can seek individual resolution of personal legal issues is through the judicial branch. The court is the only forum in which a person can present information supporting a legal position and obtain court approval and enforced legal action. In this way, the courts are the most responsive branch of government to the individual. For example, statutory law must be voted on and approved by the legislature (and to an extent the executive branch). The proposed law goes through an extensive process and if passed applies to the entire population of the jurisdiction, whereas administrative law can be created only to enforce statutory law. However, administrative law has an approval process similar in complexity to statutory law. Judicial law comes into play if someone thinks his or her rights have been invaded and files suit to have a court consider the issue and resolve it based upon applicable legal precedent or subject to common law.

☐ ASSIGNMENT 7.1

Examine each of the following situations and determine whether they would be better resolved by statutory, administrative, or judicial law.

1. Z thinks that a city ordinance (local statutory law) that prohibits more than two extended-family members (e.g., two grandparents) to reside with a family in a residence is unconstitutional, as Z's parents and his wife's parents want to live with Z and his wife in their eight-bedroom home.
2. A group of citizens wants to take action to make it illegal for minors to loiter in the parking lots of private businesses after business hours.
3. There is a statute that states that computer operators must be given "adequate rest periods" to lower the incidence of work-related eye disorders. A company is interested in knowing what is "adequate."
4. G provided professional services to T. However, T has failed to pay his bill according to the contract between G and T. T claims that G did not have a valid license as required by statutory law and that T therefore is not obligated to pay for the service.
5. Parents of a toddler want their day-care facility to be held liable for felony criminal charges if there is ever evidence of abuse of the toddler while in the care of the facility.

FUNCTIONS OF THE JUDICIARY

One of the primary functions of the judiciary is to clarify the law as it applies to specific circumstances. These interpretations of statutory or administrative

law occur anytime a statute or administrative regulation or decision is an issue in a case. If, for example, a person challenges a charge of driving under the influence, as part of the defense, that person must prove that the statute was not violated. The judge must review the statute and the facts of the case. Then, the judge must determine whether under the facts the law applies and whether it was violated. This is one example of a judicial interpretation of a statute.

Most cases have more complicated facts than addressed by the broad language of a statute. Frequently, there are specific questions not clearly answered by the statute or regulation (if an agency is involved). Judges resolve these questions by looking to the purpose of the statute and the intent of the legislature in passing the statute. Judges also look at how similar cases were treated by the courts in the past. Although no two cases are exactly alike, a judge may apply the reasoning of rulings in prior cases that have striking similarities. Such similarities may be in the facts of the case or in the legal issues involved. Judges are required to draw on their knowledge and experience to establish what is considered to be a logical and fair interpretation of the statute.

case law
Judicial opinion that interprets and applies preexisting legal standards.

commonlaw
Creation of legal standard by a court in circumstances where no applicable standard exists.

In cases where there is no applicable statute, a judge is required to establish the law. This may be done by looking to **case law** (the precedents of past similar cases) and applying the principle of stare decisis (adhering to an established legal standard). In the situation where there appears to be no judicial precedent whatsoever, a judge must create one. This is known as **commonlaw.** The term has carried over from medieval times when judges created law that applied to the "common man" rather than lords or other royalty.

Technically, commonlaw is defined as a newly established legal principle, whereas case law is the application of stare decisis. You may find, however, that some persons improperly use the terms interchangeably. The basic concept is that these terms represent judicially created law. In some instances, that law may be a specific interpretation and definition of a statute, whereas in other cases, it refers to the creation or continuation of a legal principle where no statutory language applied. Yet another instance might call for the creation of a legal standard where there is no applicable law.

Case law significantly benefits the general public. Individuals can look at existing case law in relation to their own situations. By comparing established precedents, persons involved in a lawsuit can often predict with some certainty the likely outcome of their case. In doing so, they can make an intelligent decision about whether to pursue, settle, or dismiss a dispute.

A second function of the judiciary is to protect and uphold law that is consistent with the Constitution. To accomplish this, the judiciary has the duty to impose legal liability when legal principles are violated. For example, courts have long protected free expression of political views as part of the constitutional right to free speech. Any laws that attempt to restrict such expression for reasons other than something compelling, such as public safety, are unconstitutional and not enforced by the courts. In any case, the court must decide whether the applicable legal standard is constitutional. If so, it must determine whether the standard has been violated and also determine an appropriate compensation and/or penalty for any injury caused by the violation.

To answer these questions, the court must look to cases and statutes that address the situation. The court must then determine, when the legal prin-

ciples of these cases and statutes are applied to the present situation, what result would be indicated. This would then lead the court to its judgment in the case.

CLASSIFICATIONS OF COURTS

The judicial branch exists on many levels. However, most courts serve either a primarily trial court function or an appellate court function. The **trial court** is where the parties present evidence and seek a verdict resolving their dispute. The **appellate court** is where parties take their case from the trial court on the basis that some irregularity caused an improper verdict. For example, a party may claim that during jury selection, a potential juror lied in order to be seated on the jury. Once on the jury, that person successfully pressured the other jurors to find in favor of a particular party (who happened to be a friend). Such an irregularity might serve as a claim for appeal on the basis that the jury's verdict was not based on an objective evaluation of the evidence presented.

Courts are also classified as state or federal (see Exhibit 7.1). Federal courts typically hear cases involving federal law, some office of the federal government, or disputes between citizens of different states (provided the amount sued for exceeds the statutory minimum). The latter example is known as diversity of citizenship. State courts have jurisdiction over all cases involving their respective state laws and incidents occurring within or related to the jurisdiction.

Every state has a judicial system to provide a forum for the resolution of disputes among persons and entities within the state. Such disputes typically

trial court
Court with authority to hear evidence and rule on the legal rights of parties by applying appropriate legal standards.

appellate court
Court of superior authority that reviews the application of law by a trial court.

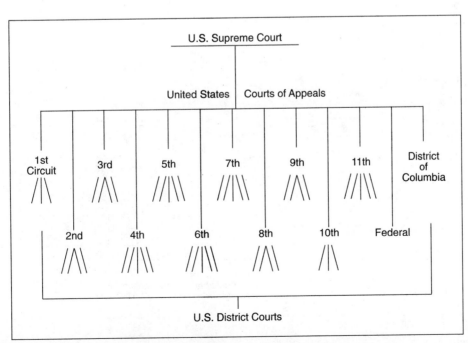

**EXHIBIT 7.1
Diagram of
Federal Courts.**

involve acts or occurrences that are controlled by state rather than federal law. State law may be case law or state legislative law. Federal courts and state courts are independent of and not subject to the authority of one another. The exception is that all courts of the nation are subject to the U.S. Supreme Court. At the state level, no state court is bound by the authority of a court from a different state. Nor is a court obligated to follow the rulings of an equivalent court. If a state court system has an intermediate appellate level made up of several courts, the opinions of these courts are not binding on one another. Rather, only the lower trial courts within the purview of authority of the particular appellate court are bound. Only the state high (supreme) court has authority over all subordinate trial and appellate courts within a state.

The states use one of two basic judicial structures (see Exhibit 7.2). The first is the three-tiered system, comparable to the federal system. The three tiers are made up of a court of last resort (the highest court of the state), an intermediate appellate court level, and a trial court level. In heavily populated states, there may be several of these intermediate appellate courts, similar to the numerous U.S. circuit courts of appeal in the federal system. At the lowest level are the trial courts, which include courts for civil and criminal trials, matters of domestic relations disputes, probate, juvenile, small claims, magistrates, and justice of the peace.

Most of the states employ the three-tiered system. A few, however, still use the two-tiered system, which consists of only one appellate (often called supreme) court and the various trial courts. Because of the increase in litigation, more states are using the three-tiered system. In the two-tiered system, appeals from the trial court are taken directly to the high court of the state, placing the total burden on a single group of judges. In the three-tiered system, appeals are taken to the intermediate appellate court first in the same manner as applied in the federal system. Then, if a party wants further review, appeal may be taken to the highest court of the state. However, most appeals

**EXHIBIT 7.2
Diagram of the
State Judicial
Systems.**

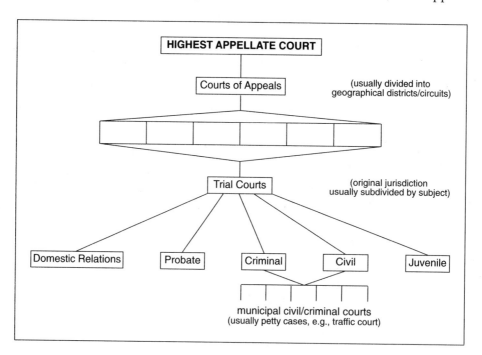

end after the first review, as the likelihood of a reversal declines dramatically with each appeal.

The terms *district court* and *circuit court* are employed in some states in the same way as in the federal system. Other states reverse these titles. The circuit court is the trial court, and the district court is the appellate court. Some states use other names entirely to describe their courts. Persons not trained in the structure of the legal system can be misled as to the importance of a judicial opinion by attaching more weight to the decision than is warranted simply because of the name of the court that rendered the opinion. What is important is that each state has a trial court level and an appellate court level and that the decisions carry greater weight in descending order from the highest appellate level to the lowest trial court.

The bottom tier, or trial courts, of the states handle more cases than any other level of state or federal court in the American legal system. These courts must therefore be organized to process the multitude of cases filed each year. Most often, state courts will divide the time of the various judges by the types of cases filed. For example, certain judges will devote their attention to domestic relations (divorce, custody, support, adoption, etc), while other judges will hear only criminal cases. These various divisions all operate together to create the trial court level. In addition, the trial courts within a particular state (usually at least one per county) are divided into geographical regions, usually bounded by county borders. Each court is responsible for the legal rights of persons and the legal issues arising from occurrences within the borders of the court's authority. By having a court within each county, the people are guaranteed reasonable access to the courts.

☐ ASSIGNMENT 7.2

Identify the information in each of the following as to whether the citation indicates federal or state judicial opinions:

1. 278 S.W. 2d, 7668 (Texas 1987).
2. 27 Cal. 3d 465, 612 P. 2d 948 (Cal. 1980).
3. 208 So. 2d 371 (Ala. 1968).
4. 306 F.2d 182 (U.S. 5th Circuit 1990).
5. 614 F. Supp. (U.S.D.Mont. 1978).
6. Mo.App.
7. U.S. District Court of Wyoming.
8. Madison County Circuit Court.
9. U.S. 8th Circuit Court of Appeals.
10. New Hampshire Supreme Court.

PUBLICATION OF JUDICIAL LAW

Chronological Publications

Published cases are predominantly appellate. The reasons for this are quite practical. First, trial courts are generally the lowest level of judicial authority. Consequently, a trial court opinion does not have to be followed by a judge in

a subsequent case because there are usually no courts below or subordinate to the trial court. However, appellate court opinions must be followed by those trial courts that are subordinate to the authority of the appellate court that issued the opinion. Also, appellate decisions are usually rendered by a panel of several appellate judges whose collective wisdom is respected by the legal community. Such opinions are seldom overturned by higher appellate courts and thus provide a stable basis for comparison of the stated legal standard to a present situation. A second reason for the limited number of published trial court opinions is cost effectiveness. There are literally hundreds of thousands of trials per year in this country. It would not be reasonable to publish all of the opinions supporting the outcome of these cases when they are of such limited authority.

report
Official publication of judicial opinions of a jurisdiction.

Judicial opinions are published in what are known as **reports** and reporters. New volumes of these books are published continuously and contain the judicial opinions as they are handed down by the courts. Thus, reports and reporters are published chronologically. Recall that publications of statutes are organized by subject and are periodically reviewed to contain changes and additions to the law. In contrast, once a judicial opinion is handed down, it remains virtually unchanged. If the verdict is altered by a higher court, that will be explained in a separate and new judicial opinion from the higher court. And the new reversing opinion will be published in a reporter at the time the opinion is given. The publication of the original opinion remains unchanged. Recall from Chapter 3 the caution that you should always validate your research because subsequent changes may not be carried back to the original publication but rather appear in later publications. This is especially true in publications of judicial law.

The usefulness of published cases is immeasurable. By having access to what opinions the courts have issued in the past, the outcome of future disputes can often be determined by the parties with great accuracy. Judges look to the cases to decide what the appropriate legal standards are and how they should be applied. The attorneys for the parties to disputes also examine the cases as an indicator of what their chances are of winning the lawsuit. In addition, it is not uncommon for parties or their lawyers to examine the cases before taking any action whatsoever. This often will guide the conduct of an individual or a business.

Official Reports

A large number of jurisdictions publish what are referred to as "official reports." These reports contain the appellate judicial opinions of the jurisdiction, and the publication is officially sanctioned by the state government. Quite often, the report is actually produced by the state printing office. Because a different publisher is responsible for the publication that contains the judicial opinions of each individual jurisdiction, the format varies. Many have no indexing system at all. Consequently, to do research, one must have the citation first. Because this system can be somewhat awkward and confined, many researchers prefer commercial publications, which have a variety of features to enable efficient and complete research on a subject even when the citation of a relevant case is not available to begin with. As you may recall, an increasing number of jurisdictions have ceased the

independent publication of their judicial opinions in favor of adopting a commercially produced publication as the official source of judicial law. By doing this, the state eliminates the cost of publication and gains multifaceted indexing and organization of its judicial law, which makes it much easier to research.

The National Reporter System

Regional and Federal Reporters.   The most comprehensive publication of state and federal judicial law in the United States is the National Reporter System. This collection of judicial opinions and indexing system by West Publishing Company is responsible for the publication of all state high court (appellate) opinions, intermediate appellate opinions, U.S. Supreme Court opinions, U.S. Court of Appeals opinions, and many U.S. District Court (trial court) and other published opinions. These opinions are categorized and regularly published under designated titles, and all are connected to the same subject indexing system, known as the key number system.

The National Reporter System consists of regional reporters and reporters for the different levels of federal courts. Each of the seven regional reporters routinely publish the new opinions of certain designated states. For example, the cases of California, Alaska, Arizona, Colorado, Hawaii, Idaho, Kansas, Montana, Nevada, New Mexico, Oklahoma, Oregon, Utah, Washington, and Wyoming are published in the Pacific Reporter Series. Opinions of other states are consistently published in a designated regional reporter as well. The reporters are Northwestern, Northeastern, Southwestern, Southeastern, Atlantic, and Southern. Once designated, a jurisdiction's opinions are always published in the same regional reporter. For example, the current cases of Nebraska are always published in Northwestern Reporter 2d series. Prior to the second series, they were published in the first series of the North West Reporter. There are also reporters for the federal courts: Supreme Court Reports (U.S. Supreme Court), Federal Reporter (U.S. Circuit Court of Appeals), and Federal Supplement (U.S. District Courts). Other West publications include the Federal Rules Decisions (federal cases with procedural issues), Bankruptcy Reporter, and various other specialized reporters.

Virtually the entire National Reporter System is currently publishing in a second series. While the state opinions continuously published in a reporter have not changed and cases continue to be published chronologically as they are issued, the volume numbers began again with volume number one as the first volume in the second series. As discussed previously, beginning a new series is the method used to denote changes in the format and features presented along with the content, in this case, judicial opinions.

Between issues of hardbound volumes (which take time to manufacture and are infrequently published in less active jurisdictions), paperback publications known as **advance sheets** are published. Advance sheets contain all the features of a reporter volume except that the advance sheet contains only those opinions in the reporter territory that have been issued since the last reporter or advance sheet. When the actual hardbound edition is issued, it will contain the same opinions in the advance sheets; as a result, the advance sheets are discarded. Because advance sheets are not cumulative, each issue should be consulted until a comprehensive volume is issued.

advance sheet
Publication of recently released judicial opinions that supplement hardbound reports/reporters.

Digests. One common thread that connects all reporters, whether first or second series, state or federal judicial opinions, is the indexing system. While many jurisdictions still publish an official report of their own judicial opinions, and other commercial reporters exist, West has the distinction of coordinating all published judicial opinions in the United States with a common format for indexing both in library and computer research.

This indexing system, known as the key number system, is quite similar to the organization of a statutory code. The key number system is published in various digests that annotate case law on national, regional, and state level. A single established list of topics (periodically updated) is arranged alphabetically in each digest. All subtopics are assigned numbers within the topic area. As necessary, these subtopics are broken down even further with additional numbers and letters assigned to create an extremely specific subject index. After each heading (e.g., topic and subtopic) are annotations commonly referred to as headnotes. What makes this system unique is that the very same topics and subtopics, and so on, are used for every jurisdictional publication. For example, if you were doing legal research in West Virginia on a particular topic, you could use the exact same topic and subtopic number to locate law on the same legal principle in the West Virginia Digest as in any other U.S. jurisdiction, such as Alaska, or the U.S. District Court. In today's mobile society, cases and the practice of law frequently are not confined to one state. The result is the need to do efficient research in a number of locations.

 APPLICATION 7.1

Jack lives in Illinois. While visiting family in Colorado, he enters a local sweepstakes. After returning to Illinois, Jack is informed that he won the sweepstakes and the grand prize trip to Florida. When Jack arrives in Florida, the hotel he is assigned to stay in is an old, dilapidated building. Nevertheless, Jack checks in. On the first day, he walks out onto the balcony adjoining his room. As Jack rests his hand on the railing, it gives way, and he falls two stories to the ground, suffering serious injuries. Jack's lawyer wants to file suit against the hotel as well as against the company that booked the trip and the organization that gave the trip as a prize. Research must be done as to where suit can be filed as well as to which jurisdiction (with authority) has the most favorable law to Jack's position. If not for a common indexing system, the search would have to be started from the beginning in every state using a different index with different terms.

APPLICATION 7.2

If you were to look for case law on the preceding example, you might locate the topic "Negligence" and the key number 32(2.3), Invitees in General. If you took this information to the digest for each jurisdiction, you would locate headnotes of cases from those jurisdictions that discussed the duty of a business owner to one invited onto the premises to conduct business.

Even with this system, however, there is so much case law—and it continues to grow—that a simple index would be too cumbersome to manage efficient research. Consequently, the digest consists of more than a basic

subject index such as you have probably used in the past. Part of each digest (which consists of multiple volumes) is called a descriptive word index (see Exhibit 7.3), which you would compare to an ordinary subject index in a book. The descriptive word index contains a variety of terms that lead you to particular information within the digest. However, in place of page numbers, key topics and numbers are given. Also, many terms are cross-referenced to make research easier. For example, if you looked up a term that was not in the West table of topics, you might find reference to the West topic or topics that are related to that term.

Once you have determined the topic and key number that would appear to address your research query (Exhibit 7.4), you can locate that topic in alphabetized topics in the other volumes of the digest. The topics included in each volume appear on the cover and binding. Once you locate the topic (Exhibit 7.5), you need only to move through the consecutive numbers until you locate the key number you have been given (Exhibits 7.6, 7.7). Once there, you will find headnotes (annotations) of cases and/or specific references to other West publications, such as *Corpus Juris Secundum.* If no headnotes are given, then as of the date of publication, no cases were published under that key number. THIS DOES NOT MEAN that no cases on your query exist. After all, your search may include other topics and key numbers. This is one reason that makes it necessary to have as many relevant terms as possible to use in your research. Also, as with all research, check supplements! West regularly publishes pocket parts for inclusion in digests. Also, validate your case law through the use of a citator for any new case law and to ensure that the cases you have found are still effective.

Topical Indexes

In addition to using the subject index method, you can conduct research through a topic index approach. This is essentially the same as the topical

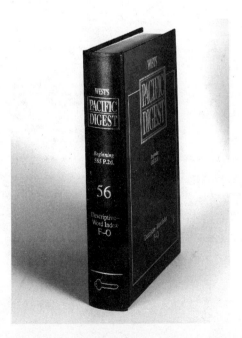

The Descriptive Word Index for Pacific Digest.

EXHIBIT 7.3
Descriptive Word
Index for the
Pacific Digest
(Volume 56,
Page 328).
Copyright 1992 by
West Publishing
Company
(1–800–328–9352).

LANDLORD

56 P.D.(585 P.2d)—328

References are to Digest Topics and Key Numbers

LANDLORD AND TENANT—Cont'd
EVIDENCE—Cont'd
Trespass to try title. Tresp to T T 40(2)
Value of lease. Evid 113(6)
Waiver of forfeiture of lease. Land & Ten 112½
EXECUTION in judicial proceedings—
Leased property subject to. Execution 34
EXECUTION of lease. Land & Ten 25(1)
EXISTENCE of property as affecting lease. Land & Ten 21
EXIT appurtenant to leased premises. Land & Ten 124(2)
EXPIRATION of term. Land & Ten 93
EXTENSION of terms. Land & Ten 82–92
EXTENT of premises. Land & Ten 122
FARM lease in general. Land & Ten 135–139
FARM subsidy programs—
Duty to comply with requirements. Land & Ten 39
FEDERAL preemption—
State laws or regulations. States 18.39
FEES, see this index Fees
FENCES, see this index Fences
FERRIES, lease of, see this index Leases
FILING mortgages of leaseholds. Land & Ten 81(4)
FINES and penalties—
Transfer of property subject to rent lien. Land & Ten 251(5)
Wrongful dispossession under law suspending remedy for recovery of possession. Land & Ten 278.17(4)
FIRE escapes, see this index Fire Escapes
FIXTURES—
Agreements between landlord and tenant. Fixt 27(2)
Between landlord and tenant and their privies. Fixt 13–17
FORCIBLE entry and detainer—
See this index Forcible Entry and Detainer
Bonds—
Pending appeal. Land & Ten 291(18)
FORECLOSURE of mortgages. Mortgages, generally, post
FORFEITURES, see this index Forfeitures
FORM of lease. Land & Ten 24
FRAUD as defense to action for rent. Land & Ten 222
FRAUD in respect to lease. Land & Ten 28
FRAUDULENT conveyance—
Retention of possession as lessee. Fraud Conv 143
GAMBLING—
Effect on validity of lease. Land & Ten 29(3)
Lease of house or place for. Gaming 76
GARNISHMENT of leased property. Garn 28
GAS as an appurtenance. Land & Ten 124
GAS leases, see this index Oil and Gas Leases
GOOD faith—
Suspension of right of reentry and recovery of possession by landlord, post
GRANTEE of reversion, rights of. Land & Ten 53(2)
GRASS, injury to by third persons. Land & Ten 142(3)
GROUND rents, see this index Ground Rents
GUARANTY of lease. Guar 36(8)
GUARDIAN'S lease of ward's property. Guard & W 44
Under order of court. Guard & W 113
Determination as to necessity. Guard & W 89
GUARDS, injuries from want of. Land & Ten 167(4)
GUESTS of tenant, injury to. Land & Ten 167(8)
HABITABILITY. Land & Ten 125
HEALTH regulations, see this index Health and Environment
HEAT, see this index Heat
HOLDING over—
Estoppel, effect on. Land & Ten 62(4)
Extension by. Land & Ten 90
Month to month tenancy. Land & Ten 115(3)
Renewal by. Land & Ten 90
Rent, amount while holding over. Land & Ten 200.9
Sufficiency to create new tenancy. Land & Ten 90(4)
Tenancy at sufferance, creation by. Land & Ten 119(2)
Tenancy at will, creation by. Land & Ten 118(4)
Year-to-year tenancy. Land & Ten 114(3)
HOMESTEAD, see this index Homestead

LANDLORD AND TENANT—Cont'd
HUSBAND and wife—
Lease of community property. Hus & W 267(3)
Administration of community. Hus & W 276(6)
Separate property of wife, see this index Separate Estate of Wife
ICE and snow—
Generally, see this index Ice and Snow
IMPLIED contracts, see this index Implied Contracts
IMPLIED covenants. Land & Ten 45
IMPLIED tenancy, see this index Implied Tenancy
IMPROVEMENTS. Land & Ten 150–161
Actions. Land & Ten 159
Claims for. Land & Ten 223(7)
Compensation. Land & Ten 157(6–8)
Damages for failure to make. Land & Ten 223(6)
Lien. Land & Ten 157(10)
Ownership in general. Land & Ten 157(2)
Remedy for failure to make. Land & Ten 159
Removal. Land & Ten 157(4)
INCOME tax, see this index Income Tax
INCUMBRANCES. Land & Ten 145–149
Reasonable rent, incumbrances as factor in determining. Land & Ten 200.25
INDORSEMENT, extension or renewal on lease. Land & Ten 89
INFANT'S property, lease of. Infants 44
INJUNCTION—
Covenants as to use of leased premises. Inj 62(2)
Disturbance of possession of tenant. Land & Ten 132(2)
Summary proceedings. Land & Ten 299
Unlawful detainer, action for. Land & Ten 290½
Violation of laws relating to suspension of right of reentry and recovery of possession by landlord. Land & Ten 278.16
Waste. Land & Ten 55(4)
INJURIES—
Criminal activities. Land & Ten 164(1)
Crop. Land & Ten 139(4)
Dangerous or defective condition. Land & Ten 162–170
Mobile home parks, see this index Trailer Parks or Camps
Employees of tenant. Land & Ten 165, 169(5)
Premises. Land & Ten 140–142
Eviction. Land & Ten 176
Terminating lease. Land & Ten 101
Property of tenant. Land & Ten 166
Property of third persons. Land & Ten 167(9)
Reversion. Land & Ten 55
Tenants or occupants. Land & Ten 164
Warranty of habitability. Land & Ten 125(1)
INNKEEPERS, see this index Innkeepers
INSANE persons, see this index Mental Health
INSOLVENCY, termination of lease. Land & Ten 101½
INSURANCE—
Covenants to insure. Land & Ten 156
Insurable interest. Insurance 115(4)
Landlord's liability insurance—
Risks and causes of loss. Insurance 435.34
Nature and cause of injury or damage. Insurance 435.35
Right to proceeds. Insurance 580(4)
INTERFERENCE with—
Possession of tenant. Land & Ten 131–133
Relationship. Land & Ten 19
Use of premises. Land & Ten 134(4), 172(2)
INTERVENTION, see this index Intervention
INTOXICATING liquors, see this index Intoxicating Liquors
INVALIDITY as affecting action for unlawful detainer. Land & Ten 290(4)
JOINT tenants, implied tenancy between. Land & Ten 8
JUDGMENT—
Conclusiveness. Judgm 684
Recovery of possession, action for. Land & Ten 285(6)

EXHIBIT 7.4
**Pacific Digest
(Volume 38,
Page 323).**
Copyright 1991 by
West Publishing
Company
(1–800–328–9352).

38 P.D.(585 P.2d)—323   **LANDLORD & TENANT**

VII. PREMISES, AND ENJOYMENT AND USE THEREOF, ☞121–180(6).

    (A) DESCRIPTION, EXTENT, AND CONDITION, ☞121–125.

    (B) POSSESSION, ENJOYMENT, AND USE, ☞126–144.

    (C) INCUMBRANCES, TAXES, AND ASSESSMENTS, ☞145–149.

    (D) REPAIRS, INSURANCE, AND IMPROVEMENTS, ☞150–161.

    (E) INJURIES FROM DANGEROUS OR DEFECTIVE CONDITION, ☞162–170.

    (F) EVICTION, ☞171–180.

VIII. RENT AND ADVANCES, ☞181–274(9).

    (A) RIGHTS AND LIABILITIES, ☞181–216.

    (B) ACTIONS, ☞217–238.

    (C) LIEN, ☞239–262½.

    (D) DISTRESS, ☞263–274.

IX. RE-ENTRY AND RECOVERY OF POSSESSION BY LANDLORD, ☞275–318(3).

X. RENTING ON SHARES, ☞319–349.

approach to statutory research or research in a legal encyclopedia, such as *Corpus Juris Secundum* (C.J.S.). Each topic begins with a breakdown of subtopics and the corresponding key numbers. If there are numerous subtopics and further subdivisions, the subtopics and numbers for the various subdivisions will be listed. Following this are pages with individual breakdowns of each subtopic and subdivision with the accompanying key numbers. Finally, the numerically arranged specific listings of titles and headnotes are included.

☐ ASSIGNMENT 7.3

Based on Application 7.2, identify the appropriate topic, subtopic, and specific key number(s) that correspond to the following query: Is a landlord required to notify a tenant of any open areas of water on the property regardless of the distance from the residential premises or the size and depth of the body of water?

Another helpful feature of the digest system is the table of case names, arranged by plaintiff and defendant (see Exhibit 7.8). If you have the name of a case, or even of one party, you can use the table of cases to locate the complete citation. In addition to providing the case citation, this table provides you with each of the key numbers that relate to subjects addressed within the case. The table is arranged by both the name of the plaintiff and the name of the defendant. Thus, only one party name is necessary to use the table. However, because many different lawsuits may involve parties of the same name, the more information you have, the more likely you will find the proper citation quickly.

EXHIBIT 7.5
Pacific Digest
(Volume 38, Page 333).
Copyright 1991 by
West Publishing
Company
(1–800–328–9352).

38 P.D.(585 P.2d)—333   **LANDLORD & TENANT**

VII. PREMISES, AND ENJOYMENT AND USE THEREOF.—Continued.

    (D) REPAIRS, INSURANCE, AND IMPROVEMENTS.—Continued.

        ☞157. Improvements by tenant and covenants therefor. Continued.

           (11). Determination of compensation.

           (12). Actions for compensation.

      158. Improvements by landlord and covenants therefor.

      159. Remedies for failure to make improvements.

           (1). Actions for breach of tenant's covenant to make improvements.

           (2). Actions for breach of landlord's covenant to make improvements.

      160. Condition of premises at termination of tenancy.

           (1). In general.

           (2). Covenants and agreements as to condition of premises on termination of tenancy.

           (3). Duty of tenant to rebuild or replace personal property.

           (4). Actions for breach of covenant.

      161. Personal property on premises at termination of tenancy.

           (1). Rights and liabilities as to property on premises in general.

           (2). Care of property left on premises by outgoing tenant.

           (3). Actions to recover property or value.

    (E) INJURIES FROM DANGEROUS OR DEFECTIVE CONDITION.

        ☞162. Nature and extent of landlord's duty to tenant.

      163. Mutual duties of tenants of different portions of same premises.

      164. Injuries to tenants or occupants.

           (1). Injuries due to defective or dangerous condition of premises in general.

           (2). Injuries due to failure to repair.

           (3). Injuries due to negligence in making repairs.

           (4). Injuries due to unlighted passageways.

           (5). Liability for injuries to subtenant.

           (6). Liability of landlord as dependent on knowledge of defects.

           (7). Notice to or knowledge of tenant as to defects.

      165. Injuries to employé of tenant.

           (1). Injuries due to defective or dangerous condition of premises in general.

           (2). Injuries due to failure to repair.

           (3). Injuries due to unlighted passageway.

           (4). Liability of landlord as dependent on knowledge of defects.

           (5). Failure to guard dangerous places.

           (6). Operation or condition of elevators.

           (7). Notice to or knowledge of tenant as to defects.

      166. Injuries to property of tenant on premises.

           (1). Nature and extent of the duties of landlord and tenant respectively.

           (2). Injuries due to defective condition of premises in general.

           (3). Injuries due to failure to repair.

           (4). Injuries due to negligence in making repairs.

           (5). Injuries due to defective water pipes or drains.

           (6). Injuries due to negligent acts of landlord.

           (7). Injuries due to negligence of third persons in general.

           (9). Injuries due to negligence of cotenant.

☞162 LANDLORD & TENANT

38 P.D.(585 P.2d)—468

For later cases see same Topic and Key Number in Pocket Part

and issue as to whether the landlord failed in that duty was a question for the jury to decide.

> Stephens v. Stearns, 678 P.2d 41, 106 Idaho 249.

A landlord's violation of a uniform building code contained in an ordinance amounts to negligence per se under section 288A of the Restatement (Second) of Torts, but the landlord may be excused from the imposition of negligence per se if he relied upon the certificates of occupancy issued by the city inspector.

> Stephens v. Stearns, 678 P.2d 41, 106 Idaho 249.

Mont. 1985. Owners of apartment complex have duty to use ordinary care to have their premises reasonably safe and to warn of any hidden or lurking danger. MCA 27–1–701.

> Limberhand v. Big Ditch Co., 706 P.2d 491, 218 Mont. 132.

Duty to others owed by landlord in management of property is to use that degree of ordinary care which reasonable persons would use under same or similar circumstances. MCA 27–1–701.

> Limberhand v. Big Ditch Co., 706 P.2d 491, 218 Mont. 132.

Mont. 1981. Common-law doctrine of caveat emptor does not apply to rental of residences. MCA 70–24–101 to 70–24–442.

> Corrigan v. Janney, 626 P.2d 838, 192 Mont. 99.

Standard of care determinative of liability of landlord was that provided by general obligation statute, i. e, owner of premises is under duty to exercise ordinary care in management of premises to avoid exposing persons thereon to unreasonable risk of harm. R.C.M.1947, § 58–607 (Repealed).

> Corrigan v. Janney, 626 P.2d 838, 192 Mont. 99.

Mont. 1980. Landlord owes duty to tenant to keep all common areas of the premises in a clean and safe condition. MCA 70–24–303.

> Rennick v. Hoover, 606 P.2d 1079, 186 Mont. 167.

N.M. 1991. Lessor may be liable for injuries resulting from lessee's activities if lessor reserves right to enter, i.e., right of control, whether or not lessor knows of lessee's specific activities and risk of harm caused thereby.

> Bober v. New Mexico State Fair, 808 P.2d 614, 111 N.M. 644.

N.M.App. 1981. Premises alone is not "product" and landlord is not subject to strict liability for renting of bare premises only.

> Begay v. Livingston, 658 P.2d 434, 99 N.M. 359, reversed 652 P.2d 734, 98 N.M. 712.

N.M.App. 1980. If landlord retains possession or control of portion of leased premises, he is charged with duty of exercising ordinary care in maintaining retained portion.

> Strong v. Shaw, 629 P.2d 784, 96 N.M. 281, certiorari quashed Reco Corp. v. Strong, 632 P.2d 1181, 96 N.M. 543.

N.M.App. 1979. Where landlord fully parts with possession of premises and retains no control or right of control over them, and does not thereafter assume control, he is under no duty to inspect their condition while a tenant remains in possession, and he is not chargeable with liability for defects not made by him or under his direction for failure to make repairs.

> Torres v. Piggly Wiggly Shop Rite Foods, Inc., 600 P.2d 1198, 93 N.M. 408, certiorari denied 604 P.2d 821, 93 N.M. 683.

Landlord is responsible for areas expressly or impliedly reserved for use in common of different tenants.

> Torres v. Piggly Wiggly Shop Rite Foods, Inc., 600 P.2d 1198, 93 N.M. 408, certiorari denied 604 P.2d 821, 93 N.M. 683.

Okl. 1986. Landlord has duty to use ordinary care to maintain common portions of leased premises, over which he has retained control, in a safe condition.

> Lay v. Dworman, 732 P.2d 455.

Or. 1988. Residential Landlord and Tenant Act does not supersede common law in all aspects of landowner's personal injury liability. ORS 91.770–91.895.

> Bellikka v. Green, 762 P.2d 997, 306 Or. 630.

Or.App. 1980. At common law, in absence of provision in lease imposing such obligation, landlord has no duty to supply fire-fighting equipment for leased premises.

> Dundas v. Lincoln County, 618 P.2d 978, 48 Or.App. 1025.

Utah 1981. Duty of landlord to use reasonable care to protect lessees may rest on common-law principles of negligence.

> Hall v. Warren, 632 P.2d 848, appeal after remand 692 P.2d 737.

Pertinent safety standards established by building codes are considered as much part of lease as if expressed in contract.

> Hall v. Warren, 632 P.2d 848, appeal after remand 692 P.2d 737.

Wash.App. 1991. Landlord may be liable for personal injury to tenant on basis of rental agreement, common law, or implied warranty

EXHIBIT 7.6
Pacific Digest (Volume 38, Page 468).
Copyright 1991 by West Publishing Company (1–800–328–9352).

LIEB

References are to Digest Topics and Key Numbers

Lieb v. Milne Intern. Sales & Service, NMApp, 625 P2d 1233, 95 NM 716. See Lieb v. Milne.

Liebelt v. Liebelt, Idaho App, 801 P2d 52, 118 Idaho 845.—App & E 1106(5); Contracts 93(8), 95(1), 96, 97(1), 99(1), 253, 256; Courts 176½; Hus & W 29(9), 34.

Liebergesell v. Evans, Wash, 613 P2d 1170, 93 Wash2d 881.—Atty & C 63; Contracts 94(1), 94(8); Estop 52.15, 55; Fraud 7; Judgm 185.3(16), 186; Phys 12; Usury 11, 12, 103.

Liebergesell v. Evans, WashApp, 597 P2d 908, 23 WashApp 357, review gr, case rev 613 P2d 1170, 93 Wash2d 881.—App & E 934(1); Joint Adv 1.1; Usury 11, 12, 18, 36, 103, 117.

Liebman v. Brunell, Mont, 689 P2d 248, 212 Mont 459.—Mand 63, 66, 73(1).

Liebmann v. Fidelity Bank, N. A., Okl-App, 635 P2d 1339.—Judgm 183, 948(2), 951(4); Release 45, 51.

Liebowitz v. Aimexco Inc., ColoApp, 701 P2d 140.—Atty & C 24; Costs 2.

Liebreich v. Cohen, OrApp, 620 P2d 975, 49 OrApp 943.—Contracts 89; Lim of Act 13; Mtg 319(1).

Liedtke v. Paccar, Inc., OrApp, 605 P2d 1377, 44 OrApp 461.—Prod Liab 88.5.

Liedtke v. Schettler, Utah, 649 P2d 80.—Const Law 213.1(2), 249(9); Courts 176½.

Lien v. Barnett, WashApp, 794 P2d 865, 58 WashApp 680.—Damag 50.10; Hus & W 323, 324; Pretrial Proc 682, 683.

Lien v. Murphy Corp., Mont, 656 P2d 804, 201 Mont 488.—Judgm 646, 650; Plead 248(9), 250.

Liese v. Smith, Idaho, 656 P2d 1359, 104 Idaho 106. See Loomis, Inc. v. Cudahy.

Liese v. Smith, Idaho, 615 P2d 128, 101 Idaho 459. See Loomis, Inc. v. Cudahy.

Liesegang v. Employment Div., OrApp, 699 P2d 203, 73 OrApp 470. See Claimant Members of Boilermakers Local 72 v. Employment Div.

Lieuallen v. Umatilla County, OrApp, 645 P2d 1074, 57 OrApp 563, review den 650 P2d 928, 293 Or 483.—App & E 1073(1).

Life Financial Inc. X v. American Guar. Financial Corp., OrApp, 704 P2d 122, 74 OrApp 497.—App & E 1041(2); Dep & Escr 17; Evid 400(2); Insurance 34; Judgm 181(29).

Life General Sec. Ins. Co. v. Patterson, OklApp, 746 P2d 696. See National Home Life Assur. Co. v. Patterson.

Life Ins. Co. of North America v. Cassidy, Cal, 676 P2d 1050, 200 CalRptr 28, 35 C3d 599.—Evid 268; Hus & W 249(3), 265, 266.2(1), 273(1); Insurance 583(1), 586(1), 593(1).

Life Ins. Co. of North America v. Evans, Mont, 637 P2d 806, 195 Mont 242.—Insurance 454, 454.2.

Life Ins. Co. of North America v. Minnequa Bank of Pueblo, ColoApp, 782 P2d 810. See Stjernholm v. Life Ins. Co. of North America.

Life Ins. Co. of North America v. Wollett, Nev, 766 P2d 893, 104 Nev 687.—Insurance 594.1.

Life of the Land v. Land Use Commission of State of Hawaii, Hawaii, 623 P2d 431, 63 Haw 166.—Action 6, 13; Admin Law 668; App & E 949; Const Law 67, 70.1(1), 72; Courts 97(1); Decl Judgm 300; Parties 1, 3, 35.1, 35.5, 35.9, 35.11, 35.13, 35.17, 35.21, 35.33, 35.69, 35.79; Zoning 571.

Life of the Land, Inc. v. City Council of City and County of Honolulu, Hawaii, 606 P2d 866, 61 Haw 390.—Elections 317; Evid 32, 83(1); Mun Corp 57, 85, 120; Statut 217.4; Zoning 35, 101, 102, 376, 633, 642, 643, 644, 646, 762.

Life of the Land, Inc. v. City Council of City and County of Honolulu, Hawaii, 592 P2d 26, 60 Haw 446.—App & E 447; Zoning 762.

Life of the Land, Inc. v. Land Use Commission, Hawaii, 594 P2d 1079, 61 Haw 3.—Admin Law 668, 722; Zoning 571, 584.

Life of the Land, Inc. v. West Beach Development Corp., Hawaii, 631 P2d 588, 63 Haw 529.—Admin Law 412; Zoning 351, 357, 358, 359, 584, 586.

Lige Dickson Co. v. Union Oil Co. of California, Wash, 635 P2d 103, 96 Wash2d 291.—Frds St of 144.

Liggett v. State Indus. Ins. System, Nev, 661 P2d 882, 99 Nev 262.—Work Comp 1174.

Light v. Cronin, Colo, 621 P2d 309.—Extrad 34, 36; Hab Corp 729.

Light v. Sheets, OrApp, 804 P2d 1197, 105 OrApp 298.—Land & Ten 187(1), 291(14).

Light's Estate, Matter of, ColoApp, 585 P2d 311, 41 ColoApp 332.—Lim of Act 48(1); Wills 441, 481, 488, 759(2).

Lighter v. Marvin, WashApp, 749 P2d 691, 50 WashApp 611. See Eubank, Matter of Estate of.

Lightly v. State, Wyo, 739 P2d 1232.—Crim Law 1216.1(2).

Lightner v. Centennial Life Ins. Co., Kan, 744 P2d 840, 242 Kan 29.—App & E 893(1); Insurance 146.1(2), 146.2, 146.3(1), 146.5(5), 146.7(1), 149, 151(2), 589.

Lightner v. Frank, Kan, 727 P2d 430, 240 Kan 21.—Autos 190, 198(4), 226(1); Joint Adv 1.2; Neglig 89(1), 135(8).

Lightning A Ranch Venture v. Tankersley, ArizApp, 779 P2d 812, 161 Ariz 497.—App & E 436, 440, 776; Courts 37(1); Joint Adv 1.14.

Lightning A Ranch Venture v. Tankersley, ArizApp, 775 P2d 1102, 161 Ariz 38, vac and superseded 779 P2d 812, 161 Ariz 497.

Lignell v. Berg, Kan, 593 P2d 800.—App & E 882(8), 964, 1177(2); Contracts 232(1), 350(1); Costs 194.32; Interest 21, 31, 68; Joint Adv 8; Jury 12(1), 25(2); Licens 1, 39.43; Parties 76(1); Princ & S 73; Trial 2.

Ligocky v. Wilcox, NMApp, 620 P2d 1300, 95 NM 275.—Poisons 6; Sales 284(1).

Ligon v. State, OklCr, 712 P2d 74.—Crim Law 274(2).

Likens, Matter of Compensation of, Or-App, 642 P2d 342, 56 OrApp 498.—Work Comp 1003, 1042, 1530, 1981.

Likens v. State Acc. Ins. Fund Corp., OrApp, 642 P2d 342. See Likens, Matter of Compensation of.

Lile, Matter of, Wash, 668 P2d 581, 100 Wash2d 224.—Crim Law 778(3), 778(5), 1173.2(5); Hab Corp 290, 481; Homic 109, 244(3).

Liles v. City of Gresham, OrApp, 672 P2d 1229, 66 OrApp 59.—Zoning 445.

Liles v. State, OklCr, 702 P2d 1025, cert den 106 SCt 2291, 476 US 1164, 90 LEd2d 732, reh den 106 SCt 3341, 478 US 1028, 92 LEd2d 749, grant of habeas corpus aff 945 F2d 333, cert den Saffle v. Liles, 112 SCt 956.—Costs 302.4; Crim Law 641.13(1), 641.13(2),

641.13(6), 706(3), 769, 795(2), 796, 865(2), 1037.1(1), 1037.2, 1038.3, 1042, 1134(2), 1144.10, 1171.1(2), 1171.8(2), 1203.3, 1208.1(6); Homic 308(2), 309(6), 311, 356, 357(4), 357(11); Jury 33(2.1).

Liles v. State, OklCr, 702 P2d 1022.—Crim Law 622.1(2), 622.2(6), 622.2(7), 622.3, 662.10, 1148, 1159.3(3); Homic 253(6).

Liles v. Wedding, OrApp, 733 P2d 952, 84 OrApp 350.—Ease 18(1), 18(6), 36(1), 44(1).

Liley, ReMine ex rel., v. District Court For City and County of Denver, Colo, 709 P2d 1379. See ReMine ex rel. Liley v. District Court for City and County of Denver.

Lilienthal v. District Court of Sixteenth Judicial Dist., Rosebud County, Mont, 650 P2d 779, 200 Mont 236.—Const Law 273; Contempt 55, 61(1), 66(5), 74; Tresp 47, 65.

Liljestrand v. Mid-Century Ins. Co., ColoApp, 598 P2d 152. See Chavez v. Zanghi.

Liljestrand v. State Farm Mut. Auto Ins. Co., WashApp, 734 P2d 945, 47 WashApp 283, review den.—App & E 125; Insurance 467.51(1), 467.51(4), 578.

Lill v. State, KanApp, 602 P2d 129, 4 KanApp2d 40.—Const Law 268.1(1); Crim Law 275, 998(7), 1030(2), 1086.4.

Lillig v. Becton-Dickinson, Wash, 717 P2d 1371, 105 Wash2d 653, reconsideration den.—Labor 1535, 1541, 1562; Libel 50, 51(1), 112(2).

Lilly v. Missouri Valley Steel, Inc., Kan, 625 P2d 1123. See Vogel v. Missouri Valley Steel, Inc.

Lilly v. Scott, OklApp, 598 P2d 279.—App & E 1060.2, 1060.6; Autos 159, 246(39); Neglig 97; Trial 110, 251(2); Witn 330(1).

Lilly v. Terwilliger, Mont, 796 P2d 199, 244 Mont 93.—Sec Tran 230, 231, 240.

Lilly and Co. v. Kirkman Laboratories, Inc., WashApp, 814 P2d 1186, 62 WashApp 451. See Hibbs v. Abbott Laboratories.

Lim v. Harvis Const., Inc., Hawaii, 647 P2d 290, 65 Haw 71.—Pretrial Proc 676, 678.

Lim v. Superior Court In and For Pima County, ArizApp, 616 P2d 941, 126 Ariz 481.—Courts 207.1; Lim of Act 55(1), 91.

Lima v. Chambers, Utah, 657 P2d 279.—Insurance 514.15; Parties 40(7), 41, 48; Trial 127; Witn 196.

Lima v. Jackson County, OrApp, 643 P2d 355, 56 OrApp 619.—Zoning 445, 570, 571.

Lima School Dist. No. 12 and Elementary School Dist. of Beaverhead County v. Simonsen, Mont, 683 P2d 471, 210 Mont 100.—App & E 169, 931(1), 1008.1(3), 1010.1(6); Domicile 1; Evid 96(2), 597; High 98; Proc 171; Schools 148(1), 159½(1), 159½(5); States 199.

Limberhand v. Big Ditch Co., Mont, 706 P2d 491, 218 Mont 132.—Judgm 181(24), 181(33); Land & Ten 162, 164(1), 167(8); Mun Corp 736; Neglig 32(2.2), 32(2.3), 33(1), 34, 39, 41, 50, 52, 136(14); Waters 260.

Limmer v. Samaritan Health Service, ArizApp, 710 P2d 1077, 147 Ariz 422.—Admin Law 686; Hosp 6.

Limpy, In re Marriage of, Mont, 636 P2d 266, 195 Mont 314.—Courts 490; Indians 27(2), 32(7).

EXHIBIT 7.8 **Pacific Digest (Volume 706, Page 491).**

LIMBERHAND v. BIG DITCH CO.   Mont. **491**
Cite as 706 P.2d 491 (Mont. 1985)

Connie **LIMBERHAND, Individually, and as Personal Representative of the Estate of Jaylon Limberhand, Deceased Minor, Plaintiff and Appellant,**

v.

BIG DITCH COMPANY; City of Billings; Ken Nicholson and Allen Nicholson, each individually and d/b/a Apple Creek Property Management, Inc., Defendants and Respondents.

No. 84–418.

Supreme Court of Montana.

Submitted May 2, 1985.

Decided Sept. 26, 1985.

Action was brought against several defendants for wrongful death of 18–month-old child who drowned in irrigation ditch. Summary judgment was entered for all defendants in the District Court, Thirteenth Judicial District, County of Yellowstone, Charles Luedke, J., and plaintiff appealed. The Supreme Court, Sheehy, J., held that: (1) doctrine of attractive nuisance did not apply to claim against owner of irrigation ditch; (2) there was material issue as to whether irrigation ditch presented peculiar danger in nature of hidden peril or trap for the unwary, thus precluding summary judgment for owner of irrigation ditch; (3) city was not liable for failing to declare commercial irrigation ditch a public nuisance and to take remedial measures; and (4) there was material issue as to whether irrigation ditch could present sufficient danger to tenants of apartment complex and their social guests so that landlords breached duty to keep premises reasonably safe by not taking remedial or warning measures, thus precluding summary judgment for landlords.

Reversed in part; affirmed in part.

1. Negligence ⬕41

Degree of care of one who maintains on his land artificial stream or body of water for useful purpose, where stream or body of water has natural characteristics, is no greater than degree of care required of one through whose land flows natural stream or contains natural body of water.

2. Negligence ⬕39, 41

Owner or user of artificial stream or body of water having natural characteristics is bound to no special duty of care or precaution for protection of children who may enter therein, unless there is in or about artificial stream or body of water some peculiar danger, in nature of hidden peril or trap for the unwary, of which owner or user has or ought to have notice.

3. Negligence ⬕32(2.2, 2.3), 33(1)

Test for determining duty owed by landowner to injured party is whether landowner exercised ordinary care under the circumstances, regardless of whether injured party is guest, invitee, or trespasser. MCA 27–1–701.

4. Waters and Water Courses ⬕260

Doctrine of attractive nuisance did not apply in action against owner of irrigation ditch for wrongful death of 18–month-old child who drowned in irrigation ditch.

5. Negligence ⬕50, 52

Landowner's duty to provide warnings, fences, or other protective devices for the unwary is measured by landowner's duty to exercise ordinary care or skill in management of his property. MCA 27–1–701.

6. Judgment ⬕181(33)

There was material issue as to whether irrigation ditch presented peculiar danger in the nature of hidden peril or trap for the unwary, thus precluding summary judgment for owner of irrigation ditch in action for wrongful death of 18–month-old child who drowned in irrigation ditch. MCA 27–1–701.

7. Municipal Corporations ⬕736

City's failure to declare commercial irrigation ditch used by 30.6% of adjoining landowners a public nuisance and to take remedial measures was not grounds for liability of city for death of 18–month-old

Once you have used the digest to locate a judicial opinion, you will find that in the reporter, the text of the opinion is preceded by the same key numbers found within the digest containing headnotes on the opinion. As you know, a headnote is a brief statement of the holding of a case on a particular issue. A headnote is prepared for every issue within an opinion. In the reporter, each of the issues is numbered 1,2,3, etc., through the opinion. At the beginning of the judicial opinion are these numbered sections followed by the topic, specific headnote title, key number, and the actual headnote that appears under that same digest title and number in the digest. Not only are the headnotes useful in the digest to locate cases that are on point with your research, but by repeating the headnotes at the beginning of the opinion, you can quickly locate the exact part of the opinion where the information you are searching for appears. However, you are cautioned to read the entire opinion, because information taken out of context may have a totally different impact than that of the complete opinion.

All West publications make reference to the key number system. For example, in a C.J.S. footnote, you may find reference to a West digest key number. However, you will also see similar alphanumerical arrangements in publications other than digests and cases that are not part of the key number system. These may even be found in other West publications. For example, the United States Code Annotated is published by West. Each statute is annotated, and the annotations are arranged by subject, with a corresponding number for each subject. However, these subjects and numbers do not correspond to the West key number system. After each statute is a cross-reference to West key numbers to be used in digest research, but they are unrelated to the statutory annotation arrangement.

🗔 ASSIGNMENT 7.4

Using Exhibits 7.4-7.9 identify the topic, subtopic, and key number that you think would be most likely to contain headnotes that address the following situation. Explain how each example can be used to assist you in your conclusion. Additionally, examine the page from the table of cases and give the citation(s) of cases that might also prove useful.

FACTS: The Jones family were tenants in a duplex on a farm just outside of town. On the farm, approximately one fourth of a mile from the duplex, was a dry creek bed. Occasionally in the spring, the creek, bed would fill with water for one to two days after the snow melted north of the farm. During one such episode, the Jones's five-year-old wandered from the duplex and fell into the creek, where she drowned.

OTHER METHODS OF JUDICIAL RESEARCH

While the most common methods of judicial research are consulting annotated statutes and digests, other sources in the law library can be valuable tools to locate applicable judicial law. Annotations provide an

extremely brief summary and citation. Other sources often give a more detailed discussion of the principle of law.

As discussed in Chapter 5, legal encyclopedias present well-established and widely accepted legal principles followed by the majority of states. An additional research feature of legal encyclopedias is their extensive footnotes. Quite often, these footnotes consist of judicial citations that are cases that exemplify the legal principle under discussion. When consulting the supplement to a legal encyclopedia, if the principle has remained unchanged, the supplement contains recent footnotes of more recent cases where the principle was discussed and applied. The only disadvantage is that the footnotes are only examples and are not exhaustive lists of case law on the topic. Therefore, the fact that a footnote does not contain a citation from your jurisdiction does not mean that no case law on the subject exists there. On the other hand, when you are conducting research on an uncommon issue, you may use a legal encyclopedia to lead you to persuasive authority on the topic when there is no primary authority from your own jurisdiction.

As with legal encyclopedias, annotated law reports (addressed in detail in Chapter 10) are an excellent research tool. Frequently, the topics and cases covered in annotated law report discussions are of new or rapidly changing areas of law. When such a report is issued, it typically contains a synopsis of all the jurisdictions that have addressed the issue and the position they have taken, complete with supporting citations. In the event you are researching an area of law that is undergoing a great deal of change or one that is relatively new, the annotated law report can be an excellent way to locate several judicial opinions that address the issue in a variety of circumstances. These opinions in turn help you to view the issue from different perspectives and assess the likely position of the court in your own case.

Two other helpful sources and often the most current are legal periodicals and looseleaf services. These publications tend to be much more regular and are very responsive to areas of law that are new or are experiencing change. Also, the editorials about the topics tend to provide you with a brief but thorough description of the law as it has been applied. Such publications tend to present the most prominent (in some cases, landmark) opinions, whereas the other collateral sources previously discussed tend to cite cases that merely demonstrate the principle. Subsequent chapters discuss further the proper methods for conducting research in annotated law reports, legal periodicals, and looseleaf reporters.

Chapter Summary

This chapter distinguished judicial publications from other types of publications. While most other publications are periodically revised to include changes, publications of judicial law are issued chronologically and are not revised. If an opinion is reversed, that information is found in the subsequent opinion that issues the reversal of the former opinion.

While official reports (often published by state printing offices) are identified as the primary publications of judicial law of a particular jurisdic-

tion, the trend is to adopt commercially prepared publications that are indexed by a system common to the publication for all jurisdictions, thereby enabling efficient research on a national scale. The largest and most comprehensive such commercial publication is the national reporter system and corresponding digests of West Publishing Company.

In addition to locating judicial law by consulting annotated statutes and digests, one can frequently find case law through legal encyclopedias, annotated law reports, legal periodicals, and looseleaf services. While these are not exhaustive sources of research, they do provide examples and often more detailed discussion of the cases.

KEY TERMS

advance sheet	case law	report
appellate court	common law	trial court

SELF-TEST

MULTIPLE CHOICE

1. The only way people can seek _____ resolution of personal legal issues is through the judicial branch.
   a) precedential
   b) individual
   c) legislative
   d) administrative

2. One of the primary functions of the judiciary is to _____ the law as it applies to specific circumstances.
   a) legislate
   b) extract
   c) interpret
   d) all of the above

3. In the situation where there appears to be no prior judicial precedent whatsoever, a judge must create _____ .
   a) legislative law
   b) administrative law
   c) commonlaw
   d) stare decisis

4. A second function of the judiciary is to _____ and uphold law that is consistent with the Constitution.
   a) create
   b) protect
   c) invalidate
   d) none of the above

5. Most courts of the judicial system serve primarily a _____ court function.
   a) trial
   b) administrative
   c) appellate
   d) legislative

TRUE/FALSE

_____ 6. The trial court is where the parties present evidence and seek a verdict resolving their dispute.

_____ 7. The appellate court is where parties take their case from the trial court on the basis that some irregularity caused an improper verdict.

_____ 8. U.S. district courts typically hear cases involving federal law, some office of the federal government, or disputes between citizens of different states (provided the amount sued for exceeds the statutory minimum).

_____ 9. State courts have jurisdiction over all cases involving their respective state

laws and incidents occurring within or related to the federal government.

_____**10.** Published cases are predominantly from the trial court.

FILL–IN THE BLANKS

11. Reports and reporters are published _____.

12. _____ reports contain the appellate judicial opinions of the jurisdiction, and the publication is sanctioned by the state government.

13. The _____ _____ _____ is a comprehensive collection of judicial opinions and an indexing system by West Publishing Company.

14. Each of the seven _____ reporters routinely publish the new opinions of certain designated states.

15. Beginning a new _____ is the method used to denote changes in the format and features presented along with the content.

16. The _____ _____ contains only those opinions in the reporter territory that have been issued since the last reporter.

17. What makes the _____ _____ _____ unique is that the very same topics and subtopics, and so on, are used for every jurisdictional publication.

18. In addition to using the subject index method, you can conduct research through a _____ _____ approach.

19. Other publications with _____ systems to organize annotations do not correspond to the West key number system.

20. Other common sources of research for judicial law include _____ _____, _____ _____, _____ _____, and _____ _____.

CHAPTER **8**

THE SEARCH FOR ADMINISTRATIVE AUTHORITY

CHAPTER OBJECTIVES

Upon completion of this chapter, you should be able to demonstrate the following competencies:

- Explain how administrative law is created.

- Discuss the functions of administrative law.

- Distinguish administrative law from statutory or judicial law.

- Explain the organization of administrative publications.

- Describe the Code of Federal Regulations.

- Explain the role of the Federal Register.

- Identify those subjects that are likely to be addressed by administrative law.

- Explain the process of research in administrative law.

- Explain the purpose of the Administrative Procedure Act.

- Discuss how reference tools could be used to assist in research in administrative law.

ROLE OF THE ADMINISTRATIVE AGENCY

An administrative agency has a unique and constantly growing place in the role of government in American society. The population of the country is so large, the geographical area so great and varied, and the system of government so complex, that it is essential to have government officials in place who can respond to the specific needs of the many facets of society. Earlier chapters have made the point that statutory law must be written broadly enough to encompass all situations designed to be addressed yet be specific enough to allow persons to know whether their actions are in compliance with or in violation of the law. Perhaps the most effective response to this dilemma has been the advent of the administrative agency, the basic role of which is to act as liaison between the Congress and the people. The agency explains what was meant by Congress in particular statutory language, clarifies and defines terms, and ultimately, under the supervision of the executive branch, enforces the law.

The president, under Article II, Section 2, of the Constitution, has the obligation to take care that the laws be faithfully executed. This responsibility to carry out and enforce the laws passed by Congress is immense. But with the assistance of administrative agencies, individuals can have access to government on a personal basis. Congress passes laws with broad goals that enable the creation of an administrative agency to define these goals. Congress then passes additional statutes that must be enforced. The president staffs and oversees the administrative agency as it clarifies, defines, and enforces the statutes passed by Congress.

Although the day-to-day operation of an administrative agency is largely within the control of the executive branch, an agency is ultimately created by the Congress. Article I, Section 8, paragraph 18 of the U.S. Constitution provides as follows:

> The Congress shall have power. . . To make all Laws which shall be necessary and proper for carrying into Execution the foregoing Powers and all other Powers vested by this Constitution in the Government of the United States, or in any Department or Officer thereof.

From this statement, Congress has drawn its authority to make laws. This statement has also been interpreted to permit Congress to enact laws that allow agencies of the government to clarify the laws through regulations and administrative decisions. The president's power to appoint federal officers allows the executive branch to staff the agencies. The duty of the executive officer (president/governor) to see that the laws are faithfully executed provides the president/governor with the authority to oversee the agencies as he or she attempts to enforce the laws passed by the Congress.

Administrative agencies have been a part of the American legal system since the 1800s because agencies can perform many legal functions that Congress, for practical reasons, cannot accomplish effectively. See Exhibit 8.1 for a partial list of existing federal agencies.

An area in which an administrative agency has been particularly effective is Social Security, administered by the Social Security Administration. Most working people in the United States pay into a Social Security fund, from which payments are made to persons who retire or become disabled from

EXHIBIT 8.1
Partial List of
Existing Federal
Agencies.

Note: The following is a partial list of existing federal agencies.

CIA–Central Intelligence Agency
CPSC—Consumer Products Safety Commission
DHHS—Department of Health and Human Services
DOD—Department of Defense
DOJ   Department of Justice
DOT—Department of Transportation
EEOC—Equal Employment Opportunity Commission
EPA—Environmental Protection Agency
FAA—Federal Aviation Administration
FBI—Federal Bureau of Investigation
FCC—Federal Communications Commission
FDA—Food and Drug Administration
FERC—Federal Energy Regulatory Commission
FRB—Federal Reserve Board
FTC—Federal Trade Commission
HUD—Department of Housing and Urban Development
ICC—Interstate Commerce Commission
INS—Immigration and Naturalization Service
IRS—Internal Revenue Service
NHTSA—National Highway and Traffic Safety Administration
NLRB—National Labor Relations Board
NRC—Nuclear Regulatory Commission
NSC—National Security Council
OSHA—Occupational Safety and Health Administration
SEC—Securities Exchange Commission
SSA—Social Security Administration
USDA—Department of Agriculture

working. Given the hundreds of millions of working-age persons in this country since the establishment of Social Security in 1935, the task of collecting and distributing the funds is incomprehensible. Such tasks can be carried out most effectively by an administrative agency, such as the Social Security Administration. In this, as in many other areas, an administrative agency is the most effective way to deal knowledgeably, efficiently, and fairly with many legal issues on an individual basis.

The following section examines the basic process for creating an administrative agency in today's legal system. It should be recognized that many additional details must be dealt with in the actual agency creation process.

◻ ASSIGNMENT 8.1

Examine the table of agencies in Exhibit 8.1 and identify subjects that you think could require regulation by an entirely new agency (i.e., an area of law that is developing rapidly and needs a great deal of specific guidelines and answers to individual issues).

CREATION OF AN ADMINISTRATIVE AGENCY

Before an agency comes into existence, Congress must pass a resolution saying that an agency is necessary to carry out the goals of certain legislation. Congress must determine that no more effective way exists to implement the

goals and that the goals of these statutes need to be enforced. When this occurs, the Congress passes what is commonly referred to as an **enabling act,** a statute that expresses the goals of Congress on a particular subject of legislation.

One such enabling act ultimately provided for the creation of the Environmental Protection Agency (EPA). The EPA carries out and enforces legislation passed by Congress to protect, enhance, or correct problems in the environment. When the National Environmental Policy Act (NEPA) was passed in 1969, as an enabling act, it was the first major environmental protection law enacted by Congress. Shortly thereafter, in 1970, President Nixon issued an executive order (a form of procedural law that implements the enabling act) calling for the creation of an agency to carry out the goals of the NEPA.

The acts that permit the creation of administrative agencies have been a great source of controversy for Congress over the years. In effect, by creating an administrative agency, Congress is giving up some of its legislative (lawmaking) authority. Early on, this was strictly prohibited by the U.S. Supreme Court. As time passed, however, and the needs of the country grew, the Court relaxed its position somewhat to permit administrative agencies to play a larger role in the legislative process. Although agencies have never been allowed to "create new law," they are permitted to create regulations to promote efficient, responsive, and effective government. Exhibit 8.2 is an example of a regulation issued by the EPA in furtherance of congressional legislation.

enabling act
Statute passed by a legislative body that sets definable goals and provides capacity for the executive branch to create an administrative agency.

Delegation Doctrine

Through cases that come before them, the courts have continued to monitor Congress and the executive branch very closely with respect to the creation and operation of administrative agencies. The chief concern of the courts with respect to the creation of administrative agencies is that the **delegation doctrine** not be violated. The delegation doctrine is based on the premise that Congress cannot be permitted to give away any of its actual lawmaking power. Rather, it can only give up or delegate the authority to clarify and enforce laws passed. The delegation of the authority to clarify and enforce is permissible even if it means that the agency must enact additional law in the form of rules and regulations as needed to clarify or enforce the original laws of Congress. However, an agency to which Congress has delegated authority is not free to make original laws of its own. All agency law must serve the function of clarification or enforcement.

delegation doctrine
Legal principle that no authority other than the legislature has the power to issue legislative law and that even the legislature cannot delegate this power to another authority.

Through its interpretations of the delegation doctrine, the Supreme Court has established several major criteria that must be followed in the creation and operation of any administrative agency. The authority delegated by Congress must not allow nonlegislative bodies to enact major laws. Therefore, the Court requires any act that enables the creation of an administrative agency to be clear in its purpose with definable limits. In this way, an agency is prevented from enacting regulations in areas other that those it was created to administer.

Criteria for Creating an Agency

When an enabling act is passed and an agency is created, it must be done in a manner that at the very least meets the following criteria:

EXHIBIT 8.2
Sample Page from
CFR Showing EPA
Regulation Section
86.502–78.

Environmental Protection Agency   **§ 86.509–78**

§ 86.502–78   Definitions.

(a) The definitions in § 86.402–78 apply to this subpart.

§ 86.503–78   Abbreviations.

(a) The abbreviations in § 86.403–78 apply to this subpart.

§ 86.504–78   Section numbering.

(a) The section numbering system described in § 86.404–78 is used in this subpart.

§ 86.505–78   Introduction; structure of subpart.

(a) This subpart describes the equipment required and the procedures to follow in order to perform exhaust emission tests on motorcycles. Subpart E sets forth the testing requirements and test intervals necessary to comply with EPA certification procedures.

(b) Three topics are addressed in this subpart. Sections 86.508 through 86.515 set forth specifications and equipment requirements; §§ 86.516 through 86.526 discuss calibration methods and frequency; test procedures and data requirements are listed (in approximate order of performance) in §§ 86.527 through 86.544.

§ 86.508–78   Dynamometer.

(a) The dynamometer shall have a single roll with a diameter of at least 0.400 metre.

(b) The dynamometer shall be equipped with a roll revolution counter for measuring actual distance traveled.

(c) Flywheels or other means shall be used to stimulate the inertia specified in § 86.529.

(d) A variable speed cooling blower shall direct air to the vehicle. The blower outlet shall be at least 0.40 m^2

(4.31 ft^2) and shall be squarely positioned between 0.3 m (0.98 ft) and 0.45 m (1.48 ft) in front of the vehicle's front wheel. The velocity of the air at the blower outlet shall be within the following limits (as a function of roll speed):

Actual roll speed	Allowable cooling air speed
0 km/h to 5 km/h	0 km/h to 10 km/h.
5 km/h to 10 km/h	0 km/h to roll speed + 5 km/h.
10 km/h to 50 km/h	Roll speed ± 5 km/h.
50 km/h to 70 km/h	Roll speed ± 10 pct.
Above 70 km/h.........................	At least 63 km/h.

(e) The dynamometer shall comply with the tolerances in § 86.529.

[42 FR 1137, Jan. 5, 1977, as amended at 42 FR 56738, Oct. 28, 1977]

§ 86.509–78   Exhaust gas sampling system.

(a)(1) *General.* The exhaust gas sampling system is designed to measure the true mass emissions of vehicle exhaust. In the CVS concept of measuring mass emissions, two conditions must be satisfied: The total volume of the mixture of exhaust and dilution air must be measured, and a continuously proportioned sample of volume must be collected for analysis. Mass emissions are determined from the sample concentration and totalized flow over the test period.

(2) *Positive Displacement Pump.* The Positive Displacement Pump-Constant Volume Sample (PDP-CVS), Figure F78–1, satisfies the first condition by metering at a constant temperature and pressure through the pump. The total volume is measured by counting the revolutions made by the calibrated positive displacement pump. The proportional sample is achieved by sampling at a constant flow rate.

567

1. The goals of the statute must be clear and have definable limits.
2. The methods the agency uses in enforcing the statutes must be fair and open to all members of the public.
3. The enforcement of the statutes must be accomplished by officers of the government, not by persons with private interests.

During the 1930s, the number of agencies increased dramatically. These agencies were part of the New Deal era, which sought to aid this country in its economic recovery from the Great Depression. Congress increased its use of administrative agencies and cooperated with the president in using them to deal quickly with the problems of the nation. Some people, however, believed that the agencies were not acting properly and within the bounds of their authority. In large part, the delegation doctrine was refined during and shortly after this time.

Administrative Procedure Act

In the years that followed, the courts became more and more involved in reviewing the efforts of the executive branch to oversee agencies, and the delegation doctrine imposed more stringent requirements upon the manner in which agencies could be created and operated. Congress responded in 1946 with the Administrative Procedure Act (APA), which was to be used in addition to each agency's enabling act. The APA included the elements necessary to satisfy the requirements of the delegation doctrine. Since that time, the APA has been modified and improved on several occasions to ensure that agencies are in compliance with the criteria the courts have established under the delegation doctrine. Thus, the APA, together with the enabling act, provides for the creation of an agency as well as for its fair and efficient operation.

CREATION OF ADMINISTRATIVE LAW

The most prominent function of administrative agencies is their authority to issue regulations. Such regulations must be necessary to achieve the goals of the enabling act or any other federal laws that the agency has the responsibility to enforce. Thus, all regulations must be derivative of legislation formerly enacted by Congress. If an agency holds a hearing and determines that a regulation has been violated, the agency may impose sanctions on the violator.

If an agency wishes to issue rules, it must follow a very specific procedure set forth in the APA. Additionally, some enabling acts dictate the precise steps an agency must take when promulgating (establishing) and publishing regulations that the public must abide by. These are known as formal rule-making procedures. They often require public hearings, the opportunity for testimony, and other input from the public before any regulations are put into force. However, most agencies are also allowed to promulgate rules through an informal process, governed by a series of detailed requirements set forth in the APA. Most agencies must adhere to the following procedures when passing

rules that will have an impact upon the public, an industry, or a subject that the agency regulates:

1. The agency must give advance notice to the public of the basic terms of the rules it proposes to enact. At the federal level, this must be done in the Federal Register, a daily publication that includes information about the actions of federal administrative agencies.
2. The agency must give the public the opportunity to participate in the agency decision by submitting comments, ideas, and suggestions regarding the proposed rules.
3. After consideration of the public comment, the agency must issue, with the final rule, a general statement of the . . . basis and purpose of the administrative agency."

After all the requirements of the APA have been satisfied, the agency issues its formal regulations and publishes them first in the Federal Register and then in the Code of Federal Regulations (CFR), where all existing regulations are located. Each subject is assigned a title similar to a title in the statutory code. Each regulation is assigned a specific section number and is placed with the other regulations under its proper title (chapter number). Also, like the statutory code, an index of the regulations within a title is included.

The APA also requires agencies to review their regulations periodically to evaluate their effectiveness and necessity. In addition, the APA gives citizens certain rights with respect to agencies. The citizens have the right of access to agency information that pertains to the public and a right to information the agency has about them personally. If business entities or individuals believe that a regulation has an unfair or adverse effect that would injure them, they may have their complaint heard by the agency. If they do not receive satisfaction, they may have the right to have the issue heard by a judge in the judicial branch of the government.

ADMINISTRATIVE LAW JUDGES

The administrative law judge functions in a totally different arena than the appellate or trial judge. The duties of administrative law judges are confined to hearing cases involving the conduct of administrative agencies and the effects of that conduct on the individual or entity that challenges the agency action.

The administrative law judge (also known as ALJ) is presumed to be an objective judicial authority who rules exclusively on issues of administrative law. The ALJ determines issues such as whether a party is subject to the authority of the agency and whether a party's conduct is in accordance with administrative rules and regulations.

Typically, administrative cases are initially filed with the agency rather than in the courts. Appeals of an administrative decision are generally made

to the trial court level in the judicial system. This is a limited instance when the trial court exercises appellate rather than original jurisdiction.

ADMINISTRATIVE LAW PUBLICATIONS

While each jurisdiction has its own method of issuing administrative pronouncements, the federal government—the most heavily consulted administrative system—regularly publishes for all administrative agencies in two sources. The first place that information about administrative agency action will appear is the Federal Register. The permanent publication is the Code of Federal Regulations.

The Federal Register

The Federal Register is a daily publication that reprints the official action of all federal administrative agencies. The information it contains includes proposed rules and regulations at the various stages of approval and administrative decisions. The primary purpose of the Federal Register is to give the general public notice of action by administrative agencies. If you are interested in the activity of several agencies you need not consult individual publications for each one. Rather, this single publication will apprise you of any imminent changes.

The disadvantage of the Federal Register is that unless you are equipped with an exact citation or at least a date of publication and the name of the issuing agency, you will have to sort through issue after issue to locate the information you are seeking. Consequently, there is a need for a single compilation of effective administrative law.

The Federal Register is cited according to Rule 14.5.1 in the bluebook. As you will note from the rule, you should include the title of the document you are citing and the volume and page of the Federal Register as well as the year in parentheses. The pages of the Federal Register are consecutively paginated through each year of publication. For example, the first issue of the year begins with page one. If that issue ends with page 110, the second issue on the following day would begin with page 111.

Because administrative agencies are actually extensions of the executive branch, the Federal Register also contains at the beginning of each issue any presidential documents, such as executive orders or proclamations. These are then followed by information from agencies that are proposing or enacting rules and regulations. You will recall that all agencies must comply with the Administrative Procedure Act when issuing administrative law. Part of the requirements under the act are that generally, proper public notice must be given of proposed regulatory law. Typically, this is done through publication in the Federal Register. Publication of proposed administrative law in the Federal Register contains not only the text of the law but also various identifying and referencing information. Exhibit 8.3 is a reproduction of a page from the Federal Register showing regulatory documents.

EXHIBIT 8.3 Reproduction of a Page from the Federal Register Showing Regulatory Documents.

51211

Rules and Regulations

Federal Register

Vol. 58, No. 189

Friday, October 1, 1993

This section of the FEDERAL REGISTER contains regulatory documents having general applicability and legal effect, most of which are keyed to and codified in the Code of Federal Regulations, which is published under 50 titles pursuant to 44 U.S.C. 1510.

The Code of Federal Regulations is sold by the Superintendent of Documents. Prices of new books are listed in the first FEDERAL REGISTER issue of each week.

OFFICE OF PERSONNEL MANAGEMENT

5 CFR Part 532

RIN 3206–AF48

Prevailing Rate Systems; Macomb, MI, Nonappropriated Fund Wage Area

AGENCY: Office of Personnel Management.

ACTION: Final rule.

SUMMARY: The Office of Personnel Management (OPM) is issuing a final rule adding Ottawa County, Michigan, as an area of application to the Macomb, Michigan, Federal Wage System (FWS) Nonappropriated Fund (NAF) wage area for pay-setting purposes. Ottawa County is not presently defined to an NAF wage area. However, OPM recently learned that there is now one NAF employee working at the Coast Guard Exchange, Grand Haven, located in Ottawa County, Michigan. The intent of this action is to officially assign Ottawa County to the proper NAF wage area for pay-setting purposes.

EFFECTIVE DATE: November 1, 1993.

FOR FURTHER INFORMATION CONTACT: Paul Shields, (202) 606–2848.

SUPPLEMENTARY INFORMATION: On June 18, 1993, OPM published an interim rule to add Ottawa County, Michigan, as an area of application to the Macomb, Michigan, FWS NAF wage area (58 FR 33499). The interim rule provided a 30-day period for public comment. OPM received no comments during the comment period. The interim rule is being adopted as a final rule.

E.O. 12291, Federal Regulation

I have determined that this is not a major rule as defined under section 1(b) of E.O. 12291, Federal Regulation.

Regulatory Flexibility Act

I certify that these regulations will not have a significant economic impact on

a substantial number of small entities because they affect only Federal agencies and employees.

List of Subjects in 5 CFR Part 532

Administrative practice and procedure, Government employees, Wages.

Accordingly, under the authority of 5 U.S.C. 5343, the interim rule amending 5 CFR part 532 published on June 18, 1993 (58 FR 33499), is adopted as final without any changes.

U.S. Office of Personnel Management

Lorraine A. Green,

Deputy Director.

[FR Doc. 93–24131 Filed 9–30–93; 8:45 am]

BILLING CODE 6325–01–M

DEPARTMENT OF AGRICULTURE

Office of the Secretary

7 CFR Part 2

Revision of Delegations of Authority

AGENCY: Department of Agriculture.

ACTION: Final rule.

SUMMARY: This document amends the delegations of authority from the Secretary of Agriculture and General Officers of the Department to delegate to the Assistant Secretary for Science and Education and to the Administrator, Agricultural Research Service, the authority to propagate bee-breeding stock and to release bee germplasm to the public pursuant to 7 U.S.C. 283.

EFFECTIVE DATE: October 1, 1993.

FOR FURTHER INFORMATION CONTACT: Marcus F. Gross, Jr., Office of the General Counsel, United States Department of Agriculture, Washington, DC (202) 720–4076.

SUPPLEMENTARY INFORMATION: This rule relates to the internal agency management. Therefore, pursuant to 5 U.S.C. 553, it is exempt from the notice and comment procedures of the Administrative Procedure Act, and this rule may be effective less than 30 days after publication in the **Federal Register**.

Further, since this rule relates to internal agency management it is exempt from the provisions of Executive Order Nos. 12291 and 12778. This action is not a rule as defined by Public Law 96–354, the Regulatory Flexibility

Act, (5 U.S.C. 601 *et seq.*) and thus is exempt from its provisions. This rule also is exempt from the requirements of the National Environmental Policy Act, as amended (42 U.S.C. 4321 *et seq.*) and the requirements of the Paperwork Reduction Act (44 U.S.C. chapter 35).

List of Subjects in 7 CFR Part 2

Authority delegations (Government agencies).

Accordingly, part 2, subtitle A, title 7, Code of Federal Regulations is amended as follows:

PART 2—DELEGATIONS OF AUTHORITY BY THE SECRETARY OF AGRICULTURE AND GENERAL OFFICERS OF THE DEPARTMENT

1. The authority citation for part 2 continues to read as follows:

Authority: 5 U.S.C. 301 and Reorganization Plan No. 2 of 1953.

Subpart C—Delegations of Authority to the Deputy Secretary, the Under Secretary for International Affairs and Commodity Programs, the Under Secretary for Small Community and Rural Development, and Assistant Secretaries

2. Section 2.30 is amended by revising the section heading and by adding a new paragraph (a)(34) to read as follows:

§ 2.30 Assistant Secretary for Science and Education.

(a) Related to science and education. * * *

(34) Propagate bee-breeding stock and release bee germplasm to the public (7 U.S.C. 283).

* * * * *

Subpart N—Delegations of Authority by the Assistant Secretary for Science and Education

(3) Section 2.106 is amended by revising the heading and adding a new paragraph (a)(64) to read as follows:

§ 2.106 Administrator, Agricultural Research Service.

(a) *Delegations.* * * *

(64) Propagate bee-breeding stock and release bee germplasm to the public (7 U.S.C. 283).

* * * * *

For subpart C.

The information that accompanies the administrative agency typically includes most or all of the following:

1. Governmental department and specific agency within the department responsible for the regulation/rule.
2. Citation to the Code of Federal Regulations where the law will be located if and when enacted and codified.
3. Title of the regulation/rule.
4. Agency responsible for the regulation/rule.
5. Type of information contained (e.g., a proposed rule, final notice, date of enactment of rule).
6. Summary (a note written by agency staff to describe the regulation/rule or other action taken by the agency). This information is not law. Rather, it is only descriptive information to better explain the agency action.
7. Text of the regulation/rule.
8. Information about effective dates and contact persons for those who wish to communicate with the agency about the rule.

The Federal Register is not a resource commonly consulted by legal researchers in general. Because the publication is daily and issues information chronologically, locating exact information is difficult. However, if you are doing research for a heavily regulated industry, the Federal Register is often the first source of information about pending law affecting the industry. Consequently, many regulated entities and persons have an interest in keeping staff personnel on top of any new proposed regulations that may affect the industry. By doing so, communication can be had with the agency to support or oppose the law before it actually takes effect.

ASSIGNMENT 8.2

Examine the pages in Exhibit 8.4 from the Federal Register and provide the following information:

1. What agencies are represented?
2. What types of executive/administrative law appear on the page?
3. Identify, if any, the actual text of administrative law on the page by giving the column, line number, and a one- or two-sentence summary of the law.
4. Identify for each item whether the law is a proposition or a final enactment/proclamation/order.

The Code of Federal Regulations

The general publication for the administrative rules and regulations for all federal agencies is the Code of Federal Regulations (CFR). This large, multivolume set contains all regulations and rules for each of the federal administrative agencies. Each subject of regulation is assigned a number, and each specific rule or regulation is also assigned a number. Because each agency is typically responsible for a different area of law, the subject categories also generally divide the code by agency as well. Within a subject,

EXHIBIT 8.4   Sample Pages from the Federal Register.

Kentucky program are being amended to implement this decision. The Director is approving these State rules with the understanding that they be promulgated in a form identical to that submitted to OSM and reviewed by the public. Any differences between these rules and the State's final promulgated rules will be processed as a separate amendment subject to public review at a later date. This final rule is being made effective immediately to expedite the State program amendment process and to encourage states to bring their programs into conformity with the Federal standards without undue delay. Consistency of State and Federal standards is required by SMCRA.

EPA Concurrence

Under 30 CFR 732.17(h)(11)(ii), the Director is required to obtain the written concurrence of the Administrator of the Environmental Protection Agency (EPA) with respect to any provisions of a State program amendment that relate to air or water quality standards promulgated under the authority of the Clean Water Act (33 U.S.C. 1251 *et seq.*) or the Clean Air Act (42 U.S.C. 7401 *et seq.*). The Director has determined that this amendment contains no provisions in these categories and the EPA's concurrence is not required.

VI. Procedural Determinations

Executive Order 12291

On July 12, 1984, the Office of Management and Budget (OMB) granted the Office of Surface Mining Reclamation and Enforcement (OSM) an exemption from Sections 3, 4, 7 and 8 of Executive Order 12291 for actions related to approval or conditional approval of State regulatory programs, actions and program amendments. Therefore, preparation of a regulatory impact analysis is not necessary and OMB regulatory review is not required.

Executive Order 12778

The Department of the Interior has conducted the reviews required by section 2 of Executive Order 12778 and has determined that, to the extent allowed by law, this rule meets the applicable standards of subsections (a) and (b) of that section. However, these standards are not applicable to the actual language of State regulatory programs and program amendments since each such program is drafted and promulgated by a specific State, not by OSM. Under sections 503 and 505 of the Surface Mining Control and Reclamation Act (SMCRA) (30 U.S.C. 1253 and 1255) and 30 CFR 730.11, 732.15 and 732.17(h)(10), decisions on

proposed State regulatory programs and program amendments submitted by the States must be based solely on a determination of whether the submittal is consistent with SMCRA and its implementing Federal regulations and whether the other requirements of 30 CFR parts 730, 731 and 732 have been met.

National Environmental Policy Act

No environmental impact statement is required for this rule since section 702(d) of SMCRA (30 U.S.C. 1292(d)) provides that agency decisions on proposed State regulatory program provisions do not constitute major Federal actions within the meaning of section 102(2)(C) of the National Environmental Policy Act, 42 U.S.C. 4332(2)(C).

Paperwork Reduction Act

This rule does not contain information collection requirements that require approval by the Office of Management and Budget under the Paperwork Reduction Act, 44 U.S.C. 3507 *et seq.*

Regulatory Flexibility Act

The Department of the Interior has determined that this rule will not have a significant economic impact on a substantial number of small entities under the Regulatory Flexibility Act (5 U.S.C. 601 *et seq.*). The State submittal which is the subject of this rule is based upon counterpart Federal regulations for which an economic analysis was prepared and certification made that such regulations would not have a significant economic effect upon a substantial number of small entities. Hence, this rule will ensure that existing requirements previously promulgated by OSM will be implemented by the State. In making the determination as to whether this rule would have a significant economic impact, the Department relied upon the data and assumptions for the counterpart Federal regulations.

List of Subjects in 30 CFR Part 917

Intergovenmental relations, Surface mining, Underground mining.

Dated: September 22, 1993.

Carl C. Close,

Assistant Director, Eastern Support Center.

For the reasons set forth in the preamble, title 30, chapter VII, subchapter T of the Code of Federal Regulations is amended as set forth below:

PART 917—KENTUCKY

1. The authority citation for Part 917 continues to read as follows:

Authority: 30 U.S.C. 1201 *et seq.*

2. 30 CFR 917.15, is amended by adding new paragraph (ss) to read as follows:

§ 917.15   Approval of regulatory program amendments.

*   *   *   *   *

(ss) The following amendment submitted to OSM on July 21, 1992, and modified and resubmitted on December 9, 1992, is approved effective October 1, 1993. The amendment consists of additions and modifications to the following provisions of the Kentucky Administrative Regulations (KAR):

405 KAR 1:007.	Termination and reassertion of jurisdiction—Interim program—surface mining.
405 KAR 3:007.	Termination and reassertion of jurisdiction—Interim program—underground mining.
405 KAR 7:030 Sec. 4.	Termination and reassertion of jurisdiction—Permanent program.

[FR Doc. 93–24149 Filed 9–30–93; 8:45 am]

BILLING CODE 4310–05–M

DEPARTMENT OF DEFENSE

Office of the Secretary

[DoD 6010.8–R]

32 CFR Part 199

RIN 0720–AA15

Civilian Health and Medical Program of the Uniformed Services (CHAMPUS); Reimbursement of Providers, Claims Filing, and Participating Provider Program

AGENCY: Office of the Secretary, DoD.

ACTION: Final rule.

SUMMARY: This final rule implements provisions of the Department of Defense Appropriations Act, 1993, section 9011, which limits increases in maximum allowable payments to physicians and other individual professional providers (including clinical laboratories), authorizes reductions in such amounts for overpriced procedures, provides special procedures to assure beneficiary access to care, and establishes limits on balance billing by providers. Also, the final rule implements a provision of the National Defense Authorization Act for Fiscal Year 1992 that requires providers to file claims on behalf of CHAMPUS beneficiaries, builds into the CHAMPUS Regulation provisions that have been in

EXHIBIT 8.4 Continued

Federal Register / Vol. 58, No. 189 / Friday, October 1, 1993 / Proposed Rules **51261**

---

14 copies of the comments must be filed with the Commission no later than November 1, 1993. Comments should be submitted to the Office of the Secretary, Federal Energy Regulatory Commission, 825 North Capitol Street, NE., Washington, DC 20426, and should refer to Docket No. RM93–24–000.

All written comments will be placed in the Commission's public files and will be available for inspection in the Commission's Public Reference Room at 941 North Capitol Street NE., Washington, DC 20426, during regular business hours.

List of Subjects in 18 CFR Part 35

Electric power rates, Electric utilities, Reporting and recordkeeping requirements.

In consideration of the foregoing, the Commission proposes to amend part 35, chapter I, Title 18, Code of Federal Regulations, as set forth below.

PART 35—FILING OF RATE SCHEDULES

1. The authority citation for part 35 continues to read as follows:

Authority: 16 U.S.C. 791a–825r, 2601–2645; 31 U.S.C. 9701; 42 U.S.C. 7101–7352.

2. Section 35.14 is amended by revising the second sentence of paragraph (a)(7) to read as follows:

§ 35.14 Fuel cost and purchased economic power adjustment clauses.

(a) * * *

(7) * * * Where the utility purchases fuel from a company-owned or controlled source, the price of which is subject to the jurisdiction of a regulatory body, and where the price of such fuel has been approved by that regulatory body, such costs shall be presumed, subject to rebuttal, to be reasonable and includable in the adjustment clause.* * *

*   *   *   *   *

By direction of the Commission.

Lois D. Cashell,

Secretary.

[FR Doc. 93–24169 Filed 9–30–93; 8:45 am]

BILLING CODE 6717-01-M

DEPARTMENT OF HOUSING AND URBAN DEVELOPMENT

Office of the Assistant Secretary for Public and Indian Housing

24 CFR Parts 905 and 990

[Docket No. R–93–1681; FR–2971–P–01]

RIN 2577–AA99

Low-Income Public Housing; Performance Funding System: Cooling Degree Days

AGENCY: Office of the Assistant Secretary for Public and Indian Housing, HUD.

ACTION: Proposed rule.

SUMMARY: This proposed rule implements Section 508 of the Cranston-Gonzalez National Affordable Housing Act requires that the Secretary of HUD include a cooling degree day adjustment factor in determining the component of subsidy eligibility relating to utility consumption under the Performance Funding System. The Act further provides that the method by which a cooling degree day adjustment factor is included shall be identical to the method by which the heating degree day factor is included.

DATES: Comments must be received by November 30, 1993 to assure their consideration.

ADDRESSES: Interested persons are invited to submit written comments regarding this proposed rule to the Office of the General Counsel, Rules Docket Clerk, room 10276, Department of Housing and Urban Development, 451 Seventh Street SW., Washington, DC 20410. Comments should refer to the above docket number and title. A copy of each comment submitted will be available for public inspection and copying during regular business hours in room 10276.

FOR FURTHER INFORMATION CONTACT: For information concerning part 990, Mr. John T. Comerford, Director, Financial Management Division, Office of Assisted Housing, Public and Indian Housing, room 4212, U.S. Department of Housing and Urban Development, 451 Seventh Street, SW., Washington DC 20410, telephone (202) 708–1872.

For information concerning part 905, Mr. Dominic Nessi, Director, Office of Native American Programs, room 4140, U.S. Department of Housing and Urban Development, 451 Seventh Street, SW., Washington DC 20410, telephone (202) 708–1015.

Hearing or speech impaired individuals may call HUD's TDD

number, (202) 708–0850. [These telephone numbers are not toll-free.]

SUPPLEMENTARY INFORMATION:

I. Paperwork Reduction Statement

The information collection requirements contained in this proposed rule have been submitted to the Office of Management and Budget for review under the Paperwork Reduction Act of 1980. Information on the estimated public reporting burden is provided in section IV. H. Comments regarding this burden or any other aspect of this collection of information, including suggestions for reducing this burden, should be sent to the U.S. Department of Housing and Urban Development, Rules Docket Clerk, 451 Seventh Street SW., room 10276, Washington DC 20410; and to the Office of Information and Regulatory Affairs, Office of Management and Budget, Washington DC 20503.

II. Statutory Requirement

Section 508 of the Cranston-Gonzalez National Affordable Housing Act of 1990 (104 Stat. 4187) directs the Department to include a cooling degree day adjustment factor to utility consumption in the Performance Funding System (PFS). The Act goes on to state that, "The method by which a cooling degree day adjustment factor is included shall be identical to the method by which the heating degree day adjustment factor is included."

Consistent with the explicit policy stated in the statute, this proposed rule contains a literal implementation of the statutory language. However, the Department is concerned that its implementation of this provision raises some basic questions and could create some major distortions in the funding system. Because of this, it has been determined appropriate to open a discussion of policy alternatives in this Notice of Proposed Rulemaking and to invite public comment on the issues surrounding implementation of this statutory provision.

Because of the potential importance of this change, and because the Department is aware that there are additional factors to consider in calculating cooling load and cost other than ambient temperatures, this Preamble describes three alternate scenarios for addressing the issue of heating and cooling degree day adjustment in the PFS formula. We are inviting public comment on these alternate approaches or suggestions of additional alternatives in anticipation of further rulemaking in the future. The Department will review any public

the rules and regulations from each agency are then grouped together. As you can see, this process is very similar to statutory compilations. In some, but not all, instances, the subject number in the Code of Federal Regulations is the same as the subject number that houses the enabling act in the United States Code. For convenience and organization, most titles are further subdivided into chapters and subchapters. However, these subdivisions are not included in the citation. The only organizational reference points in the citation are the title and specific regulation numbers.

Because the nature of administrative law is to clarify statutory law, the body of rules and regulations is quite large. As a result, the CFR is published in paperback and is revised annually. The first 16 titles (subjects) are revised and reissued before January 1, titles 17–27 are revised and reissued before April 1, revisions of titles 28–41 are completed by July 1, and Titles 42–50 are done by October 1. This staggered system of revision is necessary because of the size of the task. As a result, the various issues of CFR bear different publication dates. Also, because the revisions are not always completed on the established schedule, it is entirely possible that some issues are as much as two to three years old. This lag in revisions makes it more necessary than ever to properly shepardize your legal research.

To locate a rule or regulation for a specific agency, you can consult the CFR Index and Finding Aids. (See Exhibit 8.5.) However, this task is not as straightforward as when consulting a statutory subject index. As mentioned earlier, the volumes in a CFR collection often vary by date as much as three years. The index is published annually for the current year. Consequently, you may need to consult more than one index. However, it is important for purposes of validity to locate the most recent version of the regulation, as the regulations are often modified.

One particular difficulty in the research of administrative law is the method in which the index is organized. Unlike other statutory research where your queries and search terms need to be as specific as possible, in the CFR, specific regulations are not indexed. Rather, only broad categories, such as chapters, are indexed. Therefore, it is important that your search terms be more encompassing than in other types of research.

☐ ASSIGNMENT 8.3

Refer to the example from the CFR Index in Exhibit 8.5 and identify the likely location of regulations to answer the following questions:

1. Was there a crop disaster program in place during 1990?
2. What regulations exist regarding the handling of foreign-produced spearmint oil?
3. Can small businesses obtain loans for energy systems?
4. Is the space shuttle program regulated?
5. What food additives are considered safe?

One very helpful tool in administrative law research is part of the CFR Index and Finding Aids known as the List of CFR Sections Affected, or LSA. The LSA is a monthly update of all regulations that have been changed, cancelled, or added since the last CFR publication of volumes containing those

EXHIBIT 8.5
Sample Pages
from CFR Index.

Solar Energy and Energy Conservation Bank   **CFR Index**

Financial assistance program, 24 CFR 1800

Technical assistance and energy conservation measures, grant programs for schools, hospitals, and buildings owned by units of local government and public care institutions, 10 CFR 455

Solar Energy and Energy Conservation Bank
See Housing and Urban Development Department

Solid waste disposal
See Waste treatment and disposal

South Africa
Fair labor standards
Administrative procedures, 22 CFR 64
Definitions, 22 CFR 61
General policies and reporting requirements, 22 CFR 63
Non-adherence and penalties, 22 CFR 65
Purpose and scope of application, 22 CFR 60
Registration, 22 CFR 62
Transactions regulations, 31 CFR 545

Soybeans
Crop insurance regulations, 7 CFR 401
Loan and price support program, 7 CFR 1421
Soybean promotion, research, and consumer information, 7 CFR 1220
Sugarcane, sugar beets, soybeans, and peanuts, 1990 crop, disaster payment program, 7 CFR 777

Space transportation and exploration
Commercial Space Transportation Office
Administrative review, 14 CFR 406
Basis and scope of regulations, 14 CFR 400
Investigations and enforcement, 14 CFR 405
Launch licenses, 14 CFR 415
Licensing applications, 14 CFR 413
Licensing policy, 14 CFR 411
Organization and definitions, 14 CFR 401
Regulations and licensing requirements, 14 CFR 404
Cross-waiver of liability, 14 CFR 1266

National space grant college and fellowship program, 14 CFR 1259
Space articles, duty-free entry, 14 CFR 1217
Space shuttle, 14 CFR 1214

Spearmint oil
Marketing order regulating handling of spearmint oil produced in Far West, 7 CFR 985

Special Counsel Office
Filing of complaints and allegations, 5 CFR 1800
Investigative authority, 5 CFR 1810
Nondiscrimination on basis of handicap in federally conducted programs, 5 CFR 1850
Privacy, 5 CFR 1830
Public information, 5 CFR 1820
Subpoenas, 5 CFR 1840

Spices and flavorings
Drawback on distilled spirits used in manufacturing nonbeverage products, 27 CFR 197
Food additives, substances generally recognized as safe (GRAS), 21 CFR 182
Food dressings and flavorings, 21 CFR 169
Volatile fruit flavor concentrate, production, 27 CFR 18
Wine production and sales, 27 CFR 24

Sport fishing
See Fishing

Sporting goods
Manufacturers and retailers excise taxes, 26 CFR 48

Sports
Horseracing and dogracing industries, National Labor Relations Board, jurisdictional standards and remedial orders, 29 CFR 103

Spray cans
Self pressurized can products containing chlorofluorocarbons, requirements to provide Consumer Product Safety Commission with performance and technical data, requirements to notify consumers at point of purchase of

718

EXHIBIT 8.5
Continued

CFR Index   **State Department**

performance and technical data, 16 CFR 1401

Stamp taxes
See Excise taxes

State and local governments
Americans with Disabilities Act, nondiscrimination on basis of disability in State and local government services, 28 CFR 35
Recordkeeping and reporting requirements under Title VII and Americans with Disabilities Act, 29 CFR 1602

State Department
Acquisition regulations
Acquisition planning, 48 CFR 607
Administrative matters, 48 CFR 604
Application of labor laws to Government acquisitions, 48 CFR 622
Bonds and insurance, 48 CFR 628
Competition requirements, 48 CFR 606
Construction and architect-engineer contracts, 48 CFR 636
Contract administration, 48 CFR 642
Contract financing, 48 CFR 632
Contract modification, 48 CFR 643
Contracting by negotiation, 48 CFR 615
Contractor qualifications, 48 CFR 609
Cost accounting standards, 48 CFR 630
Definitions of words and terms, 48 CFR 602
Environment, conservation, occupational safety, and drug-free workplace, 48 CFR 623
Foreign acquisition, 48 CFR 625
Forms, 48 CFR 653
Government property, 48 CFR 645
Improper business practices and personal conflicts of interest, 48 CFR 603
Major system acquisition, 48 CFR 634
Protection of privacy and freedom of information, 48 CFR 624
Protests, disputes and appeals, 48 CFR 633
Publicizing contract actions, 48 CFR 605
Quality assurance, 48 CFR 646
Required sources of supplies and services, 48 CFR 608

Sealed bidding, 48 CFR 614
Service contracting, 48 CFR 637
Small business and small disadvantaged business concerns, 48 CFR 619
Small purchase and other simplified purchase procedures, 48 CFR 613
Solicitation provisions and contract clauses, 48 CFR 652
Special contracting methods, 48 CFR 617
Special contracting programs, 48 CFR 670
State Department Acquisition Regulations System, 48 CFR 601
Taxes, 48 CFR 629
Types of contracts, 48 CFR 616
Value engineering, 48 CFR 648
Advisory committee management, 22 CFR 8
Appellate Review Board, 22 CFR 7
Arms, international traffic
Defense articles export licenses, 22 CFR 123
Export controls administrative procedures, 22 CFR 128
General policies and provisions, 22 CFR 126
Manufacturers and exporters, registration, 22 CFR 122
Manufacturing license and technical assistance agreements, and other defense services, 22 CFR 124
Political contributions, fees, and commissions, 22 CFR 130
Purpose, background and definitions, 22 CFR 120
Technical data and classified defense articles export licenses, 22 CFR 125
United States Munitions List, 22 CFR 121
Violations and penalties, 22 CFR 127
Books, maps, newspaper purchases, etc., 22 CFR 132
Certificates of authentication, 22 CFR 131
Claims, administrative settlement of tort claims and certain property damage claims, 22 CFR 31
Collection of debts, 22 CFR 34
Collection of debts by Federal tax refund offset, 22 CFR 139

719

regulations that have been affected. Thus, when you locate a regulation that is relevant to your issue, you should also check the LSA to see that the regulation has not been altered or affected in any way that would change its impact on your issue.

The LSA is arranged in much the same way as the CFR. Information is grouped into titles containing changes, then into subcategories, and finally into specific sections. The LSA functions essentially the same as a statutory pocket part or supplement. Only that information that has been changed, added, or deleted from the Code is included, and it is organized in the same manner. However, one significant difference is that the LSA is not cumulative. You may need to consult more than one issue of the LSA to cover the time period between the issuance of the CFR volume and the current date. The LSA may refer you to particular editions of the Federal Register. At the back of the LSA is a table that indicates the dates of publication for the various editions of the Federal Register.

☐ ASSIGNMENT 8.4

From the table in Exhibit 8.6 from the LSA, determine the different types of treatment given to the various regulations affected during the name publication period of the Federal Register (e.g., proposed new rule).

ADMINISTRATIVE DECISIONS

Unlike judicial opinions, which emanate from the court systems, administrative decisions are the product of independent administrative law judges, who are included in the executive branch. If a private citizen has a dispute with an agency, or if two private citizens have a dispute over the application of administrative law, an administrative law judge may be called upon to resolve the dispute. Typically, the administrative law judge will issue a decision. In some cases, the parties appeal the verdict within the agency, and even ultimately to the judicial system. Agency appellate and, in some cases, primary decisions are published, but not within the typical judicial reporters.

Administrative decisions are published in both official and unofficial administrative reports. These documents are grouped by subject and often by agency. This is in contrast to judicial publications, which produce volumes generally arranged by jurisdiction regardless of the subject. Both administrative decisions and judicial opinions issue publications chronologically. Similarly, both issue advance sheets to apprise researchers of the most current information.

The agency decisions in official reports are sometimes indexed. However, because many of these indexes are not cumulative, several volumes must be consulted to locate the most current pronouncements. Commercially prepared unofficial reporters are usually indexed and digested much like judicial opinions, which makes the research process much simpler. However, as with all research, you should always validate your authority.

EXHIBIT 8.6
Sample Page from
the List of CFR
Sections Affected.

---

38   **LSA—LIST OF CFR SECTIONS AFFECTED**

CHANGES JANUARY 4, 1993 THROUGH AUGUST 31, 1993

TITLE 7 Chapter XVIII—Con. Page

Exhibit C amended...................... 44263
1940.551—1940.600 (Subpart L)
   Exhibit B revised; interim...... 38950
1940.590 (i) added........................... 5565
   Regulation at 58 FR 5565 con-
   firmed.......................................42639
1941.1 Amended................................ 226
1941.25 (a)(3) redesignated as
   (a)(5) and revised; new (a)(3)
   and (4) added........................... 26680
   (a) introductory text amend-
   ed; interim................................. 44752
1941.29 Heading, (b) introduc-
   tory text, (1), (2), (c) introductory text and (3) amend-
   ed; interim................................. 44747
1941.30 Revised; interim............. 44747
1941.1—1941.50 (Subpart A)
   Exhibit A amended; inter-
   im................................ 44752, 44753
1941.84 (a) and (b) amended;
   (c) through (g) redesignated
   as (d) through (h); new (c)
   added; new (d) and (g) re-
   vised..26680
1941.88 (c) amended...................... 26680
1941.92 Amended........................... 26681
1942.1 (a) amended........................226
1942.17 (q)(4)(i)(B)(1), (ii) introductory text and (B)
   heading and introductory
   text   amended;
   (q)(4)(i)(A)(2)(iii)   and
   (ii)(A) heading revised.............30102
1942.101 Amended............................ 226
1942.301 Amended............................ 226
1942.351 (a) amended......................226
1942.402 (a) amended......................226
1942.451 Amended............................ 227
1942.501 (a) amended......................227
1943.1 Amended................................ 227
1943.4 Amended............................ 26681
1943.24 (d)(1) and (2) revised......26681
1943.25 (c)(1) introductory text
   revised.......................................26681
   (c)(2) amended; interim............. 44752
1943.29 (d) amended; interim..... 44747
1943.30 Revised; interim.............. 44747
1943.32 (a) amended; interim......44752
1943.51 Amended............................ 227
1943.54 Amended............. 15072, 26681
1943.57 Added...............................15072
1943.62 (a)(3) through (7) re-
   designated as (a)(4) through
   (8) and (b)(4) through (9)

Page

   redesignated   as   (b)(5)
   through (10); (a)(1), new
   (a)(8), (b)(3) and new (b)(9)
   amended; new (a)(3), new
   (b)(4), (11), and (12) added;
   new (a)(7) and new (b)(8) re-
   vised...15072
1943.66 Revised............................ 15073
1943.67 (a), (b), and (c) redesig-
   nated as (c), (d), and (e);
   new (e) amended; new (a)
   and new (b) added...................15074
1943.68 (c) revised......................15074
1943.73 (d),   (f)(1) and   (2)
   amended; (f)(2)(iii) and (4)
   removed.....................................15074
1943.74 (d)(1) and (2) revised......26681
1943.75 (c)(1) introductory text
   revised....................................... 26681
   (c)(2) amended; interim.............44752
1943.79 (c)(1) revised................15074
   Heading, (a), (c) introductory
   text, (1) and (d) amended;
   interim.......................................44748
1943.80 Revised; interim............. 44748
1943.82 (a) amended; interim...44748,
                       44752
1944 Authority   citation   re-
   vised...227
1944.1 Amended.............................. 227
1944.24 (c)(2) amended; inter-
   im.. 44752
1944.30 (a) amended; interim......44752
1944.37 (f) and (g) amended............227
1944.39 Revised.............................. 227
1944.151 Amended........................... 227
1944.153 Amended......................... 40951
1944.157 (a)(7)(iii)   amended;
   interim.......................................44753
1944.158 (n) added...................... 38923
1944.164 (n) heading and (o)
   amended; (p) revised.............38923
1944.169 (i) heading and (2) re-
   vised.. 40951
   (a)(1)(i) amended; interim.......44752
1944.170 Introductory   text
   added.. 40951
1944.171 (d) table amended.........38923
1944.176 (d)(3) removed; (d)(4),
   (5) and (6) redesignated as
   (d)(3), (4) and (5); (d)(2) re-
   vised..38923
1944.151—1944.200 (Subpart D)
   Exhibit B amended.................. 40951
1944.201 Amended........................... 227

▌▌▌▶ STRATEGY 8.1:

Research in Administrative Law

1. Complete preparation of your query and relevant terms. Remember that in administrative research, terms should be somewhat broad.
2. Consult the CFR Index and Finding Aids. Realize that because of the staggered publication stages, you should consult each index still in effect (this may cover indexes of several years).
3. Locate by chapter the references obtained from the CFR Index. At the heading of the chapter are subchapters, which in turn are followed by specific regulations. You must examine each of these for the most applicable regulations and then make sure you examine the most current version of the regulation(s) in the soft-bound volumes.
4. Consult the List of CFR Sections Affected (LSA), a monthly update of all regulations that have been changed, cancelled, or added since the last CFR publication of volumes containing those regulations that have been affected. Consult each LSA supplement between the date of publication of the regulation you are researching and the current date.

CHAPTER SUMMARY

The focus of this chapter has been on the distinctive characteristics of administrative law that affect the research process. All administrative law is an extension of existing statutory law. Its purpose is to clarify and define broad statutory language. As a result, regulations tend to be very specific and often are quite voluminous in relation to their corresponding statute.

A daily publication of new federal regulatory law is the Federal Register, which has many features similar to a newspaper. Because there is so much regulatory law, it is permanently contained in a paperback series known as the Code of Federal Regulations, which is constantly updated on a rotating basis. The Code is indexed by broad categories; it is also supplemented with a pamphlet known as the LSA, which contains information about recently altered regulations.

Administrative decisions are published much like judicial opinions, both officially and unofficially. One distinction, however, is that administrative decisions are frequently collected and organized by the agency to which they are connected, which results in a loose collection of subjects, whereas judicial opinions are most often arranged by jurisdiction rather than by subject. Research in administrative law is quite challenging and requires some special techniques not common to other forms of legal research. However, the basic steps of identifying issue, formulating query, and validation remain constant and necessary.

KEY TERMS

administrative law   delegation doctrine   enabling act

SELF-TEST

MULTIPLE CHOICE

1. The agency _____ and _____ terms and ultimately, under the supervision of the executive branch, enforces the law.
   a) enables and creates
   b) defines and legislates
   c) creates and defines
   d) clarifies and defines

2. Congress passes an _____ with broad goals that establish the specific goal of the creation of an administrative agency to enforce them.
   a) administrative regulation
   b) enabling act
   c) administrative rule
   d) statutes

3. The _____ is a form of procedural law that implements the enabling act.
   a) administrative rule
   b) administrative decision
   c) administrative statute
   d) none of the above

4. Each area of administrative law is assigned a _____ similar to a subject in the statutory code.
   a) topic area
   b) statute number
   c) rule
   d) regulation

5. Each _____ is assigned a specific section number and is placed with the other similar administrative law.
   a) administrative decision
   b) administrative statute
   c) administrative regulation
   d) administrative opinion

TRUE/FALSE

_____ 6. Typically, administrative cases are initially filed with the agency rather than in the courts.

_____ 7. The permanent publication for administrative law is the Federal Register.

_____ 8. The Code of Federal Regulations is a daily publication that reprints the official action of all federal administrative agencies.

_____ 9. The Federal Register is cited according to Rule 1 in the bluebook.

_____ 10. The pages of the Federal Register are consecutively paginated through each year of publication.

FILL–IN THE BLANKS

11. Because each agency is typically responsible for a different area of law, the _____ of the CFR generally divide the code by agency as well.

12. In some, but not all, instances, the subject number in the Code of Federal Regulations is the same as the subject number that houses the enabling act in the _____ _____ _____ .

13. For purposes of convenience and organization, most titles are further subdivided into _____ and _____ .

14. The only organizational reference points in the CFR _____ are the title and specific regulation numbers.

15. To locate a rule or regulation for a specific agency, you can consult the _____ .

16. In the CFR, _____ _____ are not indexed. Rather, only broad categories, such as chapters, are indexed.

17. _____ is the abbreviated name for a monthly update of all regulations that have been changed, cancelled, or added since the last CFR publication of volumes containing those regulations that have been affected.

18. LSA is the abbreviation for _____ _____ _____ .

19. You can approach CFR research through a _____ approach similar to that use for statutory research.

20. Administrative decisions are often housed in collections from a _____ _____ .

CHAPTER 9

RESTATEMENTS AND TREATISES

Upon completion of this chapter, you should be able to accomplish the following competencies:

- Describe a restatement of law.

- Discuss the functions of a restatement of law.

- Distinguish a restatement of law from primary authority.

- Describe a treatise.

- Explain the role of a restatement of law as an authority.

- Explain the role of a treatise as an authority.

- Identify those subjects that are likely to be addressed by a restatement or treatise.

- Explain the process of researching a restatement of law.

- Explain the process of researching a treatise.

- Compare a treatise to primary authority.

The Nature and Function of Restatements and Treatises in Legal Research and Writing

Restatements of Law

Restatement of the Law

Publication by the American Law Institute of generally accepted principles of law on a particular topic (e.g., Restatement of the Law of Contracts).

Restatements of the Law is one of the more unique resources you may find in a law library. While they are technically secondary persuasive authority, the Restatements are the only secondary authorities that generate such respect that they are often compared against primary authority. Much of this respect comes from the origins of the Restatements, which is the American Law Institute.

Restatements as a Source of Authority.   The American Law Institute (or ALI, as it is commonly known) was formed in 1923. The original organization and its members today include some of the most well-known and respected legal scholars in the United States. The goal of the ALI when it was formed was to establish a published source of authority for generally accepted commonlaw principles. The evolution of technology occurred so rapidly in this century that many areas of law sprang up where none existed before. As a result, the courts had no guideposts and thus created a great deal of commonlaw. During this time, the legal system in this country expanded very rapidly, and because so many courts in different jurisdictions were considering similar legal issues, numerous inconsistent and even contradictory precedents were established. This development was of great concern to legal scholars, judges, and lawyers alike. The outcome of a case often was determined not only by the jurisdiction where the case was pending but also by the personal biases of the particular judge who presided over the case.

The members of the ALI formed a cohesive organization to study the legal precedents that were being issued and to formulate them into logical statements of the accepted legal principles. While the advantage of these restatements of law was that the ALI did the work of analyzing all the precedents nationally on particular issues, the obvious disadvantage was that the Restatement pronouncements were often very general—sometimes vague—and did not always reflect the specific holdings of a single jurisdiction. Nevertheless, judges who looked to the Restatements for guidance could examine commonly applied principles of law in courts faced with similar legal issues. This, coupled with the prestigious membership of the ALI, elevated the published Restatements of the Law to a respected position in the legal community.

Initially, the ALI confined its activities to examining established precedents. However, because the law is ever changing, often by the time a particular restatement was agreed upon by the membership and published, it was obsolete. In 1962, the ALI modified its goals not only to include restatements of existing precedent but also to speculate and make educated estimates as to what likely developments of law would probably occur in the near future. Whether a restatement of existing law or a proposal of what future principles might develop, the Restatements are highly regarded as legal authority.

Commonlaw Subjects of the Restatements.   The commonlaw subjects that have been addressed formally by the ALI include the following (the information after each title is a brief description and not part of the formal publication or citation):

Restatement of the Law of Agency—law applicable to circumstances where one party acts on behalf of another.

Restatement of the Law of Conflicts of Law—when courts are faced with a situation where the law of more than one jurisdiction might be applied.

Restatement of the Law of Contracts—law pertaining to agreements between parties.

Restatement of the Law of Foreign Relations Law of the United States—legal standards of agreements and treatment of laws and citizens of foreign countries.

Restatement of the Law of Judgments—enforceability and legal treatment of court orders/decisions.

Restatement of the Law of Property—law pertaining to ownership, possession, and use of tangible items and land.

Restatement of the Law of Restitution—legal principles that govern the proper legal action following damage to certain types of rights.

Restatement of the Law of Security—legal actions regarding the handling and treatment of collateral given in exchange for property or money.

Restatement of the Law of Torts—the law applicable to personal rights not governed by criminal or contract law.

Restatement of the Law of Trusts—legal standards applicable to situations where one party legally holds the property of another party.

ASSIGNMENT 9.1

Examine each of the following situations and determine which, if any, restatement would be likely to contain information about the issue.

1. A part-time driver for a delivery company causes an accident while on the job. Does the injured party have an action against the driver AND his employer?
2. Can someone provide for the financial care and upkeep of an animal shelter after his or her death, with the condition that the shelter never be moved from its present location?
3. Is it ever possible to be a party in a suit against yourself for breach of an agreement?
4. If you are injured on the job but your employer claims your injury occurred elsewhere, can you sue your employer?
5. You offer the title to your car as collateral for a loan. You have made many of the payments in cash without a receipt, and the lender, claiming you are behind in payment, wants possession of the car.

One area of law in particular that the ALI has been very active and vocal in is product liability. While principles of tort law regarding such things as

negligence and intentional tort have existed for centuries, they were somewhat simplistic and typically involved relatively straightforward situations between two parties. However, with the development of the assembly line and mass-production equipment, products were suddenly passed through various manufacturers of parts and assemblies, wholesalers, retailers, and independent salespeople, and ultimately to the consumer. In addition, many products operated mechanically and initially came with few or no instructions or warnings. As a result, countless individuals were injured, maimed, and sometimes killed as the result of malfeasance by one or more of the parties in the chain between the origin of the product and the final consumer.

Such a complicated set of facts presented courts with a variety of questions, such as, Which court has jurisdiction over all the parties involved? Can a party such as a wholesaler be held accountable for defects in a product when the wholesaler had no more involvement than to sell the product in commerce to retailers? What if the injured party did not even buy the product? Rather, if the item was borrowed, can the borrower have an action against a company with whom the party never had a business relationship? These and many other questions had to be answered. Since the Restatement of the Law of Torts was issued, countless courts have considered the sections on product liability and have often relied upon these summaries of general precedent for guidance. Exhibit 9.1 shows the section of Restatement of the Law of Torts that defines product liability.

Other Included Information. Other information is included in the restatement in addition to the commonly accepted legal principle. The principle is followed by a section called "Comment," an explanatory discussion of the meaning of the principle as interpreted by the ALI. Next are "Illustrations," descriptions of realistic circumstances that demonstrate how the principle would apply to a particular situation. Finally are citations of authority—real cases where the principle of law was applied. Additional citations and cross-references are included in a bound appendix that follows the text. All of these features are included to provide a better understanding of the legal principle and to find primary authority.

The first and second series of each restatement are valuable tools in research. While the first series may contain certain principles that are no longer the general rule, by looking at comparable sections in each series, you can see how the law has evolved. Because the restatement is a persuasive authority of great impact, knowing the development of standards by the ALI enables you to present the current standard more convincingly and to better explain why the principle should be considered applicable to a particular set of circumstances.

Arrangement of the Restatements. As with most legal authorities, the Restatements are arranged by subject. First, broad subjects of law are divided into totally distinct Restatement publications (as previously listed). Second, the restatement for each area of law is broken into individual subjects, which are then subdivided into sections. Each section contains a principle of law.

The Restatement is indexed by subject much like other legal resources. There is one comprehensive index for the combined first series Restatements. In addition, each subject area is indexed individually. The second series Restatements do not have the comprehensive index, but each subject has its

C.   Neither A nor B is liable to C in an action for negligence.

2.   A, a retail dealer, sells to B a hot water bag purchased from a reputable manufacturer. A believes the bag to be in perfect condition, although he has not inspected it, but the bag is defective in that the stopper will not screw in securely. As a result of this defect, C, the minor son of B, is severely scalded by hot water that leaks out of the bag. A is not liable to B or to C in an action for negligence.

e.   In many situations the seller who receives his goods from a reputable source of supply receives it with the firm conviction that it is free from defects; and where a chattel is of a type which is perfectly safe for use in the absence of defects, the seller who sells it with the reasonable belief that it is safe for use and represents it to be safe for use does not act negligently. Frequently, the manufacturer's literature and salesmen and his past record of sending the seller perfectly made chattels create a reasonable belief in the seller's mind that the particular chattel he is selling is made perfectly. When the seller reasonably believes that the chattel is safe, his representation in good faith to that effect is neither fraudulent, reckless, nor negligent.

Illustration:

3.   A, a retail dealer, sells to B a defective gas heater, obtained from a reputable manufacturer, which A believes to be in perfect condition, although he has not inspected it. In making the sale, and in response to B's inquiry, A says, "This heater can be used with perfect safety." The heater when used emits poisonous fumes, injuring B. A is not liable to B in an action for negligence.

TOPIC 5. STRICT LIABILITY

§ 402 A. Special Liability of Seller of Product for Physical Harm to User or Consumer

(1) One who sells any product in a defective condition unreasonably dangerous to the user or consumer or to his property is subject to liability for physical harm thereby caused to the ultimate user or consumer, or to his property, if
    (a) the seller is engaged in the business of selling such a product, and
    (b) it is expected to and does reach the user or consumer without substantial change in the condition in which it is sold.
(2) The rule stated in Subsection (1) applies although
    (a) the seller has exercised all possible care in the preparation and sale of his product, and
    (b) the user or consumer has not bought the product from or entered into any contractual relation with the seller.
See Appendix for Reporter's Notes, Court Citations, and Cross References

**EXHIBIT 9.1
Section of Restatement of the Law, Second, Which Defines Products Liability.** Copyright 1966 by the American Law Institute. Reprinted with permission of the American Law Institute.

own index. The subject indexes are usually contained in the last volume of the series. The exception to this is the Restatement of Torts 2d. The torts compilation has a subject index at the back of each of the volumes. The disadvantage to this is that each index in each volume must be consulted if you do not know the likely area where your answers will be found.

Using the Restatements. If you want to locate a particular Restatement principle, you should formulate your query and likely search terms. Next, you should take them to the appropriate Restatement. It is usually best to start with the second series to obtain the most current pronouncement. You can then refer to the first series to note any changes and the logic behind them. This may impact the way in which you present the current principle. Once you have located your search terms in the index, you will be referred to the section or sections of the Restatement that apply.

☐ ASSIGNMENT 9.2

Part I

Examine the Restatement of the Law of Contracts index pages from Exhibit 9.2. From each page, select a Restatement section number and title that is indicated and create a situation that you think might be covered by the section.

Part II

Locate and examine the section you identified in the index in the Restatement and determine whether the section does or does not address the situation you have created.

Note: Some law ibraries maintain their Restatements on reserve. To determine whether the library you are using contains the Restatement of the Law of Contracts, consult the title section of the card catalog or ask the librarian.

In addition to using the index, you can use a topical approach to the Restatement. However, unlike many other publications that contain the list of general topics within each volume and then the more specific subtopics within the particular volume, the Restatement uses a more isolated approach. Each volume contains a table of contents showing the topics, subtopics, and sections contained within that volume. However, since there is no general table of all topics, you must consult each volume until you locate the volume that includes the information for which you are looking. As you can see, the topical approach to the Restatement is not the most efficient unless you are familiar with the topics and know the exact volume to consult.

Once you have located the principle in the Restatement that is most applicable to your situation, you may want to see how the principle has been applied. While the Restatement may contain some citations, such citations are for illustrative purposes and do not compose a comprehensive or current list. In this situation, a citator can be an invaluable tool. By locating the section number in the proper Shepard's Restatement of the Law Citations, you will find a complete list of primary and limited secondary authorities that pertain to the section from the Restatement. This enables you to identify any primary authority from your own jurisdiction and other persuasive authorities. Also, because the citators indicate just how the principle was applied or not applied, you can determine whether your jurisdiction is in accord with the principle.

An alternative method of locating law relevant to the Restatement is through the use of the Restatement in the Courts for the first series of the Restatement or the appendix in the second series. The Restatement of the

INDEX

386

EXHIBIT 9.2
**Pages from a
Restatement of
the Law, Second,
Contracts Index.**
Copyright 1981 by
the American Law
Institute.
Reprinted with the
permission of the
American Law
Institute.

**EXHIBIT 9.2
Continued**

Courts is prepared with citations and headnotes about the cases cited and arranged by Restatement topic and section. Thus, unlike with a case digest, which is arranged through the key number indexing system, you must know the applicable Restatement section to obtain the benefit of the Restatement of the Courts. A disadvantage to the Restatement of the Courts to the first series Restatements is that the publication is outdated, and even at the time it was issued, it was only intermittently published. A single edition was issued for the years 1932–1944, inclusive. Subsequent volumes were issued periodically between 1948 and 1976. The second series is not supplemented with a Restatement to the Courts. Rather, this information is contained in the appendix to each volume, and periodic updates are issued annually as supplements or pocket parts.

Since 1985, a publication known as the Interim Case Citations to Restatement in the Courts has been issued on a more regular basis to provide more timely information about cases that interpret Restatement principles. Although they serve much the same purpose as an ordinary citator, the obvious benefit of these supplements over traditional citators is that headnotes are included, enabling you to be more discriminating in the full opinions that you choose to locate and read. However, as always, keep in mind that headnotes are one-sentence summaries of entire judicial opinions and may not give the full import of the decisions.

TREATISES

Standard secondary authorities in any law library are **treatises**, which are cited fairly regularly in legal documents. Treatises are especially helpful when the legal standard relied upon is one that has been established and followed for a very long time. A treatise is essentially a comprehensive collection and discussion by a noted scholar of long-established legal standards on a particular topic of law. Treatises may be prepared as national in scope or be tailored to the law of a particular jurisdiction. These commentaries usually describe the evolution of an area of law and how the principles apply in theory.

treatise
Detailed body of work about a particular subject that usually addresses the development of major concepts and theories.

Some treatises in well-developed areas of law, such as contract, have been referred to for decades (in some cases, centuries), while others in more volatile, changing, and growing areas of law are updated and new editions are issued much more frequently. Some treatises consist of multiple volumes, while others are contained within a single book.

Treatise Features

Because treatises are written by private authors and published by different companies on any number of subjects, there is no uniform format or indexing system. Most do contain subject indexes at the end of the text, but again, this is not universal, and this, along with other organizational features, depends on the publisher and often the age of the publication. More recent publications often contain more finding tools. Even if there is no index, most treatises contain a table of contents with topics and subtopics, much like any

other reference book. By referring to them you can usually determine the general area of the text where the information you are seeking lies. Some treatises even provide short summaries of subject areas within the table of contents. These descriptive statements can be very helpful in pinpointing details about your subject of research.

☐ ASSIGNMENT 9.3

Using Exhibit 9.3, determine which section of the treatise would most likely contain information about the following question: What standard is used to determine whether a party voluntarily agreed to the terms of a contract?

Using a Treatise.   Use of a treatise as an authority is most beneficial when the author or publication is well-known (e.g., Prosser on Torts). Knowing which authors are known and respected to some degree must be learned through experience. However, strong indicators of an accepted scholar are references to that scholar in other resources, such as legal encyclopedias, case law, and other publications.

When no other definitive source exists, a treatise may be the best source of authority for a clear statement on an issue. Treatises can perhaps be most easily located through the use of the traditional library card index. If you are familiar with the author or subject, this source can be consulted as in any ordinary library. The card catalog will probably not indicate that a publication is a treatise per se. Rather, the term *treatise* is a more descriptive phrase used to identify a particular type of reference book, much like the phrase "regional reporter" describes a particular type of publication of case law.

Treatises are commonly footnoted with primary authority, which can be a helpful starting point when your other methods to locate law have been futile or when you need a detailed discussion of a particular aspect of law. Citation of treatises is governed by Rule 15 of the bluebook, which addresses "Books, Pamphlets, and Other Nonperiodic Materials." The citation of specific sections or paragraphs of a treatise are addressed by Rule 3.4

Organization of Treatises.   Treatises are organized in a manner similar to other reference books, such as the one you are reading now. They generally have a table of contents at the beginning and an index at the end. Many times, the table of contents will include summaries that provide brief descriptions of the content in each major section of text. These summaries are particularly helpful in narrowing your search. Because treatises are often quite lengthy and complex discussions, you need to use every advantage to narrow your search as much as possible.

The index is probably the most useful tool to locate specific information within a treatise. Like most indexes, a treatise index will contain major and minor references to the text. Depending on the organization of the particular publication, the numbers that follow terms in the index may be page numbers or section numbers. This is usually apparent, but if not, the beginning of the index will generally state what the reference number indicates. Another helpful tool that is frequently found, especially in more recent treatises, is a table of cases. Many times, these cases are discussed within the treatise as

---

TABLE OF CONTENTS

Chapter 1

DEFINITION OF TERMS

Chapter 2

FORMAL CONTRACTS

xv

EXHIBIT 9.3 Table of Contents of Williston on Contracts, 4th Edition. Reprinted with permission of Lawyers Cooperative Publishing, a division of Thomson Legal Publishing, Inc.

applications of legal standards. Also, the table often provides you with complete citations of authority on particular points of law.

Casebooks.   A publication that is not in the traditional form of a treatise but bears many similarities is the **casebook**. Casebooks contain primarily complete or edited judicial opinions, with brief discussions of the legal standards

casebook

Collection of cases and commentary on a subject of law that has been developed and/or interpreted judicially.

EXHIBIT 9.3
Continued

applied within the decisions. Casebooks, usually more limited in scope and depth than treatises, are standard fare in law schools and are generally helpful in research to help the reader cultivate a sense of how legal theories are developed and applied to actual circumstances. Casebooks are not typically cited as authority in legal research, because they are primarily collections of case law and it is more influential to cite the primary authority of case law as published in a report rather than the secondary authority of a casebook that discusses selected cases on a given topic.

Treatise Updates.   Some treatises are updated through the use of supplements or pocket parts. Some treatises are published in binders that can accommodate supplement pages added directly to the original text. Updates may contain discussions of changes in the law and/or citations of authority that reiterate legal standards or that reflect changes in the law since the publication of the original treatise.

☐ ASSIGNMENT 9.4

Assume you are consulting a treatise and note a citation of authority from another jurisdiction but that appears to be especially relevant to the subject of your research. What is the most efficient way to locate cases from your own jurisdiction that also address this exact point of law?

▌▌▌▶ STRATEGY

Research in the Restatements

1. Identify the Restatement publication that most likely addresses the topic of your research.
2. Consult the proper subject index with relevant terms. If looking into a first series Restatement, use the comprehensive index. If looking to the second series, use the index for the particular Restatement publication. The exception to this is the Restatement of Torts, for which you must consult the subject at the back of the volume that contains the specific topic in tort law that you are researching.
3. It is best to begin with the most recent Restatement series for the most current pronouncements. However, be sure to consult prior Restatements as well because the reasons for any change may affect the impact of a Restatement section on your particular question of law.
4. Validate the Restatement section by consulting the proper citator. You may also want to consult the Restatement in the Courts (separate volume for first series sections, appendix in second series).

▌▌▌▶ STRATEGY

Treatises

1. Consult the subject or author section of the library card catalog or ask the librarian for the definitive works on the topic of your research.
2. Examine the table of contents and index (if any) to determine the proper section or sections of the treatise applicable to your topic of research.

CHAPTER SUMMARY

Restatements and treatises are somewhat different from other forms of legal authorities. Restatements are technically secondary authority but are often placed on a footing nearly equal with primary authority, especially if that primary authority is persuasive rather than mandatory or if there is no primary authority on point. The source of Restatements is the ALI, which produces the Restatements on areas of commonlaw to establish some uniformity in the generally accepted legal standards of commonlaw subjects. Because the ALI is composed of noted and respected legal scholars and the Restatements summarize generally accepted principles in a majority of jurisdictions, the publications merit and receive a great deal of deference by the judicial branch.

Treatises also are publications that often emanate from noted respected legal scholars. Unlike Restatements, treatises typically provide the history and evolution of a particular area of law in substantial detail. They are commonly cited with respect to long-established legal principles. Both treatises and Restatements are typically indexed and contain citations that provide the basis for expanded research into primary authorities.

KEY TERMS

treatise   Restatement of the Law   casebook

SELF-TEST

MULTIPLE CHOICE

1. Restatements are the only _____ authority that generates such respect that they are often compared against primary authority.
   a) judicial
   b) legislative
   c) secondary
   d) primary

2. Much of this respect for Restatements comes from their origin, which is the _____
   a) CFR
   b) ALI
   c) ALR
   d) LSI

3. Modern Restatements contain established principles of law as well as _____.
   a) anticipated changes
   b) statutes
   c) regulations
   d) opinions

4. The subjects of the Restatements include but are not limited to _____
   a) foreign relations law
   b) property
   c) torts
   d) all of the above

5. Other information included in the Restatements in addition to the actual legal principles includes _____.

a) illustrations
b) updates
c) references
d) all of the above

TRUE/FALSE

_____ 6. Additional citations and cross-references are included in an appendix that follows the text.

_____ 7. Each section of the Restatement contains a principle of statutory law.

_____ 8. The second series is served by a combined comprehensive index for all subjects.

_____ 9. The second series Restatements do not have the comprehensive index, but each subject has its own index.

_____10. The indexes are usually contained in the last volume of the subject series. The exception to this is the Restatement of Torts 2d.

FILL-IN THE BLANKS

11. By locating the section number in the proper _____

    _____ _____

    _____ _____, you will find a complete list of primary and limited secondary authorities that pertain to the section from the Restatement.

12. An alternative method to locate law relevant to a restatement is through the use of the _____

    _____ _____ for the first series of the Restatement or the appendix in the second series.

13. In addition, since 1985, the

    _____ _____

    _____ to Restatement in the Courts has been issued on a more regular basis to provide more timely information about cases that interpret Restatement principles.

14. A _____ is essentially a comprehensive collection and discussion by a noted scholar of long-established legal standards.

15. There is no _____ format or indexing system for treatises.

16. Even if there is no index, most treatises contain a _____

    _____ _____ with topics and subtopics, much like any other reference book.

17. Use of a treatise as an authority is most beneficial when the author or publication is _____ _____ (e.g., Prosser on Torts).

18. Treatises can perhaps be most easily located through the use of the traditional library _____ _____ .

19. Depending on the organization of the particular publication, the numbers that follow terms in the index may be _____ numbers or _____ numbers.

20. _____ contain primarily complete or edited judicial opinions with brief discussions of the legal standards applied within the decisions.

CHAPTER 10

ANNOTATED LAW REPORTS

CHAPTER OBJECTIVES

Upon completion of this chapter, you should be able to accomplish the following competencies:

- Describe an annotated law report.

- Discuss the method of organization of annotated law report series.

- Distinguish an annotated law report from primary authority.

- Explain the usefulness of an annotated law report.

- Distinguish an annotated law report from an annotated statute.

- Explain how an annotated law report can be used as a finding tool for primary authorities.

- Identify those subjects that are likely to be addressed by an annotated law report.

- Explain the process of research in an annotated law report.

- Describe the information contained in an annotation of an annotated law report.

- Explain the usefulness of annotated law reports updating services.

The **annotated law report** is exactly what its name implies—discussion (annotation) of published judicial opinions (law reports). The annotated law report reprints only selected judicial opinions and annotations. Somewhat of a hybrid between a digest and a reporter, the annotated law report is neither a finding tool nor a clearinghouse for judicial law. Rather, it is a very useful means to track the development of law. When citing a judicial opinion that is included in such an annotation, you should not usually cite the annotation. Rather, you should properly cite the judicial opinion to its official report. The decision of the court is primary authority. An annotation is a secondary publication of authority and thus has much less influence.

annotated law report
Selected judicial opinions followed by detailed commentary and analysis.

The most commonly used annotated law report is a publication known as the ALR series. ALR stands for American Law Reports (not to be confused with the more generic term *annotated law report*).

Thus far, there have been five series for state judicial opinions nationwide as well as a federal series for judicial opinions from the federal judicial branch. The series publications have been issued during the following intervals:

ALR 1st Series (1919–1948)
ALR 2d Series (1948–1965)
ALR 3d Series (1965–1980)
ALR 4th Series (1980–1991)
ALR 5th Series (1992–date)
ALR Fed. Series (1969–date) (Prior to 1969, federal annotations were included in the first, second, and third series.)

CHARACTERISTICS OF ANNOTATED LAW REPORTS

The ALR has a variety of characteristics that permit you to examine a subject of law that is undergoing change, locate annotations on related topics, determine whether your jurisdiction has considered a specific legal issue, and find limited citations of authority on a particular topic. As you can see, the ALR can be a source of a great deal of information and in this respect can be an extremely helpful method to confine your research to fairly narrow parameters. However, the organization of the ALR is such that if you do not follow certain procedures in accessing information, you are very likely to end up with nothing.

As a rule, the subjects addressed in the ALR are topics of law that are currently challenged in several jurisdictions, whether as the result of legal questions or factual circumstances that have generated controversy. The annotations are issued chronologically and are not arranged by subject or jurisdiction. Rather, as an area of law begins to develop or an established legal principle becomes volatile, the publishers of the ALR will select a representative judicial opinion and prepare an annotation on the topic. When several of these have accumulated, the next hardbound volume is issued in numerical sequence to the previously issued volumes (e.g., volume 101 is followed by volume 102). Because the opinions and annotations are from no one jurisdiction and are not limited to any one topic, an extensive finding tool is necessary to locate information within the ALR.

Originally, the ALR was referenced by the quick index, essentially a subject index. (See Exhibit 10.1 for sample listings.) One index was used for the first and second series and another for the third and fourth. By using research terms, you could locate annotations on relatively specific topics. The index would guide you to the series, volume, and page of the judicial opinion and subsequent annotation. While most libraries still maintain copies of the quick index for the various series, more recently, the ALR has prepared a digest that index all of the series, making the time necessary to locate annotations shorter and providing additional details about annotations. Relative to other legal resources, the ALR quick indexes and digests are very user friendly. The focus tends to be more on ordinary language than on legal terminology. Also, annotation titles are often very specific and descriptive. Thus, beginning researchers tend to have success in locating information in the ALR.

☐ ASSIGNMENT 10.1

Based on Exhibit 10.1, identify likely relevant ALR annotations for the following fact situation:

Attorney Jim Jones represented the Maryville Department of Utilities to collect past due accounts. He charged $200 per hour for the work he performed. When the department received the bill, it informed Jim that it would pay only $75 per hour. What are Jim's chances of recovering his entire fee? There is no applicable local or state law for this situation.

The ALR is not the resource of choice for all research questions. Because the publishers of the ALR concentrate on areas of changing or controversial law, well-established principles are not generally discussed in ALR annotations. Consequently, if your research is confined to basic information gathering about a subject of law, you are not likely to find helpful information unless the legal principles have been subject to change.

There are times during the research process when consulting the ALR is most beneficial: first, when you are exploring a new or controversial area of law, and second, when your research within your own jurisdiction has been fruitless. In the first instance, the ALR is often a very good source to familiarize you with how the courts have generally approached a particular issue. The discussion following the opinion is an objective analysis of the status of the legal principle in a variety of jurisdictions. Also, the actual opinion can provide you with some insight as to the application of the legal principle to a specific factual setting. In the latter circumstance, a relevant ALR annotation may in some cases provide you with citations in your own jurisdiction that you did not locate in your initial search. More often, you'll find citations from other jurisdictions that can be used as persuasive primary authority. Also, the discussion within the annotation often provides you with additional search terms and a better understanding of the subject.

The judicial opinions contained in the ALR are organized quite similarly to those published in reporters (see Exhibit 10.2). The citation information is given, along with a summary or synopsis of the decision and, finally, headnotes and corresponding paragraph numbers. These are followed by the

EXHIBIT 10.1   Sample Listings of ALR Annotations from the ALR Quick Index.
Reprinted with permission of Lawyers Cooperative Publishing, a division of
Thomson Legal Publishing, Inc.

QUICK INDEX   Attorneys' Fees

Plea of nolo contendere or non vult contendere, 89 ALR2d 540

Political campaign: attorney's conduct in campaign as ground for disciplinary action, 57
ALR2d 1362

Reinstatement of attorney after disbarment,
suspension, or resignation, 70 ALR2d 268

ATTORNEYS' FEES
§ 1. Generally
§ 2. Particular proceedings or services

---

§ 1. Generally.

Accounting: right to accounting between attorneys associated in practice, in absence of
formal partnership, 81 ALR2d 1420

Appeal
– attorneys' fees paid by appellee in resisting
unsuccessful appellate review as damages recoverable on appeal bond, 37
ALR2d 525
– contractual provision for attorneys' fees as
including allowance for services rendered upon appellate review, 52 ALR2d
863

Apportionment (this index)

Complaint, Petition, or Declaration (this index)

Conflict of Laws (this index)

Construction and operation of attorney's general or periodic retainer fee or salary contract, 43 ALR2d 677

Contingent fee
– court rules limiting amount of contingent
fees or otherwise imposing conditions
on, 77 ALR2d 411
– treatment of interest on judgment or award,
in determining, 82 ALR2d 953

Costs: attorney's fees as within statute imposing upon condemner liability for "expenses," "costs," and the like, 26 ALR2d
1295

Damages, attorney's fees as element of, see
specific lines throughout this topic.

Discharge without fault: measure or basis of
attorney's recovery on express contract
fixing noncontingent fees, where he is discharged without cause or fault on his part,
54 ALR2d 604

Discipline: amount or character of compensation as ground for disciplinary action
against attorney, 70 ALR2d 962

Former client: attorney's representation of in-

terest adverse to that of former client as
justification for refusal of compensation,
52 ALR2d 1289

Fraud: conveyance or transfer in consideration
of legal services, rendered or to be rendered, as fraudulent as against creditors,
45 ALR2d 500

Guaranty of payment as including, 4 ALR2d
138

Implied promise: what constitutes acceptance
or ratification of, or acquiescence in, services rendered by attorney so as to raise
implied promise to pay reasonable value
thereof, 78 ALR2d 318

Interpleader: allowance of attorneys' fees to
party interpleading claimants to funds or
property, 48 ALR2d 190

Limitation of actions: when statute of limitations begins to run against action by attorney, not employed on contingent fee basis,
for compensation for services, 60 ALR2d
1008

Opposing attorney: conditioning the setting
aside of judgment or grant of new trial on
payment of opposing attorney's fees, 21
ALR2d 863

Partnership: rights as to business unfinished or
fees uncollected upon withdrawal or death
of partner in law firm, 78 ALR2d 280

Splitting of fees: division of fees or compensation between co-operating attorneys, 73
ALR2d 991

Third person: right to recover as damages
attorneys' fees incurred in earlier litigation
with a third person because of involvement
therein through a tortious act of present
adversary, 45 ALR2d 1183

§ 2. Particular proceedings or services.

Alimony (this index)

Assignment for benefit of creditors: validity of
provision in deed or transfer to assignee
for benefit of creditors for payment of
attorneys fees, 79 ALR2d 513

Attachment or garnishment: right to recover
attorney's fees for wrongful attachment, 65
ALR2d 1426

Bastardy proceedings, allowance of attorneys'
fees in, 40 ALR2d 961

Bills and notes
– recovery of attorneys' fees provided for in
bill, note, or similar evidence of indeb-
tedness, as affected by opposing party's
recovery, 41 ALR2d 677
– validity of provision in promissory note or

For additional annotations, consult Quick Indexes to ALR3d and ALR4th   **53**

EXHIBIT 10.1
Continued

Public Trial   ALR2d

PUBLIC TRIAL

Exclusion of public during criminal trial, 48 ALR2d 1436

PUBLIC UTILITIES

For matters relating to particular utilities or services, such as electricity, gas, water, etc., see specific topics

§ 1. Generally
§ 2. Operation and service
§ 3. Rates and charges

---

§ 1. Generally.

Abutting owner: liability of public utility to abutting owner for destruction or injury of trees in or near highway or street, 64 ALR2d 866

Delegation of Power (this index)

Eminent domain: compensation or damages for condemning a public utility plant, 68 ALR2d 392

Relocation: constitutionality of state legislation to reimburse public utilities for cost of relocating their facilities because of highway construction, conditioned upon federal reimbursement of state under terms of Federal-Aid Highway Act [23 USC § 123], 75 ALR2d 419

Restitution and Implied Contracts (this index)

§ 2. Operation and service.

Deposit required by public utility, 43 ALR2d 1262

Discontinuance: right of public utility to discontinue line or branch on ground that it is unprofitable, 10 ALR2d 1121

Division of territory: validity of contract between public utilities other than carriers, dividing territory and customers, 70 ALR2d 1326

Municipal Corporations (this index)

Mutual association, nonprofit organization, or cooperative as under duty to furnish utilities services, 56 ALR2d 413

Strikes: validity of public utility anti-strike laws and regulations, 22 ALR2d 894

§ 3. Rates and charges.

Discrimination between property within and that outside governmental districts as to public service or utility rates, 4 ALR2d 595

Injunction: adequacy, as regards right to injunction, of other remedy for review of

order fixing public utility rates, 8 ALR2d 839

Joinder or representation of several claimants in action to recover overcharge, 1 ALR2d 160

Refund: right of customers of public utility with respect to fund representing a refund from another supplying utility upon reduction of latter's rates, 18 ALR2d 1343

Variations of utility rates based on flat and meter rates, 40 ALR2d 1331

PUBLIC WATER SUPPLY

Water Supply (this index)

PUBLIC WELFARE AND WELFARE LAWS

Poor and Poor Laws (this index)

PUBLIC WORKS AND CONTRACTS

§ 1. Generally
§ 2. Letting and award of contracts; bidding
§ 3. Construction or interpretation of contracts

---

§ 1. Generally.

Contractor's Bond (this index)

Fair Labor Standards Act: employment in connection with highway construction or repair as within federal Fair Labor Standards Act, 43 ALR2d 891

Miller Act (this index)

Obstruction, duty of highway construction contractor to provide temporary way or detour around, 29 ALR2d 876

§ 2. Letting and award of contract; bidding.

Determination of amount involved in contract within statutory provision requiring public contracts involving sums exceeding specified amount to be let to lowest bidder, 53 ALR2d 498

Differences in character or quality of materials, articles, or work as affecting acceptance of bid for public contract, 27 ALR2d 917

Mistake: rights and remedies of bidder for public contract who has not entered into a contract, where bid was based on his own mistake of fact or that of his employee, 52 ALR2d 792

Rejection of bids: right of public authorities to reject all bids for public work or contract, 31 ALR2d 469

---

506   For additional annotations, consult Quick Indexes to ALR3d and ALR4th

EXHIBIT 10.1
Continued

QUICK INDEX   **Social Security**

supplies, ladders, small tools, and like products, 78 ALR2d 696

SMOKE

Automobiles: liability for motor vehicle accident where vision of driver is obscured by smoke, dust, atmospheric condition, or unclean windshield, 42 ALR2d 13

Nuisance (this index)

SNOW AND ICE

Abutting Owners (this index)

Floors (this index)

Immunity: snow removal operations as within doctrine of governmental immunity from tort liability, 92 ALR2d 796

Landlord and Tenant (this index)

Municipal liability for injuries from snow and ice on sidewalk, 39 ALR2d 782

Power machine: liability for injury or damage caused by operation of power machine in snow removal, 81 ALR2d 519

Safety Appliance or Boiler Inspection Acts (45 USC §§ 4, 11, 23), slippery condition of grabiron, ladder, sill, or running board, as result of grease, ice, or other slippery substance as violation of, 90 ALR2d 596

Sidewalk (this index)

Stairs and Passageways (this index)

Steps: liability of proprietor of store, office, or similar business premises for injury from fall on steps made slippery by tracked-in or spilled water, oil, mud, snow, and the like, 62 ALR2d 131

Vision: liability for motor vehicle accident where vision of driver is obscured by smoke, dust, atmospheric condition, or unclean windshield, 42 ALR2d 13

SOAPBOX DERBY

Liability of operators or sponsors of soapbox derby for personal injury, 72 ALR2d 1137

SOAPS

Products Liability (this index)

SOCIAL ACTIVITIES

Discrimination or prejudice based on **Discrimination** (this index)

Liability of employer for injury resulting from games or other recreational or social activities, 18 ALR2d 1372

Libel and slander: imputation of subversive or otherwise objectionable political or social principles, 33 ALR2d 1196

SOCIAL CLUBS

Associations and Clubs (this index)

SOCIAL GUEST

Guests, Invitees, or Licensees (this index)

SOCIAL ORGANIZATIONS

Associations and Clubs (this index)

SOCIAL SECURITY

For matters dealing with unemployment compensation, see **Unemployment Compensation**

§ 1. **Generally**
§ 2. **Construction, generally**
§ 3. **Persons, employees, and employments covered or excluded**

────────

§ 1. **Generally.**

Collateral Source Rule (this index)

Conclusiveness of the records, or lack thereof, of Social Security Board respecting wages paid by employer, 6 ALR2d 954

Divorce, remarriage, or annulment, as affecting widow's social security benefits, 85 ALR2d 242

Nonoccupational disability plan, construction of benefit provisions of statutory plan, 95 ALR2d 1380

Pensions and Retirement Funds (this index)

Residence required for purposes of old age assistance, 43 ALR2d 1427

Wrongful death
– damages for wrongful death of husband or father as affected by receipt of social security benefits, 84 ALR2d 764
– pension, retirement income, social security payments, and the like, of deceased, as affecting recovery in wrongful death action, 81 ALR2d 949

Wrongful discharge: right of employer, liable for wrongful discharge or retirement, to reduce or mitigate damages by amount of social security or retirement benefits received by employee, 48 ALR2d 1293

§ 2. **Construction, generally.**

Agriculture: what constitutes "agricultural" or

For additional annotations, consult Quick Indexes to ALR3d and ALR4th   577

1095

BRUCE GRUBAUGH, Plaintiff-Appellant,

v

CITY OF ST. JOHNS, a Municipal Corporation, Defendant-Appellee

Michigan Supreme Court — November 12, 1970
384 Mich 165, 180 NW2d 778, 44 ALR3d 1095

SUMMARY OF DECISION

The plaintiff, a minor, was severely injured in an automobile accident allegedly due to the failure of the defendant municipality to maintain a public road in reasonably safe condition. Apparently, the plaintiff was so injured that he was physically incapable of giving notice of his claim against the defendant within 60 days, as required by the statute allowing such a tort claim against a municipality. However, the defendant had actual notice of the accident, since its police department had made a full investigation shortly after the occurrence. Also, notice of claim was actually filed within six months. Subsequently, the plaintiff filed suit in the Circuit Court, Clinton County, Michigan, Michael Carland, Circuit Judge sitting by designation, but the court dismissed the suit for failure to comply with the statutory notice requirement.

The Supreme Court of Michigan, T. M. Kavanagh, J., reversed the dismissal and remanded the cause for trial. The court held, inter alia, that, as applied to the plaintiff, the notice requirement arbitrarily deprived him of an accrued, vested right of action, and was therefore in violation of state and federal due process requirements.

Brennan, Ch. J., dissented.

SUBJECT OF ANNOTATION

Beginning on page 1108

Incapacity caused by accident in suit as affecting notice of claim required as condition of holding local governmental unit liable for personal injury

---

actual opinions. In ALR 5th, the opinions are placed at the end of the volume following the annotations. Keep in mind that the headnote numbers in the opinions correspond to the ALR digests rather than the West key number system. As a result, you generally cannot use the headnote titles and numbers to find information in a West digest.

The annotation begins with several preliminary components (see Exhibit 10.3) to provide you with various information relevant or collateral to the

EXHIBIT 10.3   Pages of an ALR annotation.

Reprinted with permission of Lawyers Cooperative Publishing, a division of Thomson Legal Publishing, Inc.

INDEX

Alcoholic beverage, arrest for offense involving possession or sale of, §§ 5[a], 6
Amount of permissible force, §§ 4, 7
Apparent necessity of self-defense, § 7
Armed robbery, defendants surprised by police in course of, § 8
Assault, illegal arrest as, § 3
Belief or knowledge that person was peace officer, right of resistance in event of, § 5 [a]
Civil cases, generally, § 2[b]
Deadly weapon, resistance by use of, § 4[b]
Disorderly conduct, arrest for, § 3
Drinking alcoholic beverages on public street, arrest for, § 6
English common-law right to resist unlawful arrest, § 2[a]
Exceptions to rule permitting reasonable resistance, § 8
Excessive force, arrests made with, §§ 6-8
Felony, defendants surprised by police during commission of, § 8
History and background of right to resist unlawful arrest, § 2[a]
Illegal arrests, generally, §§ 3-5
Instructions to jury, § 5[a]
Introduction, § 1
Invalidity of law allegedly being violated, resistance on ground of, § 5[b]
Killing arrester, right of resistance as including, § 4[b]
Killing while resisting arrest, § 7
Known peace officers, rule prohibiting resistance to, § 5[a]
Manslaughter while resisting arrest, § 4[b]
Minor in possession of alcoholic beverage, arrest of, § 5[a]
Model Penal Code of American Law Institute, §§ 5[a], 6

Motorist stopped for traffic violation, resistance by, § 4[a]
Narcotics agent, arrest by, § 5[a]
Personal liberty, resisting unlawful interference with right of, § 3
Physical necessities of situation as factor in determining sufficiency of force or resistance, § 4[a]
Posse, resisting "arrest" by, § 7
Practice pointers, § 2[b]
Preliminary matters, §§ 1, 2
Real necessity of self-defense, § 7
Reasonable resistance, rule permitting, §§ 3, 4, 6-8
Related matters, § 1[b]
Restatement of Torts, §§ 5[b], 6
Revenge, counterattack for purpose of, § 4 [a]
Robbery, defendants surprised by police in course of, § 8
Sale of alcoholic beverage to minor, arrest for, § 5[a]
Scope of annotation, § 1[a]
Specific maximum amount of permissible force, § 4[b]
Stabbing during resistance, § 5[a]
Statutory provision prohibiting resistance to known peace officer, § 5[a]
Sufficient force to avoid arrest, use of, § 4[a]
Summary and comment, § 2
Time interval between use of force and attack on officer, § 8
Traffic violation, resistance by motorist stopped for, § 4[a]
Unconstitutionality of law allegedly being violated, resistance on ground of, § 5[b]
Uniform Arrest Act, § 5[a]
Warrant, arrest without, § 5[b]
Weapon, resistance by use of, § 4[b]

TABLE OF JURISDICTIONS REPRESENTED
Consult POCKET PART in this volume for later case service

US	§§ 2[a], 3, 4[a, b], 5[a]	
Ala	§ 7	
Alaska	§§ 5[a], 6, 8	
Ariz	§§ 3, 4[b]	
Cal	§§ 5[a], 6	
Conn	§ 3	
Del	§ 5[a]	
DC	§§ 3, 4[b]	
Fla	§ 5[a]	
Ga	§§ 3, 4[a, b], 6	

ANNOTATION

MODERN STATUS OF RULES AS TO RIGHT TO FORCEFULLY RESIST ILLEGAL ARREST

by

Jeffrey F. Ghent, J.D.

TOTAL CLIENT-SERVICE LIBRARY® REFERENCES

5 AM JUR 2d, Arrest § 94; 6 AM JUR 2d, Assault and Battery § 79; 40 AM JUR 2d, Homicide §§ 103 et seq.
2 AM JUR PL & PR FORMS (Rev ed), Assault and Battery, Form 213
ALR DIGESTS, Assault and Battery § 38; Homicide § 39
ALR QUICK INDEX, Arrest; False Imprisonment or Arrest; Resisting an Officer

Consult POCKET PART in this volume for later case service

EXHIBIT 10.3   Continued

Top reproduction

1081 §2[a]

ILLEGAL ARREST—PRIVILEGE TO RESIST
44 ALR3d 1078

Of those jurisdictions in which the common-law right to resist an unlawful arrest has been altered,[11] most have adopted the view that a private citizen may not use force to resist a peaceful arrest by one he knows or has good reason to believe is an authorized peace officer performing his duties.[12] In other jurisdictions, the courts have made exceptions to the common-law rule where the basis for resistance is that the law allegedly violated is invalid, or that the arrest warrant is technically defective.[13]

The foregoing discussion has been confined to the situation in which the arrester does not use excessive force, since the general proposition that an arrestee may use reasonable force to defend himself against the arrester's use of greater force than is required to effect the arrest has been recognized even by courts that have limited the common-law right to resist an illegal arrest not made with excessive force.[14]

As to the amount of force that an arrestee may use to combat the excessive force of his arrester, the modern authority is sparse, but it has been held that he may kill his arrester only if he believes, and has reasonable grounds to believe, that he is in danger of death or great bodily harm at the hands of the arrester and in the exercise of reasonable judgment there are no other means of averting the real or apparent danger except to kill him.[15]

9. § 4[a], infra.

10. § 4[b], infra.

11. § 5, infra.

12. § 5[a], infra.

13. § 5[b], infra.

14. § 6, infra.

15. § 7, infra.

1080 §1[a]

ILLEGAL ARREST—PRIVILEGE TO RESIST
44 ALR3d

sist an unlawful arrest became established at least by 1710,[4] and during the nineteenth and early twentieth centuries, it became the established rule in the United States as well.[5] In Bad Elk v United States (1900) 177 US 529, 44 L Ed 874, 20 S Ct 729, for example, the United States Supreme Court held that the defendant, whose murder conviction was reversed, had the right to use such force as was absolutely necessary to resist an attempted illegal arrest.

In the modern American decisions on the question, a number of courts from a variety of jurisdictions have applied or recognized the traditional common-law rule that a person may resist an unlawful arrest by the use of reasonable force,[6] while the courts in a few jurisdictions have modified that rule.[7] Thus, although the statement in some cases that there is a trend toward limiting the right of resistance to illegal arrest[8] is true in the sense that the common-law rule has recently been modified in some jurisdictions, it is not true that the common-law rule has been abandoned more often than upheld in the modern cases.

Assuming that the use of reasonable force to resist an illegal arrest is permissible, the question arises as to how much force is reasonable. The answer most frequently given in the modern cases is whatever force is necessary to avoid the arrest,[9] short of homicide.[10]

4. The Queen v Tooley (1709) 2 Ld Raym 1296, 92 Eng Reprint 349.

5. For the historical development of the common-law right to resist an unlawful arrest, see Note.—Criminal Law: The Right to Resist an Unlawful Arrest: An Out-Dated Concept? 3 Tulsa LJ 40 (1966); and Chevigny, The Right to Resist an Unlawful Arrest. 78 Yale LJ 1128 (1969).

6. § 3, infra.

7. § 5, infra.

8. People v Briggs (1966) 25 App Div 2d 50, 266 NYS2d 546, mod on other grounds 19 NY2d 37, 277 NYS2d 662, 224 NE2d 93, United States v Heliczer (1967, CA2 NY) 373 F2d 241 (apparently applying New York law).

Bottom reproduction

1080 §1[a]

ILLEGAL ARREST—PRIVILEGE TO RESIST
44 ALR3d 1078

Ill	§ 5[a]	NY	§§ 2[a], 3, 4[a], 6
Kan	§ 3	NC	§§ 3, 5[b]
Ky	§§ 4[b], 7	Ohio	§ 3
La	§ 3	Okla	§§ 3, 4[b]
Md	§§ 3, 4[a]	Or	§ 6
Mich	§§ 3, 4[a]	SC	§§ 3, 4[b]
Minn	§§ 3, 4[a]	Tenn	§§ 3, 4[a, b], 7
Miss	§ 3	Tex	§ 6
Mo	§§ 3, 4[b], 5[b]	Va	§§ 3, 4[b]
NJ	§§ 5[a], 6–8	Eng	§ 2[a]

I. Preliminary matters

§ 1. Introduction

[a] Scope

This comment collects the modern[1] cases in which the courts have discussed the rules relating to whether, or under what circumstances, a person illegally[2] arrested may use force to resist the arrest.[3] Also covered is the question of how much force may be used in resisting the arrest.

No attempt has been made in this comment to discuss statutory provisions except insofar as they are reflected in the selected cases. The reader is advised to consult the latest enactments in his jurisdiction.

[b] Related matters

What constitutes, absent the use of actual force, offense of obstructing or resisting officer. 44 ALR3d 1018.

Criminal liability for obstructing process as affected by invalidity or irregularity of the process. 10 ALR3d 1146.

Scienter as element of offense of assaulting, resisting, or impeding federal officer. 10 ALR3d 833.

What justifies escape or attempt to escape, or assistance in that regard. 70 ALR2d 1430.

Danger or apparent danger of great bodily harm or death as condition of self-defense in civil action for assault and battery, personal injury, or death. 25 ALR2d 1215.

Danger or apparent danger of death or great bodily harm as condition of self-defense in prosecution for assault as distinguished from prosecution for homicide. 114 ALR 634.

What constitutes offense of obstructing or resisting officer. 48 ALR 746.

Right of self-defense by officer attempting illegal arrest. 46 ALR 904.

Civil liability for killing or injuring one who was attempting to make arrest. 7 ALR 313.

✦

Note.—Defiance of Unlawful Authority. 83 Harv L Rev 626 (1970).

Comment.—Criminal Law—Arrest—The Right to Resist Unlawful Arrest. 7 Natural Resources J 119 (1967).

Note.—Criminal Law: The Right to Resist an Unlawful Arrest: An Out-Dated Concept? 3 Tulsa LJ 40 (1966); and Chevigny, The Right to Resist an Unlawful Arrest. 78 Yale LJ 1128 (1969).

§ 2. Summary and comment

[a] Generally

The English common-law right to re-

1. No attempt has been made to present cases decided earlier than 1956.

2. This annotation assumes that the arrest is illegal, either in its inception (such as for lack of a necessary warrant), or by reason of the manner in which it is attempted (such as by the use of excessive force).

3. The right of a bystander or witness to aid the arrestee in his resistance involves distinct principles and is not considered here.

EXHIBIT 10.3   Continued

1083
§ 3

ILLEGAL ARREST—PRIVILEGE TO RESIST
44 ALR3d 1078

moment, rather than the result of carefully considered alternatives. (3) If a malicious or ambitious policeman can provoke a citizen to resistance, he can obtain a conviction for the resistance, if not upon the underlying charge; the more outrageous the arrest, the more likely it is to provoke resistance and lead to a conviction. (4) The freedom to refuse to obey a patently unlawful arrest is essential to the integrity of a government which purports to be one of laws, and not of men; unless it is desirable to kill the impulse to resist arbitrary authority, the rule that such an arrest is a provocation to resist must remain fundamental.

Regardless of which of the foregoing views prevails in a particular jurisdiction, counsel should remember that if the arrester can be proved to have used excessive force, the applicable rules will be much more favorable to the resisting arrestee.[6]

II. Illegal arrests, generally

§ 3. Rule permitting reasonable resistance

In a number of modern cases from a variety of jurisdictions, the courts have applied or recognized the traditional common-law rule that a person may resist an unlawful arrest by the use of reasonable force.

US—For federal cases involving state law, see state headings infra.

Ariz—State v Robinson (1967) 6 Ariz App 424, 433 P2d 75; State v Cadena (1969) 9 Ariz App 369, 452 P2d 534; State v De Ross (1969) 9 Ariz App 497, 454 P2d 167.

Conn—State v Amara (1964) 152 Conn 296, 206 A2d 438 (by implication). State v Harris (1967) 4 Conn Cir 534, 236 A2d 479.

DC—Curtis v United States (1966, Dist Col App) 222 A2d 840.

6. §§ 6-8, infra.

Abrams v United States (1956) 99 App DC 46, 237 F2d 42 (apparently applying District of Columbia law), cert den 352 US 1006, 1 L Ed 2d 554, 77 S Ct 575.

Ga—Gordy v State (1956) 93 Ga App 743, 92 SE2d 737; Finch v State (1960) 101 Ga App 73, 112 SE2d 824.

Kan—State v Goering (1964) 193 Kan 307, 392 P2d 930.

La—State v Lopez (1970) 256 La 108, 235 So 2d 394.

Md—Jenkins v State (1963) 232 Md 529, 194 A2d 618.

Jones v State (1968) 4 Md App 616, 244 A2d 459; Halcomb v State (1969) 6 Md App 32, 250 A2d 119; Lyles v State (1970) 10 Md App 265, 269 A2d 178.

Mich—People v Krum (1965) 374 Mich 356, 132 NW2d 69, cert den 381 US 935, 14 L Ed 2d 699, 85 S Ct 1765.

People v Gray (1970) 23 Mich App 139, 178 NW2d 172; People v Bonello (1970) 25 Mich App 600, 181 NW2d 652.

Minn—State v Miller (1958) 253 Minn 112, 91 NW2d 138.

Miss—Smith v State (1968, Miss) 208 So 2d 746.

Mo—For Missouri cases, see § 5[b], infra.

NY—People v Pitcher (1959) 9 App Div 2d 1016, 194 NYS2d 337; People v Dreares (1961) 15 App Div 2d 204, 221 NYS2d 819, affd 11 NY2d 906, 228 NYS 2d 467, 182 NE2d 812; People v Hamilton (1963) 18 App Div 2d 871, 237 NYS 2d 97; People v McNeil (1964) 21 App Div 2d 1, 247 NYS2d 734, affd 15 NY2d 717, 256 NYS2d 614, 204 NE2d 648; People v Briggs (1966) 25 App Div 2d 50, 266 NYS2d 546, mod on other grounds 19 NY2d 37, 277 NYS2d 662, 224 NE2d 93.

People v Tinston (1957) 6 Misc 2d 485, 163 NYS2d 554; Houghtaling v State (1958) 11 Misc 2d 1049, 175 NYS

1082
§ 2[b]

ILLEGAL ARREST—PRIVILEGE TO RESIST
44 ALR3d 1078

Even the general right of an arrestee to defend himself against excessive force has been subject to qualification in some of the cases supporting it. Thus, it has been stated that (1) where an arrestee has committed a felony which includes an immediate threat of violence, he has created a situation so fraught with peril as to preclude his claim of self-defense to any act of violence arising therefrom, unless the dangerous situation created by the felony no longer exists; and (2) if an arrestee knows that the arresting officer's unlawfully excessive force will cease if he desists from his physically defensive measures and submits to arrest, the arrestee must desist, or lose his privilege of self-defense.[16]

[b] Practice pointers

The rules relating to the right to forcefully resist an illegal arrest may become important to an attorney in a variety of contexts.[17] Thus, they may be applicable in either civil[18] or criminal[19] cases, and they may affect the outcome of cases in which the defendant is the arrester,[20] as well as cases in which the defendant is the arrestee.[1]

An attorney advocating the modification or elimination of the common-law rule permitting the use of reasonable force to resist an unlawful arrest should consider, in addition to the reasoning of

the courts that have taken that position,[2] the following arguments made by a commentator on the subject:[3] (1) It is primarily the guilty who resist unlawful arrests; (2) the resisting citizen has no sound method of gauging the legality of his conduct; (3) there is a conflict between the legally permitted uses of force by the arresting officer and the resisting citizen; and (4) the right to resist does not accomplish its purpose, since it only causes the resisting citizen to be lawfully arrested for the results of his resistance.

Similarly, counsel advocating retention of the common-law rule should consider not only the courts' reasoning,[4] but also the following arguments of another commentator:[5] (1) To formulate the question as whether the potential harms to the officers and citizen resulting from resistance are justified in light of the available alternative of submission assumes that there is no "right" to resist: the existence of other rights, such as the right to remain silent or to be free from unlawful searches, does not depend upon whether it is prudent for the individual to assert them. (2) When obeying the impulse to resist official abuse, most citizens do not consider the likelihood that they will successfully avoid arrest, any more than they consider the cost in jail time awaiting trial if they are arrested; the decision to resist is the work of a

16. § 8, infra.

17. §§ 3-8, infra.

18. See, generally, 2 Am Jur Proof of Facts 81, Assault and Battery, Proofs 4 (Defense of Persons) and 8 (Provocation).
See, particularly, the pertinent portions of the Restatement (Second) of Torts, infra §§ 5[b], 6.

19. See, generally, 7 Am Jur Trials 477, Homicide.
See, particularly, the pertinent portions of the Model Penal Code, infra §§ 5[a], 6.

20. For forms of answers alleging the use of reasonably necessary force to make ar-

rests, see 2 Am Jur Pl & Pr Forms (Rev ed), Assault and Battery, Forms 283-285.

1. For the form of an answer alleging the use of necessary force for self-protection against an unlawful arrest, see 2 Am Jur Pl & Pr Forms (Rev ed), Assault and Battery, Form 213.

2. § 5, infra.

3. Comment.—Criminal Law—Arrest—The Right to Resist Unlawful Arrest. 7 Natural Resources J 119 (1967).

4. § 3, infra.

5. Chevigny, The Right to Resist an Unlawful Arrest. 78 Yale LJ 1128 (1969).

216   LEGAL RESEARCH

EXHIBIT 10.3   Continued

§ 4. — Amount of permissible force

[a] Generally

Generally speaking,[9] an illegal arrest constitutes legal justification for the employment by the person arrested of force sufficient in amount to avoid the arrest.[10] Whether such force or resistance is more than sufficient is to be judged in terms of the physical necessities of the situation.[11] What is reasonable will vary with reference to the severity of the unlawful threat being resisted,[12] and unnecessary force may not be resorted to or means of resistance adopted which are disproportionate to the effort made to take the arrestee into custody.[13] Thus, the victim may not pursue his counterattack merely for the sake of revenge or for the infliction of needless injury,[14] and the counterattack should occur in close sequence to the unlawful arrest and as part of the resistance to it.[15] In other words, the right to forcefully resist an illegal arrest does not clothe the one wrongfully detained with the right to continue indefinitely an assaultive course of conduct, since the right to employ such combative tactics must be found to terminate at some point before the arraignment of a defendant in court, when the proceeding becomes valid without regard to the legality of the arrest[16]

For example, evidence that a motorist, after being stopped by a police officer for a traffic violation and then placed under arrest for disorderly conduct in loudly protesting the ticket, tackled the officer, removed the officer's pistol from its holster, began to leave, returned, and struck the officer twice with the pistol, causing a mild concussion and a forehead wound requiring six stitches, was held clearly sufficient to support a conviction for assault and battery, in Jones v State (1968) 4 Md App 618, 244 A2d 459, the court reasoning that even if the

9. This rule must be read in connection with the specific limitations on the maximum amount of permissible force discussed in § 4[b], infra.

10. US—For federal cases involving state law, see state headings, infra.
Ga—Finch v State (1960) 101 Ga App 73, 112 SE2d 824.
Md—Jones v State (1968) 4 Md App 616, 244 A2d 459.
Mich—People v Krum (1965) 374 Mich 356, 132 NW2d 69, cert den 381 US 935, 14 L Ed 2d 699, 85 S Ct 1765.
People v Gray (1970) 23 Mich App 139, 178 NW2d 172.
NY—People v McNeil (1964) 21 App Div 2d 1, 247 NYS2d 734, affd 15 NY2d 717, 256 NYS2d 614, 204 NE2d 648; People v Briggs (1966) 25 App Div 2d 50, 266 NYS2d 546, mod on other grounds 19 NY2d 37, 277 NYS2d 662, 224 NE2d 93.

Tenn—Long v State (1969) 223 Tenn 238, 443 SW2d 476.

11. United States v McCarthy (1966, DC NY) 249 F Supp 199 (apparently applying New York law).

12. People v Briggs (1966) 25 App Div 2d 50, 266 NYS2d 546, mod on other grounds 19 NY2d 37, 277 NYS2d 662, 224 NE2d 93.

13. State v Miller (1958) 253 Minn 112, 91 NW2d 138; Shelton v State (1970 Tenn Crim) 460 SW2d 869.

14. People v McNeil (1964) 21 App Div 2d 1, 247 NYS2d 734, affd 15 NY2d 717, 256 NYS2d 614, 204 NE2d 648; People v Briggs (1966) 25 App Div 2d 50, 266 NYS 2d 546, mod on other grounds 19 NY2d 37, 277 NYS2d 662, 224 NE2d 93; United States v McCarthy (1966, DC NY) 249 F Supp 199 (apparently applying New York law).

15. United States v McCarthy (F) supra.

16. People v McNeil (1964) 21 App Div 2d 1, 247 NYS2d 734, affd 15 NY2d 717, 256 NYS2d 614, 204 NE2d 648.

The basis for the foregoing rule has been said to be that an illegal arrest is an assault upon the person arrested,[7] or that any unlawful interference with the fundamental right of personal liberty may be resisted.[8]

Thus, a woman who was illegally arrested for allegedly disorderly conduct was held justified in violently struggling to break away from the arresting officer's grasp, in Columbus v Holmes (1958) 107 Ohio App 391, 8 Ohio Ops 2d 376, 78 Ohio L Abs 231, 152 NE2d 301, affd 169 Ohio St 251, 8 Ohio Ops 2d 253, 159 NE2d 232, the court reversing a conviction for resisting and obstructing a policeman in the execution of his office. One of the woman's tenants, being unable to drive, gave her his car, keys, and certificate of title, in consideration of her agreement to act as his chauffeur. However, no certificate of title was ever issued in the woman's name. When the tenant changed him mind about the bargain, moved out of the woman's place, and wanted the car back, the woman refused, and he called the police. A police officer arrived and attempted forcibly to transfer possession of the car, keys, and certificate of title from the woman to her former tenant; she resisted and was placed under arrest for disorderly conduct. She resisted the arrest even more vigorously, holding on first to the officer's leg, and then to a curb, in an effort to avoid going into the police car. She also made "quick little jerks" to get the officer's hand out from under her neck. The court reasoned that since a private dispute over the right to possession of personal property, the woman had rightfully refused to comply with his decision, and the arrest for disorderly conduct had been without legal foundation, no misdemeanor having been committed in the officer's presence. Adopting the view that the right of personal liberty is one of the fundamental rights guaranteed to every citizen, and that any unlawful interference with it may be resisted, the court concluded that every person has a right to resist an unlawful arrest and to use such force as may be necessary.

2d 659; People v Papp (1959) 19 Misc 2d 331, 185 NYS2d 907; People v Bomboy (1962) 32 Misc 2d 1002, 229 NYS 2d 323; People v Lasko (1964) 43 Misc 2d 693, 252 NYS2d 209.
United States v Heliczer (1967, CA2 NY) 373 F2d 241 (apparently applying New York law).
United States v McCarthy (1966, DC NY) 249 F Supp 199 (apparently applying New York law).
NC—For North Carolina cases, see § 5 [b], infra.
Ohio—Columbus v Holmes (1958) 107 Ohio App 391, 8 Ohio Ops 2d 376, 78 Ohio L Abs 231, 152 NE2d 301, affd 169 Ohio St 251, 8 Ohio Ops 2d 253, 159 NE2d 232.
Okla—Walters v State (1965, Okla Crim) 403 P2d 267.
SC—State v Poinsett (1967) 250 SC 293, 157 SE2d 570; State v DeBerry (1967) 250 SC 314, 157 SE2d 637, cert den 391 US 953, 20 L Ed 2d 867, 88 S Ct 1857.
Tenn—Long v State (1969) 223 Tenn 238, 443 SW2d 476.
Shelton v State (1970, Tenn Crim) 460 SW2d 869.
Va—United States v Moore (1971, DC Va) 332 F Supp 919 (apparently applying Virginia law).

7. DC—Curtis v United States (1966, Dist Col App) 222 A2d 840.
Ga—Finch v State (1960) 101 Ga App 73, 112 SE2d 824.

8. Columbus v Holmes (1958) text above.

NY—Houghtaling v State (1958) 11 Misc 2d 1049, 175 NYS2d 659.
8. Columbus v Holmes (1958) (Ohio) text above.

EXHIBIT 10.3 Continued

1086 §4[b] ILLEGAL ARREST—PRIVILEGE TO RESIST 44 ALR3d 1078

44 ALR3d 1078 ILLEGAL ARREST—PRIVILEGE TO RESIST 1087 §5[a]

ment other than detention, he is not justified in the use of a deadly weapon in resisting the arrest.

§ 5. Rules limiting right to resist

[a] Rule prohibiting resistance to known peace officers

Modifying the traditional common-law rule that a person may resist an unlawful arrest by the use of reasonable force,[1] the courts of a few jurisdictions have adopted the rule that a private citizen may not use force to resist a peaceable arrest by one he knows, or has good reason to believe, is an authorized peace officer performing his duties, regardless of whether the arrest is illegal in the circumstances of the occasion.

Alaska—Miller v State (1969, Alaska) 462 P2d 421; Gray v State (1970, Alaska) 463 P2d 897.

Cal—People v Curtis (1969) 70 Cal 2d 347, 74 Cal Rptr 713, 450 P2d 33.

People v Burns (1961) 198 Cal App 2d Supp 839, 18 Cal Rptr 921; Re Bacon (1966) 240 Cal App 2d 34, 49 Cal Rptr 322; People v Gaines (1966) 247 Cal App 2d 141, 55 Cal Rptr 283; People v Baca (1966) 247 Cal App 2d 487, 55 Cal Rptr 681; People v Hooker (1967) 254 Cal App 2d 878, 62 Cal Rptr 675; Pittman v Superior Court of Los Angeles County (1967) 256 Cal App 2d 795, 64 Cal Rptr 473; People v Wheeler (1968) 260 Cal App 2d 522, 67 Cal Rptr 246; People v Rhone (1968) 267 Cal App 2d 652, 73 Cal Rptr 463; People v Cannedy (1969) 270 Cal App 2d 669, 76 Cal Rptr 24; People v Soto (1969) 276 Cal App 2d 81, 80 Cal Rptr 627; People v Muniz (1970) 4 Cal App 3d 562, 84 Cal Rptr 501; People v Perez (1970) 12 Cal App 3d 232, 90 Cal Rptr 521; People v Cuevas (1971) 16 Cal App 3d 245, 93 Cal Rptr 916.

Del—State v Winsett (1964, Del) 205 A2d 510.

Fla—Daniel v State (1961, Fla App) 132 So 2d 312 (by implication).

Ill—People v Carroll (1971, Ill App) 272 NE2d 822; People v Suriwka (1971, Ill App) 276 NE2d 490.

NJ—State v Montague (1970) 55 NJ 387, 262 A2d 398; State v Mulvihill (1970) 57 NJ 151, 270 A2d 277, 44 ALR3d 1071; State v Washington (1970) 57 NJ 160, 270 A2d 282.

State v Koonce (1965) 89 NJ Super 169, 214 A2d 428; State v Owens (1968) 102 NJ Super 187, 245 A2d 736, mod on other grounds 54 NJ 153, 254 A2d 97, cert den 396 US 1021, 24 L Ed 2d 514, 90 S Ct 593.

Thus, although upholding the legality of an arrest for being a minor in possession of an alcoholic beverage, the court in Miller v State (1969, **Alaska**) 462 P2d 421, affirming a conviction for stabbing at another with intent to wound, also held that the defendant had had no right to resist with force a peaceable arrest, even if the arrest had been unlawful. Upon seeing a partly empty case of beer in the defendant's car, a police officer ordered the defendant and his girl friend to get out of the car and informed them that they were under arrest for being minors in possession of an alcoholic beverage. The girl got into the patrol car, but the defendant became argumentative, and after a scuffle, returned to his car. The officer removed the defendant forcibly from his car and managed to jostle him to the patrol car, where he was planning to handcuff him. They slipped to the ground, and the defendant came up wielding a bayonet with which he slashed at the officer, apparently knocking loose the officer's clip-on necktie. The officer then drew his gun and gained control of the situation. Concluding that the common-law rule approving reasonably forceful resistance to an unlawful arrest had little utility to recommend it under present

1. See § 3, supra.

1086 §4[b] ILLEGAL ARREST—PRIVILEGE TO RESIST 44 ALR3d 1078

44 ALR3d 1078

arrest had been illegal, the defendant motorist had had ample opportunity to escape after disarming the officer. One illegally arrested may use any reasonable means to effect his escape, even to the extent of using such force as is reasonably necessary, the court said, but the force employed may not be more than is reasonably demanded by the situation.

[b] Specific maximum

Although it has been stated that a person has a right to resist an unlawful arrest even to the extent of taking the life of the aggressor if it is necessary in order to regain his liberty,[17] in several of the modern cases the courts have taken the view that the right to resist an unlawful arrest does not extend to killing the arrester.[18] The illegality of the arrest may, however, reduce a homicide from murder to manslaughter.[19]

Drawing the outer limit of permissible resistance at a point short of killing the arrester, one court has declared that the right to resist an unlawful arrest does not extend to the infliction of such bodily harm that the officer suffers two broken ribs, a shoulder separation, and spinal injuries.[20] And another court, in the following case, placed restrictions on the use of a deadly weapon in resisting an illegal arrest.

17. State v Poinsett (1967) 250 SC 293, 157 SE2d 570.

18. US—For cases involving state law, see state headings infra.
Ariz—State v Robinson (1967) 6 Ariz App 424, 433 P2d 75; State v Cadena (1969) 9 Ariz App 369, 452 P2d 534.
DC—Abrams v United States (1956) 99 App DC 46, 237 F2d 42 (apparently applying District of Columbia law) cert den 352 US 1006, 1 L Ed 2d 554, 77 S Ct 575.
Ga—Gordy v State (1956) 93 Ga App 743, 92 SE2d 737.
Ky—Morris v Commonwealth (1967, Ky) 411 SW2d 678.
Mo—State v Messley (1963, Mo) 366 SW 2d 390.
Tenn—Long v State (1969) 223 Tenn 238, 443 SW2d 476.

The fact that police officers who had advised an arrestee who they were, and why he was being arrested, did not have a warrant in their possession, or even on file at the police station, was held not to have justified the arrestee's pulling a gun on one of the officers and attacking him, in Walters v State (1965, Okla Crim) 403 P2d 267, the court affirming a conviction for assault with a dangerous weapon. The initial arrest, for another assault, was made on a complaint signed by the defendant's wife. While en route to the police station in a car with one of the officers, the defendant pulled a gun on the officer, hitting and striking him and causing the car to jump a curb and stop against a fence. The fight continued, and the officer was shot in the stomach, but was able, with the help of a witness, to keep the defendant there until the other officer arrived to disarm him. Noting that the right to resist an unlawful arrest is limited and varies with the circumstances, the court adopted the view that if the official character of the officer is known to the person sought to be arrested, or if the officer informs him of his official character and his reason for the arrest, and if the person sought to be arrested has no reason to apprehend any treat-

Va—Banner v Commonwealth (1963) 204 Va 640, 133 SE2d 305.

19. Abrams v United States (1956) 99 App DC 46, 237 F2d 42 (apparently applying District of Columbia law), cert den 352 US 1006, 1 L Ed 2d 554, 77 S Ct 575; Long v State (1969) 223 Tenn 238, 443 SW 2d 476.
In the Long Case, it was held that a killing by means calculated to cause death, with knowledge that the intent was only to arrest, is murder, but that an unintentional killing in making such resistance, by means not calculated to cause death, is manslaughter.

20. Abrams v United States (1956) 99 App DC 46, 237 F2d 42 (apparently applying District of Columbia law), cert den 352 US 1006, 1 L Ed 2d 554, 77 S Ct 575.

EXHIBIT 10.3   Continued

1088 §5[a]   ILLEGAL ARREST—PRIVILEGE TO RESIST   44 ALR3d

44 ALR3d 1078

conditions of life, the court observed that the common-law rule had developed in a time when self-help had been a more necessary remedy to resist intrusions upon one's freedom, that the control of man's destructive and aggressive impulses is one of the great unsolved problems of modern society, that our rules of law should discourage the unnecessary use of physical force between man and man, and that any rule which promotes rather than inhibits violence should be re-examined. Along with increased sensitivity to the rights of the criminally accused, the court said, there should be a corresponding awareness of our need to develop rules which facilitate decent and peaceful behavior by all. Accordingly, the court held that a private citizen may not use force to resist peaceful arrest by one he knows or has good reason to believe is an authorized peace officer performing his duties, regardless of whether the arrest is illegal in the circumstances of the occasion. The court reasoned, first, that if a peace officer is making an illegal arrest, but is not using force, the remedy of the citizen should be that of suing the officer for false arrest, not that of resistance with force, since the legality of a peaceful arrest may frequently be a close question more properly determined by courts than by the participants in what may be a highly emotional situation. The court further reasoned that since officers will normally overcome resistance with reasonable force, the danger of escalating violence between the officer and the arrestee is great, so that what begins as an illegal misdemeanor arrest may culminate in serious bodily harm or death. Thus, the court pointed out that its rule would help to relieve the threat of physical harm to officers who in good faith, but mistakenly, perform an arrest, and that it would also minimize harm to innocent bystanders. It is not too much to ask, the court said, that one believing himself unlawfully arrested should submit to the officer and thereafter seek his legal remedies in court.

Affirming a conviction for resisting public officers in the discharge of their duties, the court in People v Burns (1961) 198 Cal App 2d Supp 839, 18 Cal Rptr 921, held that the trial judge had properly refused to instruct the jury that if an arrest is unlawful, either the person being arrested or others acting in his behalf may resist, using no more than reasonable force sufficient to prevent the unlawful arrest. Instead, the trial judge had instructed the jury, in accordance with a newly adopted statutory provision, that if a person has knowledge, or by the exercise of reasonable care should have knowledge, that he is being arrested by a peace officer, it is the duty of such person to refrain from using force or any weapon to resist such arrest. The defendants contended that the section did not deprive a person of the right to resist an unlawful arrest, but the appellate court concluded that the legislature, in adopting the new section, had clearly intended to do away with the former rule that a person could resist arrest if the attempted arrest were unlawful. Noting that the former rule had inevitably led to riots and violence by fostering a belief on the part of many people that they were the sole judges as to whether their arrest was proper, and that those persons who were inclined to resist or escape had found a ready excuse in stating that the resistance or escape was because of a belief in the unlawfulness of the arrest, the court pointed out that the new section did not eliminate the right of a person improperly arrested to pursue his lawful remedies against the peace officer, but that it merely eliminated his right to the use of force at the time of the arrest, and required him to seek his redress by resort to the courts, rather than by resort to violence. Finding nothing un-

---

ILLEGAL ARREST—PRIVILEGE TO RESIST   1089 §5[a]

44 ALR3d 1071

reasonable in the requirement that all persons should be law abiding and that they should accept duly constituted authority, even though on occasion that authority might be abused, the court emphasized that peace officers are likewise required to perform their duties in lawful fashion, redress by peaceful means being afforded to aggrieved persons. The observance of these correlative rights and obligations on both sides will, the court said, be the most conducive to the maintenance of an orderly society.

Although reversing convictions of assault and battery on police officers, because "the judicial evocation of an altered rule of criminal law should have prospective application only," the court in State v Koonce (1965) 89 NJ Super 169, 214 A2d 428, declared it to be the law of New Jersey that a private citizen may not use force to resist arrest by one he knows or has good reason to believe is an authorized police officer engaged in the performance of his duties, whether or not the arrest is illegal under the circumstances obtaining. The defendants, husband and wife, had been arrested initially for selling liquor to a minor, but they had resisted by punching the arresting officers with their fists. Stating that an appropriate accommodation of society's interests in securing the right of individual liberty, the maintenance of law enforcement, and the prevention of death or serious injury not only of the participants in an arrest fracas, but of innocent third persons, precluded tolerance of any formulation which validated an arrestee's resistance of a police officer with force merely because the arrest was ultimately adjudged to have been illegal, the court pointed out that force begets force, that escalation into bloodshed is a frequent probability, and that the right or wrong of an arrest is often a matter of close debate as to which even lawyers and judges may differ. Noting further that the concept of self-help is in decline, that such a concept is antisocial in an urbanized society, and that it is potentially dangerous to all involved, the court concluded that self-help is no longer necessary, because of the legal remedies available. In this era of constantly expanding legal protections of the rights of the accused in criminal proceedings, the court said, one deeming himself illegally arrested can reasonably be asked to submit peaceably to arrest by a police officer, and to take recourse in his legal remedies for regaining his liberty and defending the ensuing prosecution against him; at the same time, police officers attempting in good faith, although mistakenly, to perform their duties in effecting an arrest should be relieved of the threat of physical harm at the hands of the arrestee.

Article 3 § 3.04(2)(a)(i) of the American Law Institute's Model Penal Code, Tentative Draft No 8, provides that the use of force is not justifiable to resist an arrest which the actor knows is being made by a peace officer, although the arrest is unlawful. In its accompanying comments, the Institute reasons that it should be possible to provide adequate remedies against illegal arrest, without permitting the arrested person to resort to force—"a course of action highly likely to result in greater injury even to himself than the detention"—and that the reasons for demanding submission to official action, with the concomitant possibility of providing an effective civil remedy against the state or the municipality, are "obviously less persuasive in the case of private action—even for purported law enforcement."

Section 5 of the Uniform Arrest Act provides that if a person has reasonable ground to believe that he is being arrested by a peace officer, it is his duty to refrain from using force or any weapon in resisting arrest regardless of

[44 ALR3d—69]

EXHIBIT 10.3 Continued

1090
§ 5[b]   ILLEGAL ARREST—PRIVILEGE TO RESIST   44 ALR3d
44 ALR3d 1071

whether there is a legal basis for the arrest.[2]

Although an arrest by narcotics agents was held lawful, so that the arrestee had no right to resist the arrest with force, in United States v Simon (1969, CA7 Ill) 409 F2d 474, cert den 396 US 829, 24 L Ed 2d 79, 90 S Ct 79, the court, affirming a conviction for wilful, forceful assault, resistance, and interference with the agents in the performance of their official duties, stated that the additional argument by the United States that even if the arrest had been unlawful, the arrestee had had no right to resist it as he had done, had merit. The agents went to the defendant's home at night to arrest him without a warrant. When he came to the door, they announced to him that they were agents. When he admitted his identity, the agents told him that he was under arrest, whereupon he told them that he was not going anywhere with them, and struck one of the agents. The agents followed him into his house and a struggle ensued during which the defendant struck and kicked two of the agents before they put handcuffs on him. Another struggle followed, with the defendant kicking two of the agents and biting a third. Finally, the defendant again kicked one of the agents before they put him into their car. As to the government's contention that even if the arrest had been unlawful, the defendant had no right to resist it as he had done, the court observed that the consequences of accepting the de-

fendant's argument to the contrary would lead to great mischief with respect to encouraging resistance to, and endangering, arresting officers. Recognizing that law enforcement officers are frequently called on to make arrests without warrants, the court declared that such officers should not be held, so far as their personal security is concerned, to a nicety of distinctions between probable cause and lack of probable cause in differing situations of warrantless arrests. For this reason, the court expressed the belief that the force of a contrary United States Supreme Court decision[3] has been diminished. Finally, the court emphasized that in the instant case, the federal narcotics officers had identified themselves at the door of the defendant's home, and that they would not have lost that official capacity even if the arrest had been unlawful.

[b] Other rules

Although the Missouri courts have frequently reiterated the traditional common-law rule that a person may resist an unlawful arrest by the use of reasonable force,[4] in a recent Missouri case the court apparently carved out an exception to that rule by stating that it is not the right of an individual to resist arrest on the basis of a contention that the law he allegedly was violating was unconstitutional, or invalid for some other reason.[5] The court reasoned that to permit persons to resist arrest and then attack an officer, and then be excused if they successfully question the consti-

---

2. For a list of jurisdictions adopting the Uniform Laws, see Am Jur 2d Desk Book, Document 129.

3. In Bad Elk v United States (1900) 177 US 529, 44 L Ed 874, 20 S Ct 729, it was held that the defendant, whose murder conviction was reversed, had the right to use such force as was absolutely necessary to resist an attempted illegal arrest.

4. State v Messley (1963, Mo) 366 SW2d 390; St. Louis v Penrod (1960, Mo App) 332 SW2d 34; State v Parker (1964, Mo App) 378 SW2d 274; Kansas City v Mathis (1966, Mo App) 409 SW2d 280.

5. State v Briggs (1968, Mo) 435 SW2d 361.

[44 ALR3d]

---

44 ALR3d   ILLEGAL ARREST—PRIVILEGE TO RESIST   1091
44 ALR3d 1071   § 6

III. Arrests made with excessive force

tutionality or validity of a statute or ordinance, would lead to chaos and would be intolerable.[6]

Similarly, in North Carolina, general recognition of the common-law right to resist an illegal arrest[7] has apparently given way to the following more specific formulation: When an officer attempts to make an arrest without a warrant, and in so doing exceeds his lawful authority, he may be resisted as in self-defense, and in such a case the person resisting cannot be convicted of the offense of resisting an officer engaged in the discharge of his duties; but when an officer is acting under authority of process of a court, he is protected if the writ is sufficient on its face to show its purpose, even though it may be defective or irregular in some respect.[8] The court reasoned that a different rule would place in jeopardy the life of every officer in the land, by requiring them to determine, at their peril, the strict legal sufficiency of every precept placed in their hands.[9]

Comment f in § 65 of the Restatement (Second) of Torts provides in part that the use of force intended or likely to cause death or serious bodily harm is not privileged merely to prevent a confinement not itself threatening death or serious bodily harm, and that there is therefore no privilege to use such force to prevent an unlawful arrest which another is attempting otherwise than by the use or threat of deadly weapons, even where the arrestee's vastly inferior strength makes any other form of resistance obviously futile.

§ 6. Rule permitting reasonable resistance

In several modern cases, the courts have applied or recognized the general rule that an arrestee may use reasonable force to defend himself against the use of greater force by the arrester than is required to effect the arrest.[10]

Alaska—Miller v State (1969, Alaska) 463 P2d 421; Gray v State (1970, Alaska) 463 P2d 897.

Cal—People v Curtis (1969) 70 Cal 2d 347, 74 Cal Rptr 713, 450 P2d 33.

People v Soto (1969) 276 Cal App 2d 81, 80 Cal Rptr 627; People v Colbert (1970) 6 Cal App 3d 79, 85 Cal Rptr 617; People v Perez (1970) 12 Cal App 3d 232, 90 Cal Rptr 521.

Ga—Gordy v State (1956) 93 Ga App 743, 92 SE2d 737.

NJ—State v Montague (1970) 55 NJ 387, 262 A2d 398; State v Mulvihill (1970) 57 NJ 151, 270 A2d 277, 44 ALR3d 1071; State v Wahington (1970) 57 NJ 160, 270 A2d 282.

NY—People v Sanza (1971) 37 App Div 2d 632, 323 NYS2d 632.

Or—State v Laurel (1970, Or App) 476 P2d 817.

Tex—Turley v State (1961, Tex Crim) 352 SW2d 130.

Thus, a trial judge was held to have erred in eliminating, as a matter of law, the issue of self-defense from a prosecution for assault and battery on a police officer, in State v Mulvihill (1970) 57 NJ 151, 270 A2d 277, 44 ALR3d 1071,

tion also contain statements or holdings limiting the right to resist an illegal arrest not involving excessive force (see § 5, supra), it seems probable that most or all of the courts not limiting that right (see § 3, supra) would also follow the less inclusive rule stated in this section.

As to what constitutes excessive force by the arrester, see 5 Am Jur 2d, Arrest §§ 81 et seq.

---

6. State v Briggs (Mo) supra.

7. State v Morrisey (1962) 257 NC 679, 127 SE2d 283.

8. State v Wright (1968) 1 NC App 479, 162 SE2d 56, affd 274 NC 380, 163 SE2d 897.

9. State v Wright (NC) supra.

10. Since most of the cases in this sec-

EXHIBIT 10.3 Continued

---

44 ALR3d   ILLEGAL ARREST—PRIVILEGE TO RESIST   1093
44 ALR3d 1071   §8

door of the defendant's house at 5 a.m. with a shotgun in hand, in an effort to collect a $40 civil debt, was held justified, in Shine v State (1967) 44 Ala App 171, 204 So 2d 817, the court reversing a murder conviction arising out of the defendant's shooting of the deceased as he entered the house while the other two members of the posse, armed with pistols, remained outside. Stressing that the threats in the instant case had been so great as to put the defendant in fear of bodily harm or of losing his life, the court stated that he would have been required by law to submit himself to the custody of the posse only if he had been informed that the purpose of the "arrest" was to deliver him to the custody of the sheriff, and that he would not be placed in danger of bodily harm. To allow individuals, not law enforcement officers, to "arrest" debtors while armed with shotguns and pistols, the court said, could only lead to useless and unnecessary bloodshed.

§ 8. — Exceptions to rule

In some of the cases supporting the general right of an arrestee to defend himself against excessive force,[14] the courts have also qualified that right.

Thus, defendants who were surprised in the course of an armed robbery when a police officer emerged from hiding in the store were held not entitled to claim that they shot the officer in self-defense, even if the officer used excessive force in attempting to arrest them, in Gray v State (1970, Alaska) 463 P2d 897, the court affirming in pertinent part convictions for murder. Applying the rule that where an arrestee has committed a felony which includes an immediate threat of violence, he has created a situation so fraught with peril as to pre-

Comment f in § 65 of the Restatement (Second) of Torts provides in part that if a person attempts to effect the unlawful arrest of another, or to overcome the other's resistance thereto, by the use of force intended or likely to cause death or serious bodily harm, and if the other has no opportunity to submit to the arrest and so avoid the necessity of using similar force in self-defense, the other may defend himself by the use of such force, not because its use is necessary to protect him from the unlawful arrest, but because it is the only way in which he can protect himself from death or serious bodily harm.

§ 7. — Amount of permissible force

An attempt unlawfully to arrest gives the person sought to be arrested a right to resist, even to the extent of killing his opponent, if such killing is necessary to save himself from serious bodily harm; but the necessity must have been real and apparent.[11] In other words, an arrestee may kill his arrester only if he believes and has reasonable grounds to believe that he is in danger of death or great bodily harm at the hands of the arrester and in the exercise of reasonable judgment there are no other safe means of averting the real or apparent danger except to kill him.[12]

If the citizen who is arrested with excessive force employs greater force in protecting himself than reasonably appears to be necessary, then he becomes the aggressor and forfeits the right to claim self-defense to a charge of assault and battery on the officer.[13]

The use of deadly force in resisting an unlawful "arrest" by an armed posse of bonding company employees, one of whom (the deceased) broke through the back

11. Long v State (1969) 223 Tenn 238, 443 SW2d 476.

12. Morris v Commonwealth (1967, Ky) 411 SW2d 678.

13. State v Mulvihill (1970) 57 NJ 151, 270 A2d 277, 44 ALR3d 1071; State v Washington (1970) 57 NJ 160, 270 A2d 282.

14. See § 6, supra.

1092   ILLEGAL ARREST—PRIVILEGE TO RESIST   44 ALR3d
§6   44 ALR3d 1071

the court reversing the assault and battery conviction. While operating a patrol car along a public street, a police officer noticed that the defendant was standing in front of a pizzeria and pouring something from a bottle into a paper cup held by another person. Since there was a local ordinance prohibiting the drinking of alcoholic beverages on a public street, the officer stopped the car, got out, and called to the young men to come over to him. As they did so, the defendant threw the paper cup on the sidewalk. The officer asked him what was in the cup, but he did not answer. According to the facts as viewed by the appellate court in the light most favorable to the defendant, the officer grabbed him and asked to smell his breath; he held his breath and remained silent, whereupon the officer shook him "back and forth" by the shoulders and said, "I should arrest you, you punk"; the defendant tried to pull away, but the officer "jerked him back around," with the result that both men fell; they arose with the officer still holding him, and when he tried to pull free, the officer struck him on the side of the head with his gun, lacerating his scalp; the defendant then fell toward the officer, and they both went down again; by holding the officer's right hand, the defendant tried to keep the gun pointing away from himself, while the officer endeavored to direct it at him, saying "Stop or I'll shoot"; at that time the defendant was trying to avoid being shot; when the gun went off harmlessly, the defendant punched the officer in the left side of the face with his right hand. In the meantime, other officers appeared and immobilized the defendant. In concluding that the defendant had been entitled to have the issue of self-defense passed upon by the jury, the court reasoned that the jury could have found that the defendant's initial resistance had been such that the officer, in attempting to overcome it,

had employed unnecessary and excessive force in drawing his gun and striking the defendant in the head with it so as to cause a lacerated scalp, and that the jury could have found further that such excessive force had caused the defendant reasonably to feel and to fear that an effort was being made to point the gun at him and to fire it. If, in effectuating an arrest or a temporary detention, an officer employs excessive and unnecessary force, the court said, the citizen may respond or counter with the use of reasonable force to protect himself; and if in so doing the officer is injured, no criminal offense has been committed. Distinguishing the excessive force situation from an ordinary illegal arrest without excessive force, the court pointed out that in the latter situation the citizen's right to freedom from unreasonable seizure and confinement could be protected, restored, and vindicated through legal processes, whereas life or limb could not be repaired in the courtroom. Thus, the court explained that the reasons for outlawing resistance to an unlawful arrest, and requiring disputes over its legality to be resolved in the courts, had no controlling application on the right to resist an officer's excessive force.

Article 3 § 3.04(2)(a)(i) of the American Law Institute's Model Penal Code, Tentative Draft No 8, provides that the use of force is not justifiable to resist an arrest which the actor knows is being made by a peace officer, although the arrest is unlawful. However, in its accompanying comments, the Institute observes that its prohibition on the use of force for the purpose of preventing an arrest has no application when the actor apprehends bodily injury, as when the arresting officer unlawfully employs or threatens deadly force, unless the actor knows that he is in no peril greater than arrest if he submits to the assertion of authority.

subject of the annotation. These components, along with a short description of each component, are as follows:

Descriptive Title of the Annotation. Typically, annotation titles are quite detailed to enable the researcher to quickly determine whether the annotation contains the desired information. As you will note from the example in Exhibit 10.3, the annotation often describes factual as well as legal information.

Table of Contents of the Annotation. The table of contents is also usually specific. The entire annotation is broken into sections, each of which is numbered and preceded by the section symbol. Throughout the table of contents and other preliminary information, references will be made to section numbers within the annotation. Each annotation section is arranged in numerical order, and subheadings are arranged in alphabetical order. Thus, if the title preceding the symbol *3a* in the table of contents is of interest, you need only to leaf through the annotation until you reach the paragraph (a) of the third numbered section.

Total Client-Service Library® References of the Annotation. This section is an especially helpful feature to broaden your research because it directs you to very specific points in other publications, such as the legal encyclopedia American Jurisprudence. Frequently, there is also reference to locations within form books that provide examples of common legal documents that are relevant to the subject of the annotation. The client-service library section also provides you with additional research terms to consult in the ALR index and digests. For the novice researcher, this can be an excellent tool to build a research vocabulary and to assist in locating relevant information.

Index to the Annotation. The index to the annotation is comparable to a subject index to any other text. Particular words and phrases are referenced to places within the annotation where they appear. ALR volumes typically do not have individual indexes. Rather, there are the quick index, the digest, and specific annotation indexes.

Table of Jurisdictions Represented. This table is an extremely helpful feature of ALR. By using this table, you can determine at a glance every jurisdiction that has ruled on an issue, and by looking to the indicated section of the annotation following the state abbreviation in the table, you can get some idea of how each jurisdiction approached the annotation.

Scope Note. This portion of the annotation is especially helpful when the title of the annotation does not clearly and exactly address the issue of your research but seems to be related. The scope note is a brief (usually one or two paragraphs) description of the contents of the annotation and legal issues of the judicial opinion that is annotated. The note usually indicates not only what is within the annotation but also what is not addressed. Quite often, this will provide you with a definitive answer regarding whether the annotation is worth pursuing in your research.

List of Related Matters. When you are able to determine from the scope note that the annotation does not address your particular issues, you are not automatically reversed to the digest or quick index. The list of related matters provides you with other ALR citations on annotations dealing with similar but separate legal issues or factual circumstances. This list includes the titles of the annotations and their location (volume, series, page). As a practical matter, you may simply be using the wrong search terms to locate the most relevant annotation in the index or digest. However, if your terms are specific enough

to at least bring you within the proper subject area, the list of related matters can often quickly guide you to the annotation you have been looking for.

☐ ASSIGNMENT 10.2

Based on Exhibits 10.2 and 10.3, answer the following questions:

1. How many other annotations exist relevant to this topic?
2. What is the proper citation for the judicial opinion?
3. How many jurisdictions have passed on the issue that is the subject of the annotation?
4. What is the difference between the effect of the annotation and the opinion as authority?
5. How many parts are there in the annotation?

RESEARCHING WITHIN THE ANNOTATED LAW REPORT

Typically, research in the ALR version of annotated law reports is conducted much like any other legal research. You prepare your query and relevant search terms and then take them to the quick index or digest to locate annotations. As mentioned earlier, the annotations are published chronologically. There is no subject index within volumes or topic approach as with many other types of legal research. Indeed, if you are unfamiliar with the ALR and you simply pull a volume from the shelf, it appears to be a meandering text with no clear direction of content. That is because the annotations gathered within a particular volume have no more relationship to one another than that they were all topics at issue during approximately the same point in legal history.

By taking your query and search terms to the quick index or digest, you can locate specific annotation titles and references. The references to location include the volume, series, and page number. When locating the citation, be certain that you locate the volume and page within the proper series, or the citation you find will not be the annotation referenced in the index or the digest.

Once you locate the annotation, be certain to examine each of the preliminary notes (described above), giving special attention to the list of related matters. This list can refer you to additional annotations that are relevant to your research. Also, as previous indicated, the table of jurisdictions can help you to locate citations of primary authority that respond to your query. The scope note can provide immediate information regarding whether the citation is actually applicable to your research.

As with many other legal resources, the ALR is updated through the use of supplements, specifically, pocket parts. Pocket parts do not contain new or amended annotations (as do statutory supplements). Rather, they contain citations of authority that continue to interpret the issues addressed in the original annotation. Thus, when you are conducting research in ALR, you

should always check the supplements for citations, listed below a reference to the page in the volume that corresponds with the actual annotation. You should not only check pocket part supplements to gain additional citations to use in your research, but also check these citations to determine whether the position of the courts has been altered with respect to the position described in the annotation. Other supplement features of the ALR include the ALR bluebook and ALR later case service. Similar to the publication, Restatement in the Courts, used for first series Restatements publications, the ALR supplemental publications provide you with information on relevant judicial opinions that were rendered after the publication of the ALR annotation.

The citations within an annotation are not exhaustive, and the pocket parts are not a method of certain validation. Rather, they *supplement* the original annotation by way of example. The ALR is no substitute for additional proper steps of researching primary authority.

▐▌▶ STRATEGY

Researching in ALR

1. Use the relevant search terms you have identified in your query in the ALR digest (or quick index if the digest is unavailable).
2. The digest should provide you with the title, volume, series, and page number of any relevant annotations.
3. The volume, series, and page number should lead you to the proper annotations.
4. The introductory matter in the annotation should provide you with specific relevant sections, a key to discussion of any jurisdiction in which you are interested, and any other annotations of which you may not have previously been aware.

CHAPTER SUMMARY

As seen in this chapter, the annotated law report can be an excellent secondary source in legal research. The topics addressed in each volume reflect legal issues in controversy at the time of publication. The ALR is organized in such a way as to not only provide primary authority but also direct the researcher to other relevant annotations. Each annotation is divided into sections that address quite specific aspects of the legal issue. The annotations are preceded by a judicial opinion that is representative of the majority rule with respect to the legal issue(s). The exception to this format is the current ALR 5th series, which places the actual judicial opinions at the back of the volume following the annotation discussions. The opinions provide you with a very real sense of exactly how the courts have approached and dealt with the issue(s).

Research within the ALR series is done by consulting either the quick index or the digest prepared especially for the annotations. The annotations are also updated through pocket parts, which provide current citations of authority that illustrate the development of the law that was the subject of the original annotation. Annotated law reports are not exhaustive sources of

primary authority and should not be relied upon as such. Instead, the annotated law report is a source to gain a better understanding of a legal topic and to determine trends with regard to the approach of the judiciary toward topics in controversy.

KEY TERMS

annotated law report

SELF-TEST

MULTIPLE CHOICE

1. The annotated law report is a hybrid between a _____ and a
_____.
   a) statute, opinion
   b) reporter, regulation
   c) digest, reporter
   d) none of the above
2. The annotated law report is a very useful means to track the _____ of law.
   a) development
   b) creation
   c) anticipated changes
   d) legislation
3. The most common annotated law report is the _____ series.
   a) ALR
   b) CFR
   c) ALI
   d) LSI
4. When citing a _____
_____ that is included in an ALR annotation, you should not cite the annotation.
   a) commentary
   b) judicial opinion
   c) illustration
   d) none of the above
5. ALR is a _____ authority and thus has less influence.
   a) mandatory
   b) secondary

   c) primary
   d) none of the above

TRUE/FALSE

_____ 6. As a rule, the subjects addressed in the ALR are topics of law that are currently in controversy in several jurisdictions.
_____ 7. The annotations are issued in consecutively numbered volumes.
_____ 8. Each ALR volume is arranged by subject in alphabetical order.
_____ 9. Originally, the ALR was referenced by the digest, which was essentially a subject index.
_____ 10. The ALR has prepared a quick index, which indexes all of the series, making the time necessary to locate annotations shorter and providing additional details about annotations.

FILL-IN THE BLANKS

11. Because the publishers of ALR concentrate on areas of changing or controversial law, _____
_____ principles are not generally discussed in ALR annotations.
12. The annotation is arranged into several _____ to provide you with various information relevant or collateral to the subject of the annotation.

13. Typically, annotation titles are quite _____ to enable the researcher to quickly determine whether the annotation contains the desired information.

14. The entire annotation is broken into _____ _____.

15. The _____ _____ _____ _____ directs you to very specific points in other publications.

16. The _____ _____ _____ _____ is comparable to a subject index to any other text.

17. The _____ _____ _____ _____ allows you to determine every jurisdiction that has ruled on an issue.

18. _____ _____ of ALR have no subject index, as with many other types of legal research.

19. When you are conducting research in ALR, you should always check the _____ for new citations.

20. Supplements should be checked to determine whether the _____ of the courts has been altered with respect to the position described in the annotation.

CHAPTER 11

LEGAL PERIODICALS

CHAPTER OBJECTIVES

Upon completion of this chapter, you should be able to accomplish the following competencies:

- Define legal periodical.

- Discuss the primary benefits of legal periodicals.

- Describe the types of legal periodicals.

- Distinguish a legal periodical from an annotated law report.

- Explain how legal periodicals are properly used as authorities.

- Explain how a legal periodical can be used as a finding tool for primary authorities.

- Identify those subjects likely to be addressed by legal periodicals.

- Describe the process of researching legal periodicals.

- Explain how legal periodicals are updated and validated.

- Describe the variations of citation format for legal periodicals.

Characteristics of Legal Periodicals

The term **legal periodical** describes a very broad variety of publications. Essentially, a legal periodical is any regular or periodic publication of matters associated with the legal system. Technically, a legal periodical could include looseleaf services, as such services are also published on a regular basis. However, because the looseleaf publications are more similar to an updating service, and by the nature of their unique characteristics, they are dealt with separately in Chapter 12.

Legal periodicals appear in the form of newspapers, magazines, and journals. Their content ranges from comment and editorial to detailed analysis of subjects of law. The content does, however, most often focus on topics of current controversy, development, or change. Like the annotated law report, the legal periodical looks at the overall status of a challenged or new area of law. The legal periodical, however, often has the advantage of being published much more frequently. Also, legal periodicals quite often will focus on changing law in a particular jurisdiction or judicial system rather than taking the annotated law report approach to subjects national in scope.

legal periodical
Publication of information for a particular subject, jurisdiction, or interest group that is issued on a regular basis.

Sources of Legal Periodicals

Legal periodicals can come from a variety of sources, including but not limited to law schools, bar associations, and special interest groups. You will also find a section on legal issues as a regular component of various trade or professional journals, such as those published for medical professionals, industries such as air travel, accountants, and any other group whose business engenders much legislation or litigation.

Law Schools

The content of a legal periodical is usually focused by the publication's source. Law reviews and law journals issued by law schools, for example, typically contain detailed and somewhat lengthy analyses of topics of law. The articles in such publications are authored by professors, judges, lawyers, and law students. Each article typically contains a significant amount of citation of primary authority, with analysis and discussion. This makes such articles an excellent source of preliminary research to gain a basic understanding of the topic and access to a few of the relevant citations. Other previous articles may be discussed that can be used to expand your knowledge of the subject and gain additional citations.

One aspect of **law school reviews** and **journals** that may or may not be an advantage based upon the circumstances is that the articles are frequently (but not always) focused on the law of a particular jurisdiction. If this is the jurisdiction where your research is focused, the article and any included citations can be extremely helpful as a springboard for other authorities. If the article is based in another jurisdiction, the citations can still be looked up, and

law review or journal
Typically, a legal periodical issued by a school of law. Articles are usually authored by students, faculty, and invited members of the bar or bench.

you can use the same key numbers preceding the reporter opinions in the digest of your own jurisdiction to locate mandatory primary authorities.

As mentioned in chapter two on citation format, articles written by students typically will include "comment" or a similar designation in addition to or in place of the author's name. Also, because law school reviews and journals are typically issued only annually, no volume number may be given. For this and any other type of legal periodical that does not publish by volume number, you should delete the year in parentheses from the end of the citation and include the year (without parentheses) prior to the name of the journal. The article, not the title of the publication, should be underscored.

☐ ASSIGNMENT 11.1

Using Exhibit 11.1, answer the following questions:

1. Is the author a student?
2. Is the general focus of the article based on a single jurisdiction?
3. Are the supporting citations primary authority, secondary authority, or a combination?
4. Does the article advocate any changes in legal standards?
5. Prepare a citation of the article.

Bar Associations

bar association
Organization of lawyers with a common interest (e.g., state bar association or trial lawyers association).

Another source of legal periodicals is **bar associations.** Although most people are familiar with the American Bar Association, there are many other more specialized professional attorney organizations that also publish journals. Such specialized groups include state bar associations, local bar associations, and groups of attorneys who practice in particular areas of law such as domestic relations, plaintiff's lawyers, defense lawyers, criminal lawyers, public lawyers (employed by the government, such as district attorneys), probate lawyers, among others.

Typically, bar association journals have a less bookish and more commercial appearance. They include articles (usually brief) on matters of current interest to their subscribers. Some articles discuss changes in an area of law, while others provide insight on better practice, such as how to perform discovery of evidence in a particular type of case (e.g., product liability). Bar Association publications usually contain fewer citations of authority, and their approach to a topic is usually much less complex than law school publications. Thus, if your goal is to gain a very brief familiarization, review, or update of a topic, these publications can be quite helpful. They are also quite useful in keeping your practical skills current with regard to your other job duties. These journals also contain a certain amount of commercial advertising for aids in legal practice, products, and services, such as legal investigation and evidentiary aids for trial, as well as some classified advertising.

☐ ASSIGNMENT 11.2

Compare Exhibits 11.1 and 11.2 and describe the differences.

EXHIBIT 11.1 Reprint of a Law Review Article.
Nebraska Law Review, Volume 72 1993. Reprinted with permission.

Note: This article has been edited for purposes of this illustration. The text of the footnotes has also been deleted. Source Volume 72 NEBRASKA LAW REVIEW (1993). Reprinted with permission.

Spendthrift Trusts: It's Time to Codify the Compromise

by Anne S. Emanuel at Vol. 72 Nebraska Law Review

I. INTRODUCTION

The debate over the legitimacy of spendthrift provisions in trusts began well over a century ago.[1] Although it can be fairly characterized as having generated at least as much light as heat, it has generated a good deal of heat. The intensity of John Chipman Gray's reaction to Justice Miller's approval of the concept in *Nichols v. Easton*[2] can hardly be exaggerated. It has been variously described as "outrage"[3] and "trauma"[4] and his response[5] has been called a bitter denunciation,[6] a diatribe,[7] and an intemperate tirade.[8]

Gray himself expresses the astonishment, even shock, he experienced upon reading *Nichols v. Eaton's* endorsement of spendthrift provisions, which he revisited several years later upon reading *Broadway Nat'l Bank v. Adams*,[9] in which the Massachusetts Supreme Court embraced what had been dictum and confirmed it as law.[10] While Gray gives full rein to the strength of his conviction, he is ever the gentleman and colleague in the presentation of his argument even as he twists the knife.[11] However, no one lays greater claim to the traits of temperance and collegiality than the other major writer on the topic, Erwin Griswold.[12]

As early as 1895, Gray conceded defeat when he recognized the readiness of courts and legislatures to follow the lead of the United States Supreme Court and the Supreme Court of the Commonwealth of Massachusetts and place their imprimatur upon the concept of the spendthrift trust.[13] Gray had lost the major battle. *Nichols v. Eaton* and *Broadway Nat'l Bank* were relied upon to establish the legitimacy of spendthrift provisions, and received overwhelming acceptance.[14] Creditors of beneficiaries of spendthrift trusts have not given up, however. Instead, they have waged a war of attrition. The result in many jurisdictions is a general rule confirming the validity of spendthrift provisions, but subjecting them to a hodgepodge of exceptions.[15]

The time has come to codify the compromise that has evolved through over a century of litigation.[20] The settlor of a trust for another person should be allowed to insulate the assets and distributions of the trust form the beneficiaries' creditors, but only up to a point. Some claims compel recognition on policy grounds. It is economically counterproductive to require that each claimant litigate her entitlement;[21] at the same time, however, it is impossible to classify claims so as to uniformly separate just claims from unjust claims. Given the virtually universal recognition of spendthrift provisions, the best solution treats all enforceable claims equally and permits them to be satisfied in a manner that does not jeopardize the existence of the trust, or, in most cases, the fulfillment of its purpose.[22]

II. RESTRAINTS ON THE ALIENATION OF INTERESTS IN TRUST

An express trust arises when a settlor puts property (the corpus of the trust) in the hands of a trustee for the benefit of a beneficiary. The trustee is given legal title, and the beneficiary is given equitable title. If we assume one of the simplest and most common arrangements, we may postulate a trust corpus comprised of income producing investments. We may also assume that the settlor has directed the trustee to pay the income to the settlor's children, and upon the death of the last child, to divide the remainder among the grandchildren or their surviving issue.[23]

The parent who makes such an arrangement does so with the hope that the plan will endure. Disruption may occur, though. What if a child or a grandchild incurs an enormous liability? May the creditor satisfy its claim out of the trust income or assets? Might that result in the children and grandchildren being left economically unprotected? The parent/settlor who wants to avoid this possibility has several options. Prime among them is a spendthrift provision. Alternatives include protective provisions and discretionary and support trusts. All have one thing in common: they act to restrain the beneficiary from effectively alienating any interest in the trust. Spendthrift provisions directly restrain the beneficiary, while protective, discretionary and support trusts limit the assets in which the beneficiary has an interest.

A. Spendthrift Provisions

A spendthrift provision prohibits the beneficiary from voluntarily or involuntarily transferring her interest in the trust.[24] It restrains the power of the beneficiary to alienate the beneficial interest, and at the same time directs the trustee to continue distributions to the beneficiary notwithstanding any attempted alienation.[25] The following suggested language appears in a corporate trustee's form book:

> The interest of any beneficiary in any trust created under this Will shall not be transferred, assigned or conveyed and shall not be subject to the claims of any creditors of such beneficiary, and the Trustee shall continue distributing trust property directly to or for the benefit of such beneficiary as provided for herein notwithstanding any transfer, assignment or conveyance, or action by creditors.[26]

Arguments for and against the validity of such a provision will be discussed in section III, *infra*. Suffice it to say that while the proponents have won the day for the most part in this country, English courts rejected the concept.[27]

B. Protective, Discretionary and Support Provisions as Alternatives

The major problem with a spendthrift provision is that it might not be honored. Some jurisdictions have refused to approve spendthrift provisions on policy grounds.[30] Even if judicial decisions indicate that spendthrift provisions are

EXHIBIT 11.1   Continued

valid, further decisions may create exceptions that limit the protection afforded to the income and assets of the trust on policy grounds.[31] Likewise, a statute approving spendthrift provisions may be subject to the interpretation that it is not meant to bar certain claims.[32] When the validity of spendthrift provisions is litigated, the claimant who wins the sympathy of the court may win the lawsuit.[33]

If the settlor is primarily concerned with protecting the income and corpus of the trust from creditors of beneficiaries, a protective provision offers a highly effective alternative to a spendthrift provision. Protective provisions insulate the trust by terminating the interest of the beneficiary.[34] The settlor who uses a protective provision simply makes a conditional gift. When the condition is breached, the gift terminates. Many settlors, however, are presumably as interested in protecting the beneficiary as in protecting the trust. If the major purpose of the trust is to provide guaranteed lifetime support to a beneficiary, the protective provision is unsatisfactory.

A protective provision need not entirely terminate the interest of the beneficiary. Put more simply, a protective provision may turn the trust into a discretionary trust with respect to the beneficiary at issue.

The spendthrift provision insulates the asset even though it belongs to the beneficiary. The protective provision terminates the interest of the beneficiary. The discretionary trust, conversely, creates no interest in the beneficiary. The creditor of a beneficiary can only reach the property of that beneficiary. Where the beneficiary has no right to the trust income or corpus, neither, *a fortiori*, does a creditor of the beneficiary. Again, however, the beneficiary is unprotected. If the trustee who holds a discretionary power to distribute income decides not to distribute to a beneficiary, that beneficiary has no remedy and no right to compel a distribution. It is, after all, the beneficiary's inability to reach the income or assets of the trust that renders the beneficiary's creditor unable to do so as well.[35]

Similarly, a support trust that directs the trustee to distribute income to the beneficiary as necessary for support is inaccessible to creditors of the beneficiaries, unless the creditors supplied the necessaries.[36] However, the beneficiary will be relegated to such distributions as are necessary for support, and the settlor may wish to guarantee more.

III. THE CONTOURS OF THE DEBATE

Nothing, it seems, works quite like the magic of a spendthrift provision. Nothing else allows the settlor to determine exactly how much the beneficiary shall receive, to direct the trustee to distribute that amount to the beneficiary, and to direct the trustee to ignore all claimants, even judgment creditors. Nothing else allows a beneficiary to enjoy a stream of income no matter how impecuniously he has behaved, while foreclosing any attachment or levy on the interest in trust. Thus, spendthrift provisions enjoy increasing popularity, and engender increasing controversy.

A. Arguments Pro and Con: *Proponents of Spendthrift Provisions v. The Loyal Opposition*

1. Dicta as Historical Imperative

When *Nichols V. Eaton*[37] reached the United States Supreme Court in 1875, American courts seemed committed to the venerable English common law rule invalidating spendthrift provisions.[38] The case did not, on its facts, implicate that rule because no spendthrift provision was involved.

The case involved assets held in a trust established by the will of Sarah Eaton. Sarah Eaton's will made her four children the income beneficiaries of a protective trust; should a son's interest terminate because of the attempted alienation or disposition of the income, including the son's insolvency or bankruptcy, that son's share of the income would become payable to his wife and children. If there were no spouse or children the income accumulated, provided that following the termination of a son's right to income the trustee had the discretion to distribute all or any part of that income to the son and/or his wife and children.[40]

After Sarah Eaton's death one of her sons, Amasa, became insolvent. Amasa, who was unmarried, made a general assignment of all his property for the benefit of his creditors to Charles A. Nichols. Subsequently, Nichols was appointed his assignee in bankruptcy. Nichols brought suit against the executors and trustees of Sarah Eaton's will and trust to recover the income which Amasa had forfeited, and which was now payable to him at the discretion of the trustees, for the benefit of Amasa's creditors.[41]

With reference to the termination of Amasa's interest, Sarah Eaton's will had been carefully drafted to fall within the English rule on protective trusts:

> Taking for our guide the cases decided in the English courts, the doctrine of the case of *Brandon v. Robinson* seems to be pretty well established. It is equally well settled that a devise of the income of property, to cease on the insolvency or bankruptcy of the devisee, is good, and that the limitation is valid.[42]

In converting the trust to a discretionary trust of which Amasa was a potential beneficiary, however, she went a step further.[43] Nichols argued that the discretionary provisions were merely a sham, a way to "evade the policy of the law already mentioned; that the discretion vested in the trustees is equivalent to a direction, and that it was well known it would be exercised in favor of the bankrupt."[44] The Court disagreed, and applied the standard rule for discretionary trusts. Under the instrument, the trustees were given absolute discretion; Amasa could not in fact compel its exercise in his favor. Therefore, he had no interest his creditors could reach.[45]

Having decided the case, Justice Miller, who wrote for a unanimous Court, went on in dicta to lay the foundation for the approval of spendthrift trusts in the United States. . . . he articulated three rationales for approving spendthrift provisions. First, in every state, debtors were empowered by statute to exempt some portion of their property form creditors'; claims; spendthrift trust provisions simply worked an analogous exemption which in no way violated public policy. Second, a creditor relies at her own risk on income or assets which, due to the recordation of wills and

EXHIBIT 11.1   Continued

testamentary trusts, she is on notice are not available to satisfy her claims. Finally, the owner of property as an incident of ownership should be able to attach conditions for the protection of a donee.[47]

Gray responded by authoring his classic treatise, Restraints on the Alienation of Property.[48] He sought to establish that "[t]he current of law has for centuries been in favor of removing old restraints on alienation," and that this was especially true with reference to "compelling a debtor to apply to his debts all property which he could use for himself or give at his pleasure to others."[49]

2. Should Spendthrift Provisions Be Treated as Invalid Restraints on Alienation?

The argument relying on the general prohibition of restraints on alienation has not aged well, at least with regard to trusts.[50] Two of the significant evils of restraints on alienation-perpetuating the dead hand's control of property and removing property interests from the stream of commerce-are substantially ameliorated by the rise of the modern trust in which the trustee has virtually all the power over the legal title to the property that an owner would have.[51] Passive trustees, who might well lack the power to sell or even lease trust property, were once the rule.[52] Now they are archaic exceptions. Trustee's powers are still held somewhat in check, though. While the trustee typically has the power to buy or sell, invest or reinvest trust property, the trustee must ordinarily act with a degree of caution not incumbent on an absolute owner.[53] Put simply, trust capital is not risk capital.

Nonetheless, the alienability of the legal title of most property held in trust supports Justice Miller's position. Yet Justice Miller does not allude to alienability, and at the time he wrote it may well have been common for trustees to have only limited powers to sell. What argument, or policy, obvious at the turn of the century, drove the enthusiastic embrace of the concept of spendthrift provisions?

Viewing spendthrift provisions from the perspective of the law's general antipathy to restraints against alienation helps clarify why spendthrift provisions were accepted in American courts. The disallowance of restraints against alienation has its roots in the ancient rules of property law relating to seisin. If one has a fee interest, one must have the entire bundle of rights that comprise the interest, including the power to alienate it. Therefore, any restriction on a fee is "repugnant" to the grant of the fee and void.[54]

Notwithstanding this theoretical concept, as early as the 12th century, English law imposed considerable restraints on property. As early as the 13th century, however, English law began to remove those restraints.[55] Gray identifies the forces in favor of restraints on alienation as "[f]amily and ecclesiastical pride and natural dishonesty."[56] Gray should have added governmental interests. As he points out, "[t]he abolition [in 1660] of military tenures and of fines to the Crown did away with the last restraints upon the transfer of estates in fee simple. . . ."[57]

Restraints on alienation tend to preserve the status quo by freezing the situation. They are consistent with the requisites of a society with an economy completely controlled, and largely owned, by church and state. Restraints are inconsistent with an entrepreneurial, free market society.[58] Commerce cannot thrive if the critical property cannot be transferred. The invalidation of restraints in general was essential to the economic development of England and the United States.

What, then, accounts for the American approval of a classic restraint on alienation, the spendthrift provision? I would submit that the very interests which must invalidate restraints in order to thrive suddenly find that this particular restraint suits their personal interests quite nicely. That is, the successful entrepreneur utilizes the free market concept to amass a fortune. Once he has amassed his fortune, the protection provided by a restraint on alienation suddenly becomes appealing.[59]

Costigan, who castigated Gray for his reaction to *Nichols v. Eaton*,[60] defended the concept somewhat smugly:

> When one thinks of the boost to plutocracy given to the possessors of property by those devices of practical exemption form full legal and financial responsibility for business venture failures, known as limited partnerships and corporations . . . he has to smile at the great to-do made over trusts designed by a trustor to give [an income] to a favored cestui que trust, for a lifetime or less, out of the trustor's property, to which the cestui's creditors in no way contributed. . . .[61]

The disingenuousness of this position has resulted in one virtually universal exception. A settlor cannot obtain this protection for herself. "A man cannot put his own property beyond the reach of creditors and at the same time reserve substantial interest in it or control over it."[62] As early as 1930, Dean Griswold observed, "The cases are uniform in holding that . . . a person cannot create a spendthrift trust for himself which shall be effective against the rights of his subsequent creditors."[63]

In his sometime biting response to John Chipman Gray, George Costigan points out that while the common law is replete with denunciations of restraints on alienation, even Gray recognized that common law courts had simultaneously approved of certain restraints.[64] Thus, Costigan argues, no universal rule invalidating restraints on alienation exists, and "whether restraints on alienation, voluntary or involuntary, or both, shall be permitted, are purely questions of humanity and of wise public policy."[65] Wise policy he maintains, while validating spendthrift trust provisions to a great extent, would focus on "the need of the beneficiary, and not the prideful and lordly disposition of the donor. . . ."[66] Furthermore, while a needs test would destroy much of the utility of the spendthrift provision to the rich and answer the criticism that one should not enjoy a luxurious income while not meeting one's obligations, a needs test would also impose intolerable transaction costs by requiring the claimant to establish that the beneficiary was not needy enough to qualify for a public policy exception. Finally, a needs test will inevitably force courts of equity to fashion inequitable remedies. The beneficiary who lives a life reflecting high social status will need more income to meet his basic expenses than will the beneficiary of more modest means. As Gray said of the New York "station in life" rule,

EXHIBIT 11.1   Continued

> To say that whatever money is given to a man cannot be taken by his creditors is bad enough; at any rate, however, it is law for the rich and poor alike; but to say that from a sum which creditors can reach one man, who has lived simply and plainly, can deduct but a small sum, while a large sum may be deducted by another man because he is "of high social standing," or beucase "his associations are chiefly with men of leisure," or because he " is connected with a number of clubs," is to descend to a depth of as shameless snobbishness as any into which the justice of a country was ever plunged.[67]

Finally, Justice Miller relied in large part on exemption statutes to establish that public policy supports restraints on alienation. As one commentator notes, however, exemption statues may be thoroughly distinguished form spendthrift provisions:

> Exemption laws seek to strengthen the integrity of the debtor by keeping him from absolute poverty, to benefit the community by keeping him off the welfare rolls and to protect the debtor's family from starvation, while still enabling the maximum payment to the creditors. Spendthrift trusts, on the other hand, permit children of rich men to live in debt and luxury at the same time, while the claims of their creditors remain unsatisfied.[68]

3. The Notice Argument

Justice Miller's second rationale, the notice argument, stands on both the shakiest of footings and the firmest of foundations. He observed that creditors of the beneficiary of a spendthrift trust had little to complain of because testamentary trusts, as part of probated wills, are recorded public documents. Anyone who extends credit despite being on notice that the debtor's income is insulated by a spendthrift provision acts at her own risk:

> When . . . it appears by the record of a will that the devisee holds this life-estate or income, dividends, or rents of real or personal property, payable to him alone, to the exclusion of the alienee or creditor, the latter knows, that, in creating a debt with such person, he has no right to look to that income as a means of discharging it. He is neither misled nor defrauded when the object of the testator is carried out by excluding him from any benefit of such a devise.[69]

This argument fails on two grounds. First, while testamentary trusts are public records, inter vivos trusts are not; the point simply does not apply to a significant number of trusts. Second, the creditor did not necessarily "recklessly" extend credit. The creditor might hold a tort judgment, or a claim for child support or unpaid taxes.[70]

With reference to contract creditors, however, the spirit of Justice Miller's observation continues to prevail. Contract claimants are unlikely to obtain satisfaction from assets protected by a spendthrift provision. This result turns not on the argument that the creditor is on constructive notice of the provisions of a testamentary trust, but rather on the argument that the creditor should identify security before extending credit.[71] The creditor who relies on apparent affluence without determining its source does so at his own risk.

4. The Incident of Ownership Argument

Justice Miller's final argument continues to provoke enthusiastic agreement and astonished disagreement. Harking to the American tradition recognizing private property, with its assumption that the owner of property may do with it as he will, Justice Miller waxed both eloquent and sentimental:

> Nor do we see any reason, *in the recognized nature and tenure of property* and its transfer by will, why a testator who gives . . . may not attach to that gift the incident of continued use, of uninterrupted benefit of the gift, during the life of the donee. Why a parent, or one who loves another, and wishes to use *his own property* in securing the object of his affection, as far as property can do it, from the ills of life, the vicissitudes of fortune, and even his own improvidence, or incapacity for self-protection, should not be permitted to do so, is not readily perceived.[73]

Simply stated, Justice Miller's position seems to be, "It's the settlor's property; the settlor can do as he wishes with it." The response is obvious: it is not the settlor's property; rather, it is the beneficiary's property. When questions about the enforceability of spendthrift provisions arise, the property held in trust and at issue "belongs" to the beneficiary. Otherwise, the beneficiary's creditor has no basis for a claim against the trust. To say it is the settlor's property both begs the question and confuses the analysis. It once was the settlor's property, but it no longer is. That argument, therefore, reduces itself to the fundamental question of whether the law should allow a person who once owned property to convey it subject to restraints on its alienation[74] The law's answer, for the most part, is no. With respect to spendthrift provisions, however, the answer is generally yes.[75] Whether this is wise remains highly debatable. No one has answered Gray's fundamental objection that the law should not allow a person to enjoy a stream of income, however lavish, that is not subject to claims for just debts.

B. Where the Dust Has Settled

1. Claimants Likely to Prevail-the Restatement List

The overwhelming acceptance of the validity of spendthrift provisions in principle has been ameliorated in most jurisdictions by a concomitant recognition of exceptions. Certain creditors may present such compelling claims that public policy demands recognition. The Restatement lists the claims typically recognized:

> Although a trust is a spendthrift trust or a trust for support, the interest of the beneficiary can be reached in satisfaction of an enforceable claim against the beneficiary,
> (a) by the wife or child of the beneficiary for support, or by the wife for alimony;
> (b) for necessary services rendered to the beneficiary or necessary supplies furnished to him;
> (c) for services rendered and materials furnished which preserve or benefit the interest of the beneficiary;
> (d) by the United States or a State to satisfy a claim against the beneficiary.[76]

EXHIBIT 11.1   Continued

Claims for necessaries present one of the conundrums of this area of the law. While there has been limited litigation of this issue, most courts agree that those who provide necessaries to the beneficiary can recover from the assets of the trust, a spendthrift provision notwithstanding.[81] The commentators are virtually unanimous.[82] Courts and commentators reason that allowing claimants for necessaries to recover is consistent with the purpose of the trust, which is presumably to provide for the beneficiary.[83]

For those who oppose spendthrift provisions on principle, however, the claimant for necessities presents a peculiar problem. Public policy surely must recognize as meritorious the interest of a settlor in providing permanent economic protection to a disabled beneficiary. Yet the disabled beneficiary is especially likely to incur high expenses for necessaries such as living expenses in a personal care home and medical expenses. To complicate the matter, the claimant may both be a provider of necessaries and a governmental entity.[84] It is ironic that the one class of beneficiaries for whom a strong policy argument can be made supporting the validity of spendthrift provisions in its favor-the disabled beneficiary-is likely to incur substantial claims from two classes of creditors who are likely to prevail when they assert claims against the trust.

The Restatement's third exception is "for services rendered and materials furnished which preserve or benefit the interest of the beneficiary."[88] This exception exists in part because it would be counterproductive not to recognize it. The exception assures that the beneficiary's interest in the trust will not be diminished or lost because the person in a position to protect it declines to do so for fear her efforts would be uncompensated. Additionally, this exception involves benefits conferred by the claimant; denying recovery would result in unjust enrichment of the trust.[89] Recovery for a benefit conferred presents a different issue than recovery from the assets contributed by the settlor. Finally, as the Restatement notes, in many such cases, recovery could be had on a contract theory: "[T]he person rendering the services and furnishing the materials would have a claim against the trustee if he contracted for such services and materials, and the trustee would be entitled to indemnity out of the trust property."[90]

The fourth and final exception enumerated by the Restatement is for claims by the United States or a state. While the federal government ordinarily defers to state law on the issue of whether a debtor holds any property interest, whether that interest is subject to levy on a federal claim is a question of federal law.[91] With respect to tax liens, the answer is both clear and predictable; an otherwise valid spendthrift provision will not prevent levy by the Internal Revenue Service for satisfaction of a tax lien.[92] In fact, governmental claims in general, whether state or federal, prevail.[93]

What of those claims not listed in the Restatement, most notably tort claims and contract claims? While tort claims are not listed as recognized exceptions because of the paucity of decisional authority,[94] comment "a" addresses them:

> The interest of the beneficiary of a spendthrift trust . . . may be reached in cases other that those herein enumerated, if considerations of public policy so require. Thus it is possible that a person who has a claim in tort against the beneficiary of a spendthrift trust may be able to reach his interest under the trust.[95]

Notwithstanding early approval of the theory that tort claimants should be allowed to recover pursuant to a public policy exception,[96] a recent commentator concluded, "Cases addressing whether tort creditors should be able to reach the beneficial interest in a spendthrift trust, although scarce, overwhelmingly reject an exception for tort victims"[97]

Pity the poor contract creditor. Those commentators who express sympathy for the tort creditor-after all, one can't check the credit of the driver of a car about to hit oneself[101]-reserve none for the contract creditor. "It has frequently been suggested that [ordinary contract creditors] have only themselves to blame if they extend credit to [the beneficiary of a spendthrift trust] without first ascertaining the amount of his resources that are available for the discharge of his debts."[102]

2. Pensions and Retirement Plans: The Erisa Exception

No discussion of spendthrift provisions is complete without a consideration of the impact of ERISA, the Employee Retirement Income Security Act of 1974.[104] Congress enacted ERISA as part of a comprehensive plan to safeguard the retirement income of the nation's workers.[105] In return for submitting to federal regulations, employers who establish tax qualified ERISA plans gain a number of advantages.

In order to be tax qualified, an ERISA plan must have a spendthrift provision. "A trust shall not constitute a qualified trust under this section unless the plan of which such trust is a part provides that benefits provided under the plan may not be assigned or alienated."[107] The facial clarity of this provision notwithstanding, creditors of beneficiaries of ERISA qualified plans have been predictably aggressive in seeking to overcome this barrier to recovery from their debtor's interest in the trust.

Alimony and child support creditors have been successful.[108] ERISA, when first enacted, contained a blanket anti-alienation provision and no alimony or child support exception. Nonetheless, virtually every court confronting this issue found that an exception existed.[109] Congress concurred in this construction of the ERISA anti-alienation provision when it enacted the Retirement Equity Act of 1984[110] and included an exception for "qualified domestic relations orders."[111]

Notwithstanding over a decade of contentious litigation, and the adoption by the lower courts of a number of "implied exceptions,"[112] it now appears the ERISA spendthrift provisions are virtually impregnable. In two recent cases, the Supreme Court decisively resolved two major issues in favor of the trusts.[113] Even more critically, the Court staked its position by describing itself as "vigorously [enforcing] ERISA's prohibition on the assignment or alienation of pension benefits, [and] declining to recognize any implied exceptions to the broad statutory bar."[114]

EXHIBIT 11.1   Continued

In *Guidry v. Sheet Metal Workers National Pension Fund*,[115] Curtis Guidry pled guilty to embezzling funds from the sheet metal workers union of which he served as an officer. Guidry also served as a trustee for one of three union pension funds from which he was eligible to receive benefits. While serving his sentence for embezzlement, Guidry filed suit against two of the plans alleging that they were wrongfully withholding his benefits. He did not sue the third because he had reached a settlement with it. He did not sue the third because he had reached a settlement with it. The union intervened, joined the third plan, and obtained a $275,000 judgment against Guidry.[116]

The union sought to recover on the judgment by imposing a constructive trust on Guidry's interests in the plans.

The Tenth Circuit was not alone in concluding that criminal misconduct by the employee justified imposition of an equitable remedy on the employee's interest in the company's pension fund.[120] The Supreme Court disagreed, however. Recognizing that "there may be a natural distaste for the result we reach here,"[121] the Court held firm to the statutory bar on alienation: "[The identification of any exception should be left to Congress."[122]

One scenario may, however, fit a statutory exception. In *Guidry*, the Tenth Circuit relied on section 409(a) of ERISA,[123] finding that it created a statutory exception. That section provides that when a plan fiduciary breaches a fiduciary duty to the plan she "shall be personally liable to make good to such plan any losses to the plan resulting from each such breach . . . and shall be subject to such other equitable or remedial relief as the court made deem appropriate." The Supreme Court's disagreement was based on the facts of the case. Finding that Guidry, who had been convicted of embezzling from the union, had "not been found to have breached any duty to the plans themselves,"[124] the Court concluded that § 409(a) was not applicable. The Supreme Court did not decide whether this provision could present an exception to the anti-alienation bar.

The other hotly contested alleged exception arose when plan participants went bankrupt. The Bankruptcy Code allows a debtor to exclude from his bankruptcy estate property subject to a spendthrift provision which is enforceable under "applicable nonbankruptcy law."[127] Despite the facial clarity of that provision, a substantial number of courts concluded that " applicable nonbankruptcy law" described only state law, not federal law.[128] If participants in ERISA plans went bankrupt and the court concluded that neither ERISA's spendthrift provisions nor applicable state law protected the plan, the result would be that a creditor could reach the plan assets. In *Patterson v. Shumate*,[129] the district court reached just that conclusion, and ordered the trustee to turn the participant's interest in the plan over to his bankruptcy estate.[130] Somewhat surprisingly, rulings like this persisted even after the Internal Revenue Service took the position that a breach of the ERISA-required spendthrift provision disqualified the *entire* plan.[131]

The Supreme Court opinion in *Patterson* makes short work of the interminable and extraordinarily complex debate over the relationship between the Bankruptcy Code and ERISA with reference to spendthrift provisions.[132] In *Patterson*, the Supreme Court described itself as having "vigorously . . . enforced ERISA's prohibition on the assignment or alienation of pension benefits, declining to recognize any implied exceptions to the broad statutory bar."[133]

Guidry and *Patterson* highlight the complexity of law making and decision rendering. These opinions resolved conflicting issues in a manner consistent with our notions of separation of powers, yet also consistent with rational public policy choices, of which separation of powers is itself one, albeit one made by the Constitution. They decisively effectuated an important act of Congress. They should deter litigious attempts to breach ERISA's anti-alienation provision by their announcement of a clear rule: there are no exceptions unless Congress creates them. Yet it is somewhat disconcerting that this "rule" is explained in part by a footnote reference to the congressionally created exception of qualified domestic relations orders,[138] an exception which most likely would not exist but for the determined, persistent efforts of litigants. The message of *Guidry* and *Patterson* seems to be, "Don't go to court, go to Congress." *Quaere* whether political lobbying will prove as efficacious in illuminating and correcting inappropriate policy choices as has litigation.

IV. CODIFYING THE COMPROMISE
A. The Wheels of Justice Grind Slowly

In jurisdictions where the validity of spendthrift provisions has been established by judicial decision, exceptions are recognized in a continuing patchwork of decisions. The evolution of the Florida law on the alimony exception exemplifies this situation.[139]

In 1947, the Florida Supreme Court recognized the validity of spendthrift provisions.[140] By 1984, when *White v. Bacardi*[141] reached the Court of Appeals for the third district, no legislation limiting or qualifying the validity of spendthrift provisions had been enacted.[142] The trust at issue had been created in 1971, during the defendant's first marriage, by the defendant's father. The income beneficiaries were the defendant and his three children. The marriage between the defendant and the petitioner had lasted for two years. They had no children. In the property settlement incorporated in the divorce decree, the defendant had agreed to pay his wife alimony of $2000.00 per month. Armed with judgments for unpaid alimony in the amount of $14,000 and attorney's fees in the amount of $1,000, the petitioner had obtained an order authorizing a continuing garnishment against the trust income.[143]

The *Bacardi* court recognized that the Restatement position, which would have allowed the claim, purported to represent the majority view in 1935. Citing critics of that position, however, the court "align[ed] with what appears to be both the modern trend and the best reasoned view,"[144] holding that a divorced wife would only reach trust assets in the hands of the trustee if she could show "by competent and substantial evidence that it was the settlor's intent that she participate as a beneficiary."[145]

Had Florida law been settled, the calm would have been remarkably short lived. A scant three days later the District Court of Appeal for the second district reached a contrary decision. In *Gilbert v. Gilbert*,[147] the court dealt with a claim

EXHIBIT 11.1   Continued

by an ex-wife for $50,500 arrearages in alimony and medical expenses, and $18,000 in attorney's fees. The opinion offers scant facts about the relationship between the parties, but the wife's medical expenses were attributable to her multiple sclerosis, and the husband is described as having "fled the jurisdiction."[148]

Faced with these compelling facts, the court held that the former wife could reach the trust assets, the spendthrift provision notwithstanding, and that a continuing garnishment would lie.[151] He also would "specifically limit the application of this decision to the trust now before us, to other existing spendthrift trusts which are revocable and can be changed, and to spendthrift trusts created after the date of this decision."[153]

A year later the Florida Supreme Court affirmed *Gilbert*[154] and reversed *Bacardi*.[155] Two theories underlie decisions allowing claims for alimony against assets protected by spendthrift provisions. The first theory is that the claimant is within the class the settlor sought to favor or expected to benefit. The second theory is that, notwithstanding the settlor's intent not to allow this claimant to reach the assets, public policy demands an exception be made. The *Bacardi* court chose the latter theory. The court also affirmed the right of the claimant to collect attorney's fees as well as alimony arrearages, and to use a continuing garnishment in these circumstances. However, the court restricted the breadth of its opinion by adopting Judge Lehan's view that spendthrift trust assets could only be reached when all other means had failed. The retroactivity issue was not discussed.[156]

The inevitable complexity of litigation emerges strikingly in these two cases. It is notable that Florida recognized spendthrift provisions in 1947[157] and nearly 40 years elapsed before this fundamental question-whether the spendthrift provision bars alimony claimants-was decided. Furthermore, while the decisions resolve three basic issues-alimony claims are public policy exceptions, a continuing garnishment will lie, and attorney's fees may be included-they leave open the question of retroactivity, and create the "other assets are available" defense, which is certain to protract litigation in some cases.

A judicially created exception grounded in public policy may also exist when the spendthrift provision derives its validity from a statute, at least where the statute itself contains no exceptions. When the statute addresses the problem by providing certain exceptions, a strong argument can be made that the public policy issues have been resolved by the legislature, and the court has no room in which to act. Where no exceptions are provided, however, a court may conclude that the legislature did not address the issue, and did not intend to preclude certain claims. ERISA, for example, when first enacted, contained a blanket anti-alienation provision and no alimony or child support exception. Nonetheless, virtually every court which confronted this issue found that a child support exception existed[158] Congress concurred in this construction of the ERISA anti-alienation provision when it enacted the Retirement Equity Act of 1984[159] and included an exception for "qualified domestic relations orders."[160]

The history of domestic relations claimants' success against spendthrift provisions-even in the teeth of federal regulation-indicates that the common law works. It does. Unfortunately, it works slowly and at great cost. The economic cost of litigation does not fall solely on the claimant. In some cases, particularly those involving domestic relations orders, the claimants attorney's fees may be recoverable form the trust.[161] In all cases, the expenses of defending the lawsuit on behalf of the trust are borne by the trust.[162] Society itself incurs significant costs in providing the forum and the adjudicator.

Granted, some "enforceable" claims probably should not be allowed. Were Solomon to resurrect himself, he would pick out worthy claims and dismiss unworthy ones. However, once it has been established that a claim is "enforceable" and that a debt is "legitimate," sorting out those that public policy demands approval of from those less compelling is a game not worth the price of the ticket. The costs are simply too high.

B. A Proposal for a Statutory Solution

More that 50 years ago Erwin Griswold proposed a model spendthrift trust statute. Quickly adopted in Louisiana and Oklahoma, it then fell into desuetude.[165] The Griswold proposal first provides that spendthrift provisions are valid and enforceable, and then severely limits their reach. All income over $5000, and 10% of income over $12 per week can be alienated or attached.[166] Even those protections are overridden when the claim is for alimony, child support, necessaries, or a tort; then the court can allow the creditor to reach whatever trust income the court finds to be "just under the circumstances."[167] The spendthrift provision does not protect the beneficiary's interest in the principal, only in the income.[168]

The Griswold proposal has not proven politically viable, perhaps because it gives with one hand and takes away with the other. Spendthrift provisions are valid, but only the first $5,000 of income is protected, and the provision may be *completely overridden* for certain claimants. Whatever the merits of this plan in terms of fairness, it does not satisfy the proponents of spendthrift provisions. It also suffers from two other significant flaws. First, by using sum certains ($5,000 per year and $12.00 per week) to determine what amounts are protected in the first instance, the statute is vulnerable to becoming outdated by inflation or recession.[169] Second, by providing that favored claimants can recover what a court determines to be just, it forces them into litigation they may not be able to afford. If the matter is litigated, the trust itself will be further depleted by its share of the costs.

Several things are now clear. First, most jurisdictions approve spendthrift provisions in concept. Second, those that do find certain creditors' claims compelling. Any class of creditors can present an individual with a claim that equity finds overwhelming. What of the paralyzed father/construction worker, unable to support his family, injured by a reckless driver with a long history of traffic violations? What of the widow/shopkeeper, struggling to keep her own family afloat, who has extended credit on account to the seemingly affluent scion of the town's most substantial family? They are tort and contract creditors, ordinarily less favored by the law of spendthrift provisions.

EXHIBIT 11.1   **Continued**

The converse is true as well-a class ordinarily favored may include an unworthy claimant. An alimony claimant may have been a contributing partner in a long standing marriage, or may be a schemer who marries and quickly divorces a vulnerable, albeit wealthy, beneficiary. *Quaere* whether it makes sense to separate out claimants with enforceable claims according to the class of creditor to which they belong. Enforceability itself should insure some measure of "justness." Forcing virtually every claimant to litigate the merits of her claim is both grossly inefficient and grossly unfair.

A true compromise is called for-a compromise that constricts, if not eliminates, the need for litigation of claims and provides creditors with an efficient method of obtaining some satisfaction of their claims, but a compromise that also protects the essence of the spendthrift provision by insulating a significant portion of the beneficiary's interest in the trust. True compromise requires giving something up. If my proposal were enacted, the creditor would lose the right to seek the recovery of more than the statutory limit, that is, to ask the court to order a transfer of however much is "just under the circumstances," even if that be the beneficiary's entire interest. In return, the creditor is freed of the burden of litigating his claim. To make that bargain worthwhile, in cases where the obduracy of the trustee results in the creditor being forced to litigate, the creditor should be entitled to recover the costs of the litigation, including attorney fees.

I would retain the venerable rule that a settlor cannot create a valid spendthrift provision for her own benefit.

V. CONCLUSION

"The life of the law has not been logic: it has been experience."[178] Logic, to my mind, impels the conclusion that spendthrift provisions are invalid. Gray's arguments carry the day. Experience, on the other hand, teaches that they are valid. The current of history has swept away Gray's position without refuting it. Spendthrift provisions may be theoretically suspect; they are, nonetheless, not only valid but also thriving.

Special Interest Groups

Some special interest groups also publish legal periodicals. These groups may include members of public advocacy, such as environmental groups, or members of a particular industry or profession that is heavily legislated, regulated, and litigated. As you would expect, these publications have a specific focus. They typically do not concentrate on the law of a particular jurisdiction (as is common in law school publications) or on practical aspects of law practice (as seen in legal trade publications). Instead, this type of journal usually tracks the development of law on very specific topics. Other articles comment on the activity of subscribers with respect to the law, be it in litigation or advocacy regarding legislation or regulation of the industry or profession. While publications by law schools and bar associations tend to focus on the significance of changing law for the practice of lawyers and their staff, special interest group publications analyze the meaning of developing law for the citizenry, in particular, the members of the group.

⚖ APPLICATION 11.1

A new law is passed that requires proposed lawsuits against physicians to first be reviewed by a panel of lawyers, doctors, and laypersons, who issue an opinion as to the merit of the suit. Immediately, publications issue articles on this law. The law school law review article may approach the development and rationale of the law with some examination into how other similar laws in other jurisdictions have impacted malpractice suits. The bar association journal will likely examine the constitutionality of the law. The special interest publication, such as one on medical malpractice or a state medical association journal, will tend to focus on what the law means to physicians in terms of how it affects pretrial publicity, insurance rates, likelihood of judgments, and settlement of claims.

EXHIBIT 11.2   Reprint of Article from Trial Magazine.

Negotiating a Small Personal Injury Claim

Fifteen Points to Remember

Ellsworth T. Rundlett, III

There is no one simple and concise theory of negotiation when it comes to personal injury cases. Every attorney negotiates differently. Some are masters of the art of negotiation; others will never master it.

Practicing in this area of law requires your best bargaining skills. You will be dealing with defense attorneys who have tuned negotiating to a fine art. And keep in mind that usually they represent companies that will spare no expense to avoid paying a claim.

The following 15 axioms may help guide you safely through the discussions, conferences, and compromises that invariably accompany negotiating small personal injury cases. Ideally, they will also help you know when to settle and when to litigate.

1. Insurance companies are not afraid of being sued in small personal injury claims.

The cost of defending these claims usually will not be very high compared with the outside chance of a substantial verdict against the carrier. An insurance company would rather not pay $6,000 to defend a claim worth $10,000 but will do so if it has to. The company would rather make you litigate a case to completion or at least to the courthouse steps than give the impression that it will settle a claim just to avoid litigation. If liability is a big issue, the company will spend $10,000 to defend a case that could have settled for $3,000. So, remember, threatening to sue in a small case is not going to make either insurance adjusters or their supervisors shake in their boots.

2. Insurance adjusters prefer to close files, but they will not do so at the expense of settling a small claim for much more than it's worth.

Insurance adjusters are in some ways no different from other negotiators, including plaintiffs' lawyers. They want to close cases, put the files away, and move on to other things. Closing files is a goal of adjusters just as moving crowded dockets along is a goal of judges. However, insurance adjusters or their supervisors will go to trial rather than substantially compromise the value of small claims. When suit begins, the adjuster simply refers the file to the company's defense attorney. The two stay in touch, but the defense firm does the hard work.

3. Every insurance adjuster or claims supervisor must justify any settlement to at least one superior.

Even a senior adjuster or claims manager will have to consult someone higher in the company before a settlement can be offered. This means that adjusters can always talk about "getting authority." They realize a settlement could be questioned at a later date and that their own careers might suffer as a result. Today, most adjusters will not authorize any payment without appropriate justification and documentation.

The reluctance of insurance company employees to risk job security just to close a file or avoid litigation means that the days of settling a case with one letter and two telephone calls are over. Even a small personal injury claim requires substantial documentation and support. Therefore, the plaintiff's attorney must provide facts and figures that cannot be disputed.

4. Some insurance companies seldom settle small to medium cases for a fair amount. With these companies you have to file suit and perhaps go through a full trial.

If you are new to the practice of personal injury law, there are only two ways to find out which companies don't settle cases easily. Either you spend a few years learning through experience, or you ask two or three lawyers with experience in litigating small personal injury cases to tell you strategies and tactics that have worked for them. I recommend the latter approach because it will save you countless hours of frustration and effort and widen your circle of acquaintances in the profession as well.

Plaintiffs' lawyers have found that national and statewide companies are extremely conservative when it comes to settling personal injury claims. They have a philosophy that seems to keep them from admitting that there is such a thing as a just claim and even a formal procedure for settling claims. In small to medium range cases, especially soft-tissue cases, management of conservative insurance carriers makes it clear to their supervisors and adjusters that soft-tissue damages are to be minimized. Lower-level insurance adjusters have little authority for non-economic damages like pain and suffering. These adjusters must continue asking for authority for limited amounts in small cases and are instructed to let the cases go to suit even if the parties are a few hundred to a few thousand dollars apart.

The companies will seldom make a reasonable offer to settle small personal injury claims, especially those involving soft-tissue injuries. And when on occasion they move toward settlement, their offers demean the victims. They know that most people who are unrepresented by counsel will succumb to the "take it or leave it approach." Most individual claimants believe or are forced to believe that they must accept an adjuster's offer.

The carriers also know that the majority of attorneys who represent the plaintiffs in theses cases will usually settle claims rather than take the time, effort, and expense to go to trial.

For example, our law firm represented three cousins over the course of several years, each of whom had soft-tissue injuries from an automobile collision. Liability in each case was clear.

A nationally known conservative carrier insured two of the tortfeasors. A more reasonable carrier insured the potential defendant responsible for the third cousin's injuries. The claims of the first two were each worth

Ellsworth T. Rundlett, III, is a partner in the Portland, Maine, law firm of Childs, Emerson, Rundlett, Fifield & Childs. This article was adapted with permission from Maximizing Damages in Small Personal injury Cases *(James Publishing 1991).*

EXHIBIT 11.2   Continued

approximately $20,000 at the time of the first letter of demand. In both cases, the conservative carrier made final offers of less than $10,000. Efforts to compromise were fruitless and the carriers were not averse to litigation. After a two-year period between filing suit and the eve of trial, the carrier settled each case on the courthouse steps for close to $25,000.

By that time the carrier realized that trial was imminent, the plaintiffs were prepared for trial, liability was clear, and the plaintiffs had proved to be potentially good witnesses during discovery. Court costs, defense costs, and a potentially high verdict for each plaintiff prompted the carriers to settle for more than the original value before suit.

The philosophy that 'a case settled is a case won' is appropriate in small personal injury claims.

Our firm estimated the claim for the third cousin's injuries at approximately $30,000. The final settlement after the original letter of demand and a few courteous follow-up letters was $33,000.

The moral of this story: Know the carriers you are negotiating with-some insurance companies settle; most don't.

5. Preparing for negotiation or settlement with the insurance companies referred to in axiom 4 above is a waste of time.

When you are asked to represent a person with a small personal injury claim, you should first find out whether the insurance company has a history of not settling without litigation. If so, you must decide the merits of accepting the case. If you accept, commit yourself to litigation.

If you have a soft-tissue injury case with subjective complaints or one in which the victim underwent substantial chiropractic treatment, you can count on certain insurance carriers paying little for pain and suffering. The adjuster will question everything in the file. If there is even the slightest liability question, you will be lucky if the offer approaches the special damages. Often it will be much less. Don't waste you time trying to convince the carrier with letters, phone calls, documentation, and settlement brochures. You will merely delay the inevitable.

In a soft-tissue injury of medium-range settlement value ($25,000 range or more), file suit right after the initial investigation and preparation. Litigation and verdicts are the only language conservative carriers really respect.

6. Insurance defense attorneys make more money by litigating cases over as long a period as possible than they do by settling cases soon after suit.

The large law firms that insurance companies generally retain to represent them earn the bulk of their fees through litigation. They do not work on commissions, and they are not paid to settle cases early. They bill an insurance company on an hourly basis. The more hours they bill, the higher their fees.

If you start litigation in a small case, be prepared to do some work. Even if defense attorneys know that you may be willing to settle for much less than the figure you gave initially, they won't beg you to do so. Be prepared to take you case to trial if necessary.

7. Insurance carriers are more impressed with special damages like medical bills and well-documented loss of income than with dissertations about pain, suffering, loss of consortium, and mental anguish.

Do not try to build your case with elaborations of these intangibles. Insurance companies are moved only by facts, figures and objective measurements of injury. Substantial documentation is what you need to convince carriers to settle.

Imagine a rear-end collision case in which absolute liability and substantial collision damages were factors for the two passengers who were in the back seat of the car. Mr. Jones and Mr. Smith are the same age and same weight, and they work for the same company. The impact they received in the accidents was essentially the same, and they suffered essentially the same injuries. Mr. Jones consulted a medical doctor who prescribed six weeks of physical therapy. He took approximately eight weeks to recover from his acute injuries and missed work for six weeks. His medical bills and physical therapy fees are approximately $2,500, and his lost wages are approximately $1,800. His residual injuries are minimal, and he has virtually recovered after six months.

Mr. Smith went to the local hospital emergency ward. The doctor who examined him recommended that he see a specialist. Instead, he had four or five chiropractic treatments. Because of his determination not to miss work, he lost only five days' pay. However, he is in considerable pain, is unable to interact with his family, has difficulty performing work assignments, and has been unable to participate in leisure activities for almost a year. His medical bills total approximately $500 and his lost wages approximately $300. Many friends, relatives, and work associates have written letters concerning the incredible pain and difficulties he has experienced since the accident.

The insurance company will settle Mr. Jones's case for approximately $12,000 or more, but they will offer Mr. Smith no more than $3,000 to $5,000-if he is lucky. Moral of the story: Adequate medical treatment and documentation are all-important. Insurance companies believe facts and figures more than they believe letters from friends about pain and suffering.

8. Most capable defense attorneys can find weaknesses in your case that the adjuster overlooked or could have discovered without formal discovery.

When you try to settle your case directly with an adjuster, you control most of the information. Once litigation begins, however, the defense attorney will scrutinize your case to spot weaknesses. Formal discovery records like medical authorization forms, independent medical examinations, depositions, interrogatories, and requests for production of documents will disclose some, if not many, weaknesses of your case. Therefore, unless your case is very strong, the defense attorney may be able to successfully attack it after you file suit. If you are aware of potential weaknesses such as the plaintiff's having had a number of prior injuries, previous permanent impairment claims, admissible convictions, or other problems, do you best to settle the case prior to litigation.

9. Defense attorneys usually have more settlement authority or knowledge of settlement authority than they will admit to.

During negotiations after litigation starts, the defense attorney will almost always refer to the need to get permission or authority from the carrier. In fact, most defense attorneys have a good idea about the range of figures

EXHIBIT 11.2 Continued

within which the carrier is willing to settle and may already have authority to quote the range. In order to get the defense attorney at least to disclose the potential range, I suggest asking this question: "Mr. Defense Attorney, what would you do if you were in my place? What do you think this case is worth?"

If the defense attorney gives you a figure, add another 50 to 100 percent. The exact amount, of course, will depend on the size of the case, the nature of liability, and the extent of documented damages. As the case approaches trial, the figure from the defense attorney may approach reality. But the defense attorney will always try to save the carrier money.

10. Defense attorneys obtain and maintain insurance company clients by settling cases for less than the maximum authority given to them by the carrier and by winning defense verdicts.

Defense attorneys will agree to pay top authority only if they believe they may get docked with a substantial verdict at trial. For a defense attorney who believes a win on liability or damages is probable, the roll of the dice will be much more attractive. Thus, while some defense attorneys will tell you how hard they are working to get a settlement, do not count the money until your client has received it.

11. If an adjuster makes an offer that he or she says your client "can't refuse," it is almost never the best you can obtain.

We all recall Marlon Brando's famous line in the movie "The Godfather" where he tells his subordinate to "make an offer they can't refuse." Insurance adjusters will often indicate that they are making such an offer. It may sound like you are going to be offered the maximum value of the claim. What you are really getting is the best offer the adjuster has to make at the time. If the adjuster makes an offer your client "can't refuse," it is almost never the best that you can obtain.

An offer that can't be refused can be used by either party in settlement negotiations. If you have a case with strong liability, well-documented damages, and an appealing plaintiff, ask the adjuster to make an offer *no one* would refuse. In weaker cases, you should probably advise you client to consider taking an offer the adjuster says can't be refused.

12. Clients who settle their cases without litigation may always have second thoughts, but they may be happier than clients who go trial.

The philosophy that "a case settled is a case won" is appropriate in small personal injury claims. Just as divorce clients often complain about their settlements, some personal injury clients will always doubt the adequacy of their settlements. Remind them that the difficulty and emotional stress of litigation are seldom worth the few thousand dollars' difference a verdict may bring.

13. Plaintiffs' attorneys may make a living by settling cases, but they can settle cases only if they also known how to litigate.

You can settle cases for maximum damages only if you also know how to litigate. If you plan to practice personal injury law and you intend to accept small to medium cases, prepare yourself for litigation.

Successful litigation requires thorough investigation and complete understanding of the facts and nuances of a case. You will need to decided on a case theme and develop it through painstaking-and sometimes expensive-discovery. Throughout trial, you must use every skill you have to bring jurors around to thinking that fault lies with the defendant-not with your client. Emphasizing evidence that your client's injury is worthy of an award will help to convince them. In the case of a soft-tissue injury, for example, document how it will cause life-long suffering. Then you must establish a reasonable figure for general damages to compensate the victim. If you are unwilling or unable to make such a commitment, I suggest you either move to another area of law or refer to yourself as a settling attorney.

14. A verdict that is close to or equal to the amount offered before trial is not really a win, but it may help your practice.

A verdict that is close to the final offer before trial may not be considered an absolute win. Thus, at trial you must ask for an award somewhat in excess of the final offer-but it must be an amount you think is fair. If you arguments have convinced jurors that your client's injuries warrant an award, they are likely to view your request as reasonable.

15. Insurance companies as entities are not fair, logical, predictable, or understandable, but the insurance adjusters who work for these companies are almost always ordinary, likable human beings.

It is as impossible to figure out insurance companies as it is to figure out the opposite sex. It is important to remember, however, that adjusters and their supervisors are human just like you. Treat them with the same respect that you like to receive.

Source: Adapted form *Minimizing Damages in Small Personal Injury Cases* by Ellsworth T. Rundlett, III, James Publishing, Inc. Costa Mesa, CA (714)755-5450. This adaptation appeared in "*Negotiating a Small Personal Injury Claim*", TRIAL, October 1991.

Legal Newspapers

Frequent legal periodicals, such as **legal newspapers** (See Exhibit 11.3) that are issued daily or weekly, tend to appear in a format quite similar to ordinary newspapers. Articles are short, and advertising may be heavy. The articles typically track the development of law as it is issued from the courts, legislators, and administrative agencies. Also frequently included is action in the courts, such as case filings, property transactions, and probate court action. Legal newspapers can be a tremendous benefit because information

legal newspaper
Newspaper published with format similar to ordinary newspaper except that articles and advertising are directed toward legal matters.

EXHIBIT 11.3   A Page from the National Law Journal.
Reprinted with the permission of *The National Law Journal* copyright 1994, The New York Law Publishing Company.

THE NATIONAL LAW JOURNAL

VOL. 16, NO. 41 © 1994 THE NEW YORK LAW PUBLISHING COMPANY   *The Weekly Newspaper for the Profession*   PRICE $3.00 • MONDAY, JUNE 13, 1994

Counsel's Counsel

Suing Lawyers Brings Growth To Shadow Bar

Malpractice attorneys cater to their sensitive clients and rarely go public.

BY THOM WEIDLICH
NATIONAL LAW JOURNAL STAFF REPORTER

TO WRITE THE FIRST edition of his treatise "Legal Malpractice" in the 1970s, Ronald E. Mallen read upwards of 600 cases—all that there were.

He now reads 700 a year to prepare the supplements. Suing lawyers is a growth industry. According to the book, co-authored with Jeffrey M. Smith, there were more published appellate decisions concerning legal malpractice during the 1970s—the decade such actions

Who's Who and What's Next
Assembling a roster of leading practitioners in legal malpractice is no easy matter; environmental law may be the next snare for the unwary; and how to avoid malpractice mistakes. *See pages A24-A26.*

became a serious concern to lawyers—than "in the previous history of American jurisprudence."

And yet, an organized bar of legal malpractice attorneys has never appeared—and never will, according to those who work in the area.

For several reasons, including the sensitive nature of the field, malpractice attorneys are not very clubby.

Strong Defense
The World Cup symbol shown here is the event's prime asset, and organizers are using U.S. law to confiscate counterfeit jackets, T-shirts and other merchandise expected to bring revenue worth millions.

U.S. Trademark Law Is World Cup Penalty Kick

(e.g., case summaries) appears in them quite often weeks or even months before the opinions are published in reports or statutory compilations.

⚖ APPLICATION 11.2

The law in a particular jurisdiction states that if a motion to admit facts is not responded to within 30 days of receipt, the information in the motion is presumed admitted by the receiving party and cannot later be denied.

Party A is suing Party B (an insurance company) for failure to pay a claim on a home fire. Party B sends a motion to admit facts based on its insurance agent's representation that Party A had not paid the premium due for insurance in the month preceding the fire. The failure to pay would have caused the policy to lapse. Party A's lawyer receives the motion but the next day suffers a heart attack. Party A is unaware of the motion but in fact has cancelled checks to prove payment of all premiums. The

lawyer for Party A returns to work 33 days later. According to the law, Party A can no longer deny the claim of Party B and thus cannot introduce evidence that the premium was paid and the insurance was valid. The result would be that Party A would probably lose the suit and the cost of the total loss of its home would not be covered by insurance. This could quite possibly bankrupt the average client and cause a malpractice suit against the lawyer. The lawyer, in reading the daily legal newspaper discovers a two-paragraph story about a failure to timely respond to a motion to admit facts in which the state supreme court held that if the failure is corrected in a reasonable time, is not unfair to the opposition, and is based on sufficient circumstances, the trial court has discretion to accept the response late. (In some publications, such a change in the law would result in publication of the full opinion.)

In this case, the lawyer's sudden health condition would more than likely meet the standards set out by the court. However, if not for the legal newspaper, the synopsis of the opinion would not be available even in advance sheets for probably a month or more. By this early indication, the lawyer can contact the court and request an immediate slip copy (single case publication) to be sent for submission to the trial court along with the response to the motion to admit genuineness and a motion to accept the response.

◻ ASSIGNMENT 11.3

Identify three specific situations in which a legal newspaper could be helpful in legal research.

CONDUCTING RESEARCH IN LEGAL PERIODICALS

Researching legal periodicals is not necessarily more difficult, but it is typically conducted differently than other types of legal research. Unlike with reporters, there is no digest system. Unlike with statutes or regulations, there is often no subject index for each type or issue of publication. Also, the large number of publications of legal periodicals and the frequency with which they are issued require special features in finding tools.

Using Indexes

In addition to the computer-assisted research methods discussed in Chapter 14, legal periodicals have a number of general subject indexes that appear both in hardbound issues (with supplements) and on microfiche as well as on computer. Both types are accessed by simply using research queries and relevant search terms, much like any other type of subject index research. The indexes are heavily cross-referenced to assist the researcher in locating relevant information even when not using the exact word or phrase under which the information is located. The hardbound indexes are published periodically, with frequent paperback supplements to accommodate the constant inundation of newly released information. The disadvantage of these indexes is that they are not cumulative. As a result, one must check each year of publication and each monthly or weekly supplement for the current year. Some publications do issue cumulative supplements for the current year. One

can determine this by examining the cover to determine the period of time covered by the supplement.

A number of different indexes are available for legal periodical research. The distinction is typically in the type of periodicals indexed, such as law reviews and journals, bar association publications, legal newspapers, special interest periodicals, and other trade journals with legal components. You should note that most legal periodical indexes do not reference local publications or, in many cases, even state publications. Thus, if you are looking for articles from a particular jurisdictional bar association or special interest group, you may need to consult the table of contents of the publication's issues or a specially prepared index (if one exists) for that publication.

The most broad based legal index is the Legal Resource Index, or LRI (see Exhibit 11.4). Published since 1980, this index contains references to law reviews and journals, bar association journals, special interest law reviews, six legal newspapers, a variety of general publication newspapers (e.g., *The Washington Post*), and many popular magazines with articles relevant to law. The LRI is also available on microfilm or laser disk (called Info/Trak). The system indexes well over 700 publications. Information is indexed by author, title, subject, cases, and statutes. A weekly supplement is the Current Index to Legal Periodicals, which can be consulted for the most recent information.

Another common index is the Current Law Index, or CLI. This publication is quite similar to the LRI except that legal and general newspapers and popular magazines are not included. The oldest index is the Index to Legal Periodicals, first published in 1908. This publication references 460 law reviews, special interest publications, and bar association journals. Information is indexed by author/subject, cases, statutes, and book reviews of legal texts. While somewhat more limited in scope, this is the only publication that provides reviews of legal texts, which can be helpful when looking for a method to analyze a number of treatises on a topic rather than evaluating each treatise individually. Other indexes include publications that reference foreign country legal periodicals and more concentrated subject or geographical areas of publication. Most are arranged in a similar format, with indexes by subject, author, case, and statute.

Consulting Citators

As a final step in your periodical research, you should consult a citator. This can be extremely helpful to determine whether the article has met with opposition or has been included in the opinion of any court. Shepard's Law Review Citations is one example (see Exhibit 11.5). By locating the journal, then volume, then first page of the article, you can quickly determine whether the article has been addressed in any way subsequent to its publication.

IIII▶ STRATEGY

Researching in Legal Periodicals

1. Determine whether your research must be confined to a particular jurisdiction or whether it can be done on a national scale.

EXHIBIT 11.4
Sample Page from
the Index to Legal
Periodicals, Vol-
ume 86, No. 5.
Copyright 1993 by
the H.W. Wilson
Company. Material
reproduced with
the permission of
the publisher.

SUBJECT AND AUTHOR INDEX   **69**

Employment discrimination—*cont.*

Sex

Feminist or foe? Justice Sandra Day O'Connor, Title VII sex-discrimination, and support for women's rights. B. Palmer. 13 *Women's Rts. L. Rep.* 159-70 Summ/Fall '91

Fetal hazards, gender justice, and the justices: the limits of equality. D. L. Kirp. 34 *Wm. & Mary L. Rev.* 101-38 Fall '92

Fetal protection policies no longer a bona fide occupational qualificaton defense? International Union, UAW v. Johnson Controls, 111 S. Ct. 1196 (1991). T. M. Scannell, student author. 75 *Marq. L. Rev.* 489-507 Wint '92

Fetal protection: valid employer concern or disguise for discrimination? International Union, UAW v. Johnson Controls, Inc., 111 S. Ct. 1196 (1991). G. N. L. Hagan, student author. 12 *Miss. C. L. Rev.* 533-58 Spr '92

The impact of employment arbitration agreements on sex discrimination claims: the trend toward nonjudicial resolution. R. A. Shearer. 18 *Empl. Rel. L.J.* 479-88 Wint '92/'93

International Union, UAW v. Johnson Controls, Inc. [111 S. Ct. 1196 (1991)]: death toll of fetal protection in business. L. S. Hootman, student author. 36 *St. Louis U. L.J.* 187-211 Fall '91

Labor pains: the rights of the pregnant employee. P. J. Bejarano. 43 *Lab. L.J.* 780-90 D '92

Law firm partnership selection and Title VII. E. B. Cogan. 43 *Lab. L.J.* 801-5 D '92

The status of sex-specific fetal protection policies. E. A. Phillips, student author. 57 *Mo. L. Rev.* 979-1001 Summ '92

Canada

Paramètres de l'égalité: quelques réflexions sur la loi des grands nombres. M.-F. Bich. 17 *Queen's L.J.* 54-90 Spr '92

Russia (Republic)

The worker's paradise lost: the role and status of Russian and American women in the workplace. M. B. Gottesfeld, student author. 14 *Comp. Lab. L.J.* 68-95 Fall '92

States (U.S.)

State ERAs and employment discrimination. B. E. Altschuler. 65 *Temp. L. Rev.* 1267-78 Wint '92

Canada

A proposal for legislative intervention in Canadian human rights law. I. B. McKenna. 21 *Man. L.J.* 325-39 '92

Great Britain

Victimisation of applicants. E. Ellis. 142 *New L.J.* 1406-8 O 16 '92

New Jersey

Federal and New Jersey state fair employment laws. E. Grosek. 43 *Lab. L.J.* 791-800 D '92

New Zealand

The Human Rights Commission Amendment Act 1992. G. Williams, student author. 7 *Auckland U. L. Rev.* 202-7 '92

States (U.S.)

Smokers' rights legislation: should the state "butt out" of the workplace? T. W. Sculco, student author. 33 *B.C. L. Rev.* 879-902 Jl '92

United States

Federal and New Jersey state fair employment laws. E. Grosek. 43 *Lab. L.J.* 791-800 D '92

Employment of undocumented aliens

The employer sanctions provision of IRCA: deterrence or discrimination? S. M. Kaplan, student author. 6 *Geo. Immigr. L.J.* 545-65 O '92

EMU *See* European Monetary Union

Endangered species

See also
Animals

The anti-baiting regulation pursuant to the Migratory Bird Treaty Act: have the federal courts flown the coop, or is the regulation for the birds? A. E. Schmalz, student author. 14 *Geo. Mason U. L. Rev.* 407-26 Wint '91

Critical habitat designations: a legal tool for Endangered Species Act Section 9 investigations. G. Guinta, Jr. 2 *U. Balt. J. Envtl. L.* 183-94 Summ '92

The tarnishing of an environmental jewel: the Endangered Species Act and the northern spotted owl. E. A. Foley. 8 *J. Land Use & Envtl. L.* 253-83 Fall '92

Australia

Biodiversity legislation: species, vegetation, habitat—a response to John Bradsen. [9 *Envtl. & Plan. L.J.* 175-80 Je '92] T. Dendy. 9 *Envtl. & Plan. L.J.* 475-9 D '92

Idaho

Just water over the dam? A look at the Endangered Species Act and the impact of hydroelectric facilities on anadromous fish runs of the Northwest. A. S. Noonan, student author. 28 *Idaho L. Rev.* 781-802 '91/'92

Saving Idaho's salmon: a history of failure and a dubious future. M. C. Blumm. 28 *Idaho L. Rev.* 667-713 '91/'92

States (U.S.)

The hybrids howl: legislators listen—these animals aren't crying wolf. B. J. Kramek, student author. 23 *Rutgers L.J.* 633-56 Spr '92

Victoria (Australia)

Guaranteeing the survival and evolution of endangered species: an analysis of the Flora and Fauna Guarantee Act (Victoria). S. Edmonds, J. Giddings. 9 *Envtl. & Plan. L.J.* 421-44 D '92

Washington (State)

Fish gotta swim: establishing legal rights to instream flows through the Endangered Species Act and the public trust doctrine. S. W. Reed. 28 *Idaho L. Rev.* 645-66 '91/'92

Energy resources

See also
Electricity
Mines and minerals
Nuclear energy
Oil and gas

An international perspective on energy. R. J. Zedalis. 27 *Tulsa L.J.* 473-7 Summ '92

The national energy strategy—an illusive quest for energy security. C. L. Van Orman. 13 *Energy L.J.* 251-64 '92

Enforcement of judgments abroad

Commercial claims in Europe. S. Cromie. 142 *New L.J.* 1423-5 O 16 '92

L'exécution des jugements et des sentences. A. Prujiner. 22 *Rev. Gén.* 453-7 Je '91

Enforcement of taxation *See* Tax enforcement

Engfer, Victoria L.

By-products of prosperity: transborder hazardous waste issues confronting the maquiladora industry; by V. L. Engfer, G. A. Partida, T. C. Vernon, A. Toulet, D. A. Renas. 28 *San Diego L. Rev.* 819-51 N/D '91

Engineers *See* Architects and engineers

Engineers Corps *See* United States. Army. Corps of Engineers

Eagle, Eric

FCC regulation of political broadcasting: a critical legal studies perspective. 14 *Comm. & L.* 3-40 S '92

Engle, Karen

Female subjects of public international law: human rights and the exotic other female. 26 *New Eng. L. Rev.* 1509-26 Summ '92

English, David M.

The UPC and the new durable powers. 27 *Real Prop. Prob. & Tr. J.* 333-405 Summ '92

Entertainment

See also
Motion pictures
Radio and television
Sports

Are samplers getting a bum rap?: Copyright infringement or technological creativity? S. C. Hampel, student author. 1992 *U. Ill. L. Rev.* 559-91 '92

Exiled on Main Street: a ticket scalper's dilemma. B. M. Pukier, student author. 50 *U. Toronto Fac. L. Rev.* 280-300 Spr '92

Legislating canned performances. J. Boessenecker, student author. 14 *Hastings Comm. & Ent. L.J.* 545-66 Summ '92

---

2. If the research must be confined, consult the publications for the jurisdiction (e.g., law school reviews or journals, bar association journals, local legal periodical publications such as state, county, and city legal newspapers). Often, these are not indexed, and it may be more expedient to use national index sources but confine your search in them to local publications.

EXHIBIT 11.5 Sample Page from Shepard's Law Review Citations.
Reproduced by permission of Shepard's McGraw-Hill, Inc. Further reproduction is strictly prohibited.

HARVARD LAW REVIEW Vol. 71

– 630 –
491F2d311
242CA2d665
33WAp625
Alk
457P2d647
Calif
51CaR716
Wash
657P2d332
22AkL289
7AlkR209
21AzL1072
23AzL774
2BCR206
38BL51
39BUR5
50BURS145
60BUR207
62BUR911
1980BYU725
1980BYU785
1980BYU812
49CaL617
68CaL209
68CaL266
71CaL40
73CaL1182
7Cap40
8Cap2
51ChL803
46CK9
7CLA592
10CLA786
26CLA1267
29CLA812
29CM727
32CM393
6CnL45
16CnL713
56Cor437
66Cor873
67Cor823
68Cor660
69Cor1007
61CR213
65CR1333
73CR1533
78CR1430
6Cum39
46CUR368
19CWL564
23CWL279
23CWL317
8Day732
24DeP851
31DeP802
36DLJ242
37DLJ227
66DLR295
1961DuL362
1963DuL650
34FLR483
36FR514
3GaL686
11GaL1071
11GaL1350
11GaL1375
15GaL118
71Geo1552
41GW190
16HLJ391
10Hof676
10Hof722
11Hof859
89HLR1764
90HLR839
91HLR940
92HLR437
98HLR965
14HUL633
15HUL85
27HWL146
67IBJ428
36ILJ426
42ILJ528
43ILJ422
50ILJ231
51ILJ476
53ILJ19
53ILJ638
67ILR717
45JUL575
57JUL966
52KLJ347
7KLR469
37LCP7
1962LF364
1979LF841
42LJ5
75McL486
36MdL106
43MdL664
31Mer525
25MiL396
36MiL400
45MnL898
60MnL430
62MnL277
29MoL2
40MoL579
46NbL762
54NbL356
56NbL284
40NCL669
34NDL547
54NDL53
60NwL28
76NwL76
33NYL780
35NYL1023
41NYL869
52NYL564
52NYL1332
56NYL375
52OLR128
107PaL160
113PaL671
116PaL1061
117PaL34
126PaL796
130PaL1297
130PaL1494
133PaL712
45PitL10
45PitL608
46PitL388
2PLR285
8RCL589
38RJ355
43RJ12
13RLR526
14RLR9
23RLR70
24RLR293
36RLR776
41SCL9
45SCL454
54SCL179
58SCL304
16SLJ200
17SLJ205
11StLJ550
22StLJ324
26StLJ217
12StnL809
18StnL613
28StnL105
52TLQ17
53TLQ268
9Tol48
1970Tol24
37TuL682
52TuL117
38TxL572
40TxL761
33UCR174
49UCR35
53UCR696
51VaL253
65VaL490
65VaL1068
17Val383
15VLR327
18VLR946
3VR466
10VR641
10VR664
27W&L267
22W&M635
1962WLR
[416
12WnL727
28WnL143
22Wsb432
35WsL13
45WsL343
51WsL57
52WsL29
60WsL245
71YLJ1046
77YLJ416
87YLJ507
90YLJ975
90YLJ1027
90YLJ1169

– 674 –
56McL853
115PaL498
13RLR553

– 687 –
253F2d860
223Md218
Md
163A2d456
43CLQ372
11FLR562
31FR324
45ILR107
46ILR519
35JBK148
57McL660
68McL23
18MdL277
41MqL358
48NbL977
34NYL218
38OBJ1117
20OR248
13RLR296
32RMR333
16VLR352
15W&L18
1958WLQ
[393

– 712 –
259F2d939
261F2d206
167FS799
1960DuL391
1962DuL31
41FR365
72HLR301
16NYF596
12SR21
13StnL508
52VaL248
12VLR384
13VLR437

– 728 –
271F2d203
14RLR751

– 732 –
34NYL24

– 734 –
35FRD77
42FRD394
11AzL443
40DJ199
74HLR1021
34TuL80

– 735 –
45FRD276

– 736 –
DC
145A2d581
13NYF249

– 744 –
14MiL634

– 750 –
47ABA1178
38GW435
12VLR259

– 754 –
34NYL416

– 769 –
259F2d169
293F2d229
295F2d447
296F2d695
302F2d721
373F2d693
416F2d537
258Md342
228Or436
Md
265A2d870
Ore
365P2d860
65CR62
1983DuL343
28FR12
74HLR234
74HLR698
74HLR1303
76HLR866
39ILJ202
50ILJ715
68McL870
27MdL41
50MnL277
54NwL20
34NYL19
19OR403
13SCQ440
49TuL95
68VaL21
8VR3
20VR3
1959WLR98
69WVL254
72YLJ1295
75YLJ568

– 815 –
610F2d1071
1982BYU907
66CR462
97HLR1849
58ILR47
50NYL286
52NYL991
28PitL188
45TxL667
50VaL580
51VaL273
76YLJ335

– 843 –
44CLQ313
72HLR1241
81HLR1210
10KLR21
109PaL959
42TxL448
46TxL342

– 874 –
404US536
30LE693
92SC635
263F2d741
265F2d54
265F2d811
270F2d370
300F2d589
345F2d670
350F2d553
358F2d214
374F2d822
403F2d942
472F2d267
160FS660
167FS926
172FS293
174FS590
177FS552
185FS811
204FS305
223FS536
248FS509
254FS579
260FS1009
268FS269
22FRD88
25FRD266
28FRD326
36FRD222
41FRD73
43FRD498
47FRD103
52FRD269
6AzA286
18AzA236
58C2d285
67C2d708
101NH376
103NH246
58NJS79
60NJS136
94NJS280
207Va629
Ariz
431P2d927
501P2d412
Calif
23CaR767
63CaR734
373P2d855
La
279So2d675
Minn
169NW220
NH
143A2d431
169A2d633
NJ
155A2d272
158A2d354
228A2d81
Va
151SE432
10BCR546
49BUR443
36ChL24
71CR628
1967DuL289
1968DuL
[1131
3GaL510
73HLR958
75HLR1494
76HLR1084
77HLR630
81HLR362
81HLR594
40ILJ349
46ILR499
48ILR273
1960LF60
1967LF209
1967LF277
30LLR291
60McL910
18MiL78
38MoL182
22SLJ767
35StJ23
11StnL227
16StnL45
54VaL394
8VR521
19W&L167
1969WLR41
74YLJ412

– 1001 –
41DLJ409
22LJ501
8SDR58
18StnL161
43TxL893
12VLR32

– 1057 –
369US207
7LE679
82SC704
270F2d605
202FS753
41A1A498
341Mas272
360Mch44
228Md432
104NH108
104NH247
33NJ21
Ala
139So2d355
Mass
168NE485
Md
180A2d666
Mich
104NW85
NH
179A2d291
182A2d900
NJ
161A2d715
51CaL558
9Cap40
51CBJ243
29ChL678
37ChL475
46CLQ130
38Dic331
29FR559
30FR594
32FR3
73HLR8
18HWL618
12KLR367
31KLR122
24Law69
27LCP333
27LCP405
27LCP432
39LCP(3)30
1962LF357
61McL140
61McL671
47MLJ946
28MR4
33NDL545
38NDL395
38NDL411
38NDL506
34NYL122
34NYL1217
36OBJ1441
16OR60
34SCL182
11SDR19
15StLJ542
47VaL1331
16Val451
13VLR1030
15VLR1267
24W&L227
8WnL46
9WnL46
71WVL114
72YLJ16
72YLJ40
72YLJ76
72YLJ93
73YLJ289
75YLJ536
86YLJ1610

– 1102 –
46CaL683
45CLQ417
36JBC409
26LCP649
1959LF239
17RLR389

– 1122 –
282F2d240
353Mas619
Mass
233NE752
49KLJ310
33LJ549
71McL774
45NDR365
49TxL671

– 1133 –
29Ap2d958
13Msc2d984
NY
174NYS2d
[484
289NYS2d
[329
11Buf535
54NwL292
21SR544
13VLR211
41WsL245

– 1143 –
267F2d519
92Ida252
242Md497
245Md298
87NJS512
Idaho
441P2d162
Md
219A2d812
226A2d311
NJ
210A2d92
3BCR117
25BL281
44CLQ47
27MdL256
53NwL144
34NYL211
35TLQ289
53VaL333

– 1152 –
188FS595
2Wsb232

– 1154 –
1966DuL900
53ILR416
34NYL358

– 1163 –
299F2d571

– 1169 –
260F2d455
220Or107
Ore
348P2d1114
59CR273
24MdL252
41NCL2

– 1172 –
220Or107
Ore
348P2d1114
59CR279
29FR301
48ILR246
41NCL4

505

3. If the research is national, consult a national indexing system such as the LRI by using your relevant search terms. Start with the most recent issues and move backward through prior issues.
4. The index should provide you with volumes, abbreviated publication names, pages, and often exact dates of issue. If you are unable to decipher the publication name, consult the index table of abbreviations.
5. Use the information from the index to locate the proper issue and page of the periodical. Most are arranged alphabetically in the library. If the publication or issue is absent, consult the librarian. The publication may have been put on microfiche or a computer database or may have been sent with other issues to be bound into a hardcover volume, or it may simply be placed out of order or be off the shelf.

CHAPTER SUMMARY

This chapter has demonstrated the benefits of legal periodicals, a quick and interesting source of information about a variety of topics of law. Legal periodicals often provide the most current information and frequently include citations of primary authority. The disadvantage is, of course, that they are often too broad or too narrow in scope for use as an authority, and their secondary authority influence is often minimally persuasive on a court. However, the use of legal periodicals to familiarize or update your knowledge of a subject is indisputable. The citations of primary authority can also be a quick entry method to the key numbers that will serve you in research of primary judicial authority.

Locating information within legal periodicals is a somewhat cumbersome task, as it often requires the use of a single publication for hundreds of periodicals. Because of the complexity of the index, however, most terms are heavily cross-referenced to give you as the researcher a broad array of terms that will ultimately lead you to the articles relevant to your research. Unlike many other types of legal research indexes, in addition to having hardbound and computer sources, legal periodicals are often indexed on microfilm, which is often a faster and simpler method for accessing information than the numerous hardbound volumes or computer systems that require basic computer research skills.

KEY TERMS

legal periodical	bar association	legal newspaper
law review or journal		

SELF-TEST

MULTIPLE CHOICE

1. Legal periodicals can come from a variety of sources, including but not limited to _____and _____ .

a) bar association, judicial branch
b) bar association, legislative branch
c) law schools, bar associations
d) law schools, administrative agencies

2. Articles written by students typically will include _____ or a similar designation in addition to or in place of the author's name.
   a) "3rd-year student"
   b) "author anonymous"
   c) "comment"
   d) no special designation is used

3. If no _____ _____ is given, you should delete the year in parentheses from the end of the citation and include the year (without parentheses) prior to the name of the journal.
   a) volume number
   b) page number
   c) article title
   d) name of author

4. The _____ and not the title of the publication should be underscored.
   a) journal
   b) article title
   c) name of author
   d) none of the above

5. Bar association journals usually contain fewer references to _____ , but the approach to the topic is usually much less complex than law school publications.
   a) author
   b) annotations
   c) authority
   d) statutes

TRUE/FALSE

_____ 6. Law school reviews and journals usually track the development of law on very specific topics.

_____ 7. Special interest group publications analyze the meaning of developing law for the particular jurisdiction or topic of special interest.

_____ 8. Legal newspapers frequently include court actions such as case filings, dismissals, probate court orders, legal notices, and property transactions.

_____ 9. Legal periodicals are available on computer, in hardbound form, or on microfilm/laser disk.

_____ 10. Legal periodicals are usually heavily indexed to maximize the opportunity for the researcher to locate relevant articles.

FILL-IN THE BLANKS

11. Often _____ _____ to legal periodical indexes are not cumulative.

12. The primary _____ in legal periodical index publications is typically the type of periodicals indexed.

13. The most broad based legal index is the _____ _____ _____ .

14. The laser disk system of LRI is called _____ .

15. The oldest index is the _____ _____ _____ , first published in 1908.

16. The Index to Legal Periodicals is the only publication that provides reviews of _____ _____ .

17. Book reviews can assist you in evaluating _____ on a topic.

18. As a final step in your periodical research, you should consult a _____ .

19. Legal periodicals often provide the most _____ source of information on a topic of law.

20. Legal periodical citators can allow you to determine whether the article has been considered in a _____ _____ .

CHAPTER 12

LOOSELEAF SERVICES

CHAPTER OBJECTIVES

Upon completion of this chapter, you should be able to accomplish the following competencies:

- Describe a looseleaf service.
- Discuss the primary benefits of looseleaf services.
- Describe the types of looseleaf services.
- Distinguish a looseleaf service from other types of legal research resources.
- Explain how looseleaf services are properly used as authorities.
- Explain how a looseleaf service can be used as a finding tool for primary authorities.
- Identify those subjects likely to be addressed by looseleaf services.
- Describe the process of researching looseleaf services.
- Explain how looseleaf services are updated and validated.
- Describe the variations of indexing for looseleaf services.

Looseleaf Services As A Resource

looseleaf service
Periodic publication that can be updated through replacement pages. Usually prepared for subjects of law that change frequently.

commentary
Discussion of various aspects regarding a particular concept or topic.

The **looseleaf service** is a unique legal research resource. It combines primary and secondary authorities into a constantly updated **commentary** on law. Each looseleaf publication is dedicated to a particular topic of law or source of authority. The topics that looseleaf services usually address are those that are heavily litigated, legislated and regulated and subject to frequent change or interpretation. One such area that is very heavily covered by looseleaf service publications is tax. With tax laws and regulations constantly subject to change and interpretation and the vast array of circumstances that affect how tax laws are applied, the public and professionals affected (e.g., lawyers, accountants, and businesspeople) are very interested in knowing the very latest information about tax law developments. Thus, the looseleaf, with its perpetual and frequent updating service, is an especially useful tool. Other similar topics are also popular because of this advantage.

Although each looseleaf publication is tailored to the specific characteristics and needs of a current publication for the specific topic, some basic components are generally present. As previously indicated, a looseleaf service is often a combination of primary and secondary authority. The primary authority—statutes, regulations, and selected judicial opinions relevant to the topic—is included as a means of consolidating relevant laws in a single location. It is also quite often accompanied by commentary on the meaning and application of the legal standards and any variations that different circumstances might produce. The commentary is especially helpful to the novice researcher because quite often the law is so complex that it is difficult to adequately break down and interpret. However, even the experienced researcher can reap benefits from the commentary because it often saves the reader a great deal of time, as the author of the commentary has already done much of the work of legal analysis of the standards.

In addition to providing the actual reprint of many of the relevant primary authorities, the looseleaf service frequently provides citations of additional relevant primary and secondary authorities that are not fully reproduced in the looseleaf. This feature often allows the researcher to use the looseleaf as a stepping stone into additional research resources.

☐ ASSIGNMENT 12.1

Using Exhibit 12.1, identify whether each of the authorities designated by a circled letter (e.g., a, b, c) is primary or secondary authority. If the item is primary authority, indicate what type of primary authority.

Updating

Perhaps the most unique and advantageous characteristic of the looseleaf service is the updating system. While some looseleafs are updated annually (much like other types of legal research resources), most often, the updates

EXHIBIT 12.1 Sample Pages from BNA's Americans with Disabilities Act Manual.
Copyright by the Bureau of National Affairs, Inc. (800-372-1033).

(5) New direct connections to commercial, retail, or residential facilities shall, to the maximum extent feasible, have an accessible route complying with 4.3 from the point of connection to boarding platforms and all transportation system elements used by the public. Any elements provided to facilitate future direct connections shall be on an accessible route connecting boarding platforms and all transportation system elements used by the public.

10.3.3 Existing Facilities: Alterations.

(1) For the purpose of complying with 4.1.6(2) Alterations to an Area Containing a Primary Function, an area of primary function shall be as defined by applicable provisions of 49 CFR 37.43(c) (Department of Transportation's ADA Rule) or 28 CFR 36.403 (Department of Justice's ADA Rule).

10.4. Airports.

10.4.1 New Construction.

(1) Elements such as ramps, elevators or other vertical circulation devices, ticketing areas, security checkpoints, or passenger waiting areas shall be placed to minimize the distance which wheelchair users and other persons who cannot negotiate steps may have to travel compared to the general public.

(2) The circulation path, including an accessible entrance and an accessible route, for persons with disabilities shall, to the maximum extent practicable, coincide with the circulation path for the general public. Where the circulation path is different, directional signage complying with 4.30.1, 4.30.2, 4.30.3 and 4.30.5 shall be provided which indicates the location of the nearest accessible entrance and its accessible route.

(3) Ticketing areas shall permit persons with disabilities to obtain a ticket and check baggage and shall comply with 7.2.

(4) Where public pay telephones are provided, and at least one is at an interior location, a public text telephone shall be provided in compliance with 4.31.9. Additionally, if four or more public pay telephones are located

in any of the following locations, at least one public text telephone shall also be provided in that location:

(a) a main terminal outside the security areas;
(b) a concourse within the security areas; or
(c) a baggage claim area in a terminal.

Compliance with this section constitutes compliance with section 4.1.3(17)(c).

(5) Baggage check-in and retrieval systems shall be on an accessible route complying with 4.3, and shall have space immediately adjacent complying with 4.2.4. If unattended security barriers are provided, at least one gate shall comply with 4.13. Gates which must be pushed open by wheelchair or mobility aid users shall have a smooth continuous surface extending from 2 inches above the floor to 27 inches above the floor.

(6) Terminal information systems which broadcast information to the general public through a public address system shall provide a means to provide the same or equivalent information to persons with a hearing loss or who are deaf. Such methods may include, but are not limited to, visual paging systems using video monitors and computer technology. For persons with certain types of hearing loss such methods may include, but are not limited to, an assistive listening system complying with 4.33.7.

(7) Where clocks are provided for use by the general public the clock face shall be uncluttered so that its elements are clearly visible. Hands, numerals, and/or digits shall contrast with their background either light-on-dark or dark-on-light. Where clocks are mounted overhead, numerals and/or digits shall comply with 4.30.3. Clocks shall be placed in uniform locations throughout the facility to the maximum extent practicable.

(8) Security Systems. [Reserved]

10.5 Boat and Ferry Docks.
[Reserved]

are issued monthly or weekly. This provides a much more current source of information than the standard judicial report, statutory publication, or updated secondary resource. Another updating feature is the method by which the current text is supplemented. As you are well aware by now, most updating is done through paperback, hardbound, or pocket part supplements. This requires you as the researcher to check the original publication and all current supplements each time you consult the resource. However, as the name implies, the looseleaf service is typically contained in a binder that can be opened for insertion or removal of pages. This allows obsolete information

EXHIBIT 12.1   Continued

that individuals with disabilities receive the benefits and services of the program.

Curb Ramps

Public entities that are responsible for streets, roads, or walkways must prepare a schedule for providing curb ramps where pedestrian walkways cross curbs.

TAM
p. 90:0716

First priority must be given to walkways used by public employees and those serving state and local government offices and facilities, transportation, and places of public accommodation, and then to walkways serving other purposes. The schedule for providing ramps must be included as part of the public entity's transition plan (see p. 25:0008).

Historic Preservation Programs

Historic preservation programs are those conducted by a public entity that have preservation of historic properties as a primary purpose.

28 CFR §35.150 (a)(2)
p. 70:2031
TAM
p. 90:0716

Historic properties are places that are listed or eligible for listing in the National Register of Historic Places or those designated as historic under state or local law.

Public entities must give priority to methods that provide physical access to individuals with disabilities, so that they may experience the historic property itself. However, no action is required that would threaten or destroy the historic significance of the property. If physical access cannot be provided because of this special limitation, or because an undue financial burden or fundamental alteration would result, the public entity must undertake alternative measures to achieve accessibility.

Ⓒ —— For example, if installing an elevator in an historic house, which is maintained as a museum, would destroy architectural features of historic significance, the public entity could provide an audio-visual display of the contents of the upstairs rooms in an accessible location on the first floor.

Ⓓ **Accessibility Standards**

All public facilities on which construction or alteration began after Jan. 26, 1992, must be "readily accessible and usable" by individuals with disabilities.

28 CFR §35.151(c)
p. 70:2032
TAM
p. 90:0717

Ⓔ —— This means that the facility must be designed, constructed, or altered in strict compliance with a design standard. Public entities may choose either the Uniform Federal Accessibility Standards (UFAS) or the ADA Accessibility Guidelines for Buildings and Facilities (ADAAG)(p. 70:0201). Many public entities that are recipients of federal funds are already subject to UFAS, which is the accessibility standard referenced

4-92   15

to be removed and new or additional information to be added. Thus, the looseleaf service is always current, and the time required to research a topic may be shortened.

Because of the extensive and frequent updating, many subscribers to numerous looseleaf services (lawyers, accountants, real estate firms, etc.) often employ individuals who have no other duty than to remove and replace pages as the updates arrive. Each update contains a directory to indicate which, if any, pages are to be removed and the proper location for any new pages. Because the pages are frequently removed and replaced, the paper quality is

EXHIBIT 12.2
Sample Page of
CCH Medicare
and Medicaid
Guide.
Published and
copyrighted by
CCH,
INCORPORATED,
2700 Lake Cook
Rd., Riverwoods,
IL 60015.
Reproduced with
permission.

28,882   New Developments   683   1-92

in 1978 U.S. Code Cong. & Admin. News 5787, 5815. At the time of the Bankruptcy Code's passage, Congress was aware that its prior enactments, such as the FTCA, had already prescribed certain conditions for the government's waiver of sovereign immunity. The legislative history of section 106 indicates that Congress meant to alter this landscape by subjecting the government to an automatic exposure to liability as the price of its participation in the distribution of the bankruptcy estate. *See id.*

AFFIRMED.

[¶ 39,749]   Eric Kranz, M.D. v. The Inspector General.

HHS Departmental Appeals Board, Civil Remedies Division, No. CR148, Aug. 1, 1991.

Medicare/Medicaid: Exclusion for Program-Related Abuses

Fraud and abuse—Exclusion for program-related abuses—Revocation of license—Determining "professional competence, professional performance, or financial integrity".— Failure of a physician to advise a state licensing board that another state had denied his application to practice medicine is an act of dishonesty relating to the physician's professional competence as that term is used in the exclusion law. The physician was licensed to practice medicine in the District of Columbia and in the States of Pennsylvania and West Virginia. West Virginia revoked the physician's license after finding that he had engaged in unprofessional conduct for failing to disclose that the State of Ohio had denied his license application. Ohio denied the physician's license application after finding that he (1) offered to sell the answers to the Medical Council of Canada's examination to applicants planning to take the examination, (2) falsely stated in his application that he had been licensed to practice by the Medical Council of Canada, and (3) had previously been denied a license to practice in Pennsylvania and in Oklahoma.

The term "professional performance" is not defined in the exclusion law. However, that term plainly subsumes elements of professional deportment which include honesty and integrity in the discharge of professional duties. A provider's professional duties include compliance with applicable state laws and regulations concerning licensure and license renewals. A requirement by a state licensing board that a provider honestly and fully report the status of his licensure applications to the board is an integral element of professional performance.

See ¶ 13,927.67.

Fraud and abuse—Exclusion for program-related abuses—Revocation of license—Reasonableness of period of exclusion.—The Inspector General's determination excluding a physician from program participation until his license to practice was restored in West Virginia was unreasonable because the determination did not bear a rational relationship to the remedial purpose of the exclusion law. West Virginia revoked the physician's license after concluding that he had engaged in unprofessional conduct by failing to disclose that the State of Ohio had denied his license application.

The remedial purpose of the exclusion law is to enable the Secretary to protect federally funded health care programs and their beneficiaries and recipients from individuals and entities who have proven by their misconduct that they are untrustworthy. Even though the physician's explanations for the events which resulted in disciplinary actions by several state licensing boards were glib and self-serving, it cannot be concluded that he actually lied in his testimony. It is conceivable, from the license board revocation decision, that West Virginia might never determine to restore the physician's license. Both Pennsylvania and the District of Columbia have reviewed essentially the same record and have concluded that the physician is sufficiently trustworthy to be permitted to practice in those jurisdictions. Accordingly, the remedial purposes of the law will be served by an exclusion from program participation for one year.

See ¶ 13,927.65.

[Text of Decision]

KESSEL, Administrative Law Judge: On September 24, 1990, the Inspector General (I.G.) notified Petitioner that he was being excluded from participation in the Medicare and State health care programs.[1] The I.G. told Petitioner that he was being excluded because his license to practice medicine in West Virginia had been revoked by that state's licensing authority. The I.G. cited section 1128(b)(4) of the Social Secu-

[1] "State health care program" is defined by section 1128(h) of the Social Security Act to cover three types of federally-financed health care programs, including Medi- caid. I use the term "Medicaid" hereafter to represent all State health care programs from which Petitioner was excluded.

¶ 39,749   ©1992, Commerce Clearing House, Inc.

typically not as good as that found in hardbound publications. Also, the pages are hole punched (usually for three- or five-ring binders) and have a tendency to tear. Consequently, the entire contents of a looseleaf are periodically moved into what is commonly known as a transfer binder. Quite often a transfer

binder is prepared annually, and an entirely new and current set of pages is issued for the looseleaf, which begins the updating service over again. If you are researching in a looseleaf and the information you are seeking is possibly old or no longer effective, you can consult the transfer binders. However, all current information will be included in the current looseleaf publication.

LOOSELEAF SERVICES AS AN AUTHORITY

The looseleaf service is not commonly seen within the context of published judicial opinions, because looseleaf services are not the properly cited source for primary authority and the commentary is frequently of less influence than many other types of secondary authority. You may, however, frequently see looseleafs relied upon in legal documents presented by parties to the court because they are often the only source available for the most current pronouncements and commentary on legal standards. However, the primary function of the looseleaf is one of explanation to the researcher and as a finding tool for other authority that can be properly cited by both the parties and the courts.

As discussed in previous chapters, primary authority should be cited by referring to the official publication. Even if the primary authority has not yet been codified or published in an official reporter, the reference should be made to that source or the source of the authority (e.g., Public Law 94-1006). This is true even though the authority may be reprinted in part or whole within a looseleaf service. The reason is that the looseleaf is not considered an official publication for primary authority. This is because it is an incomplete repository of the authority and has the central purpose of serving as a commercial publication of secondary authority (i.e., commentary on changes in primary authority).

☐ ASSIGNMENT 12.2

Examine Exhibit 12.3 and select and cite each primary authority and any secondary authorities that might be listed that are from sources other than the looseleaf.

ORGANIZATION AND RESEARCH

While each looseleaf is organized in a manner suited to the type of material contained, certain basic elements are typically found as part of the internal components. Because looseleafs are often multivolume sets, a common feature is consecutive pagination; that is, each volume is numbered and the pages within each volume are a continuation from the last page number of the preceding volume rather than the more traditional approach of beginning each volume with page number one. Also, each topic within the looseleaf and

EXHIBIT 12.3   A Sample Page From the *U.S. Law Week General Law* Looseleaf Service by BNA.
Reprinted with permission from *The United States Law Week.* Copyright by the Bureau of National Affairs, Inc. (800-372-1033).

The United States
Law Week

Court Decisions
Agency Rulings

June 30, 1992   •   THE BUREAU OF NATIONAL AFFAIRS, INC., WASHINGTON, D.C.   •   Volume 60, No.51

NEW COURT DECISIONS
Digests of Significant Opinions Not Yet Generally Reported

Attorneys

RIGHT TO PRACTICE—

Law firm's separation agreement that denies termination compensation to departing members who, within one year of departure, represent firm's clients or solicit firm's lawyers or staff is void in New Jersey as indirect restriction on practice of law.

(*Jacob v. Norris, McLaughlin & Marcus*, NJ SupCt, No. A-67/68, 5/28/92)

The two plaintiffs and an associate left the defendant law firm (a professional corporation) to establish their own firm. They took with them a number of associates, a paralegal, and clients who had generated about $500,000 in annual billings for the firm. The plaintiffs were paid their equity interest in the firm under a Buy-Sell Agreement. However, they were denied termination compensation under the firm's Service Termination Agreement, which denies such compensation to members who perform legal services for any firm client within one year of departure or who solicit any lawyer or paraprofessional to leave the firm.

Contracts that violate the Rules of Professional Conduct violate public policy and are unenforceable. Any provision, whether direct or indirect, that restricts a lawyer's post-termination practice contravenes Rule 5.6. The rule's purpose is to ensure the freedom of clients to select counsel of their choice, and it precludes commercial arrangements that interfere with that goal.

Outright prohibitions on the practice of law are clearly forbidden. Indirect restrictions on the practice of law, such as the financial disincentives at issue in this case, likewise violate both the language and spirit of Rule 5.6. Any provision penalizing an attorney for undertaking certain representations restricts the right of a lawyer to practice law within the meaning of the rule. By forcing lawyers to choose between compensation and continued service to their clients, financial disincentive provisions may encourage lawyers to give up their clients, thereby interfering with the lawyer-client relationship and, more importantly, with clients' free choice of counsel. Those provisions thus cause indirectly the same objec-

tionable restraints on the free practice of law as more direct restrictive covenants.

The defendant firm argues that this court should distinguish between agreements that require departing lawyers to forfeit their equity interest in a firm and those that merely deprive them of additional compensation unrelated to their vested interest. Regardless of whether the compensation in question represents "earned" or "additional" compensation, to condition payment on refraining from practice violates the rule. The operative question is not what income the departing partner has a "right" to receive, it is the effect of the terms of payment on the lawyer's decision to decline or accept those clients who wish to choose him or her as counsel.

The firm argues its agreement presents a reasonable economic arrangement that recognizes the detriment to the firm when a former member competes with it. This argument both ignores the underlying meaning of the rule and misrepresents the practical effects of the financial disincentive provisions. The disciplinary rules govern the practice of law based on ethical standards, not commercial desires. The commercial concerns of the firm and of the departing lawyer are secondary to the need to preserve client choice. The more lenient test used to determine the enforceability of a restrictive covenant in a commercial setting is not appropriate in the legal context.

The court is not unmindful of the potential detrimental effect of the departure of a partner or partners on those remaining. In computing a withdrawing partner's equity interest in the former firm, accounting for the effect of the partner's departure on the firm's value is not unreasonable. Although the departing partners always have a right to receive the value of their capital accounts, in computing the value of any additional interest they have in the firm, the value they contributed can be offset by the decrease in the firm's value their departure causes. Good will is an element of the value of a partner's interest in a law firm, and can be translated into prospective earnings. Accordingly, if a partner's departure will result in a decrease in the probability of a client's return and a consequent decrease in prospective earnings, that departure may

decrease the value of the firm's good will. It would not be inappropriate therefore for law partners to take that specific effect into account in determining the shares due a departing partner.

In an issue of first impression in New Jersey, the firm argues that the provision discouraging partners from contacting the firm's professional and paraprofessional staff does not violate Rule 5.6. However, the "practice of law" includes not only lawyers' interactions with their clients but also their interactions with colleagues. Agreements discouraging departing lawyers from contacting those lawyers with whom they would like to associate violate Rule 5.6. Restrictive agreements have a similarly unfair effect on paraprofessionals.

Lastly, the firm argues that equitable principles should bar the plaintiffs from receiving the agreement's benefits. True, the plaintiffs violated Rule 5.6 as did the firm by making this agreement, and the plaintiffs will get a "windfall" by receiving compensation despite their violation. But the issue is not simply which party is more or less innocent, but which outcome best serves the public interest.—Garibaldi, J.

Banking and Finance

INSURANCE SERVICES—

Section 92 of National Bank Act implicitly bars national banks located in towns with more than 5,000 inhabitants from selling insurance, including title insurance, and "incidental" powers granted banks under Section 24 (Seventh) do not alter this outcome.

(*American Land Title Association v. Clarke*, CA 2, No. 91-6235, 6/15/92)

Two title insurance associations brought suit against the Office of the Comptroller of the Currency, seeking to void an OCC decision permitting a bank to engage in the title insurance agency business. The district court upheld OCC's determination.

The associations argue that the district court erred in upholding the OCC's view that Section 92 of the National Bank Act,

the many subtopics and further specific breakdown of subject matter are assigned section or paragraph numbers. Some older publications also employ a decimal number system to further subdivide information. Thus, when you are consulting a looseleaf, it is important that you look for the section number within the proper section or subtopic, or the information you locate may have little resemblance to what you are seeking. Because the topics commonly addressed in looseleafs are usually so complex, you must be quite specific in your research and the section numbers you consult to find exact information relevant to a particular question.

The specific method by which information is contained in a looseleaf depends in large part on the publisher. Unlike the uniformity of the national reporter system or the common practices used in arranging statutory compilations, looseleafs are put together by a variety of publishers. And because there are so many possible combinations of content, such as regulatory, statutory, judicial, commentary, and forms, the need for a logical arrangement is somewhat dictated by the amount and variety of information presented. More extensive publications often contain a "How to Use" section at the beginning of the publication to describe organization and explain how to access specific information.

One of the most prolific publishers of looseleaf services is an organization known as Commerce Clearing House, or CCH. You will frequently see CCH black-with-gold-letter binders with the letters "CCH" in law libraries and other types of businesses that subscribe to looseleaf services. Because CCH publishes so many looseleafs, its indexing system is very well developed and defined. For purposes of illustration, that indexing system is examined in the paragraphs that follow. If you encounter another looseleaf publication (e.g., Matthew Bender), you will find that the indexing system probably has the same logical pattern as that of CCH publications.

The indexing system for a looseleaf is somewhat more complex than a standard subject index. Quite often, the index is so extensive that it is maintained in a separate index binder. This is especially common in multi-volume looseleaf services. Some looseleafs also provide a separate smaller index for each major section or for each volume. Because looseleaf publications often consist of many thousands of pages, there may be a shortened index (e.g., CCH's Rapid Finder Index). These shortened indexes precede the longer index and do not contain as much detail. Rather, they are confined to major headings. The topical or subject index compares to other subject indexes you have used in the past. The beginning of each index is a description of the meaning of references. Most often these references are to sections rather than to page numbers. Because the looseleaf contains so many sections and subparagraphs, the numbers are often quite lengthy. But keep in mind that the page numbers are only a guide to the volumes and consecutive section numbers. Quite often the individual volumes contain separate tabs on page dividers that signal major sections. The binding of the volumes often contains descriptive information that indicates the sections or headings contained within. A table of contents is generally included at the opening of each volume.

When looking at a page from a looseleaf service, be sure you are looking at the section number rather than the page number, as both will appear in the margin. By using the index to identify the major section and any specific subparagraph, you can then locate the proper section and specific point of

EXHIBIT 12.4   Sample Pages from the Environment Reporter Looseleaf Service by BNA.
Reprinted with permission from the *Environment Reporter.* Copyright by the Bureau of National Affairs, Inc.
(800-372-1033).

ENVIRONMENT REPORTER

Current Developments

A weekly review of pollution control and related environmental management problems

Volume 25, Number 10   THE BUREAU OF NATIONAL AFFAIRS, INC.   July 8, 1994

TWO-MONTH
INDEX-SUMMARY
COVERING VOLUME 25, Nos. 1-8
PAGES 1-432
MAY 6, 1994 through JUNE 24, 1994

> **FILE behind white Index tab in Current Developments binder. For material in other binders, see MASTER INDEX in Federal Laws binder, and MINING MASTER INDEX in Mining Binder No. 1.**

How to Use This Index

This topical index provides references to the material in **ENVIRONMENT REPORTER CURRENT DEVELOPMENTS.**

The index is arranged alphabetically word-by-word. For example, the heading ENVIRONMENTAL PROTECTION AGENCY precedes the heading ENVIRONMENTALIST GROUPS. Numbers are treated as if spelled out, e.g., 1993 will appear in the "Ns." Acronyms other than those taken from the EPA Glossary of Environmental Terms and Acronym List are explained within the index.

Editor's Notes [*Ed. Note:*] appear under some headings to explain the scope of the heading and, where appropriate, refer the researcher to related headings.

Numbers in parentheses after boldfaced chemical substance names are Chemical Abstracts Service (CAS) Registry Numbers.

Cross references link related information within the index as illustrated below:

LAND DISPOSAL OF HAZARDOUS WASTE
Ignitable, corrosive, and reactive wastes,
  see Third-third rule, *this heading* ◄————————— | Referring to another entry under the same main heading |

MOTOR VEHICLES
Commuting, *see* TRANSPORTATION CONTROL PLANS ◄——— | Referring to another main heading |

LAND USE
Future use, *see* SUPERFUND, *subheading:* Future use of sites ◄— | Referring to specific entry under another main heading |

A cumulative index is issued every 2 months, with a final index every 12 months.

ALSO IN THIS INDEX

See TABLE OF MATERIALS PUBLISHED IN FULL TEXT, SPEAKERS AND AUTHORS, PUBLICATIONS, *and* TABLE OF CASES

ANALYSIS AND PERSPECTIVE

Corporate environmental compliance program guidance, 325

Superfund, federal courts crisis, case study, 139

A

ABOVE-GROUND STORAGE TANKS
Abandoned sites, Fla. cleanup program outlined, 324
Control tightening
—Introduced bills, *see* LEGISLATION, FEDERAL, HR 1360, S 588

—Regulatory and legislative options, EPA recommendations, conference, 55

Hazardous substances, N.Y. approves rules, 28

Hazardous waste organic air emissions, draft RCRA rule due in May, 46

HON (hazardous organic NESHAP) rule, medium tanks must meet "higher floor interpretation," EPA final rule, 276

EXHIBIT 12.4 Continued

ER-CURRENT DEVELOPMENTS

Current Developments

ENVIRONMENT REPORT

No claims have been settled by Exxon since 1990, Coe said. The amounts paid by the company to fishermen in 1989 are far less than the losses they incurred since then, he added. Much of the trial's second phase will involve debate over how much the fisheries were damaged, Coe said. This is an area of much dispute between Exxon and the plaintiffs.

Other evidence will come from representatives of the many fishermen involved in the suit, Coe said. Declining catches and fishery closures have cut into incomes, and drops in fish prices have hurt more, he said. These developments have led some 300 people to sell their fishing licenses, he said.

If the jury decides punitive damages are warranted, those damages will be set in Phase III of the trial, Coe said. This may entail a substantial sum, because Exxon is so large that a fine that "sounds like a lot to the public" could easily be absorbed by the company, Coe said.

Lynch painted a different picture in his opening statement: "The plaintiffs and their lawyers are interested in recovering more than full and fair compensation, much more. They are asking you, in the guise of the interest of protecting the public or somehow promoting oil spill prevention or something, to award them very large sums of money which they pocket."

"Unfortunately, in all our activities, even judging, mistakes are made, errors are made, and not every mistake, not every error justifies an award of punitive damages," he said.

Radioactive Waste

COMMITTEE PASSES BILL TO BAN OCEAN DUMPING; LOW-LEVEL RADIOACTIVITY OK FOR DREDGED MATERIAL

The House Merchant Marine and Fisheries Committee approved a measure May 11 that would ban dumping of all types of radioactive waste into oceans.

The bill (HR 3982), would amend Title I of the Marine Protection Research and Sanctuaries Act of 1972, known as the Ocean Dumping Act, to bring it into conformity with an international agreement banning the dumping of all radioactive wastes.

Russia is the only country in the world with no prohibition on ocean disposal of radioactive waste, he said.

"We want them to work with us so eventually they'll take the same position," he said.

According to the committee statement, the State Department and the Commerce Department support the bill.

Solid Waste

PUBLIC MEETINGS PLANNED ON ALTERNATIVES TO GROUND WATER MONITORING FOR LANDFILLS

The Environmental Protection Agency May 6 announced a series of public meetings to gather information on possible alternatives to requirements for ground water monitoring at certain small municipal solid waste landfills.

The agency said it wants comments on alternatives to costly ground water monitoring requirements for small municipal solid waste landfills that must still meet stringent rules adopted by the agency in 1991 (40 CFR Part 258).

The final rule established minimum criteria for landfills, including location restrictions, facility design and operating criteria, ground water monitoring requirements, corrective action requirements, financial assurance requirements, and closure and post-closure care requirements. In addition, it provided an exemption for small landfills from certain requirements, including the ground water monitoring provisions. To qualify for the exemption, the landfill had to meet certain requirements, including accepting less than 20 tons of waste per day annually and exhibiting no evidence of ground water contamination.

However, the exemption for ground water monitoring for small facilities was vacated by a federal appeals court following an environmental group's challenge (*Sierra Club v. EPA*, 992 F.2d 337, 36 ERC 1819, CA DC, 1993).

Effective Date Delayed

EPA said it issued a final rule delaying the effective date of the landfill criteria on Oct. 1, 1993, and rescinded the small

reference through the page dividers and subject tabs. Be sure, too, that you are within the proper major heading or volume of the looseleaf service. In some instances, if the looseleaf is tied to a legislative or regulatory subject, the subject numbers correspond to statutes or regulations. This cannot be counted upon, however, and you should confine your research method to the indexing system prepared for the particular service.

If you are quite familiar with the subject or the looseleaf service, you may obtain some benefit from the table of contents (and sometimes each heading) found at the beginning of each volume. However, these tend to be more general and are not especially helpful in locating specific pronouncements. Following the table of contents may be a correlator, a very brief summary of the legal standards, with corresponding section numbers. The numbers enable you to scan the correlator and then go directly to a point of reference.

Many looseleaf services also publish a supplemental binder even though the existing pages are updated regularly. This serves a valuable purpose. The supplemental binder typically contains information about significant additions or changes to the law that can be helpful when you are not well versed in the subject and may not know all of the sections that are relevant. Secondly, the supplemental binder is a means to keep yourself updated quite easily by regularly checking this portion of the looseleaf for reference to changes that are discussed more fully within the context of the other more comprehensive volumes.

When conducting research in a looseleaf, remember that the service's basic purpose is one of commentary and as a finding tool to locate relevant authority. Consequently, you will not typically cite a looseleaf service. However, you should still, as always, validate any authority you obtain from the looseleaf (e.g., new legislation).

IIII➤ STRATEGY

Researching in a Looseleaf Service

1. If you are uncertain as to which looseleaf publication to consult for your query, go to the card catalog subject index or ask the librarian for the most pertinent looseleaf publication.
2. If the looseleaf contains a "How to Use" section, consult it to familiarize yourself with the organization. For example, is information referenced by page or by section?
3. Using the index, your relevant terms should lead you to the location of specific information. An alternative is to use the correlator (if any) following the table of contents to locate information on particular points of law.
4. Consult the supplemental binder (if any) for recent changes.

CHAPTER SUMMARY

The focus of this chapter has been on the maximum use and benefit of looseleaf services. Looseleafs are the only publication that routinely combine legislative, judicial, regulatory, and secondary authority into a single format.

Because of its physical housing (looseleaf temporary binders), the looseleaf publication is generally more current than many other authorities. However, the looseleaf is neither an official nor an exhaustive source of primary authority and thus is not the source of choice for citation. The looseleaf can, however, through its commentary, provide information to the researcher about the topic, any rationale and background, and additional sources of research. The looseleaf services are most often published for heavily legislated, regulated, and litigated subjects of law. As a result, the publications often are quite complex and consist of tens of thousands of pages. A variety of indexing methods makes the information within the looseleaf manageable. However, information that you locate and intend to rely upon should be validated through the use of an appropriate citator.

Key Terms

commentary   looseleaf service

Self-Test

MULTIPLE CHOICE

1. The looseleaf service is designed to combine _____ and _____ authorities.
   a) primary, secondary
   b) mandatory, precedential
   c) primary, mandatory
   d) mandatory, secondary
2. Each looseleaf publication is dedicated to a particular _____ or _____ .
   a) reporter, periodical
   b) regulation, statute
   c) topic of law, source of authority
   d) restatement, citator
3. The topics addressed by looseleaf services are those that are heavily _____ and subject to frequent change or interpretation.
   a) litigated
   b) legislated
   c) regulated
   d) all of the above
4. The _____ in a looseleaf service is especially helpful to the novice researcher because quite often the law is so complex that it is difficult to adequately break down and interpret.
   a) numbering system
   b) volumes and tab dividers
   c) "How to Use" section
   d) none of the above
5. The looseleaf service also frequently provides _____ of additional relevant primary and secondary authorities that are not fully reproduced in the looseleaf. This feature often allows you as the researcher to use the looseleaf as a stepping stone into additional research resources.
   a) citations
   b) judicial opinions
   c) statutes
   d) none of the above

TRUE/FALSE

____ 6. The most unique and advantageous characteristic of the looseleaf service is the updating system.
____ 7. The looseleaf service updating system is usually much more current

than the standard supplemented authority or updated secondary resource.

_____ 8. Periodically, the contents of the looseleaf are moved into what is commonly known as an annual report.

_____ 9. The looseleaf service is commonly seen as a citation of authority within the context of published judicial opinions because they are the properly cited source for secondary authority.

_____10. You may frequently see looseleafs relied upon in legal documents presented by parties to the court because they are often the only source available for the most current pronouncements and commentary on legal standards.

FILL–IN THE BLANKS

11. Because looseleafs are often multivolume sets, a common feature is consecutive _____ .

12. Each topic within the looseleaf and the many subtopics and further specific breakdown of subject matter are assigned _____ .

13. The _____ _____ for a looseleaf is somewhat more complex than a standard subject index because of the combined types of primary and secondary authority.

14. The index is often maintained in a separate _____ _____ .

15. A shortened index may precede the longer index and does not contain as much _____ .

16. Most indexes provide references to _____ rather than page numbers.

17. Individual volumes may contain separate tabs on page dividers that signal _____ _____ .

18. The binding of the volumes often contain descriptive information that indicates the _____ or _____ contained within.

19. A _____ is a very brief summary of the legal standards, with corresponding section numbers.

20. Many looseleaf services also publish a _____ binder of new information even though the existing pages are updated regularly.

CHAPTER 13

REFERENCE BOOKS

CHAPTER OBJECTIVES

Upon completion of this chapter, you should be able to accomplish the following competencies:

- Describe a reference book.

- Discuss the primary benefits of reference books.

- Describe the types of reference books.

- Distinguish a reference book from other types of legal research resources.

- Explain how reference books are properly used as authorities.

- Explain how a reference book can be used as a finding tool for primary authorities.

- Identify those subjects likely to be addressed by reference books.

- Describe the process of researching reference books.

- Explain how reference books are updated and validated.

- Describe the variations of indexing for reference books.

REFERENCE BOOKS AS A RESOURCE

While the general term **reference book** can encompass a vast array of subjects, the scope of this chapter is limited to those reference materials not addressed specifically in other portions of the text and those that provide assistance to the legal researcher and professional. A reference book can include anything that provides basic information on a subject (See Exhibit 13.1). In the law library, however, the reference section is usually one of the smaller collections of publications. Most of the law library consists of reports, reporters, digests, statutory compilations, regulatory materials, looseleaf services, citators, and finding tools. Certain reference materials, such as legal encyclopedias, treatises, and periodicals, are also commonplace. True reference books are often limited, however, because these books are secondary authority and often much less influential than established treatises or primary authorities. This does not mean that you should exclude the reference section of the library from your research. To the contrary, you will very often find that this collection is the most likely site for answers to specific questions about practical situations. The types of books included in the reference section not previously discussed in depth include casebooks, general subject books on various topics of law, and form books (See Exhibit 13.2).

As mentioned in chapter one, casebooks consist of selected cases on a topic and brief commentary on the rulings in the opinions. General subject books are much like those found in any ordinary library on a given topic. In the law library, these books may be quite general or they may give specific information on a particular type of case, area of law, or jurisdiction.

A source frequently consulted in the work of the legal professional is the **form book.** Form books are published on virtually every aspect of practice and save the legal professional from the task of reinventing the wheel. They provide basic forms for legal documents, pleadings, jury instructions, deposi-

reference book
Publication of general information on a topic.

form book
Publication of commonly used documents. In law, form books often contain a variety of frequently used pleadings or other documents (e.g., contracts).

EXHIBIT 13.1
A Reference Book.

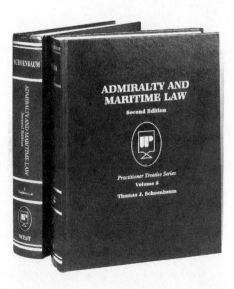

**EXHIBIT 13.2
M.Bender, Personal Injury
Litigation.**

**EXHIBIT 13.3
A Reference/Form
Book.**

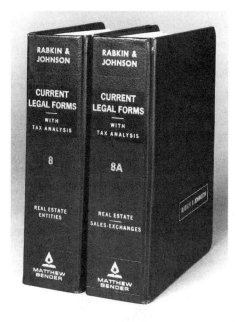

tion questions, and other repetitive steps in litigation (See Exhibit 13.4). While every situation is unique, and although even forms from these books often require some tailoring, the forms do provide the basis for a sound document or procedure by including the necessary basics common to all similar situations whether it be a real estate purchase agreement or questions for a deposition in a train accident case. Some form books consist strictly of forms, while others combine commentary on general aspects with specific procedures for a particular topic of litigation.

☐ ASSIGNMENT 13.1

Explain how each of the exhibits 13.1-13.4 could be helpful in practice.

EXHIBIT 13.4   Federal Jury Practice and Instructions.
Copyright 1994 West Publishing Company (1-800-328-9352).

§ 43A.03   INSTRUCTIONS—SPECIFIC CRIMES   Pt. 3

the statute is not limited to perjury as defined by statute but includes false testimony or declaration before a grand jury or court.)

Fifth Circuit

Perjury is an essential element of subornation of perjury. United States v. Brumley, 560 F.2d 1268, 1278 n. 5 (5th Cir.1977).

Eighth Circuit

Form Jury Instruction

"The crime of suborning perjury, as charged in [Count _____ of] the indictment, has three essential elements, which are:

One, the defendant voluntarily and intentionally persuaded (name of witness) to commit perjury;

Two, the defendant did so with the intent that (name of witness) would deceive the [court] [jury]; and

Three, (name of witness) committed a perjury in that:

(a) He testified under oath or affirmation at (describe proceeding, e.g., the trial of United States v. Doe) that [insert false testimony];

(b) the testimony given was false;

(c) at the time he testified, the witness knew his testimony was false;

(d) the witness gave such testimony voluntarily and intentionally."

Manual of Model Criminal Jury Instructions for the District Courts of the Eighth Circuit, Instruction No. 6.18.1622 (1994). The Eighth Circuit Committee refers the user to its Comments at § 6.18.1621 and cites Segal v. United States, 246 F.2d 814, 816 (8th Cir.), cert. denied, 355 U.S. 894, 78 S.Ct. 269, 2 L.Ed.2d 192 (1957).

Ninth Circuit

"The defendant is charged in [Count _____ of] the indictment with subornation of perjury in violation of Section 1622 of Title 18 of the United States Code. In order for the defendant to be found guilty of that charge, the government must prove each of the following elements beyond a reasonable doubt:

First, the defendant persuaded _____ to testify falsely before [*insert name of tribunal*];

Second, _____ falsely testified under oath that _____; and

Third, _____ knew the testimony was false."

Manual of Model Criminal Jury Instructions for the Ninth Circuit, Instruction No. 8.29B (1992).

146

§ 3:117   **Premises**

§ 3:117   Elevator—Defendant to Deponent

TOTAL CLIENT-SERVICE LIBRARY® REFERENCES

Am Jur:
  26 Am Jur 2d, Elevators and Escalators §§ 1 et seq.

ALR Annotations:
  Products liability: elevators. 7 ALR4th 852.

Auto-Cite®:
  Any case citation pertinent to this material can be checked for form, parallel references, later history, and annotation references through the Auto-Cite computer research system.

1. Elevator involved in occurrence
   (a) location
       (1) building
       (2) floors served
       (3) distance of shaft from fixed objects and other shafts
       (4) whether automatic
   (b) operator
       (1) physical description
       (2) name and address
       (3) employee number
   (c) plaintiff's prior experience with elevator
       (1) number of previous times used (annually)
2. Description of occurrence
   (a) location of plaintiff
       (1) floor
       (2) distance from fixed objects (feet)
       (3) position of body
   (b) position of elevator or doors
       (1) floor at or above
       (2) distance above floor (feet, inches)
   (c) movement of plaintiff
       (1) direction
       (2) speed
       (3) what plaintiff doing
       (4) whether entering or leaving elevator
   (d) movement of elevator or doors
       (1) direction

720

EXHIBIT 13.5
Continued

Chapter 3   **§ 3:118**

      (2) speed

    (e) whether any warning given about movement or position or elevator of elevator or doors

      (1) time before occurrence (seconds)

      (2) substance

      (3) reason occurrence happened despite warning

    (f) manner in which elevator caused occurrence

    (g) description of any defective condition of elevator

    (h) description of any faulty conduct of operator

    (i) number of people in elevator at time of occurrence, and description of any faulty conduct of people in elevator at time of occurrence

  3. Rescue

    (a) parts of body or clothing caught by elevator or doors

    (b) time period during which plaintiff caught in or by elevator or doors (began, ended)

    (c) steps taken by plaintiff to notify of entrapment (time, description, effectiveness)

    (d) steps taken by others to rescue plaintiff

  4. See §§ 3:51–3:77

§ 3:118   Escalator—Plaintiff to Deponent

TOTAL CLIENT-SERVICE LIBRARY® REFERENCES

Am Jur:
    26 Am Jur 2d, Elevators and Escalators §§ 78 et seq.

ALR Annotations:
    Liability for injury on, or in connection with, escalator. 1 ALR4th 144.

Auto-Cite®:
    Any case citation pertinent to this material can be checked for form, parallel references, later history, and annotation references through the Auto-Cite computer research system.

  1. Description

    (a) number of steps

    (b) width of steps

    (c) height of the risers

    (d) incline of each riser

    (e) material from which constructed

    (f) slipperiness

    (g) length of escalator

EXHIBIT 13.6
Pleadings from 21
AmJur Proof of
Facts Pleading
and Practice
Forms.
Reprinted with
permission of
Lawyers
Cooperative
Publishing, a
division of
Thomson Legal
Publishing, Inc.

RAILROADS   **Form 387**

Notes

Injuries to animals on track. 65 Am Jur 2d RAILROADS §§ 574, 588.

Form 386 Complaint, petition, or declaration—Collision of train with
animals straying onto tracks—Excessive speed at crossing

[Caption, Introduction, see CAPTIONS, PRAYERS, ETC.]

I

Plaintiff is, and at all times mentioned in this instrument was, residing at
....1............ *[address],* ....2............ *[city],* ....3............ County, ...4............ *[state].*

II

Defendant ....5............ *[railroad]* is, and at all times mentioned in this instrument was, a corporation organized and existing under the laws of ....6............
[state], with its principal office located at ....7............ *[address],* ....8............ *[city],*
....9............ County, ...10............ *[state].*

III

At all times mentioned in this instrument, defendant owned and operated a
railroad from ....11............ *[city]* to ....12............ *[city],* which railroad ran through
....13............ County, in ....14............ *[state].*

IV

On ....15............ *[date],* in ....16............ County, ...17............ *[state],* defendant, its
agents, servants and employees, carelessly and negligently ran defendant's
train, train No. ....18...., against and ....19............ [injured *or* killed] ....20............
[describe animal or animals] of the value of $....21...., the property of plaintiff,
damaging plaintiff in the sum of $....22.....

V

The place where the above-mentioned ....23............ *[animal or animals]* came
onto the track and ....24............ [was *or* were] ....25............ [killed *or* injured] was
at the ....26............ crossing at ....27............ *[specify location].*

VI

Defendant, through its agents, servants and employees operating the above-
mentioned train, negligently ran the train at a great rate of speed, and
negligently failed to sound its whistle or ring its bell prior to the above-
described collision. In consequence, plaintiff's ....28............ *[animal or animals]*
....29............ [was *or* were] ....30............ [injured *or* killed].

Wherefore, plaintiff requests judgment against defendant for the sum of
$....31...., costs of suit, and such other and further relief as the court deems just
and proper.

[Signature, Verification, see CAPTIONS, PRAYERS, ETC.]

Notes

Injuries to animals because of excessive speed of train. 65 Am Jur 2d RAILROADS §§ 587, 588.

Form 387 Complaint, petition, or declaration—Collision of train with
animals straying onto tracks—Negligent construction of
crossing and failure to give warning signal

[Caption, Introduction, see CAPTIONS, PRAYERS, ETC.]

I

Plaintiff is, and at all times mentioned in this instrument was, residing at
....1............ *[address],* ....2............ *[city],* ....3............ County, ...4............ *[state].*

327

Reference Books As an Authority

General reference books are not widely used as cited authorities for several reasons. First, they are secondary authority, which always places them in a subordinate position to controlling primary authority. Primary authority, as a matter of course, should be cited whenever possible because it has greater influence even when persuasive rather than mandatory. Second, as a secondary resource, general reference books tend to be less influential than other sources, such as treatises or restatements. Third, the material contained in many reference books often is more suited to providing background information than presenting specific points of law to be relied upon as authority. For example, the form book would serve no purpose as an authority even though it may be an invaluable resource in assisting you to draft a complaint that will withstand a motion to dismiss by the opposition. In some instances, however, a general reference book will be cited. When this occurs, the proper citation form is the same for other books, as covered by Rules 15–17 of the bluebook.

Organization

The organization of reference books varies widely among publishers and is affected to some extent by content. For example, books consisting predominately of commentary may be organized by chapter, while casebooks may be arranged much like a judicial reporter, and a pure form book may consist of little more than an extensive collection of sample documents associated with a particular subject or aspect of litigation. However, two features common to most general reference books regardless of the type or publisher are a detailed table of contents and a subject index. You will recall the statement at the beginning of this text that virtually every legal resource is indexed in some manner by subject; general reference books are no exception. Quite often, the book contains an index to the contents, and even those that do not will at the very least have a table of contents to assist you in locating specific information within the text. From a more general perspective, general reference books are catalogued in the law library by subject and author, much like the books of any ordinary library.

Methods of Research

The catalog system of indexing general reference books by subject and author makes this area of the library one of the most appealing to the novice researcher because of the similarity to research done previously in other libraries. Typically, the library will contain a card catalog arranged by topic and author. Armed with either of these, you can identify those specific cards

that represent particular authorities within the library and indicate their location. Once information is located, general reference books frequently contain citations to other forms of primary and secondary authority. The disadvantage is that the reference citations are often dated and the authority may not indicate the most current status of a legal principle.

A second method to locate general reference books is through citation found in other authorities, such as legal encyclopedias and periodicals. When a general reference book is cited, the author, title, and publication information should be included. With this information, you can consult the card catalog to obtain the specific location within the law library of the text. While reporters, statutes, digests, and other law library authorities tend to be placed together respectively and arranged in alphabetical order by title, general reference books are arranged under the standard decimal system used in other libraries. As a result, consulting the card catalog can save quite a bit of time in determining the exact location of the reference book.

▐▐▐▶ STRATEGY

Researching Reference Books

1. Use your query to locate pertinent reference books in the subject index of the card catalog.
2. Use the standard library decimal coding system to locate the specific books.
3. Check the back of the book for a subject index and use your relevant search terms to locate specific information. If no subject index is provided, use the table of contents to lead you to particular points of discussion that bear on your query.

Chapter Summary

The general reference book can be a valuable source in understanding a topic. It can also provide necessary practical information that can be employed after the research is complete. General reference books include those discussed in previous chapters as well as casebooks, books of commentary, and form books. General reference books are catalogued by subject and author and arranged under the decimal system common to ordinary libraries. Most general reference books are also internally indexed and at the very least contain a table of contents. The arrangement of information within a general reference book is controlled by the publisher and the nature of the book's content.

Key Terms

form book   reference book

SELF-TEST

MULTIPLE CHOICE

1. A _____ _____
   can include anything that provides basic
   information on a subject.
   a. reference book
   b. form book
   c. case book
   d. none of the above

2. In the law library, the books in the
   reference section are most easily accessed
   by _____.
   a. card catalog
   b. digest
   c. subject indexes
   d. quick index

3. Reference books are _____
   _____ and often much less
   influential than established treatises or
   primary authorities.
   a. primary authority
   b. mandatory authority
   c. persuasive authority
   d. none of the above

4. The reference collection is often the most
   likely site for answers to _____
   _____ about practical
   situations.
   a. legislative questions
   b. specific questions
   c. judicial questions
   d. none of the above

5. The types of books commonly included in
   the reference section include
   _____.
   a. general subject
   b. casebook
   c. form book
   d. all of the above

TRUE/FALSE

_____ 6. General subject reference books
   consist of selected cases on a topic
   and brief commentary on the
   rulings in the opinions.

_____ 7. A source frequently consulted in the
   daily work of the legal professional
   is the form book.

_____ 8. Form books provide basic forms for
   documents in legal situations.

_____ 9. Forms in form books provide the
   basis for a sound document or
   procedure by including the
   necessary basics common to all
   similar situations.

_____ 10. Casebooks are not widely used as
   cited authorities.

FILL–IN THE BLANKS

11. Reference books are secondary authority,
   which always places them in a
   _____ position to primary
   authority.

12. As a secondary resource, general reference
   books tend to be less influential than
   other sources, such as_____
   or _____ .

13. The material contained in many reference
   books often is more suited to providing
   background information than specific
   _____ _____
   _____ to be relied upon as
   authority.

14. When a general reference book is cited,
   the proper citation form is the same for
   other books, as covered by _____
   _____–_____ of the
   bluebook.

15. The _____ of reference books
   varies widely among publishers and is
   affected to some extent by content.

16. Two features common to most general
   reference books regardless of the type or
   publisher are a detailed _____
   _____ and a _____
   _____ .

17. General reference books are catalogued in
   the law library by _____ and
   _____ .

18. The _____ system of indexing
   general reference books is similar to
   research done in other libraries.

19. _____ may be pure forms or
   combined with commentary.

20. Form books exist for _____
   and _____ _____
   _____ , such as contracts.

CHAPTER **14**

COMPUTER ASSISTED RESEARCH

CHAPTER OBJECTIVES

Upon completion of this chapter, you should be able to accomplish the following competencies:

- Explain how computer research is advantageous.

- Describe the hardware components used in computer research.

- Distinguish between the three major categories of software.

- Discuss how software is used in computer research.

- Distinguish between database and CD ROM research.

- Explain the individual advantages of CD ROM and database research.

- Describe the steps in conducting computer research.

- Describe the features of computer research.

- Explain how computer research queries vary from traditional research queries.

- Distinguish floppy disc hardware systems from hard-drive systems.

THE ROLE OF COMPUTER TECHNOLOGY IN LEGAL RESEARCH

Until now, the focus of this text has been on the traditional law library setting. Each chapter dealt with a different aspect of legal publications and the use of such publications to locate current and valid answers to legal issues. The objective of using computer research is essentially the same. The distinction, however, is that rather than consulting various bound publications, you use a computer, monitor (screen), and keyboard to access information stored in a database.

Until relatively recent times, all research was conducted in the traditional law library. In the latter part of this century, however, the rapid advancement of computer technology allowed legal research to be more current and easily done than ever before through the use of automated systems. A major expense of law practices is space, and even the minimal law library can occupy a large area. Additionally, the cost of creating a law library is often prohibitive for the smaller firm. Updating services alone for even a few statutory and reporter/digest collections can easily run into the thousands annually. Consequently, many legal professionals had to expend not only the actual time in the law library but also the travel time to and from a more comprehensive law library, such as those typically found in courts and law schools.

With the advent of computer-assisted research, the work could be done in the office, little or no additional space was needed, and often the cost of subscribing to a computer research service (database or CD ROM) was (and still is) often less than that of subscribing to bound publications. Also, no manpower is required to complete updating through placement of pocket parts, supplements, and looseleaf pages. The computer and legal research are essentially a perfect marriage, given one crucial condition: the researcher must have adequate computer research skills, or the necessary information may exist but never be found.

COMPONENTS OF COMPUTER-ASSISTED LEGAL RESEARCH: HARDWARE AND SOFTWARE

It may be helpful to begin by defining a few basic terms. **Hardware** consists of the actual equipment used in computer technology. **Software** is the programs that allow the computer to accept commands from the keyboard and respond by performing certain functions, such as those described here. One type of software is the **database,** a general computer phrase that essentially describes a particular type of stored information. In the case of legal research, a database is a law library contained in a computer memory that is accessible by computer through either a modem or CD ROM (explained below). This, in addition to word-processing (clerical) programs and spreadsheet (accounting) programs makes up the most common computer software.

hardware
Physical components of a computer system (e.g., monitor, processing unit, printer).

software
System that enables use of hardware to perform specific functions (e.g., database).

database
Collection of information, much like a library, that can be accessed through use of a computer.

With respect to hardware, there are many variations and special feature components; however, the most common and necessary are described here. The **computer** is the actual machine that processes and stores information and enables communication with other computers. The **monitor** is the screen upon which you view the information you are accessing, inputting, or storing. The **keyboard** (similar, but not identical, to that of a typewriter) is the means by which you inject commands to the computer. The **printer** is connected to the main computer by what is commonly known as the basic cable. This cable is used to transmit electronic bits of information into a temporary memory in the printer until the information is translated electronically into letters and symbols and printed out on paper, often referred to as the hard copy of the information that you initially input into the computer.

Computers are operated by a program (a particular set of symbols understood by the computer, such as DOS, Windows). The collection of symbols is often referred to as a program. When you input commands on the keyboard that coordinate with the set of symbols, the computer will respond appropriately to your command. For example, if you input a command by striking certain keys telling the computer that you wish to access a database to do research, the computer would respond by attempting to contact the database.

Programs can be used with a floppy disk (available in two sizes), a hard drive, or both. A **floppy disk** is a removable magnetic cartridge that contains information accessed on the computer. The **hard drive** is contained within the computer and permits the same function. Many computers have a hard drive and a receptacle for floppy disks. The advantage of the floppy disk is that you never run out of storage space, because new discs can always be added to your collection, of which you use only one or two at a time. The advantage of a hard drive is that you generally do not need to be concerned about damage or loss of the stored information by external elements, as is the case with floppy disks.

modem
Hardware that can be used to permit communication between separate computer systems.

A **modem** is a device that is mounted internally or externally on the computer and enables you to contact other computer systems via a telephone line. Typically, a phone line will plug into the wall at one end and into a jack on the modem at the other end. After inputting certain commands (including passwords) to the computer, a telephone number is dialed, and when the call is answered, you have access to the stored information of another computer system. This is especially helpful in research because you can contact database law libraries and complete all necessary steps of research without ever leaving your desk. Also, computer research via modem is perhaps the most current and time efficient method of research if you have adequate computer research skills.

CD ROM
Hardware that permits access to a limited database contained on a compact disc.

A **CD ROM** is a device connected to the computer by which you can place a specially designed compact disc (similar to those used in the music industry) into the CD ROM and then use the computer to access the information stored on the disk. This allows you to contain virtually entire libraries on a series of discs and to use them only when needed without taking up valuable storage space on your computer. While updated CDs are issued periodically, they are not as current as research using a modem to contact a computer library. The CD ROM system is often much more cost efficient, although with the CD ROM, you may have to consult several discs because

each contains different information (e.g., statutes, cases, regulations, secondary sources).

☐ ASSIGNMENT 14.1

Complete the following sentences:

1. The advantage of the CD ROM is _____ .
2. The advantage of modem research is _____ .
3. The advantages of computer-assisted research over traditional library research are _____ .
4. The difference between a hard drive and floppy disc is _____ .
5. The function of a modem is _____ .

BASIC RESEARCH FUNCTIONS

The goal of this section is to familiarize you with computer-assisted research and to enable you to complete a basic research query by consulting a database. You will see in the following subsections that virtually all of your research can be fully and adequately completed through the use of a comprehensive software program.

Features of Computer Research Software

While more than one database for legal research, such as WESTLAW and LEXIS, is on the market, the primary focus of this chapter is on the features and uses of WESTLAW in order to present a more thorough approach to the actual steps necessary to locate information and to provide you at the conclusion of the chapter with practical skills that you can employ. Other programs, such as LEXIS, function quite similarly and are relatively easy to use once you are familiar with the proper commands.

WESTLAW is a commercial research service offered by West Publishing, which also publishes the National Reporter System, its parallel digests, various statutory publications such as USCA, and a large number of secondary resources. WESTLAW is designed to incorporate many of the same techniques used in traditional research so that the researcher with even minimal skill can locate information. An example is the key number system. If you can use this system in the digest, you can locate information on cases in WESTLAW by using key numbers.

Some of the more common features of various databases available through computer-assisted research include the following:

Judicial law arranged by state and the levels of federal courts.
Statutory law arranged by state and the federal Congress.
Administrative law arranged by state and the CFR.
Legal encyclopedia and the ALR.

Some legal periodicals and looseleaf services.
Citators.

Getting Started in Computer Research

If you have computer experience, you can get started in *computer research* quite easily. However, if you have not used a computer in the past, doing so can be your first achievement in becoming computer literate. In the most basic sense, the first step in computer research is to turn on the equipment. Often, the computer, monitor, and printer have separate switches. Some systems have combined these items, and simply turning the computer switch on will automatically turn on the other components.

Once the computer is on, you may have to boot up the software. This is simply the process of telling the computer which software program you intend to use. For purposes of clarity, the DOS software system will be used in this discussion. Other programs operate in a similar manner but simply require different commands to obtain the desired function. If your computer contains a floppy disc drive, you may need to insert the proper disc before the computer can retrieve any information if the information is not on a hard drive. If it is, and you need to boot up a particular program, instructions should appear on the screen. Once a letter and caret symbol (>) appear, you then need to access the particular function you wish to use, whether it is accounting, clerical, or research. If the letter and caret do not appear on the screen, enter the proper drive letter and a caret symbol (e.g., C>).

The letter represents the proper drive; for example, computers with floppy disc and hard drive assign a letter to represent each drive. If the program is on the hard drive, you will enter the letter for the hard drive, followed by the caret. If you are going to do computer research, you should enter the letter for the drive that contains the software necessary to utilize the modem to contact the database. For example, WESTMATE is the software program used by the computer and modem to contact the WESTLAW service. This is done by your computer's placing a telephone call to the mainframe computer that contains the database (in this case, Westlaw). Generally, the program with this ability to contact and communicate with other computers is on a hard drive located internally in your computer. Following the caret you should enter the name or proper abbreviation for the accessing software. The proper command to follow the drive letter and caret is contained in the reference manual provided when you subscribe to a particular software program (e.g., C>WESTMATE\WESTMATE).

Press and release the ENTER key. Your modem will accept a proper command and begin the process to contact the database. You will see instructions on the screen on which steps to take next. Often the next step is to identify yourself through the use of a password. This password, which can be numbers, letters, or a combination of both, is used by the database service to identify you for billing purposes. It is also a security measure to prevent others from misusing your account for their own research. The database may also ask you to identify the research. Thus, when billed, you can easily identify for which client the research was performed and consequently assign the bill to the proper account in your own expense and billing system.

After your password and research identifiers have been entered, you will be provided with a directory of services available in the database. This typically includes all of the publications contained in the database; each of

these is followed by a number/letter. By typing the number/letter and pressing the ENTER key, a more detailed description of the particular service will appear. At this point, you are ready to begin your research.

Additional Computer Training

The first step is, of course, to understand how the system works. While the query process will be explained in this chapter, if you anticipate using a computer research system, you should obtain additional training through tutorial, reference manual such as the WESTLAW Reference Manual, or other method designed especially for the computer research system you plan to use. As with traditional library research, experience will provide a degree of skill if you first have a working knowledge of the necessary steps to locate the relevant legal principles in the most influential and current authorities.

Many commercial computer database systems have tutorials. Often tutorials can be used on any personal computer with a floppy disc drive regardless of whether there is actual access to the database. The tutorial disc is simply placed in the disc drive, and after the proper beginning commands are given, the user is walked through each of the services of a database. This includes primary and secondary authorities. The tutorial can be utilized at your own pace and at convenient times. You can stop and start when you like and repeat the process as many times as necessary to help you feel comfortable with the preparation of queries and consultation of the various library services. Because this is done through the use of a floppy disc rather than actual connection to the database, the expense is limited to the one time purchase of the tutorial rather than your being billed for the time accessed to a database.

Process of Computer Research

The process of legal research is quite similar for most systems. For the purpose of demonstration, however, reference will be made to the WESTLAW system. The first step is to identify the jurisdiction whose authority you seek. For example, if research is being done for a case pending in the state of California, you would be focused on the legal standards issued by the courts and legislature of that state. In computer research this step is known as identifying the field. Once the correct field has been entered into the computer, all queries will be directed to the law of that field.

To further narrow your research, you should determine whether the legal standards that address your issue are likely to be statutory or judicial. This is done by utilizing the same methods discussed previously in the text. Once you have identified the jurisdiction by entering the proper letter/number for that field, you will be given the option of the various courts, legislatures, and administrative branches of that jurisdiction. Select the proper branch and enter the corresponding letter/number. You are now ready to enter your actual query.

Because computer research is charged on a time increment basis and because research needs to be efficient for other practical reasons, you should adequately prepare your query prior to accessing the computer research system. As with other research, you should prepare a specific query. You can

always broaden the scope if necessary. After you determine the issue with as much specificity as possible and select the most relevant terms, you must arrange them in a manner that will be accepted by WESTLAW and that will locate the most appropriate information.

In WESTLAW, your general query can be prepared in two ways: (1) natural (also known as WIN) and (2) terms and connectors. The natural system is fairly recent and is designed to make the system more user friendly. By selecting this method of research, you enter a query much as you would state the question in ordinary English. This is opposed to terms and connectors, which actually looks for the same terms in your query as they appear verbatim within the text of legal authorities. While the natural method is somewhat easier to employ, there exists the danger of locating numerous authorities on the same topic that are not relevant to your exact query. Again, specificity is a must. The terms and connectors method will find authorities using the exact language of your query, but if you select terms that do not appear in relevant authorities and do not include alternatives, you may miss important authorities entirely. To avoid this, you should include any reasonable alternative terms and use the root expander method, which looks for variations of tense or form of a particular term. To use the root expander, you should type in the root of the word followed by an asterisk for each additional letter that might appear (e.g., norm*****). Also, you may employ another method, such as the key number system, or one of the citators available.

Using Terms and Connectors Method

The terms and connectors method enables you to locate legal authorities that pertain to the issue based on the presence in the authority (e.g., a judicial opinion of the key terms that you include in your search query). Because the search is for verbatim language, you should identify variations or synonyms of the terms that may also appear in the authorities through the inclusion of alternative terms or the use of proper symbols to indicate term variation, such as past, present, or future tense and plurality.

Your query terms should be written in such a way that the search will produce authorities containing variations of the terms you have chosen. For example, "normal" could also be represented by "normality," "normalcy," "normalize," or "normalization." You should begin with the root of the term and follow it immediately with an exclamation point (!). This will instruct the database to produce all authorities in the field that contain the root of the word and any variation. If the only relevant variations contain only a few letters in difference (e.g., the letters *tion* as a suffix), an asterisk (*) can be used within the original term at any place where a different letter might appear in a variation. Be aware that the system will automatically search for plurals; therefore, these need not be identified as variations.

☐ ASSIGNMENT 14.2

Prepare each of the following words for use in a computer research query. List each of the variations of the term you would expect to find with the query as you have prepared it.

active	insane
bankrupt	pollute
corrupt	reasonable
determine	secure
discriminate	testate

After the terms and their variations are selected, you must properly connect the terms. Connectors are symbols that the computer interprets to mean how closely terms in the query must appear to one another to be retrieved. The way in which you do this will cause the terms to be located either together or as mutually exclusive alternatives. Proper use of connectors helps you to limit the information retrieved to authorities relevant to your query. For example, the system interprets a blank space between letters as *or* (e.g., *malicious prosecution*). The system would interpret this query to mean locate any authority that contains the word *malicious* or the word *prosecution* but not both within the same authority. Therefore, be especially aware of all spaces that appear in your query. On the contrary, the ampersand (&) is used to locate terms that appear together somewhere within the same authority. Additional symbols discussed in the following paragraph are used to locate terms within greater proximity. Within the actual text of this book, spaces may be used between terms and connectors for the purpose of making illustrations more clear.

Common Hardware Components of a Computer System.

The symbol "/s" between two terms signifies that the terms must appear within the same sentence of an authority before the system will retrieve it. Similarly, the symbol "/p" means that the terms must appear within the same paragraph of an authority before the system will retrieve it. Often, the "/s" symbol is so limiting that relevant cases or statutes may be missed. However, the "/p" symbol may cause numerous irrelevant authorities to appear. You should use the "/s" symbol for terms you are searching that generally appear together, such as *gross negligence.* Similarly, the "/p" symbol is used when the terms may not be used as a common phrase but are integrally part of the same topic, such as *codicil /p will.* Finally, the combination of the backslash and a number will locate terms that appear within the signified number of words; for example, *codicil /5 will* would require that codicil and will appear within five words of each other.

Entire phrases can be enclosed in quotation marks (" ") exactly as the term should appear in the authority. Terms within quotation marks are not subject to the use of additional connecting symbols. The quotation marks are the signal to locate the terms in the order given with no other terms included (e.g., "Motion for Judgment Notwithstanding the Verdict"). As you develop a knowledge of the subject matter, you will become more adept at identifying terms that are likely to appear within the same sentence or paragraph or phrases that should be included within quotations. As a result, your research will become more efficient.

Exhibit 14.1 presents a list of all the terms and connectors that can be employed in WESTLAW. Gaining a thorough knowledge of these is essential in developing skill at accessing information.

▢ ASSIGNMENT 14.3

For each of the following series of terms, prepare the following queries: 1) terms that are mutually exclusive, 2) terms that appear within the same sentence, and 3) terms that appear within the same paragraph. (Terms not separated by comma are phrases.)

age, discriminate, protected class, civil rights

custody, visitation, religion, parental rights

constructive, eviction, habitability, tenant, landlord

contract, consideration, duress, breach

federal jurisdiction, removal, remand

Citations Method

If you begin your research with a specific citation of a relevant authority, you can summon the cited authority without going through the query process by the use of the find (Fi) function. Also, to validate and examine the history of a case, you can utilize insta-cite. For insta-cite, you must include the term *cite* followed by the identifying volume/page, chapter/section, or other relevant indicators in the citation and publication. If you have only the name of the

EXHIBIT 14.1   Table of Connectors for WESTLAW.

Use	To retrieve documents with:	For example:	Would retrieve:
& (and)	Search terms in the same document	automobile & alcohol	all documents that contain both the word *automobile* and the word *alcohol* anywhere in them.
space bar (or)	One search term or the other	frisk search	all documents that contain either the word *frisk* or the word *search*
/s	Search terms in the same sentence	automobile /s alcohol	all documents that contain both the word *automobile* and the word *alcohol* in the same sentence
/p	Search terms in the same paragraph	automobile /p alcohol	all documents that contain both the word *automobile* and the word *alcohol* in the same paragraph
/n	Search terms within "n" words of each other (where "n" is a number)	blood w/3 alcohol	All documents that contain both the word *blood* and the word *alcohol* within three words of each other
+n	One search term preceding the other by "n" words (where "n" is a number)	automobile +5 alcohol	All documents where the word *automobile* precedes the word alcohol by 5 words
" "	Search terms appearing in the same order as in the quotation marks	"doctor patient"	All documents where the exact phrase "doctor patient" occurs

statute, case, or secondary authority, the computer retrieves all authorities in the field by that name. But if the volume and page are available, a specific case can be summoned. Additionally, if you are using insta-cite rather than a general directory field, such as the law of a particular jurisdiction, insta-cite will provide you with any subsequent actions taken with respect to the authority (i.e., validation).

As in all legal research, you have to select the authorities that are most pertinent and influential and then verify their validity. To verify an authority, you can use the Shepard's Citations or insta-cite feature of the WESTLAW database. As with the bound copies of Shepard's, the information that appears on the screen will be all subsequent references to the citation by later authorities. You will also be provided with abbreviations in these subsequent citations to indicate the position of the later authority with respect to the authority you are checking; for example, *J* would indicate that a later court dissented from the holding.

⚖️ **APPLICATION 14.1**

FACTS: A delivery truck driver offers a ride to a hitchhiker. This is strictly prohibited by the delivery company. An accident occurs and the passenger is seriously injured. Is the delivery company liable as the principal of the agent driver?

    NATURAL QUERY: Can a principal be held responsible for the acts of an agent when the agent's activity was expressly prohibited by the principal?

    TERMS AND CONNECTORS QUERY: "Scope of Authority" /p Principal & Agent

---

Whatever feature of WESTLAW, LEXIS, or any other computer-assisted research program that you are using, an essential prerequisite is a working knowledge of the system. As mentioned earlier, this can be gained through computer tutorials, books compatible with the system, or personal training. Regardless of the method you use, without a base level of skill at formulating queries and accessing information, computer research can be a costly and inaccurate method of research.

CD ROM Research

Another component of computer-assisted research is the CD ROM library, commercially prepared compact discs that can be played on a special receiver, known as a CD ROM, that is compatible with the computer. Information is transmitted from the CD ROM through the computer to the monitor and the printer. Development of this system has made computer research affordable for virtually any size firm or organization. The concept is quite simple. A compact disc player is connected to a personal computer, and compact discs containing research materials for a particular subject of law or jurisdiction can be loaded into the disc player and retrieved on the computer. Similar to WESTLAW, you can retrieve headnotes, cases, statutes, etc. However, because only those discs necessary to personal research needs are required, there is no cost for access through telephone lines to a database, nor is there the cost for access to all published statutes and cases nationally as well as the other peripheral features of a database. As your library needs increase, additional discs can be purchased. Also, new discs are issued periodically to update the information, much as the pocket part and looseleaf updating services keep bound publications current. Because approximately 300,000 pages of information can be contained on a single disc, the space requirements are extremely low when compared to a standard library. CD ROM also has word-processing capabilities that enable you to lift information from the disc and incorporate it into a brief or other document you may be preparing.

    As the efficiency and cost of computer research continue to improve, the use of such research is becoming more and more widespread. The legal profession is rapidly approaching the time where computer research is more cost effective than the expense of book space and updates of hard volumes in the ever-expanding subject of law. Thus, all legal professionals or individuals whose work requires an element of legal research should be prepared to develop computer research skills as a basic part of job readiness.

IIII➡ S T R A T E G Y

Computer Assisted Research

Note: Because different businesses utilize a variety of databases, the strategy will be confined to basic steps.

1. Familiarize yourself with the hardware and commands necessary to access the software.
2. Prepare your query, relevant search terms, and any citations of authority you may have in a format that is acceptable to the software program. This should be completed before you access the database.
3. Begin with the most specific searches and broaden them if necessary.
4. Validate any authority you may need.
5. Print out citations of authority rather than writing them down (this is faster and requires less billable time on the computer). Check with your supervisor regarding whether the whole authority (e.g., judicial opinion) should be printed or whether the cite should be used to locate the opinion in a reporter. Lengthy or numerous authorities could generate quite a bit of expense in computer time necessary to print them in full.

Chapter Summary

As you have seen, computer research is a rapidly expanding and growing element of the practice of law. This form of research is both cost and time efficient and has become almost commonplace. Computer research can be performed through access to a database or on a more limited scale through CD ROM. Both provide current and complete libraries. However, a base level of skill in query formulation is absolutely necessary to properly and completely access the information sought. The WESTLAW database and CD ROM systems contain a variety of features to represent all the components of a traditional library. A variety of methods, including natural, terms and connectors, and citations, can be employed to obtain information. Tutorials, books, and personal training can be used to develop skills at query formulation for these or other commercially prepared database and CD ROM systems.

Key Terms

CD ROM
database

hardware
modem

software

SELF-TEST

MULTIPLE CHOICE

1. Traditional law libraries require significant continuous expense for _____ .
   a) supplementation
   b) pocket parts
   c) looseleaf services
   d) all of the above

2. The researcher must have adequate _____ _____ or the necessary information may exist but never be found.
   a) computer skills
   b) computer research skills
   c) command of terminology
   d) all of the above

3. _____ consists of the actual equipment used in computer technology.
   a) Software
   b) Hardware
   c) Database
   d) External modem

4. _____ is the program that allows the computer to accept commands from the keyboard and respond by performing certain functions.
   a) CD ROM
   b) Word processor
   c) Software
   d) Database

5. One type of software is _____ , which describes a library of stored information.
   a) word processor
   b) modem
   c) spreadsheet
   d) database

TRUE/FALSE

_____ 6. A modem is a device that is mounted internally or externally on the computer and enables you to contact other computer systems via a phone line.

_____ 7. A monitor is a device that is connected to the computer by which you can place a specially designed compact disc (similar to those used in the music industry) into a special player and then access information.

_____ 8. You may need to access or boot up the software program by inputting a command after the drive letter and caret symbol.

_____ 9. A modem tells the computer who you are for billing purposes and acts as a security measure to prevent other users from billing time on your account.

_____ 10. A law library database typically contains all of the features of a traditional law library.

FILL-IN THE BLANK

11. Training for computer research can be obtained through _____ , _____ , and _____ .

12. A _____ is a resource (publication) feature within a database.

13. Because computer research is charged on a _____ _____ basis, you should adequately prepare your query prior to accessing the computer research system.

14. In WESTLAW, your general query can be prepared in two ways: _____ and _____ .

15. With the _____ system, you enter a query much as you would state it in ordinary English.

16. The _____ method looks for the same terms in your query as they appear verbatim within the text of legal authorities.

17. With terms and connectors, you should include any reasonable _____ terms.

18. Proper _____ determine whether how the elements of your query are searched in relationship to one another.

19. The _____ method of research allows you to locate an authority by inputting its proper citation or even parts thereof.

20. The final step in computer research is to _____ your authorities through the use of a citator.

NOTES ABOUT LEGAL WRITING

There are many different types of legal documents. Most people are aware of the basic legal forms used to initiate and defend against lawsuits. However, virtually all significant steps in litigation before and after a suit is filed are evidenced by some type of writing. This may begin with an opinion letter from an attorney advising a potential client. Once the chain of legal writing has begun, it may continue as far as an appellate brief, which presents the legal arguments over the correctness of a judicial decision.

The form, content, and tone of a legal writing depend in large part on two factors: the audience to whom the document is directed and the reason behind the creation of the document. If, for example, you are writing to a client, you would probably be careful to use language that makes your point clear without being condescending. If the document is directed to a court in an attempt to win some aspect of a case, your tone would be strongly persuasive and your language would incorporate appropriate legal terminology. However, the nature of the document must also be respectful, and even though it may be highly persuasive, it should not appear to be demanding. Rather, the document should always be organized in a logical manner so that it reasonably draws the reader to your intended conclusion.

Another consideration in legal writing is the objectivity of your writing. When communicating with other legal professionals who are on the same side of an issue, it is usually acceptable to be very objective, that is, to bluntly examine both the strengths and the weaknesses of your position. However, when you are attempting to persuade the opposition, or a court, or both, you would assume a more subjective attitude. While still presenting all of the applicable authority, you would do so in a manner that tends to emphasize the strengths of your case and draw the focus away from any significant weaknesses while still including them in the argument. Chapter 4 of this text presents a number of examples of different types of legal writing. When preparing your first samples of legal writing, you may want to refer to them for an idea of how objective and subjective tones influence the way in which the information is presented. Also, the following paragraphs offer some brief instructions for preparing certain types of legal documents.

With regard to legal writing, your grammar should be a careful consideration. Proper spelling, punctuation, and structure are imperative. Sentences should not be so long as to become confusing. A good rule of thumb (but subject to exception) is that your average sentence should not exceed 35

words. If it is significantly longer, consider presenting the idea in two or more sentences. Take care, however, that sentences are not so short that the document sounds choppy.

Each paragraph should convey a single concept. If you are presenting a thorough discussion of several different aspects of an idea, do so in several paragraphs.

Avoid overuse of legal terminology. The trend in recent years has been to make legal writing more "reader friendly." As a result, much of the flowery and often redundant language has been eliminated. Rather, information should be presented clearly and concisely. Legal terms should be incorporated when they are directly relevant to the issues and where substitution of more common terms might alter the legal meaning.

There is a preferred form for certain types of legal documents. For example, documents presented to a court should be preceded by a case heading, which identifies the parties to suit, the court, docket number, and any other information routinely included in documents for that particular court. The arrangement of content under particular headings or in a particular order (e.g., Jurisdiction, Facts, Issues, Argument, Conclusion) can be determined by examining other similar documents and court rules/forms.

Some legal documents follow legally prescribed instructions as to format, presentation, and even type and length. The most common example is the appellate brief. The state and federal courts have specific published rules of procedure for these documents, and close adherence is required or the document may be rejected by the court for deficiency in form regardless of the content. Consequently, you should always consult state or federal as well as local rules for preparation of any documents that will be submitted to the court. Until you are familiar with the requirements, you may find it helpful to follow other similar documents as models. These can be found in the files of the law office or on record as part of the case files at the office of the clerk of the court. Some law libraries also contain collections of appellate briefs that are extremely helpful as examples of the court rules.

Basic Review of Common Legal Documents

Note: Examples of many of these are found in Chapter 4.

Internal Memorandum of Law

Written to another legal professional on the same side of the issue.
Purpose is informative.
Tone is objective.

Generally, length is short and little explanation is required. Give an extremely brief recitation of the facts to refamiliarize the reader with the case. Indicate what law is relevant and how it applies to the current situation. Close by making suggestions and/or asking for further action to be taken on the matter.

External Memorandum of Law

Written for external use. Generally directed to opposing counsel and/or the courts.
Purpose is almost always persuasive as well as informative.
Tone is subjective.

Since these documents can influence the outcome of a lawsuit, it is imperative that research be accurate and on point. Also, it is necessary for the analysis to be realistic as well as complete (strengths and weaknesses). It is imperative that the documents be well organized.

The memorandum should be presented in such a manner that a discussion of the facts logically lead the reader to the issue at hand. The issue should be resolved by addressing strengths and weaknesses in a positive manner. The conclusion should reemphasize the strengths. The desired result should be indicated at this point as the only logical outcome.

Appellate Brief

Written for external use. Directed to other legal professionals and the courts.
Audience is legal.
Purpose is always persuasive.
Tone is subjective.

Since these documents greatly influence the outcome of a lawsuit, it is imperative that research be accurate and on point. Also, it is necessary for the analysis to be realistic and for the writing to be persuasive but concise (to the point) and extremely well organized. Headings should be used exactly as indicated by the statutes (rules of appellate procedure).

In most jurisdictions, rules require that the statement of facts NOT be written in a persuasive manner. Rather, they should be presented objectively. All relevant facts should be mentioned. To avoid persuasiveness, avoid the overuse of adjectives. The facts should logically lead the reader to the issue at hand.

The issue or issues should be presented so as to clearly identify the alleged error in the lower court. This typically involves not the guilt or innocence of a party but rather some allegedly incorrect action or actions by the court that influenced the outcome of the case. The latter are the questions that the appellate court must answer.

The argument is presented in a persuasive manner that emphasizes strengths and minimizes weaknesses, citing all applicable law that is on point.

In some jurisdictions, the conclusion reemphasizes the strengths. In others, this summation is done in the argument, and only the desired result is indicated. Whatever the form, the result is pointed to as the only logical outcome.

Opinion Letter

Written for external use. Generally directed to existing or potential client to advise legal standing on an issue.
Purpose is generally informative.
Tone is objective.

These documents typically examine the primary points of law on a particular issue and advise as to the appropriate legal action. Such a letter may also accept or decline an offer of representation. Because of legal ethical considerations, opinion letters should generally advise the client as to the next possible step. Even if an attorney declines to represent a client, the attorney should close by making this clear and further advising the client of the opportunity to seek other representation within any applicable statute of limitations. If a statute of limitations or other time requirement does apply, it is generally good form to indicate the last date for action by the client.

ASSIGNMENTS

☐ ASSIGNMENT B.1

This assignment should better acquaint you with how terms are located and presented in both their legal and their ordinary meaning. For each term, locate a legal definition or interpretation and prepare a definition so that a client would understand the meaning of the term when used in a discussion. After each definition, give the citation to the source of your answer. If a term or phrase has multiple definitions, select only one.

1. bailment
2. assignment
3. delegation
4. annulment
5. novation
6. intestate succession
7. discovery
8. reasonable man
9. fixture
10. equity
11. proximate cause
12. par value
13. respondeat superior
14. relevant
15. stare decisis
16. venue
17. life estate
18. negotiable instrument
19. hearsay
20. joint and several
21. liquidated damages
22. res judicata
23. quid pro quo
24. sua sponte
25. voir dire

☐ ASSIGNMENT B.2

General Research Questions
(do not require access to a law library)

1. If I want to know generally about a subject but am not concerned with recent developments, where should I go? Why?

2. With respect to the following, would each instance most likely be covered by statute or by case law? Why?

    a. A client wants to prevent his girlfriend from having an abortion.

    b. A client wants to force a neighbor to cut down a 150-year-old tree because the tree's sap drips onto his property and damages the paint on his car.

    c. A client wants to have his child support obligation suspended while he is unemployed.

    d. A client's son drowned at a state park lake, and the client wants to sue the state for not posting warning signs near an area with large submerged rocks.

    e. A client was rendered a quadraplegic during a touch football game with friends that was played on base where he was stationed with the Air Force, and he wants the Air Force to pay his bills for life.

    f. A client wants to have her father declared legally incompetent because sometimes he exercises poor judgment and acts irrationally.

    g. A client wants to incorporate her rent-a-prom-dress business.

    h. A client wants to find out whether the FBI has a file on him and wants to obtain a copy of any existing file.

    i. A client wants to defend herself against an aggravated assault charge on the basis of insanity because she was suffering from PMS.

    j. A client wants to establish visitation rights with her grandchildren, who are in the custody of her ex-daughter-in-law.

    k. A client wants to claim loss of companionship because of the death of his son in an auto accident caused by someone else.

    l. A client wants to sue his landlord because the landlord refused to repair a hole in the roof and as a result, the utility bills were so high that the client was forced to move and forfeit his deposit.

    m. A client purchased a lemon car and wants to force the dealer to replace the vehicle or refund her money.

    n. A client's boyfriend broke their engagement and wants the engagement ring back, and the client wants to keep the ring because it was also a birthday gift.

    o. A client built a fence around his yard 17 years ago, and the new neighbors want the client to remove it because they claim it comes eight feet across their property line.

    p. A client was assaulted by a server at a fast-food restaurant drive-up window for ordering something not on the menu, and the client wants to sue the restaurant company.

    q. A client wants a divorce. She is pregnant by a man other than her husband. She says she has been separated for two years and does not know the whereabouts of her husband. Can the court grant a divorce and deny the husband the right to claim paternity?

r. A client slips and falls in a grocery store in an area marked "WET FLOOR" and wants to sue the store for her injuries because she says the sign faced the other direction.

s. A client wants to sue her mother's dentist because the mother was anesthetized for a common procedure and never woke up.

☐ ASSIGNMENT B.3

General Research

Locate a specific example of each of the following items and prepare the complete citation:

1. A federal statute. (Because U.S.C.A. contains the same federal statutes as U.S.C. and has an identical numbering system, you may cite from either.)
2. A term from Words and Phrases.
3. A treatise or casebook.
4. Three cases from different state courts.
5. A state statute.

☐ ASSIGNMENT B.4

General Validation Research

By using the information available in the library and in your textbook, answer the following questions:

1. By using Shepard's Citations, can you determine whether a federal court has cited a particular article in a leading law review? If so, how would you find that information?
2. Does Shepard's Citations cover the court rules of the state? If so, where?
3. Give three examples of letter abbreviations used to indicate history or treatment in Shepard's Citations and explain their meanings.
4. By starting with Shepard's, locate and give the complete and proper citation for a state case that has been cited in a legal periodical. It is not necessary to give the legal periodical complete cite; you need only include the information given about it in the citator.
5. Does Shepard's have a citator for citations to rules and regulations issued by federal administrative agencies, boards, and commissions? If so, what citator would include this information?

☐ ASSIGNMENT B.5

General Judicial Research Questions

Locate a judicial opinion that addresses each of the following issues. Cite the case and brief (analyze) it. These topics are generally addressed in a majority of jurisdictions and consequently should be available in the jurisdictional materials available to you (e.g., your regional or state reporters).

1. Admissibility of a former conviction of a witness (not the defendant) in a criminal trial used to impeach the witness.
2. Are courts limited in the amount of time they have to revoke someone's probation?
3. If a rape occurs in County A of your state, after the victim was brought forcibly from County B of your state, should the rape trial be held in County A or County B?
4. Can your state prosecutors file interrogatories (i.e., require answers under oath to questions about the case) with defendants or their counsel in criminal cases?
5. What is the burden of proof one must meet when seeking to have a party held in contempt of court?
6. What is considered civil contempt in your state?
7. Can one who is seeking to have another held in civil contempt of court also seek damages in the contempt proceeding?
8. What is the liability of a partner for the acts of the other partner that are performed on behalf of the partnership?
9. Are nudity and obscenity considered synonymous by your state courts?
10. Person A puts her own life in danger to save Person B and, as a result, is injured. Person A sues Person B for damages. Can Person B claim Person A was contributorily negligent?
11. What is a licensee in your state?
12. What is a riparian owner in your state?

☐ ASSIGNMENT B.6

Federal Case Research

Locate a case of your choosing in the Federal Digest table of cases and complete the following information on it:

1. Complete citation.
2. All key numbers.
3. The subject and section number in corpus juris secundum that discusses the primary issue involved in the case.
4. The page in Shepard's where the case is or should be located.

☐ ASSIGNMENT B.7

Federal Statutory Research

Use federal statutory publication U.S.C. or U.S.C.A. to locate the statutes that address each of the following questions. Prepare a proper citation of authority for each answer.

1. Can fortified parboiled rice be given to schools?
2. Do American troops ever protect Yosemite National Park?
3. When is kidnapping presumed as a matter of law?
4. Are there government benefits for anyone with black lung?
5. Is there a penalty for arming a shipping vessel against a friendly nation?

6. Are there restrictions for shipping plutonium by air?
7. Can an air carrier (airline company) refuse to transport a passenger?
8. What is a public aircraft?
9. Are babysitters entitled to minimum wage?
10. Can student loans be avoided by filing for bankruptcy?
11. Is it illegal to use the American flag as a bed covering?
12. Is it illegal to put up a billboard in Cuyahoga National Recreation Area?
13. When was the bald eagle adopted as the national bird?
14. What are the boundaries of the Big Cypress National Preserve?

☐ ASSIGNMENT B.8

Basic Statutory Research

Locate and give the proper citation for the statute in your jurisdiction for the questions. Analyze the statute and report on its contents. (That is, what is necessary for the statute to apply and its requirements to be met?) Do not quote the statute. Rather, interpret its meaning. You may give examples as part of your interpretation to clarify your answer.

1. You work for a bank. You are asked to write a procedure for bank employees that explains when information about a client's account may be released to third parties.
2. You are preparing an annual report for a business corporation. What should it contain?
3. You are researching any limitations on creation of a corporation's name.
4. What are the boundaries of a state county?
5. What are the procedures for erecting a statue in a state park?
6. You want to be a sheriff. You even bought yourself a badge. What are your duties?
7. You want to sue a particular person who is very rich and frequently travels outside the jurisdiction of your state. Under what circumstances can you serve the summons on the attorney who represents this person in business dealings in this town?
8. You're considering becoming a small claims court judge someday. Before going to the trouble of law school, find out what cases you would hear as this type of judge.
9. You want to become a licensed practicing embalmer. What must you do?
10. You work for an attorney who handles adoptions. You are asked to prepare an adoption decree. What should it contain?
11. You want to provide day care for five tots who belong to the five other people who live on your street. Do you need a license?
12. You wish to open a boarding house. Do you need a license?
13. You are a state court employee and know of a judge who is so old she is completely senile. Can she be forced to retire?
14. You are adopted. You know who your biological parents are. Your biological father is now a wealthy rancher. Can you inherit from your biological father when he dies?

15. What is required before a passenger is considered a guest in another person's automobile (for purposes of suing the driver after an accident)?
16. Is it a criminal offense to give a police officer false information?
17. If your spouse dies of natural causes in a hospital, can you orally consent to an autopsy? If you won't consent, can one be performed anyway?
18. If you get a job as a bellboy at the Red Lion Hotel, are you entitled to a minimum wage, or must you live off of tips?
19. You want to open your own cemetery. What state law procedures, if any, must you follow?
20. If you are a witness in a trial and refuse to answer questions for reasons other than self-incrimination, can you be convicted of a crime for your refusal?
21. You want to start your own corporation. Must you have a president, or can you just go with the flow?
22. Who is considered to be a neglected child?
23. You have a lovely shnitzerdale dog that hates physical restraints of any kind. Must you subject it to a leash?

ASSIGNMENT B.9

General Research

Answer each of the following questions under your state law. (Be as current as possible.) Give the citation that supports your answer.

1. May a police officer under appropriate circumstances approach a person for purposes of investigating possible criminal behavior even though there is no probable cause to make an arrest?
2. What constitutes substantial performance of a building contract?
3. Is intent to deceive a necessary element of a cause of action for fraudulent misrepresentation or deceit?
4. If the statute of limitations is asserted as a defense, which party has the burden to prove a defense?
5. Is a workers' compensation court bound by the same rules of evidence as other courts?
6. Do premeditation and deliberation have to exist for any particular period of time to substantiate a charge of murder?
7. May a trespass be committed by explosions or blasting operations?
8. Does state law recognize the formation of a commonlaw marriage?
9. Can a 12-year-old make a valid will?
10. When is contributory negligence a bar to any recovery whatsoever by the plaintiff?

ASSIGNMENT B.10

Answer each of the following questions under your state law. (Be as current as possible.) Give the citation that supports your answer.

1. What is the *current* statute of limitations for sexual assault?
2. May a police officer under appropriate circumstances approach a person for purposes of investigating possible criminal behavior even though there is no probable cause to make an arrest?
3. Does state law recognize holographic wills? If so, what are the conditions to make them valid?
4. What is the definition of murder?
5. What is the definition of manslaughter?
6. What is the penalty for a second drunken driving offense?
7. What is the time period for adverse possession in this state?
8. Can nurses working for dentists administer general anesthesia in the office?
9. Can blood-alcohol test results be admitted in a civil case?
10. When can an order of child support be modified?
11. Does state law recognize surrogate mother contracts?
12. What characteristics of individuals are considered to be discriminatory when used in such decisions as whether to employ an individual?
13. When a car and an individual are both entering an unmarked intersection, who must yield the right of way?
14. What is comparative negligence?
15. When, if ever, are state courts required to apply the doctrine of contributory negligence?
16. Does the driver of an automobile have any duty toward children in the roadway ahead?
17. Is it necessary to install curbs in a cemetery?
18. What statute requires males to register for the draft?
19. What statute governs the sale, possession, and purchase of bald eagles?
20. Is the federal government authorized to repair and replace sidewalks surrounding federal buildings?
21. What is the liability of the owner of a nationally accepted charge card or plate for unauthorized use?
22. Is a defendant in the United States District Court required to reasonably investigate the claims of a plaintiff before the defendant can base his or her answer on a lack of information?
23. What is necessary to be a seaman under the terms of the Jones Act?
24. Locate the *Miranda v. Arizona* decision of the U.S. Supreme Court. (No written answer need be provided; the complete proper citation is sufficient.)

☐ **ASSIGNMENT B.11**

General (State and Federal) Research

Locate the answer to the following questions. For each answer, provide a list of all sources consulted and the approximate time spent on each source. The source and time portions of your answer will not be graded. Rather, they provide your instructor with information necessary to assist you in improving your research skills. The questions may be addressed by state or

federal law. In some jurisdictions, a particular question may not be addressed. If this is the case, document your research as described above and state that no applicable law exists on the topic in your jurisdiction or at the federal level.

1. Must cows be tested for tuberculosis?
2. Must podiatrists take continuing education courses?
3. Is it illegal to kill a muskrat?
4. Can lanterns be used to hunt raccoons?
5. How is jaywalking defined?
6. Can you stuff animals without a license?
7. Are there limits on hours a taxi driver can work?
8. How do I go about donating my spleen to a university?
9. Who is entitled to a public defender?
10. Can convicts be forced to work in rock quarries?
11. When can parental rights be terminated?
12. What is the state tree?
13. How are people notified to serve for jury duty?
14. Do you need a license to operate an ambulance?
15. Where are the state boundaries on bridges that connect two states?
16. What is considered bribery of a sheriff?
17. Can each county sheriff choose what color his or her uniform will be?
18. Can you sell cemetery crypts without a license?
19. Must a train have a caboose?
20. Can a posthumuous child inherit?
21. Can you erect a billboard in your yard if you live adjacent to an interstate highway?
22. Can embalmers solicit business by television advertising?
23. What type of offense (e.g., felony, misdemeanor) is committed if you operate a car without a valid driver's license?
24. What type of offense is committed by a minor who transports beer?
25. Is it a criminal offense to leave a child unattended in a car?
26. What is an injury that is eligible for workers' compensation?
27. In a will, does the word *issue* include grandchildren?
28. What are percolating waters?
29. What is an excise tax?
30. What type of case is appropriate for the remedy of specific performance?
31. When can you sue a manufacturer for defective design of a product?
32. Who is housed in a county jail?
33. What does the court consider when awarding attorney's fees in a divorce case?
34. When can new evidence be cause for a new trial?
35. Can a layperson give opinion evidence at trial?
36. What are the guardian's rights over a minor if no parents are alive?
37. Can an employer be sued for libel if the statement is made to one employee about another?
38. When can a bank foreclose on a mortgage?

39. What is the primary consideration of the court when awarding temporary custody?
40. If a job requires you to stay on site during lunch, are you entitled to wages for that time?
41. What is insurance?
42. When is summary judgment proper in a medical malpractice case?
43. Is a tenant who doesn't read the terms of a lease bound by the lease?
44. What is eminent domain?
45. What determines who is an infant under state law?

☐ ASSIGNMENT B.12

Looseleaf Service Research

Consult five different looseleaf service reports; for each one, answer the following questions:

1. Number of volumes.
2. Number of transer binders (if any).
3. Does the subject index indicate page or section numbers where information is located?
4. Is information arranged by topic, or does it correspond to numbers of codified laws?
5. In what volume and on what page are instructions for the use of the looseleaf?
6. Provide the correct citation for each of the looseleaf services.

☐ ASSIGNMENT B.13

Closed Opinion Letter Assignment

Write a brief opinion letter based on the following facts and authority. No additional research is required. Assume the only authority is that which is provided.

FACTS: Joe and Joann Jones have two children, aged 8 and 10. Joe and Joann love the nightlife. They have gone disco dancing every night for the past year. Once a month, Joe buys 60 pot pies and 2 boxes of cereal. The children are expected to have this as their sole nourishment. The children are given no money for lunch, although Joe and Joann have a substantial income. All money over and above the groceries mentioned above, rent, and utilities for the one-bedroom apartment is spent on sequined disco clothes. The parents do not care whether the children attend school, and often the children do not attend because they are too dirty, weak, or embarrassed.

Some know-it-all social worker has petitioned through the district attorney to have Joe and Joann's children taken away from them permanently. Joe and Joann have come to your office for help. They maintain that the children are provided with basic food, clothing, and a roof over their heads. Further, the children are given the opportunity to go to school. Joe and Joann will not consider changing their lifestyle.

Based on the following authority (AND NOT ON PERSONAL FEEL-INGS), do Joe and Joann have a valid fight for custody?

AUTHORITY: Xenia Rev. Stat. Sec. 43-292(3) provides that parental rights may be terminated when ... "The parents, being financially able, have willfully neglected to provide the juvenile with the necessary subsistance [sic] education, or other care when legal custody of the juvenile is lodged with others and such payment ordered by the court; ... "

☐ ASSIGNMENT B.14

Closed Opinion Letter Assignment

Based on the following facts and authority, identify the primary issue and address it in an opinion letter to the client. Write your answer on the next page.

FACTS: Client Brian Morgan was a passenger in a car driven by Paul McElroy. The men were returning home on the evening of March 3 from an out-of-town business seminar. Brian is employed by Paul. In addition, Paul regularly provides transportation for Brian to and from the office each day in exchange for $15 per week. The seminar was on a workday, but Brian paid no extra money for transportation to it. Freezing rain had fallen since March 2, and the roads were treacherous. Brian and Paul heard on the car radio that the interstate highway should be avoided. However, it would be several miles out of Paul's way to take Brian home by any other route. Brian agreed with Paul that the interstate would be the fastest route, but he voiced concern about the safety of the interstate. After travelling about four miles of the five-mile trip on the interstate, Paul lost control of the car and struck an embankment. Brian now seeks to recover from Paul for injuries received in the accident.

AUTHORITY: 1986 Xenia Revised Statutes Chapter 21, Section 6101 (a), "No person transported by the operator of a motor vehicle ... as a passenger without payment for such transportation shall have a cause of action for damages against such operator for injury suffered in an accident arising out of such transportation, unless the accident was intentional on the part of the operator or caused by willful and wanton disregard for others by the operator.

AUTHORITY: "The purpose of the statute is to protect one who, without receiving any benefit, transports another in his or her vehicle." *Engle v. Poland,* Volume 275, page 326, of the Xenia Reports, page 468, Volume 375, of the Midwestern Reporter Second Series, Xenia Supreme Court issued in 1994.

☐ ASSIGNMENT B.15

Opinion Letter Assignment

Prepare an opinion letter to the client. The letter should be concise but should give sufficient explanation of the law on the issue(s). You may use statutes, cases, or secondary authority.

FACTS: You are employed as a paralegal by John Guadalupe, attorney-at-law. Mr. Guadalupe has been contacted by Miriam Sensless for representation. It appears that Miriam has a problem. Two years ago, Miriam married Marvin Sensless. They had a wonderful honeymoon, after which Marvin brought Miriam's belongings to an apartment to use as their marital home. Miriam has continued to reside there day in and day out for the past two years. Marvin stays with his mother and father fifty miles away during the week. He comes

to the apartment every weekend. On Mondays, he leaves for work and then returns to his parents' home for the week. The rent and utilities on the apartment (which is in Marvin and Miriam's name) are $400 per month. Marvin gives Miriam exactly $475. He says she should have a little pocket change and grocery money. Miriam is a member of a fundamentalist religion that does not believe a wife should work under any circumstances or should ever consider divorce. However, Miriam has been virtually dependent on the kindness of family and strangers for assistance ever since that fateful night that Marvin first wooed her.

Miriam is adamant that she does not want to start a divorce proceeding or even a legal separation. She does not want to go to work to assist in the support of the marital home. She believes her duty is to keep the home ready for the times that Marvin resides there. She does, however, wish to eat regularly and purchase necessary clothing. She has purchased nothing for herself or the apartment since her marriage to Marvin.

According to Miriam, Marvin works as an oral surgeon for pets and earns in excess of $95,000 per year. Marvin does not care whether Miriam works or not. He says no matter what, he will continue his "generous" allowance.

ASSIGNMENT: Mr. Guadalupe has told Miriam that he will look into her rights in this matter and will respond to her in a letter that details her options. He then calls you in and asks you to research the issues and prepare the letter to Miriam. Specifically, you are to address whether Miriam could expect court-ordered maintenance or alimony as a married woman, in a divorce, or in a legal separation.

☐ ASSIGNMENT B.16

Opinion Letter Assignment

Prepare an opinion letter to the client. The letter should be concise but should give sufficient explanation of the law on the issue(s). You may use statutes, cases, or secondary authority. Assume that the facts take place in Nebraska unless otherwise stated.

FACTS: Sandra Soo Sizemore married Merle Meeker Munucci. Sandra, an attorney, offered to assist Merle's parents with their estate planning. She assisted extensively in the preparation of the wills of Merle's parents. Only three months after the will of each parent was executed, Merle's parents died a horrifying death in a single accident.

At the funeral, Merle's sister and brother both appeared. This was quite a surprise, since they had run away to be married more than 10 years prior and had not been seen or heard from since. Merle's parents had never really gotten over the marriage of their son and daughter (to each other). However, they did want to leave them something. In their wills, the parents agreed that Sandra would receive 20% of the estate, Merle would receive 75% of the estate, and Mike and Michelle would each receive 2 1/2% of the estate.

It is one week after the funeral. Mike and Michelle anticipate that their parents' wills are going to be filed with the probate court very soon. They disagree with the wills and feel that Sandra exercised her feminine wiles on their father and her charming coyishness on their mother to get a portion of the estate for herself. They realize Merle may be entitled to a greater share, but they do not think Sandra should share the wealth. They want to challenge the will.

In an opinion letter to Mike and Michelle, you are to address the following issues:

1. Is there a significant chance that the will can be declared invalid?
2. If the will is declared invalid, what share of the estate would Mike and Michelle each be entitled to?
3. What is your recommendation?
   Legal Research and Writing

☐ ASSIGNMENT B.17

Closed Memo Assignment

You work in a law office. You have been assigned to work on the case whose facts are described below. Do not add or assume additional facts. Approach the case from position A or position B. Complete an appropriate closed internal memorandum (an internal memo using only the authority given).

The following are the facts that both parties agree took place:

Mary Lou's fiance was going on a business trip to Tahiti. She accompanied her fiance Jim to the airport. After Jim boarded the plane, Mary Lou watched longingly from her car as the plane taxied and took off. The plane disappeared into the clouds. Almost immediately thereafter, Mary Lou heard a very loud noise and saw burning debris falling from the sky. She returned to the terminal and within minutes was informed that the plane had self-destructed.

Distraught, Mary Lou began to drive home. On the way, her car hit a tree. Mary Lou was hospitalized for her injuries from the accident which included the loss of her sight. She became very depressed about her fiance's death and was subsequently placed in a psychiatric ward. She is confined there now and does nothing more than sit and mumble that she and Jim will never go birdwatching again.

ISSUE: Does Mary Lou have a viable lawsuit in your state against the airline company for (1) injuries received in the auto accident and (2) injuries received as a result of the death of her fiance.

ASSIGNMENT A: You work for the office that is preparing the defense for the airline company. Your memorandum is addressed to attorney Bill Burpee, who is assigned to handle the case.

ASSIGNMENT B: You work for the office that is preparing the plaintiff's case for Mary Lou. Your memorandum is addressed to attorney Sam Slurper, who is assigned to handle the case.

Legal Authority for Closed Memo Assignment

Restatement (Second) of Torts (1965)

Section 436.   (1) If the actor's conduct is negligent as violating a duty of care designed to protect another from a fright or other emotional disturbance which the actor should recognize as involving an unreasonable risk of bodily harm, the fact that the harm results solely through the internal operation of the fright or other emotional disturbance does not protect the actor from liability.

(2) If the actor's conduct is negligent as creating an unreasonable risk of causing bodily harm to another otherwise than by subjecting him to fright,

shock, or other similar and immediate emotional disturbance, the fact that such harm results solely from the internal operation of fright or other emotional disturbance does not protect the actor from liability.

(3) The rule stated in Subsection (2) applies where the bodily harm to the other results from his shock or fright at harm or peril to a member of his immediate family occurring in his presence.

Section 436A. If the actor's conduct is negligent as creating an unreasonable risk of causing either bodily harm or emotional disturbance to another and it results in such emotional disturbance alone, without bodily harm or other compensable damage, the actor is not liable for such emotional disturbance.

☐ ASSIGNMENT B.18

Memorandum of Law Assignment

Prepare a persuasive legal document to be used in support of or in opposition to a motion before the court. This memorandum of law is for use externally (outside the office) and thus should present an accurate but carefully written description of the case, issue(s), and legal authorities (both positive and adverse). It should further logically lead the reader to a suggested conclusion of the issue(s) based on the information presented.

The document should be typewritten. It should bear appropriate headings, such as Facts, Issues Before the Court, Argument, and Conclusion. You are not confined to these headings. Use whatever headings you think will make an orderly presentation of the information in the document.

When citing legal authorities, give not only the first page of the case but also the page of the decision where your specific point of authority lies. This page should immediately follow the first page of the case in your cite. The only time you would not do this is when you are making reference to the decision in its entirety and not making any particular point. (If you have questions about citation, refer to your bluebook.)

In a case where there are multiple issues or multiple parts of a single issue (i.e., different questions that must be resolved or a two- or three-pronged test that resolves the issue), it is generally best to address each part fully and make a conclusory statement at the end of that portion of your discussion. This includes the following information:

1. Discussion of the positive authorities in support of your position.
2. Discussion of the negative authorities in such a way that they appear inapplicable to your client's case, or at least not as influential as your positive authorities.
3. Conclusory statement indicating what resolution the authorities indicate for this issue or this part of the issue.

After this is completed for each issue or portion of an issue, prepare a strong conclusory paragraph for the entire document that summarizes the conclusory statements made previously and the total of which indicates your final conclusion as to what the outcome of the motion (which this memorandum supports) should be.

(*Hint:* The outcome you suggest should be in favor of your client.)

FACTS: On March 13, 1992, Mary Sighner was cleaning the exterior of the windows on the second story of her home. While cleaning, Mary slipped and

fell from the ladder on which she was standing. She was taken by ambulance to a nearby hospital for treatment of her injuries. In the emergency room, she was seen by Dr. Mark Walston, who is qualified as a board-certified specialist in the field of plastic surgery.

Dr. Walston examined Mary and ordered morphine to suppress the pain she was suffering. The morphine was administered, and shortly thereafter, Dr. Walston explained to Mary that her face would need to be sutured and there was a possibility of scars remaining. Dr. Walston further explained to Mary that she was lucky that he was a plastic surgeon. Mary made no response. She was asked to sign a consent form to allow Dr. Walston to repair the facial lacerations suffered in her fall. Mary signed her name, and Dr. Walston immediately began suturing her injuries.

During the procedure, Dr. Walston was informed that another patient had entered the emergency room and required the doctor's attention. Dr. Walston hurriedly completed suturing Mary's facial wounds on the right side of her face and went to attend the other patient. The doctor did not return or see Mary again. He left instructions that Mary should see her family physician in one week to have the sutures removed. Mary has no recollection from the time the morphine was administered until she awoke the next morning and was discharged from the hospital. Mary's home and the hospital are in a community of approximately 20,000 people.

Approximately one week later, Mary went to her family physician in accordance with Dr. Walston's instructions. When the sutures were removed, she was shocked at the scarring on the right side of her face. Her physician explained that there is often scarring immediately after an injury such as hers, but it generally fades quite a bit within a few months. After six months, Mary's facial scars were no better. Mary finally could stand the staring and comments by the public no longer. On September 22, 1995, she sought the advice of a board-certified plastic surgeon in New York City who indicated that some of the sutures had been poorly placed and this was the reason for her scars. Further, the doctor informed Mary that additional surgery would be required to minimize the damage caused by the manner in which the lacerations on the right side had been sutured.

Mary sought the advice of an attorney, who agreed to represent her in an action against Dr. Walston. An action was initiated on September 22, 1996. Subsequently, suit was filed and is now pending in the county trial court. Dr. Walston has filed a motion to dismiss in the court seeking dismissal of Mary's claims. He alleges that (1) Mary voluntarily consented to the treatment after being informed of the risks; (2) Mary's claim is barred by the statute of limitations, as she did not initiate her action until after the statute from the date on which she claims she was injured (March 13, 1992); and (3) the allegation of negligence in the manner in which the sutures were administered is unfounded, as the sutures were administered in accordance with the standards of other plastic surgeons in the local area.

▢ ASSIGNMENT B.19

Memorandum of Law Assignment

Select one side (Team A or Team B) of the case and prepare an external memorandum of law regarding the following issue and the viability of your case. Unless otherwise instructed, assume all relevant facts occur within your state jurisdiction. Use proper citation form for all authorities.

FACTS: Stacey Maddly is an 18-year-old resident of Douglas County. Stacey spends most of her time at the homes of friends, although her primary residence is still that of her parents. Unable to deal with what they consider to be Stacey's bizarre behavior, Stacey's parents had Stacey committed six months ago to the mental ward of a local hospital. Stacey ran away from the hospital a few days later, and she was arrested shortly thereafter on the nearby interstate highway wearing nothing but a throw rug (the arrest was for indecent exposure). Stacey was readmitted to the mental ward by the police but was released the next day as an outpatient. Stacey's parents are convinced that Stacey is dangerous and should be committed on a long-term basis for intensive treatment. Stacey has retained an attorney, who maintains that (1) Stacey is not dangerous and (2) she cannot be involuntarily committed on the circumstances of her arrest because it was over three months ago and no hearing was ever held.

Stacey's "bizarre" behavior includes constantly dressing in black and writing poetry about the glamours of mass suicide and murder. Stacey goes into extensive detail and writes that suicide and murder would make her a figure in history. To date, Stacey has taken no known steps toward completion of her ideas. Several friends have said that Stacey acts this way simply to upset her parents and she really doesn't mean it. Stacey recently told her parents that they should be honored because they were at the "top of the list." When questioned, she refused to state what the list was about. Her parents think they have a good idea.

On the other hand, Stacey, attends college, is an "A" student, and works part-time at the college. Her instructors have not noticed anything unusual. However, the average class size is 80–120 students. Stacey's job is alone on the switchboard at night. Therefore, no co-workers can give information regarding job performance or unusual behavior.

Team A works for the county attorney. Specifically, your boss is Mr. D. L. Duerite, who will assist Mr. and Mrs. Maddly in having Stacey committed.

Team B works for Stacey's attorney, S. A. Ruels, who is assisting Stacey in her fight against involuntary commitment.

ASSIGNMENT B.20

Appellate Brief Assignment

Based on the following facts, prepare an appellate brief for your state high appellate court. Follow proper rules of the court for format as to the organization and content of the brief. Your instructor may grant exceptions with respect to certain elements that may be omitted (e.g., a copy of the record). Your instructor may provide you with additional supportive materials as he or she deems appropriate. You may choose either side for your brief.

On August 21, 1993, Sue Bee Homely, a 17-year-old, gave birth to her first child, Amanda Sue. At the time of the birth, Sue Bee was not married. The father of the child, Wilbur Valley, was aware of the pregnancy but was under the impression that Sue was not going to continue with the pregnancy. Further, he was not informed of the date of the birth. Wilbur's job required travel for extended periods of time, and Wilbur was out of town during the period of August 10–September 29. On September 30, 1993, Sue Bee placed

Amanda Sue for adoption with the Newton State Children's Home. Sue Bee undertook to place her child for adoption under the threat of being kicked out of her parents' home and left with no place to live. During the short time Amanda was in Sue Bee's custody, virtually all caretaking of the child was performed by Sue Bee's older sister Gertrude. Sue Bee did visit with the child daily but did not spend an extensive amount of time with her. At no time during the meeting with the agency in which Sue Bee relinquished her rights did she mention the threat of her parents or exhibit any other behavior that would indicate she was not acting voluntarily in relinquishing the child.

On October 15, 1993, Wilbur Valley had an attack of conscience and became aware of his real love for Sue Bee. Wilbur went to Sue Bee and offered to take her into his home and to marry her. It was only then that Wilbur Valley became aware that the child had been born and later given up for adoption. On October 20, 1993, Wilbur and Sue Bee appeared at the Newton agency to request the return of Amanda Sue. All papers had already been properly formalized at the agency, and Amanda had been placed with adoptive parents. However, no decree of adoption had been entered by the courts as of that date. The agency refused to return the child to Sue Bee and Wilbur.

On November 10, 1993, Sue Bee and Wilbur filed an action in the trial court. Sue Bee claims that she was forced into the decision by the threat of being homeless and unable to support her child. Wilbur claims that he was unaware of the birth and thus was unable to assert his parental rights. Further, Wilbur contests the adoption on the basis that he never relinquished his rights to the agency.

On January 10, 1994, the court entered an order of summary judgment against Sue Bee and Wilbur. The couple has appealed.

☐ ASSIGNMENT B.21

Appellate Brief Assignment

Prepare an appellate brief for the following case that complies with the state rules of appellate procedure. You may choose either side of the case. Because the case is one in which summary judgment was granted, there is no trial record and no need for reference to such.

PARTIES: Millie Cook, Plaintiff

Graham Simpson, Defendant

COURT: Douglas County District Court, Your State

DOCKET: 91-11183

BACKGROUND: Graham Simpson is a local attorney. He employs Jan Bean as his paralegal. Recently, Graham undertook the representation of Millie Cook, who intended to sue a local doctor for malpractice. Graham left town for an extended trial in another state. Among the assignments he left for Jan was a complaint in the Cook case. Jan was to file the case and arrange for service of process on the physician. The office was extremely busy in Graham's absence. In the hectic atmosphere, Jan failed to file the complaint on time. The complaint was filed three days after the statute of limitations expired. The defense immediately filed for a motion for summary judgment in Millie's case. This was granted, and Millie's medical malpractice case was dismissed with prejudice.

Two months later, Millie Cook filed suit against Graham Simpson for professional malpractice. After discovery, Millie's lawyer filed a motion for summary judgment against Graham. The court found that no genuine issue existed as to Graham's malfeasance. It further found that the only issue to be determined was that of damages. The court issued an order of summary judgment against Graham in the legal malpractice case and set the case for trial on the question of damage that Graham would be required to pay Millie.

Graham has filed an appeal from the order of summary judgment in his legal malpractice case. His claim is that there is a genuine issue of fact with respect to the element of injury to Millie Cook as the result of his malfeasance. Graham's position is that it is speculative as to whether Millie would have even won the medical malpractice case. Therefore, how can the court find as a matter of law that Millie was injured by Graham's failure to properly file her suit?

SELF-TEST ANSWERS

CHAPTER 1: SELF-TEST ANSWERS

1. a
2. c
3. a
4. d
5. a
6. T
7. F
8. T
9. T
10. F
11. degree of influence
12. adverse authority
13. whether the authorities are current
14. Persuasive
15. report
16. Statutory
17. statutory, judicial, administrative
18. chronologically
19. supplements
20. law

CHAPTER 2: SELF-TEST ANSWERS

1. d
2. b
3. a
4. c
5. c
6. T
7. F
8. F
9. F
10. T
11. supplements, procedural
12. most current
13. agency
14. title
15. underline
16. U.S. Supreme Court

17. restatement
18. treatise
19. point of law
20. volume number

CHAPTER 3: SELF-TEST ANSWERS

1. d
2. d
3. a
4. d
5. c
6. F
7. F
8. T
9. T
10. F
11. cumulative
12. jurisdiction
13. frequently
14. secondary authorities
15. computer
16. above and to the right of
17. Letters
18. weekly, quarterly, annually
19. cumulative
20. descriptive

CHAPTER 4: SELF-TEST ANSWERS

1. b
2. c
3. c
4. a
5. d
6. F
7. F
8. T
9. T
10. F
11. authority

12. query
13. distinguish
14. legal analysis
15. primary, persuasive
16. prioritization
17. en banc
18. landmark
19. legal standard
20. validation

CHAPTER 5: SELF-TEST ANSWERS

1. a
2. c
3. a
4. d
5. b
6. T
7. F
8. T
9. T
10. F
11. synonyms, antonyms
12. subject index
13. topical arrangements
14. alphabetically
15. subheadings
16. supplemented
17. efficient
18. annually cumulative
19. supplement or pocket part
20. substantive

CHAPTER 6: SELF-TEST ANSWERS

1. c
2. b
3. a
4. d
5. a
6. T
7. T
8. F
9. T
10. T
11. Substantive law
12. procedural law
13. criminal
14. administrative regulation
15. unique
16. volumes
17. numerical

18. topic indexing
19. Popular Name Tables, Law Finders
20. Deskbooks

CHAPTER 7: SELF-TEST ANSWERS

1. b
2. c
3. c
4. b
5. a
6. T
7. T
8. T
9. F
10. F
11. chronologically
12. official
13. National Reporter System
14. regional
15. series
16. advance sheet
17. key number system
18. topic index
19. alphanumerical
20. legal encyclopedias, annotated law reports, legal periodicals, looseleaf services

CHAPTER 8: SELF-TEST ANSWERS

1. d
2. b
3. a
4. a
5. c
6. T
7. F
8. F
9. F
10. T
11. subjects
12. United States Code
13. chapters, subchapters
14. citation
15. CFR Index and Finding Aids
16. specific regulations
17. LSA
18. List of CFR Sections Affected
19. topical
20. particular agency

CHAPTER 9: SELF-TEST ANSWERS

1. c
2. b
3. a
4. d
5. d
6. T
7. F
8. F
9. T
10. T
11. Shepard's Restatement of the Law Citations
12. Restatement of the Courts
13. Interim Case Citations
14. treatise
15. uniform
16. table of contents
17. well-known
18. card index
19. page, section
20. Casebooks

CHAPTER 10: SELF-TEST ANSWERS

1. c
2. a
3. a
4. b
5. b
6. T
7. T
8. F
9. F
10. F
11. well-established
12. components
13. detailed
14. numbered sections
15. total client-library service
16. index to the annotation
17. table of jurisdictions represented
18. single volumes
19. supplements
20. position

CHAPTER 11: SELF-TEST ANSWERS

1. c
2. c
3. a
4. b
5. c
6. T
7. T
8. T
9. T
10. T
11. paperback supplements
12. distinction
13. Legal Resource Index
14. Info/Trak
15. Index to Legal Periodicals
16. legal texts
17. treatises
18. citator
19. current
20. judicial opinion

CHAPTER 12: SELF-TEST ANSWERS

1. a
2. c
3. d
4. c
5. a
6. T
7. T
8. F
9. F
10. T
11. pagination
12. section numbers
13. indexing system
14. index binder
15. detail
16. sections
17. major sections
18. sections, headings
19. correlator
20. supplemental

CHAPTER 13: SELF-TEST ANSWERS

1. a
2. a
3. c
4. b
5. d
6. F
7. T
8. T
9. T

10. T

11. subordinate

12. treatises, restatements

13. points of law

14. Rules 15–17

15. organization

16. table of contents, subject index

17. subject, author

18. catalog

19. form books

20. litigation, common legal situations

CHAPTER 14: SELF-TEST ANSWERS

1. d

2. d

3. b

4. c

5. d

6. T

7. F

8. T

9. T

10. T

11. tutorials, books, personal training

12. field

13. time increment

14. natural, terms and connectors

15. natural

16. terms and connectors

17. alternative

18. connectors

19. citation

20. validate

GLOSSARY

Administrative law legal standards including regulations, rules, and administrative decisions that issue from administrative agencies as a function of the executive branch's duty to enforce the law.

Advance sheet publication of recently released judicial opinions that supplement hardbound reports/reporters.

Annotated law report selected judicial opinions followed by detailed commentary and analysis.

Annotated statutes statutory compilation with accompanying headnotes (annotations) of judicial opinions that have applied and/or interpreted the statute.

Annotation see Headnote.

Appellate court court of superior authority that reviews the application of law by a trial court.

Argumentative method used to persuade in which language is presented in a fashion that leads the audience and indicates the desired result.

Bar Association organization of lawyers with a common interest (e.g., state bar association or trial lawyers association).

Casebook collection of cases and commentary on a subject of law that has been developed and/or interpreted judicially.

Case brief legal analysis of a judicial opinion.

Case of first impression a case whose legal issues are considered by the court for the first time. No other primary interpretative authority exists on the issue within the jurisdiction.

Case law judicial opinion that interprets and applies preexisting legal standards.

CD Rom hardware that permits access to a limited database contained on a compact disc.

Citation a reference note containing information necessary to locate an authority.

Citator a publication used to provide reference to all authorities that have referred to a prior authority.

Commentary discussion of various aspects regarding a particular concept or topic.

Commonlaw creation of legal standard by a court in circumstances where no applicable standard exists.

Database collection of information, much like a library, that can be accessed through use of a computer.

Delegation doctrine legal principle that no authority other than the legislature has the power to issue legislative law and that even the legislature cannot delegate this power to another authority.

Deskbook condensed statutory compilation of current procedural laws for a jurisdiction.

Enabling act statute passed by a legislative body that sets definable goals and provides capacity for the executive branch to create an administrative agency.

Form book publication of commonly used documents. In law, form books often contain a variety of frequently used pleadings or other documents (e.g., contracts).

Hardware physical components of a computer system, such as monitor, processing unit, and printer.

Headnote also known as an annotation. A brief summary of a judicial opinion.

Judicial law legal standards established by the judicial branch in the form of court orders and judicial opinions.

Jurisdiction   limits of authority of a particular court or branch of government.

Law review or journal   legal periodical often issued by a school of law or other legal organization.

Legal analysis   method of extracting significant information from a legal authority for comparison purposes.

Legal newspaper   a newspaper published with format similar to an ordinary newspaper, except that articles and advertising are directed toward legal matters.

Legal periodical   a publication of legal information for a particular subject, jurisdiction, or interest group that is issued on a regular basis.

Legal standard   a principal of law.

Legislation   statutory law created by an elected legislative body (e.g., Congress).

Legislative history   information about the background and rationale for legislation.

Looseleaf service   periodic publication that can be updated through replacement pages and that is usually prepared for subjects of law that change frequently.

Mandatory authority   primary authority or law that comes from a superior source and that must be adhered to.

Modem   hardware that can be used to permit communication between separate computer systems.

Objective   unbiased presentation of facts.

Persuasive authority   primary or secondary authority from a collateral or subordinate source that may be given deference.

Pocket part   a method of updating an authority by preparing a pamphlet of updated information for the authority which fits into a pocket inside the cover of the book in which the original authority is contained.

Primary authority   a legal standard having the effect of law.

Procedural law   laws designed to move legal issues fairly and efficiently through a branch of government (e.g., judicial system).

Reference book   publication of general information on a topic.

Report   official publication of judicial law for a jurisdiction.

Research issue   general question to be addressed by research.

Research query   words, phrases, and questions used in sources of authority to obtain the answer to a research issue.

Restatement of the law   publication by the American Law Institute of generally accepted principles of law on a particular topic (e.g., Restatement of the Law of Contracts).

Secondary authority   published reference from a private (nongovernmental) source that does not have the effect of law but can be used as persuasive authority.

Series   continuation of a chronological publication. A subsequent series does not change the content, but rather revises the format of presentation.

Session law   a statute that has been passed during a specific term of a legislative body (e.g., the 95th Congress).

Slip law   singular publication of a statute that generally is not published but must be requested or subscribed to from the clerk of the legislature.

Software   system that enables use of hardware to perform specific functions (e.g., database).

Statutes at large   publication of all session laws passed in a given term of a legislative body.

Statutory law   primary authority created by a legislative body that has the effect of law that is generally superior to other types of primary authority.

Supplement   method used to update materials without total revision of a publication. A pocket part is a type of supplement.

Terms of art   language, words, or phrases that have a particular meaning when used within the context of a certain subject, such as law.

Treatise   detailed body of work about a particular subject that usually addresses the development of major concepts and theories.

Trial court   court with authority to hear evidence and rule on the legal rights of parties by applying appropriate legal standards.

Validation   the process of establishing through the use of a citator whether an authority is current and effective or whether it has been subsequently reversed, overruled, repealed, or amended.

Veto   authority of the executive branch to cancel or reject recently enacted legislation.

Subject Index